The Marital Knot

BRANDEIS SERIES ON GENDER, CULTURE, RELIGION, AND LAW
Series editors: Lisa Fishbayn Joffe and Sylvia Neil

This series focuses on the conflict between women's claims to gender equality and legal norms justified in terms of religious and cultural traditions. It seeks work that develops new theoretical tools for conceptualizing feminist projects for transforming the interpretation and justification of religious law, examines the interaction or application of civil law or remedies to gender issues in a religious context, and engages in analysis of conflicts over gender and culture/religion in a particular religious legal tradition, cultural community, or nation. Created under the auspices of the Hadassah-Brandeis Institute in conjunction with its Project on Gender, Culture, Religion, and the Law, this series emphasizes cross-cultural and interdisciplinary scholarship concerning Judaism, Islam, Christianity, and other religious traditions.

For a complete list of books that are available in the series, visit brandeisuniversitypress.com/series-list.

Noa Shashar, *The Marital Knot: Agunot in the Ashkenazi Realm, 1648–1850*

Ronit Irshai and Tanya Zion-Waldoks, *Holy Rebellion: Religious Feminism and the Transformation of Judaism and Women's Rights in Israel*

Mark Goldfeder, *Legalizing Plural Marriage: The Next Frontier in Family Law*

Samia Bano, editor, *Gender and Justice in Family Law Disputes: Women, Mediation, and Religious Arbitration*

Kimba Allie Tichenor, *Religious Crisis and Civic Transformation: How Conflicts over Gender and Sexuality Changed the West German Church*

Margalit Shilo, *Girls of Liberty: The Struggle for Suffrage in Mandatory Palestine*

Susan M. Weiss and Netty C. Gross-Horowitz, *Marriage and Divorce in the Jewish State: Israel's Civil War*

Lisa Fishbayn Joffe and Sylvia Neil, editors, *Gender, Religion, and Family Law: Theorizing Conflicts between Women's Rights and Cultural Traditions*

Chitra Raghavan and James P. Levine, editors, *Self-Determination and Women's Rights in Muslim Societies*

Janet Bennion, *Polygamy in Primetime: Media, Gender, and Politics in Mormon Fundamentalism*

THE TAUBER INSTITUTE SERIES
FOR THE STUDY OF EUROPEAN JEWRY
Jehuda Reinharz, General Editor
ChaeRan Y. Freeze, Associate Editor
Sylvia Fuks Fried, Associate Editor
Eugene R. Sheppard, Associate Editor

The Tauber Institute Series is dedicated to publishing compelling and innovative approaches to the study of modern European Jewish history, thought, culture, and society. The series features scholarly works related to the Enlightenment, modern Judaism and the struggle for emancipation, the rise of nationalism and the spread of antisemitism, the Holocaust and its aftermath, as well as the contemporary Jewish experience. The series is published under the auspices of the Tauber Institute for the Study of European Jewry—established by a gift to Brandeis University from Dr. Laszlo N. Tauber—and is supported, in part, by the Tauber Foundation and the Valya and Robert Shapiro Endowment.

For the complete list of books that are available in this series, please see https://brandeisuniversitypress.com/series/tauber

Noa Shashar, *The Marital Knot: Agunot in the Ashkenazi Realm, 1648–1850*

Jehuda Reinharz and Motti Golani, *Chaim Weizmann: A Biography*

Scott Ury and Guy Miron, editors, *Antisemitism and the Politics of History*

Jeremy Fogel, *Jewish Universalisms: Mendelssohn, Cohen, and Humanity's Highest Good*

Stefan Vogt, Derek Penslar, and Arieh Saposnik, editors, *Unacknowledged Kinships: Postcolonial Studies and the Historiography of Zionism*

Joseph A. Skloot, *First Impressions: Sefer Hasidim and Early Modern Hebrew Printing*

Marat Grinberg, *The Soviet Jewish Bookshelf: Jewish Culture and Identity Between the Lines*

Susan Martha Kahn, *Canine Pioneer: The Extraordinary Life of Rudolphina Menzel*

Arthur Green, *Defender of the Faithful: The Life and Thought of Rabbi Levi Yitshak of Berdychiv*

Gilad Sharvit, *Dynamic Repetition: History and Messianism in Modern Jewish Thought*

The Marital Knot

Agunot in the Ashkenazi Realm, 1648–1850

NOA SHASHAR

TRANSLATED BY SARA FRIEDMAN

BRANDEIS UNIVERSITY PRESS
Waltham, Massachusetts

Brandeis University Press
© 2024 by Noa Shashar
All rights reserved
Manufactured in the USA
Designed by Richard Hendel
Typeset in Arno type by Passumpsic Publishing

For permission to reproduce any of the material in this book, contact Brandeis University Press, 415 South Street, Waltham MA 02453, or visit brandeisuniversitypress.com

Originally published as *Gevarim ne'elamim: 'agunot ba-merḥav ha-Ashkenazi, 1648–1850* (Jerusalem: Carmel, 2020)

Library of Congress Cataloging-in-publishing Data

NAMES: Shashar, Noa, author. | Friedman, Sara P., translator.
TITLE: The marital knot: Agunot in the Ashkenazi realm, 1648–1850 / Noa Shashar; translated by Sara Friedman.
OTHER TITLES: Gevarim ne'elamim. English
DESCRIPTION: Waltham: Brandeis University Press, [2024] |
SERIES: The Tauber Institute series for the study of European Jewry | Includes bibliographical references and index. | SUMMARY: "What kind of reality was imposed on Jewish women who found themselves agunot, literally 'chained women,' and what could they do to extricate themselves from their plight? How did rabbinic experts with the authority to free agunot discharge their task and what were the outcomes of the fact that the agunot were dependent on the male rabbinic establishment?" — Provided by publisher.
IDENTIFIERS: LCCN 2024021997 (print) |
LCCN 2024021998 (ebook) | ISBN 9781684582402 (paperback) | ISBN 9781684582419 (cloth) | ISBN 9781684582396 (ebook)
SUBJECTS: LCSH: Agunahs. | Marriage — Annulment (Jewish law) | Jewish women — Legal status, laws, etc. — Europe — History — 17th century. | Jewish women — Legal status, laws, etc. — Europe — History — 18th century. | Jewish women — Legal status, laws, etc. — Europe — History — 19th century. | BISAC: HISTORY / Jewish | HISTORY / Social History
CLASSIFICATION: LCC KBM550.5 .S5313 2024 (print) | LCC KBM550.5 (ebook) | DDC 296.4/440940902 — dc23/eng/20240527
LC record available at https://lccn.loc.gov/2024021997
LC ebook record available at https://lccn.loc.gov/2024021998

5 4 3 2 1

*For my beloved children,
Ehud, Reut, David, Avinoam, and Yair,
who displayed patience and humor
throughout my wanderings in distant lands
or in my imagination.
And for my beloved mother, Estelle,
and in memory of my dear father, Michael,
both of whom inspire my life and thoughts.*

CONTENTS

Preface and Acknowledgments *xi*

Introduction *xv*

PART I. WIDOWS AND YEVAMOT IN THE ASHKENAZIC WORLD IN THE EARLY MODERN AGE

Chapter 1: Widows in the Ashkenazic World, 1648–1850 *3*

Chapter 2: Yibum and Halitzah: The Halakhic Basis for Freeing an Agunah Awaiting Halitzah *41*

Chapter 3: The Halitzah Trap *51*

PART II. DEAD MEN, CHAINED WOMEN

Chapter 4: Bitterly She Wails: Agunot in Times of Persecution and War *77*

Chapter 5: Two Tales of Murder *90*

Chapter 6: Identifying the Dead in the Interest of Freeing the Agunah and Taking Revenge *102*

Chapter 7: "Nothing of Him Was Ever Found Save a Shoe and Belt": Freeing an Agunah When the Corpse Is Missing *108*

Chapter 8: The Agunah Wife of Lemli Wimpe of Metz *127*

Chapter 9: Death of a Merchant: Gutta and Avraham Heckscher of Hamburg *133*

PART III. TROUBLED MARRIAGES

Chapter 10: Scenes from Marriages in Conflict 141

Chapter 11: "Concerning the Agunah Whose Husband Left for Distant Parts" 174

PART IV. THE RIDDLE OF THE SOURCES

Chapter 12: Heterei Agunah in Beit Din Records and Responsa Literature 223

Afterword: The Agunah, the Decisor, and the Suffering 255

Glossary 269

Notes 271

Bibliography 325

Index 349

PREFACE AND ACKNOWLEDGMENTS

This book tells the family stories of men and women who lived hundreds of years ago. Focusing on *agunot*,[1] literally "chained women," who were often considered a marginal group, it sheds light on Jewish family life in the early modern era and on the activity of *poskim* (rabbis who gave Jewish legal rulings, hereafter called "decisors") who dealt with agunot.

Research for this book was conducted from 2007 to 2012, as my journey took me to archives in Israel and overseas. I found notebooks and documents in the literary estates of rabbis and lay leaders and in the treasures of Jewish communities large and small. Searching for agunot among these pages was a quest for something that may not exist. The exultation of discovery, familiar to historians who enjoy their Sisyphean labor digging in archives, contrasted starkly with the content I found and with the fate of the agunot I was following. As often happens, historical sources converge with current events. As the Hebrew edition of this book was going to press, three agunot in Israel were freed and permitted to remarry, one after about two decades of being an *agunah*. As this English edition is being prepared for publication, recent events in Israel raise, among others, the issue of *iggun*.[2] During the massacre of October 7, 2023, terrorists from Gaza infiltrated Israeli territory, murdering and kidnapping hundreds of men, women, and children, most of them Jewish. Some of the men have not been found, and many bodies remain unidentifiable. As some of these men were married, their wives now remain in the uncertain state of iggun. Public interest in the fate of agunot and the road they travel to obtain their freedom raise a number of questions regarding halakhic activity on the topic of agunot and regarding the danger lurking in store for women who marry in accordance with *halakhah* (Jewish law). This discussion is taking place as more and more Israeli couples seek to secure the rights of both spouses by signing prenuptial agreements. The need for such agreements can be quite controversial. In turning the research into a book, I deliberated whether to include only family stories from the past or to also provide the reader with a detailed account of the *halakhot* that pertain to marriage and to the release of agunot, as well as information regarding the development of these halakhot. Not wanting to overburden the contemporary reader, I nevertheless realized the real need to equip the interested public with knowledge of the choices and crossroads that decisors faced over the ages in handling agunah cases. I also wanted readers to realize the implications that their decisions had on the lives of Jewish men and women from then until today. To serve this purpose, some sections explicate terms and points of Jewish law.

In my PhD dissertation, submitted to the Hebrew University in 2012, I traced the lives of agunot. I have many people to thank for making my research possible. Heartfelt thanks to Professor Immanuel Etkes for getting me started; guiding me on the often tortuous road with wisdom, generosity, and devotion; and giving generously of his time, knowledge, and efforts throughout. This book would never have come into being without him. A three-year Scholion grant enabled me to carry out most of my research; for a long time, this multidisciplinary center became my home. I am grateful to Professor Israel Yuval and Zohar Marcovich, who created a special atmosphere and were always willing to offer advice and help. My fellow doctoral students in the research group dubbed "wisdom and sorrow"—Dr. Michal Altbauer-Rudnik, Dr. Omri Herzog, and Dr. Naama Cohen-Hanegbi—accompanied me from the start, sharing ideas and hesitations and bearing with me in moments of happiness and crisis. Professor Edward (Ted) Fram read parts of the manuscript and generously shared his knowledge, helping me greatly. Professor Avriel Bar-Levav, Professor Jay Berkovitz, Professor Elisheva Carlebach, Blu Greenberg, Shlomit Davidov, Dr. Dori Haneman, Professor Motti Zalkin, Professor Chava Turniansky, Professor Adam Teller, Hagay Lahav, Dr. Stefan Litt, Dr. Rachel Furst, Dr. Oren Roman, Professor Daniel Schwartz, Professor Debra Kaplan, and many others were generous with their knowledge and time. I thank them all.

Much of my research was conducted at the Central Archives for the History of the Jewish People in Jerusalem. Thanks to its staff, I was able to track down agunot in long-forgotten places. The now-retired archives director Hadassah Assouline drew my attention to important sources and expressed interest in my work; the staff—Eli Ben-Yosef, Yaacov Tsabach, and others—made every effort to assist me. I owe them all a debt of gratitude.

Generous grants from the Guggenheim Foundation for Research in Jewish Ethics, the international Leo Baeck Fellowship Programme of Germany, and the Israel Science Foundation allowed me to devote my time to research. Grants from the Yitzhak Averbuch Foundation at the Hebrew University of Jerusalem and the Elsa De Beer Foundation enabled me to trace agunot and vanishing men who left their mark in distant archives.

I am deeply indebted to Naama Cifrony, who edited the Hebrew book; to the translator, Sara Friedman; and to Adina Yoffie, the style editor of this English edition, who enriched the volume with her wisdom and textual and personal sensitivity. Special thanks to Nava Finkelman for her thorough proofreading and helpful advice and to Gershon Klapper for assisting in preparing the book for press. My deepest gratitude to Dr. Lisa Fishbayn Joffe and to Sylvia Fuks Fried, without whom the publication of this English edition would not have been possible.

More than anyone, my immediate and extended family accompanied me on my journey, helping in many ways. My beloved mother, Estelle Shashar, labored with me in translating sources from several languages, providing spiritual and material support. Her profound wisdom, curiosity, breadth of knowledge, and good nature have left their mark on my work. I learned much from my nephew Dr. Matan Fischer, who gladly tackled any challenge. My aunt and uncle Annette and Professor Stephen Hochstein expressed ongoing interest in my work and lent a helping hand to enable me to complete it.

I lost two loved ones in the course of this project. My father, Michael Shashar z"l, instilled in me a love of knowledge and encouraged me to engage in research. He died suddenly before the project was realized. My grandmother Toni Reinhold Schiff z"l, practical and wise, died at a ripe old age in 2011. Both were a source of inspiration for this book, and I miss them very much. This book is dedicated to their memory.

Jerusalem, December 2023

INTRODUCTION

One Thursday, a Jew came to town and told how he had seen Yehiel, the innkeeper, lying murdered in the forest; and the whole congregation mourned and brought him to town. The rabbi sent to tell us not to mourn, nor was I to say the Mourner's Prayer, until it had been proven by reliable and decisive evidence who the slain man was. But it was not simple to identify; the head had been hacked off the body. So my mother was left a widow, and not only a widow, but also a desolate forsaken wife [Hebrew, *agunah shomemah*];[1] while I was not even permitted to repeat the Mourner's Prayer. But Brody is a city of scholars and scribes; they began to exchange questions and responses and finally decided that in this special case, the possibly forsaken woman [agunah] might remarry. But truth to tell, that permission served no practical purpose save to magnify the Torah and glorify it; for my mother had taken sick with grief and pain.
— S. Y. Agnon, *The Bridal Canopy*, 14

S. Y. Agnon's protagonist in *Hahnasat kalah* gives ironic expression to the gulf between the agunah and her fatherless son, on the one hand, and the halakhic authorities charged with freeing her from the chains of her marriage, on the other. As the forlorn agunah falls ill with grief, the "scholars" and "scribes" are concerned solely with extolling and enhancing the Torah. *Hahnasat kalah* is a literary work, not a historical source,[2] yet Agnon's depiction accords with the criticism Jewish society levelled against halakhah (Jewish law) and the poskim who dealt in freeing agunot. Judah Leib Gordon (Vilnius, 1830–St. Petersburg, 1892), in his well-known poem "Kotzo shel yod" (published 1876), attacked rabbis for focusing on trivialities while ignoring the distress of agunot.[3] Although Gordon, like Agnon, represents a type of Jew that developed later than the period under discussion in the present study (1648–1850), the criticism expressed in his poem had been voiced already many years earlier. In the controversy known as "the Cleves *get* [writ of divorce] affair" (1766–1767), those involved in the controversy accused the decisors of acting out of foreign motives and not purely halakhic considerations.[4] What was the background behind this kind of criticism? This is one of the questions that are discussed in this book.

Jewish law determines that marriage takes place by the free will of both parties and can end in only one of two ways: the death of one spouse or divorce. The term "agunah" denotes a woman who is precluded from remarrying because she is still in a marital bond that has not come to an end in accordance with halakhic requirements. "Agunah" (Hebr., "chained") denotes a unique halakhic category, referring to a woman whose husband is absent, whether of his own volition or not, and who will not or cannot divorce her in accordance with Jewish law. An agunah is also a woman (as in Agnon's *Hahnasat kalah*) whose husband is dead but whose body has not been identified in accordance with Jewish law. "Agunah" also refers to a woman whose husband refuses to divorce her despite her unwillingness to continue in the marriage. Finally, it is used to describe a widow whose husband died childless; she is therefore required to undergo the *halitzah* ceremony, in which her husband's brother publicly refuses to marry her (see below), before she can remarry someone else. Women finding themselves in these situations sometimes shared a common fate, yet each type of iggun (roughly, "agunah situation") imposes its unique hardships on the agunah. These difficulties, and the implications that the halakhot dealing with the situation of iggun had on the lives of Jewish women in early modernity, lie at the center of this book.

Many cultures recognize the phenomenon of deserted women, whether the husband has met with an accident or has left for his own reasons. Great works of literature, from ancient Greece to this day, mention this phenomenon and describe its consequences.[5] However, within every culture, each of the situations enumerated above manifests itself with different practical and symbolic significance. In certain cultures, in the event of the husband's prolonged absence or deviant conduct, a marriage can be ended in the presence of the wife alone,[6] thereby allowing the woman to start anew. By contrast, the halakhic category of iggun, which renders the wife unable to remarry, leaves her socially marginalized in many respects. Traditional Jewish culture has always considered marriage and childbearing a woman's primary vocation, and a woman who fails to realize this potential is liable to experience great suffering.

The sources show that iggun was probably quite common in this period. Who were the women in this situation, and who were the men who caused it? How did Jewish society deal with the danger of a woman's becoming an agunah? What kind of reality was imposed on women who found themselves agunot, and what could they do to extricate themselves from their plight? How did decisors—the rabbinic experts with the authority to free agunot—discharge their task during this period, and what were the outcomes of the fact that the agunot were dependent on the male rabbinic establishment?

The present study has a twofold aim: to fill a void in the scholarship on agunot by describing the lives of agunot and of the men who brought this about. The second is to reexamine the halakhic activity concerning the freeing of agunot in this period and to propose a new assessment of the attitude that decisors displayed toward the freeing of agunot. These issues, which previously have met with only slight scholarly attention, merit extensive investigation.

AGUNOT AS A RESEARCH TOPIC

There is a long list of studies on iggun. The foundations of scholarly investigation into this subject were laid by Yitzhak Ze'ev (Y. Z.) Kahana as early as 1946.[7] At that time, the extent of the Holocaust was just beginning to emerge and there was pressing need for a solution for freeing married women from iggun, women who returned alone from the horror. Kahana's study, beyond the theoretical aspect, provided a timely response to an urgent need. An expanded version, published in 1954,[8] serves to this day as a starting point for any scholarly discussion of the agunah problem. In his volume, Kahana compiled the basic texts underlying any halakhic inquiry into the problem of iggun, listed the halakhic works treating the subject, and noted many of the responsa dealing with this issue composed by decisors over generations. Being a compilation of primary sources, his *Sefer haagunot* (lit., *Book of Agunot*) was not intended as a practical guide for halakhic ruling in actual cases, as Kahana explains in his introduction.[9] It becomes immediately evident that Kahana assumed that the decisors he was citing, he himself, and his readers all subscribed to the binding force of Jewish law on the agunah issue.

Some subsequent scholars have addressed only the theoretical aspect, while others have sought practical solutions for freeing actual agunot or for preventing more women from entering this category. Since the publication of *Sefer haagunot*, the halakhic issues relating to freeing an agunah have been addressed in scholarly publications as well as by those interested in halakhic guidelines.[10]

In the State of Israel, matters of marriage and divorce are governed by Jewish law. As a result, even people who are not necessarily committed to halakhah have become interested in iggun. Feminist trends also began to leave their mark on society and scholarship, influencing the freeing of agunot. Kahana's book came to be consulted by scholars who no longer subscribed to the binding force of Jewish law. Rather, they were seeking to apply critical tools to the halakhot in order to improve the status of women in halakhah and in society.[11] Today, men and women from all parts of the religious spectrum in Israel and elsewhere are publishing on halakhic and legal aspects of iggun. Fruitful conversation on the subject is taking place in academic, political, and social forums.[12] In 2004, Jewish-British law professor Bernard Jackson founded the Agunah Research Unit at the University of Manchester. Researchers at the unit set out to promote a global solution to what is sometimes known in English as "the agunah problem": a husband's refusing to divorce his wife.[13] In 2009, after a series of publications dealing with various aspects of the agunah problem, the unit submitted its concluding report with a proposal for a solution and its implementation.[14] Jackson presented the report at a 2010 conference in New York, which was attended by rabbis and scholars from several countries; in the ensuing debate, however, many speakers rejected the proposed solutions on the grounds that the Orthodox establishment would never accept them.

There are far fewer studies about agunot in specific historical contexts. These can be divided into those that touch on agunot as part of another subject and a very few focusing on agunot or specific agunot in a given historical period.[15] Yet, there has never been a study devoted to a systematic, comprehensive investigation of the circumstances of daily life of agunot from 1648 to 1850 in Ashkenazic culture. The goal of the current study is to fill in part of that gap.

THE GEOGRAPHICAL AREA OF ASHKENAZ

The Ashkenazic world, as defined by Jacob Katz, extends from Poland-Lithuania in the east to Alsace in the west. In our period, this vast territory was divided among many ruling powers.[16] The areas of German culture comprised nearly three hundred independent political entities, some monarchies, others free cities. The Crown of Poland-Lithuania, where many villages and towns belonged to the great magnate families, underwent great turmoil in this period until its dissolution in the late eighteenth century, when its territories passed to Russia, Austria, and Prussia.

The decision to cover such a large territory is by no means self-evident.[17] It is precisely the topic of agunot that justifies relating the entire expanse of Ashkenazic culture, for several reasons. The first is that halakhah in general, and the halakhah relating to agunot in particular, had binding force among all Ashkenazic Jewry for most of this period. Second, iggun is, in many respects, an essentially geographical phenomenon; in many cases, iggun was caused by men who travelled in search of livelihood, who wandered to follow spiritual or intellectual trends, or who left for personal reasons. Thus, the legal and social conditions of wherever her husband happened to be on his wanderings had the power to influence the agunah's life. In fact, the *heter agunah* (rabbinic written order to free an agunah, which she needed if she wished to remarry) was often made possible thanks to community ties throughout the Ashkenazic world and its inhabitants' shared views of marriage in halakhah. Centers of Jewish life in eastern and western Europe maintained strong ties: youths from Poland went to study halls in Germany, while rabbis, religious officials, and teachers from Poland held positions in Germany and vice versa. Toward the end of the eighteenth century, young people throughout the Ashkenazic world travelled to the Haskalah (Jewish Enlightenment) centers in Germany, and, somewhat later, to those in eastern Europe. Marriage ties linked families in the Ashkenazic world throughout this period (trends of differentiation between the Jews of central Europe and those of eastern Europe emerged only in the latter part of the century, and even then, the division was not comprehensive). Third, lively correspondence among decisors, including about agunot, in the entire area justifies treating the Ashkenazic world as a unity.[18] It was not unusual for the fate of an agunah in eastern Europe to be sealed by a rabbi in Germany. In many cases, decisors from the entire Ashkenazic world were involved in raging controversies over agunah issues. These correspondences and controversies show that decisors regarded themselves as subject to a single halakhic system in this matter, with shared responsibility for the collective of the Jewish people. The decision to deal with the fate of agunot and the stances of decisors throughout the entire Ashkenazic world thus accords with the self-perception of the halakhic authorities themselves.

TIMEFRAME

The period of 1648–1850 was one of great upheaval in the Jewish-Ashkenazic society in Europe, which affected Jewish family life as well. Significant demographic changes for Jews in the entire region followed upon The Thirty Years' War (1618–1648), which ended at the point that our study begins: the massacres of 1648–1649; the series of wars waged between the Poles, the Cossacks, the Russians, and the Swedes; and later on the partition of Poland. The changes affected the size and dispersion of Jewish communities, as well as their relations with their non-Jewish surroundings.[19] In addition, at this time, far-reaching spiritual change was sweeping Jewish society. Traditional authority was undermined by the Shabtai Tzvi affair in the late seventeenth century; the rise of Hasidism in eastern Europe in the latter part of the eighteenth century and the opposition it incurred; and the Haskalah, emancipation, and exposure to modernity that began in western and central Europe during the late eighteenth century and reached eastern Europe in the nineteenth century. These trends impacted all areas of Jewish life, due mainly to changed perception of individual autonomy vis-à-vis authority wielded by the community. Some of these had gender implications: changes occurred in family size and in women's status and education. The change did not happen all at once: alongside trends of progress and secularization, centuries-old customs and beliefs would remain in place for a long time yet. Throughout this period, for example, it continued to be the case that the only Jews who could be rabbis or study in Talmudic academies (*yeshivot*) to obtain halakhic knowledge were men, though a few women from the Jewish elite might learn some halakhah and study texts within their families. However, these changes did not take place all at once. Alongside trends of change or secularization, the traditions and beliefs that had taken root within Jewish society for hundreds of years remained

Introduction ::: xxi

steadfast. Further, although iggun had existed throughout the course of Jewish history, the sources show that the persecutions and massacres of 1648–1649 unbalanced the family as an institution. More than ever, decisors were now called upon to free agunot. I chose these persecutions as a point of departure for my discussion of agunot because they were indelibly seared into Jewish consciousness and affected the generations that followed. The end point of 1850 was chosen in recognition of the change in scope and nature of iggun that took place in the second half of the nineteenth century, mainly in light of the mass migration to the United States. This justifies a separate discussion of the phenomenon as it took place before the great migration.

THE SOURCES

The paucity of sources written by women, including agunot, is one of the striking difficulties in this book. We are forced to rely on texts by men — rabbis or community officials — for cases revolving around women. The resulting picture will of necessity be merely partial. However, we have a variety of sources from which we can extract information concerning agunot; we even have female voices discussing their experiences as agunot. Here are the sources that were used in this book.

Community Records

Like non-Jewish organizations and institutions in Europe in the early modern (and modern) age, Ashkenazic Jewish communities kept records of different kinds.[20] Record books (*pinkasim*) included details of institutions, budgets, enactments, decisions, and events in the lives of individuals and the community. Some of these records are extant and available.[21] Reading and analyzing the records of *batei din* (rabbinic courts; singular, *beit din*) has not been simple. Many beit din records, housed in archives all over the world, have only recently come to the attention of scholars as invaluable sources of information about everyday life in Jewish society in the early modern era. The overwhelming majority of these records have not been systematically studied; no comprehensive list has been made of all record books, and very few have been published in scholarly editions. There are different types of sources that fit into this "community records" category.

The first are beit din record books. The rabbinic courts (batei din) were a central institution in Jewish life in the early modern and modern eras.[22] Such courts were scattered throughout the region, with one beit din serving several local communities. The rabbi of the city headed the tribunal, assisted by rabbinic court judges (*dayanim*) and other leaders of the community. The beit din convened at regular intervals, usually twice a week, generally in a room adjacent to the synagogue or in the home of the rabbi.[23] Litigants paid fees to the judges, and these formed a major part of their salary. Beit din work focused on collecting testimony. Dayanim would question witnesses, occasionally calling upon an expert witness in a given profession. Testimony at the beit din, including for freeing agunot, was usually given in the local Yiddish vernacular of everyday life,[24] though proceedings were written down in Hebrew by the dayanim until at least the early nineteenth century.

The beit din handled financial lawsuits, business disputes, and family matters. The tribunal would hear the litigants and sometimes additional evidence. Its activity was documented in beit din record books or in the personal notebooks of the judges, and occasionally in both. Records of rabbinic courts (or of rabbinic judges) have survived from large and small Jewish communities, including Metz, Prague, Altona-Hamburg, Frankfurt, Kraków, Niedernai, Heidingsfeld, Romanswiller, and elsewhere.[25] The record books (pinkasim) date for the most part to the latter half of the eighteenth century.[26] Jay Berkovitz, author of an exhaustive study on the Metz beit din record books, has remarked: "beit din records represent a culture of law consumers rather than of lawmakers." The Metz beit din record books, he suggests, should be regarded as a kind of memoir, preserving not only legal principles but also stories.[27]

The second type of source is community documents. Many are extant; they document various community decisions, appointment of officials, enactments, and various events. A community scribe, or sometimes a rabbi or lay leader, would take down the particulars. These documents come in assorted formats and sizes; some have been published, while others are still languishing in archives. Aside from these archival documents, there is also a treasury of edited printed volumes, including works of homiletic/exegetical literature (midrash),[28] books of customs, and memory books, in Hebrew and Yiddish. I used some of these for my research as well.

A third source type comprises records of the community treasurer (*gabai*) and fee collector. Records of these community officials contain financial data concerning fees paid by members, as well as donations, charity, and fees for the use of communal facilities (e.g., the ritual bath, or mikveh, and cemetery), including money distributed to the needy from communal charity funds.

Placards are a fourth source. These placards were posted in the community to announce events or to disseminate policies and decisions made by rabbis, lay leaders, or the non-Jewish authorities.

What remains are other community records. Community archives and the literary estates of community rabbis contain additional documents: letters, marriage contracts (ketubot), betrothal agreements, and assorted notes. These texts can provide invaluable information about everyday life in the Jewish community or about a specific individual.

Shulhan arukh

Many of the legal decisions made by decisors who dealt with the cases that appear in this book are based on the law code that was already considered authoritative in the period under discussion (and to this day) called the *Shulhan arukh* (lit., "set table"), written by Rabbi Joseph Karo. This law code summarizes the legal decisions made in the Talmud and by its subsequent commentators so that the (usually rabbinic) reader could use it for reference without having to engage with the centuries of arguments it took to arrive at a particular law. It was in the early modern period that the *Shulhan arukh*, first printed in Venice in 1565, became the authoritative law code in Ashkenaz. Since Rabbi Karo was Sephardic, Ashkenazic decisors read the code alongside the glosses (collectively called the *Mapah*) of Rabbi Moshe Isserles of Poland, whose comments and opinions reflected Ashkenazic custom. Also relevant for our purposes is that the *Shulhan arukh* and *Mapah* were divided into four sections by topic: *Orah hayim* (daily *mitzvot*, Sabbath, and festivals); *Yoreh deah* (miscellaneous subjects, including the laws of kashrut, purity, charging interest, and mourning); *Even haezer* (marriage, divorce, and connected subjects); and *Hoshen mishpat* (legal issues, both civil and criminal).[29] The influence of these works was so great that many decisors who read them later divided their own collections of responsa or other writings into these same four sections. The reader, therefore, will notice frequent citations of Even haezer, whether from the writings of Karo, Isserles, or other early modern decisors who arranged their work similarly.

Responsa Literature

Responsa (Hebr., *she'elot utshuvot* lit., "questions and answers") were answers, typically in the form of letters, written by rabbis in response to questions they had received from their congregants, colleagues, and other followers. We have responsa about practical halakhic matters regarding specific agunot and on theoretical aspects of the agunah problem. The printing revolution that began in the early sixteenth century generated a great number of responsa volumes, and their distribution increased steadily after that.[30] For the present book, I studied over four hundred responsa written by fifty-six decisors in Ashkenazic society during the relevant period.[31]

We must also note the theoretical question of the extent of the usefulness of responsa as historical sources (see also the discussion in chapter 12 regarding methodological questions affecting the book at large). The clear methodological problem of how to select responsa on a certain issue that are representative of the period's halakhic activity is discussed in part 4.

Yet, historians and scholars of halakhah analyze these case histories on the assumption that the narrative as constructed by the writer reflects the range of possibilities envisioned by the questioner. These descriptions and opinions provide a wealth of information about everyday life, as well as insights into the writer's own worldview. The task of the historian is to extract information from the sources and anchor it in a broader context by cross-referencing it with other available sources. This is what I have tried to do in this book.

Other Printed Jewish Sources

Various books in Hebrew and Yiddish, among them books of homiletics, books of customs, and memoirs, were annotated, edited, and brought to print by scholars researching the Jewish communities in Ashkenazic lands. I used several of these for the current study.

Census Data

Population censuses began in parts of the area under discussion in the eighteenth century. Some are extant and partly or wholly available. The census was part of the attempt by authorities to regulate the population, particularly the Jewish population. The census served, inter alia, tax collection purposes. In certain localities, the community as such had to declare its assets; in others, non-Jewish officials recorded the data. Scholarship on these census reports generally considers them to be reliable.[32] At the same time, they are not uniform in format or type of data, and using them raises methodological problems, as will be discussed in context. In researching this book, I used published volumes of census reports or online databases: the census of the Jews of Poland, 1764, published by Raphael Mahler;[33] census reports from different localities in Prussia over the eighteenth century, published by Selma Stern;[34] and the census of the Jews of Alsace, from the latter half of the eighteenth century, published on the website of the Nouvelle Gallia Judaica project.[35]

Tombstone Inscriptions

In the region under discussion, it was customary to inscribe gravestones with the name of the deceased and their date of death, and also with biographical details, such as place of birth, occupation, and father's name. Some gravestones bear a form of elegy or remembrance of the nature and deeds of the deceased or details of the circumstances of death. While obviously not objective descriptions of the deceased, gravestone inscriptions do provide the biographical information of historical people and the values and norms of their particular society.[36]

Through this diverse set of sources, we can access what was considered appropriate conduct in a given society, as reflected in enactments and homilies; from sources such as beit din records, we can follow actual behavior. Jay Berkovitz, who studied the beit din from Metz, wrote that they generally represent a culture of law abiders more than a culture of lawmakers. Therefore, they should be viewed as a kind of memoir, which preserves not only legal issues but also stories.[37] Yet, each source type mentioned above presents its own methodological problems. These are treated in this book with respect to specific texts. For the present, in addition to those I have already mentioned, I will note a few primary methodological problems with using these sources.

First, caution is necessary when using halakhic literature in general, and responsa literature in particular, for the purpose of drawing historical conclusions. On the one hand, valuable historical information is embedded in this literature, including the referencing of specific people and places by name. Like many legal documents, for example, they reference previous legal documents, often word for word, and frequently use technical terms. These conventions often make it difficult to distinguish the reality of the responsa's author-decisor from that of his predecessors or to discern which statements reflect realia and which are stock phrases and images.[38] In analyzing this literature, I have tried to make the necessary distinctions. Even if the decisor does not cite concrete details, still, the premises that guided him, and the way in which his rulings were guided by these premises, may reveal the reality in which he was active. This is especially valid when data taken from one source can be read in light of information from another source.

In addition, since all the extant texts used in this book were written almost solely by men, they express almost exclusively the male, authoritative voice for anything to do with halakhic matters. The female voice that is sometimes heard through them is not the primary voice. This well-known problem has been thoroughly studied in women's history, Jewish and non-Jewish alike.[39] Along with the attempt to derive the woman's point of view from the text, we are assuming that the decisors were guided by deeply rooted gender perceptions; as such, these texts do provide information, albeit partial, about experiences of women in that world.

We find difficulty of a different sort in sources of what has been called the "ego-document" type: memoirs, letters, wills, and other texts penned by private individuals.[40] These may have been biased by the author's personality, age, experience, and purpose in writing. We must ask whether a specific text is representative of its time, again by comparing the information derived from it with data from other sources and in scholarly research.

RESEARCH METHODS AND METHODOLOGICAL ASSUMPTIONS

This book is essentially a historical study attempting to answer the question, What happened? Scholars of microhistory, beginning with the field's pioneer, Carlo Ginzburg, have defended the attempt to grasp the general picture of a society from the lives of individuals not necessarily of its hegemonic, or dominant, group. I have combined this approach with the assumption of Fernand Braudel that structures, including social structures, change slowly; they restrain but also allow people to act.[41]

This assertion about social structures is certainly valid for those laws regarded in traditional Jewish society as the foundation of its existence, including the laws of agunot.

Historical analysis profits from the application of methods and assumptions originating in other disciplines, such as anthropology, sociology, hermeneutics, jurisprudence, study of Jewish law, and gender studies. Several basic assumptions for this study should be mentioned in this context.

1. A careful reading of the sources presented in this book obliges us to relate not only to the specific social contexts in which they were written but also to their use of metaphor, idioms, phrases, quotations, narrative, and rhetoric. Examining them allows us to discern conscious or unconscious ideological biases that stem from the worldview of the author's contemporaries. Hans-Georg Gadamer's fusing of horizons — the world of the author and that of his predecessors, their worlds and ours — may lead to insights as to the meanings of texts in their original contexts as we analyze them centuries after they were written.[42]

2. Since the publication of Sherry Ortner's influential article introducing the distinction between "sex" as a biological fact and "gender" as a cultural one (1974),[43] a generation of scholars, both women and men, have deepened our understanding of this subject. Sociopolitical and psychological meanings derive from the fact that gender identities are fluid, constructed by different cultures in different ways. We have learned that gender identity, like many other aspects of human existence, is not permanent but time- and culture-dependent. Tendencies, qualities, roles, and practices regarded in the past as deterministic "nature" are now seen as raw material for social interactions influenced by powerful social forces. As the feminist attorney Catherine MacKinnon has said: "Social inequality is substantially created and enforced — that is, done — through words and images. Social hierarchy cannot and does not exist without being embodied in meanings and expressed in communications."[44]

3. For a study on agunot, it is additionally helpful to use studies

in anthropology, especially those focusing on symbols and their role in organizing the social order, as well as studies on attitudes to marriage and its termination as culture-dependent, and as reflecting various models of the power struggle of the sexes.[45]

OVERVIEW OF HALAKHAH RELEVANT TO AGUNOT

The many specific agunah cases discussed in this book are more easily understood in light of some important halakhot relating to most situations of iggun. These laws will be introduced in general terms here, though details may reappear in connection with specific cases. For most of the period in question, rabbinic authorities, through the beit din, adjudicated Jewish marriage and divorce. Even after 1850, matters of personal status generally were handled by Jewish courts. Jewish law, unlike canon law and other legal systems that partially or totally rejected divorce,[46] recognizes the possibility of ending a marriage by a get. The get is the legal document with which a husband may divorce his wife. The source is in biblical law: "A man takes a wife and possesses her. She fails to please him because he finds something obnoxious about her, and he writes her a bill of divorcement, hands it to her, and sends her away from his house; she leaves his household and becomes the wife of another man" (Deut. 24:1–2).[47] These verses give only the husband the right to end the marriage by initiating divorce. The precise circumstances under which a man may exercise this right have been much debated. The eleventh-century rabbinic enactment known as *herem derabeinu Gershom* restricted the husband's right by decreeing that he may not divorce his wife unless she accepts the get of her own free will. Since then, practically speaking, as long as the husband has not freely given, and the wife freely received, the get, the couple is still married and neither party may marry anyone else. In a few specific cases, discussed in more detail in part 3, a beit din could force a husband to give a get or (more commonly) a wife to accept one, but this option was exercised rarely. Though the beit din typically agreed when both spouses wanted to divorce, the asymmetry in divorce law favoring the husband gave the rabbinic court a fair amount of power when there was a dispute. Marital disputes and their impact on iggun will be discussed in more detail in part 3.

Jewish divorce has monetary consequences: the husband is required to return the woman's property and pay her the money specified in her *ketubah* (marriage contract) and dowry. Poverty does not exempt a husband from this obligation or from the requirement in Jewish law that he pay child support. Not granting a get, then, was one option a husband could use when he did not want to pay his wife. Without a divorce, a ketubah could not be paid.

Divorce also followed automatically upon the death of either spouse. If a husband died naturally at home or some other place in his town, allowing his wife to marry again was almost never an issue. But one reason why many women became agunot in this period is that their husbands' whereabouts were unknown, including because they disappeared or died in a manner that could not be proven under halakhah. It was not uncommon for early modern Jewish men to die while traveling for business or studies — travelers at that time risked murder, drowning, and other similar fates — or during persecution or war. The wife of such a missing man was an agunah. She could receive the beit din's permission to remarry only on the strength of witnesses to the man's death or, more rarely, circumstantial evidence that would satisfy the court. Typically, the beit din required at least two Jewish witnesses (who could be men or women) to testify to the man's death.[48] The many complicated and specific Jewish laws on testimony, including the almost total exclusion of non-Jewish witnesses (even though non-Jewish authorities often took possession of the body of a crime victim and/or foreigner and performed an inquest); the preference for the witnesses' having seen the man's actual death, not just his body, and if his body, only soon after the death; and the difficulty of securing witness testimony across the far-flung European Jewish diaspora, despite the efforts of many a beit din to contact distant colleagues by letter or even to send emissaries to a witness's house, meant that many women whose husbands were very likely dead could be denied permission to remarry.

Even when the evidence satisfied all these rules, some rabbis still feared freeing agunot. Their nightmare scenario was allowing a woman to remarry and then discovering that her husband was still alive. In that case, she had committed adultery; any children born of this marriage were *mamzerim*, which meant that they could not marry within the Jewish community. Though a beit din always warned witnesses to testify truthfully, in agunah cases, additional warning was sometimes provided, indicating these concerns. In one case, to be detailed in part 2, the judge's report reads: "We cautioned him: it is no small matter to free a married woman so that she is free to marry anyone she chooses—based on your word! Only if you are absolutely certain that it was indeed [the man in question whose body you saw]."[49] Some dayanim cross-checked the testimony of different witnesses in an attempt to identify contradictions. Many rabbis would only free agunot if a certain number of their rabbinic colleagues (often two, but as many as ten or more) would sign onto their decisions.

BOOK STRUCTURE AND CONTENTS

"Agunah" as a halakhic category blurs distinctions since, in fact, it refers to women in various situations. The structure of this book lifts the veil on agunah as a category. "Agunah" includes widows in need of halitzah (a ceremony voiding the need to perform levirate marriage; see part 1), women whose husbands disappeared without a trace, abandoned wives, and married women who wished to untie the marital knot against their husband's will. We will focus not only on the agunot, but on the men who brought them to that state as well. As we shall see, the category of "agunah" permeated other areas of life. Where men are concerned, moreover, the category left plenty of room to maneuver, whereas it posed a constant threat to women's liberty. A folk saying, cited later in this book, illuminates the point: "Today a slattern, tomorrow—an agunah."[50]

The book comprises four parts. The first part traces the state of widows in Ashkenazic society, given that the first category of iggun refers to women awaiting halitzah; all such women were widows. Like agunot, the subject of Jewish widows in early modern times has met with very little scholarly attention.[51] The first part starts by detailing the personal and social significance of widowhood. It is premised on the halakhic foundation of a widow's legal status. Key concepts related to a widow in need of halitzah are also explained, and the fate of widows awaiting halitzah, who had agunah status in the interim, is described. The book here explores attitudes to halitzah, depicts the attitude of Jewish society toward women awaiting halitzah, and goes into the details of the ceremony itself.

The second and third parts of the book present stories of agunot in their social context. Part 2 tells the stories of women who became agunot because the body of the dead husband was either never found or was not identified in compliance with halakhah. Relevant principles of Jewish law regarding this type of iggun are explained in detail: the identity and validity of witnesses, testimony for freeing an agunah, identification of a corpse, pronouncing death on grounds of circumstantial evidence, and laws relating to the process of freeing an agunah. Next, we look at two kinds of agunah cases: first, women who became agunot through persecution or massacre, focusing on the difficulty of obtaining testimony to prove the husband's death to a beit din's satisfaction and procedures for obtaining a rabbinic court's formal permission to remarry (heter agunah; plural, *heterei agunah*). We then turn to women who lost their husbands during relatively ordinary life. We look at agunah cases resulting from murder, drowning, and fire, elaborating the social and economic consequences. We will discuss both the various means the agunah had at her disposal to extricate herself from her state and her community's willingness to assist her. The attitude of non-Jewish authorities also had a bearing on the agunah's chances of obtaining permission to remarry, as did gender-related and social factors. The complex role of gossip in the lives of premodern communities, with special attention to agunot, is examined as well.

Part 3 of the book is devoted to the agunah who was abandoned by her husband. We begin with marital disputes, tracing the dynamics culminating in a husband's desertion of his wife. The community's involvement in family and marital life is explained. We also look at how Jewish society generally regarded marriage and marital crises. This analysis will provide the basis for my claim that a man sometimes consciously chose to make his wife an agunah, because society treated these men with impunity. The last chapter of this part traces men who abandoned their wives, inquiring into the circumstances that led them to the decision. Finally, we will survey the ways in which deserted women coped with the need to locate their missing husbands and clarify the dangers this task involved.

The fourth and final part of the book focuses on decisors and their attitudes toward agunot. I begin with the odd discrepancy I found between the small number of heterei agunah in beit din record books as compared to the large number of responsa concluding with giving permission to the agunah to remarry. The riddle is solved in this part. I present an overview of approaches decisors used to free agunot in this period, paying special attention to the factors that could influence the halakhic process. I revisit the claim made by some scholars that decisors tended to leniency in freeing agunot. My conclusion: this claim is not borne out by the contemporary sources.

The broad range of topics in this book illuminate facets of Jewish family life in the Ashkenazic world from 1648 to 1850. Addressing such a broad range of topics across a vast geographical area, for such an extended period of time, is liable to lead to generalizations instead of sensitivity to nuances and difference. Yet, I am convinced that this methodological approach is necessary to achieve an in-depth, multidimensional understanding of the fate of agunot. In the time that passed since I conducted the research for this book, a number of new studies have been published on relevant topics. Some of these focus on Jews within specific communities, while others attempt to trace practices that were shared by various Jewish communities. Verena Kasper-Marienberg and Edward Fram presented cases that, like some of the cases in this book, show that Jews —women and men—often navigated between both Jewish and non-Jewish courts more extensively than was assumed in the scholarship.[52] Debra Kaplan illuminates various aspects of life in Jewish communities in Germany during the modern era.[53] In her book, readers will find valuable information about the lives of Jews from different social strata and the relationships between them, including attitudes toward widows (as discussed in the first part of my book). Her book also includes important information about community records, a genre that I used extensively when conducting the research for this book. Jay Berkovitz's comprehensive work about the records of the Metz beit din is especially relevant to the topics discussed in this book.[54] Here, readers will find much information regarding widows, legal guardians, divorce disputes, and petitioning non-Jewish courts. Among others, Berkovitz presents cases in which Jews—men and women, ordinary members of the community as well as decisors in the local batei din—conducted themselves differently from the protagonists of the cases I describe in my book. While these studies do not, to my understanding, question the validity of the arguments that I present, they can certainly illuminate aspects of the issues that I have dealt with only briefly. Particularly noteworthy is Berkovitz's claim that the Metz beit din "approved the appointment of women as guardians over the property of orphans, despite the misgivings expressed in codified halakhic sources," and that it employed mechanisms to allocate parts of the inheritance to daughters.[55] Berkovitz highlights the ways in which the Metz beit din differed from rabbinic courts in other locales, emphasizing its collaborative relationship with the French civil court system and noting that "the urgency of resolving the dissonance between the Jewish and general legal systems was likely more pronounced in Metz than in rabbinic courts of similar stature in the eighteenth century."[56] While I have also presented cases in which batei din exhibited some flexibility in implementing Jewish law, the sources I analyzed show that this was the exception rather than the rule. Nevertheless, Berkovitz's findings suggest that the legal status of women may be better in cases where rabbinic courts are subordinate to state civil law, or where rabbis acknowledge the interdependence of cases brought before rabbinic and civil courts, than in situations where rabbis rule solely on the basis of Jewish law. This hypothesis (which is consistent with the thesis presented in the fourth part of this book) warrants further research. I believe that the growing number of studies that focus on rabbinic and civil court records will eventually lead to a well-founded conclusion on this topic. I hope that this book will contribute to the ongoing discussion and inspire future research on the lives of Jewish women in general and of agunot in particular.

Part One

Widows and Yevamot in the Ashkenazic World in the Early Modern Age

1 : WIDOWS IN THE ASHKENAZIC WORLD, 1648–1850

A pitiful widow who abruptly loses such royalty!
— Chava Turniansky, *Glikl: Memoirs 1691–1719*

Widows have a strong presence in historical texts of all periods, including in the early modern and modern periods. Lacking a spouse, a widow (or an agent acting on her behalf) had to carry out legal and financial acts normally reserved for men. Some widows required financial aid from the community. Hence, their visibility in historical documents is more pronounced than that of either married women or widowers.[1] Yet, while the subject of widows in non-Jewish society has been extensively researched,[2] that of Jewish widows in the early modern and modern periods has not.[3] Given that many agunot were actually widows, let us begin by expanding upon aspects of widowhood in the period in question, with particular attention to agunot awaiting halitzah. These were women whose husbands had died without leaving living offspring; biblical law (Deut. 25:5–10) mandated that a woman in that position either marry her deceased husband's brother or participate in a halitzah ceremony, in which the brother formally refuses to marry her and thus frees her to marry someone else. At the same time, we need to understand the situation of agunot in other categories as well. First, the responsa literature deals with cases of women classified as agunot due to some procedural error in identifying the husband's remains or in the presentation of the evidence required by Jewish law for verification of death, while the woman herself already knew that she was, in fact, already a widow. Second, abandoned and separated wives have often been classed as widows since demographic data were entered under the name of the householder. While women do appear as householders in their own right, the circumstances leading up to that status are usually unknown. Since the halakhic term "agunah" was an internal, Jewish category, one not recognized as an official demographic one, a woman recognized as an agunah in Jewish law would be registered by non-Jewish authorities as a widow or divorcée. Finally, many societal norms applied to widows were also relevant to agunot, either as generalization or as a way of marginalization.

Agunot and widows shared certain characteristics and differed in others. Before we turn to the differences, we must understand the status of each group in the context of its society. In discussing agunot awaiting halitzah, I will chiefly address aspects of widowhood that are not related to motherhood, since many such young women did not yet have children. Widows awaiting halitzah and other categories of agunah occasionally include widows who married bachelors, or even widows who had children from a previous marriage who then remarried and were widowed again without having had children from their second husband. As we shall see, the patterns of marriage and remarriage in the society under discussion at times necessitated complex maneuvering. Therefore, the discussion will include cases of widowed mothers, which are indicative of the different attitudes contemporaries afforded widows, in general, and widows with children, in particular.

THE DUALITY OF WIDOWHOOD

In her memoir, the businesswoman Glikl Hamel (Hamburg, 1645– Metz, 1724) documented, in rich detail, various aspects of Jewish life.[4] No other widow in seventeenth- to eighteenth-century Germany left us such detailed descriptions. Glikl impresses the reader as an educated, well-informed woman with strong opinions who wished to determine her own fate and those of her children according to her values, beliefs, and memories. We cannot help but admire her penetrating insights into her own world along with her candid criticism. Her writing, originally intended for her numerous descendants, is peppered with didactic aphorisms and poignant anecdotes, her innermost musings, and moments of joy and crisis. The document affords us a better understanding of how Glikl's society treated widows.[5] As a minority, Jews were influenced in their views of widows both by Jewish tradition and by patterns of behavior in neighboring non-Jewish societies.

It will be recalled that the geographical area in question was divided into many principalities, territories, and jurisdictions. Separate legal systems operated alongside each other, with many implementing independent policies. This greatly impacted the socioeconomic status of women, and widows in particular.[6] Two parallel legal models operated in different areas of Germany at the time. In one model, joint marital property was owned nominally by both spouses, but the husband alone was entitled to manage it (i.e., buy and sell). In the second model, a wife could own private property and use it as she liked, including carrying out relevant legal actions. In the same way, inheritance law for women in German territories followed several approaches. In certain areas, the husband inherited two-thirds of his wife's property, should she predecease him, while she stood to inherit only a third of his property should he predecease her; the rest of the estate was divided among their children. The law in other areas was more like Jewish law: the wife's right to claim her dowry took precedence over any of the husband's debts and over the rights of other heirs. Both models allowed the husband to cut his wife off completely from the inheritance if he so wished. In Poland as well, diverse legal models operated side by side. Women were generally considered incompetent for the purpose of managing their own property. In fact, however, many women of the aristocracy managed family estates during their married life. In urban society, a woman's situation largely depended on local civil law, which differed from one city to another. Under Kulm law (or Chełmno law), a married woman was essentially dependent on her husband, since he held the right to manage their joint property, unless she could prove that his behavior was irresponsible or harmful. Under Magdeburg law, any property a wife brought to the marriage was somewhat protected; if widowed, her claim had priority over those of other heirs or creditors.[7] In the early modern era, there was a growing trend of authorities' restricting women's legal and financial rights in different parts of Europe. This had severe repercussions, especially for widows.[8]

In contrast to the diverse legal models operating in non-Jewish society, Jewish society was guided in the treatment of widows primarily by requirements of halakhah and tradition. Uniformity in patterns of behavior in Jewish communities was strengthened by marriage among families from all over the Ashkenazic world. Despite this, Jewish documents show that communities also differed in their treatment of widows depending on the size of the community, its financial situation, and other factors that will be mentioned in context.[9]

Glikl, twice widowed, tells of other widows of varying ages and circumstances: Her grandmother was left a penniless widow with two daughters still living at home; Glikl's own mother was widowed at age forty-four with three unmarried orphans living at home. Yente, Glikl's sister-in-law, was widowed at a young age, and Glikl's bachelor servant married a widow.[10] In our discussion of widows, we must therefore take into account age, social position, number of children, financial situation of the late husband and of the widow's family of origin, and family and community support networks. We should also look at demographics and patterns of marriage. Yet none of these affords an understanding of the personal experience of becoming a widow. The uniqueness of Glikl's memoir lies in the glimpse it allows into the personal dimension of one widow among many.

Glikl began writing her memoirs after the death of her first husband and resumed after being widowed for the second time in 1712.[11] In describing and analyzing other widows, Glikl drew on her own experiences and firsthand knowledge. Bearing in mind that Glikl intended her memoirs for her children, we may assume that her presentation of events and characters was influenced by her perception of their significance for her intended readers.[12]

Glikl describes her actions, thoughts, and emotions in the weeks following the death of her husband. Chaim Hamel died on January 16, 1689:

> He was buried on Sunday, 24 Tevet 5449, *with a good name.* Such distress and consternation throughout the community cannot be put in writing, for the tragedy was, due to our great sins, so sudden, alas. So, with my children around me, I sat for the woeful week of mourning, thinking what a woeful situation it was, what a sight: I, a desolate widow, here with my twelve fatherless orphans—may they live a long life—apart from him. We assembled a regular quorum for prayer right away, and I arranged for men to study regularly at my house, night and day, that entire year, and other things, may God remember them in my favor. My children recited the mourner's prayer diligently. Not a single man or woman failed to pay a condolence visit every day, nor were we lacking in tears. You can imagine how we got through the week of mourning. *I was fed tears as daily bread, made to drink great measures of tears . . . I have been cast down from heaven to earth,*[13] alas. My children, my brothers and

sisters and other relatives, all consoled me as well as they could, but one by one they all went home with their loved ones, while I and my orphans were left grief-stricken. That beloved man was mine for thirty years, and I enjoyed all the good a decent woman could or should wish for; he even ensured I would be provided for after his death.... He was fortunate to depart this sinful world a prosperous man, much respected.... But he abandoned me and my unmarried and married children to sorrow, pain and grief, sorrow and grief increased every day, disaster overtook disaster as my friends and relations stood far off. But what can I and my lamenting do? It was all due to my sins, for those do I weep, my eyes flow with tears, I will not forget him to the end of my days for he is engraved on my heart. My dear mother and my brothers and sisters consoled me.... But alas, these condolences only made my grief worse by the day; such condolences only poured oil on the flames, which rose higher and higher, and my anguish and heartbreak only grew worse. The condolences and encouragement lasted two or three weeks; after that no one knew me anymore. In fact, those we had greatly assisted repaid us with nothing but evil; that's the way of the world. At least that's how it seemed to me in the mood I was in, the brooding of a pitiful widow who abruptly loses such royalty—how can one forget that?—in our great sins it seemed to us, wrongly perhaps, that no one is doing the right thing by us. May God forgive me for this.[14]

One of the first thoughts Glikl ascribes to herself is awareness of her situation and how it looks to others. Besides her grief at losing her beloved husband—the image for the misery she feels is an object flung from heaven to earth, a natural response to the loss of a beloved husband—she is keenly aware of how the bereaved widow and family are perceived by others. The tableau of painful separation from husband and father is depicted visually. Glikl describes the reactions of relatives and acquaintances: the entire community is dismayed and shocked, as her siblings and relatives console her. Ultimately, however, grief and bereavement are hers and her children's alone. Glikl seems to be troubled by how her bereaved family must look to friendly, or perhaps curious, eyes, as observers scrutinize the grief-stricken wife and children even as they offer condolences.

Were acquaintances and relatives really more interested in the appearance of the bereaved family than in their actual situation? Or was that merely subjective interpretation? Glikl herself raises this possibility. Does evidence from historical documents support her feeling? What did a widow in that society and time look like? Put another way, let us ask, How was she expected to look?

WIDOW'S GARB

Special garments worn by widows are mentioned already in the Bible. When Tamar sets out to seduce Judah, "She took off her widow's garb" (Gen. 38:14, 19). On taking captives in war, the text states, "And you see among the captives a beautiful woman and you desire her and would take her [into your household] as your wife, and [she shall] discard her captive's garb" (Deut. 21:11–13). A midrash takes this to mean that the captive woman must discard her own nice clothes and don "widow's garb."[15] Very few Jewish historical sources describe widows' garments, and changes in wearing mourning clothes in Jewish society have scarcely been studied.[16] In a brief discussion of widows' apparel in non-Jewish German society in early modernity, Britta-Juliane Kruse found that in medieval times, only some groups among the aristocracy wore special garments of mourning. Mourning customs became more widespread in the sixteenth century among all classes and included special garments in black or white and special hats or headscarves.[17] Early modern Jewish society, too, underwent accelerated ritualization of death and mourning customs, influenced by kabbalistic imagery, as shown by Avriel Bar-Levav.[18] Belief that devils kept company with the deceased led to customs for warding off their baleful designs on mortals. Did these developments also leave their mark on widows' clothing?

It should be recalled that the sartorial customs of Jews generally resembled those of their non-Jewish neighbors. The exceptions were specific articles of clothing that Jews in certain places were required to wear to externalize their Jewishness.[19] In Ashkenazic communities of this period, costume symbolized social status and degree of affiliation with the community.[20] One's apparel was (supposedly) not a matter of personal choice. Regulations in many Jewish communities reflect the importance of clothing for the social order.[21] These regulations were prescriptive in nature (not descriptive, as were works of Jewish customs)[22] and thus were similar to *Kleiderordnungen*—restrictions on certain kinds of clothing in non-Jewish society. By regulating dress, community leadership sought to set proper moral standards and monitor its members.[23] These occasionally specifically related to a particular social class, gender, or occupation, as can be seen in the regulation from Moravia (1703) that stipulates that community dignitaries must appear at meetings respectably attired in cloak and turban or overcoat and hat. The same holds for anyone requesting an audience with community or state dignitaries.[24]

Thus, respect for social status had to be reflected in one's costume. The 1686 regulations of the communities of Altona, Hamburg, and Wandsbek (AHW) even explicitly stipulate that anyone attending synagogue or a communal meal not dressed according to regulation may be thrown out.[25] Extant documents do not contain any requirement for widows to wear any specific mourning garment, but articles of clothing for widows in mourning are mentioned in works of Jewish custom and other contemporary sources.[26] Yosefe Manspach, a *shamash* (a layperson who assisted in the synagogue with religious services and also sometimes kept communal records) in Worms from 1648 to 1678, notes the custom in Ashkenaz for men and women alike to wear special garments throughout the year of mourning.[27] Of special interest are the relevant customs recorded in the book of customs of the community of Fürth, printed in 1767. The work contains detailed instructions for the appropriate mourning attire according to degree of blood relationship to the deceased: A woman mourning her father or mother wears weekday clothes during the year, but on Rosh Hashanah and Yom Kippur may not don a *kittel* (a white robe worn on special occasions, such as on the High Holidays and at weddings). A woman in mourning for her husband substitutes white garments for her black ones after thirty days. She may don a kittel over her mourning garments on Rosh Hashanah and Yom Kippur. If she marries during the year of mourning, she discards her garments of mourning immediately after the wedding.[28]

It emerges that a widow, like other mourners, was distinguishable by garments worn throughout the first year of mourning, unless she remarried within that year. During the first thirty days of mourning (*sheloshim*), a widow would cover her head with a black kerchief,[29] which was then replaced by a white one for the remainder of that year. In premodern Europe, garments of black and white, colors of purity and modesty, were deemed effective for warding off evil spirits.[30] The choice of these colors for Jewish widows was probably based on similar considerations.

Given that widows in this period were recognizable by their manner of dress, any deviation from custom was liable to be noticed, as society expected the widow to display outward mourning and grief for her husband.[31]

WIDOWS: IMAGE AND REALITY

Imagery of the widow has been extensively researched in literary criticism, art history, anthropology, and history.[32] Images tend to the extreme: widows embody threat, being free of male domination; or conversely, images emphasize their vulnerability and helplessness.[33] Contradictory images of the widow are found in nearly all cultures, including Jewish culture and tradition. Jacob Katz has observed that for Jews in the sixteenth to seventeenth centuries, it made no difference whether a specific custom, outlook, or rule derived from Talmudic times or from the late Middle Ages.[34] Indeed, the traditional sources that are the focus of our study are based on halakhic and philosophical works spanning centuries. New ideas intertwine with old until they can no longer be easily separated. Halakhah regarded the widow as both a potential threat and needy person, with a similar picture emerging from other popular genres in Ashkenazic Jewry in the relevant period.[35]

Glikl's account of how her widowed mother married off Glikl's siblings shows a facet of the widow image as perceived by contemporary society: "My mother held such elegant, lavish weddings that no one could tell that she was a widow, poor thing; it was all as though my father, of blessed memory, were still alive."[36] The fact that a wretched widow could organize a lavish wedding reception was apparently not taken for granted. A widow's status may be apparent, for example, in the celebrations she hosts. Family celebrations, as Glikl reiterates, required heavy expenditure,[37] and the quoted description most probably alludes to the widow's anticipated financial difficulties. In a society where social position is commensurate with financial status,[38] loss of property means loss of social prestige. It is likely that Glikl's mother endeavored to keep up appearances of wealth in order to maintain the family's social status even when she became a widow.

Glikl speaks admiringly of her mother. To Glikl, her mother embodied the dignified, respectable model of widowhood. Her mother's misery as a widow was undeniable, but whether it would show outwardly depended, in Glikl's view, on the widow's own life choices. This ideal of widowhood—the widow masterfully running an efficient household while keeping up the family's prestige—draws on the lives of Glikl's mother and grandmother, both widowed at a young age.[39] Glikl's point of view is perhaps not representative of her milieu but rather of the women in her family and their self-imposed standards. At the same time, it is worth asking how the ideal held up by this extraordinary woman reflects her own strategies for coping with opinions and remarks voiced by others. Indeed, other contemporary sources show that there was a gap between the ways in which Jewish widows presented themselves and the ways in which some of them lived.

Ostensibly, society could be expected to maintain an image of the fragile widow in the interest of preserving the social order. Independent, strong widows conceivably could undermine the institution of marriage. On the other hand, destitute women would become a drain on communal resources. The inherent duality in the treatment of widows thus led to polarized views, with a widow perceived simultaneously as strong and dangerous or weak and in need of protection. As women internalized this duality, they developed coping strategies according to individual ability and circumstances.

The view that a woman who loses her husband also loses her protection and livelihood, and consequently merits pity, is found as early as the Bible: "you shall not take a widow's garment in pawn" (Deut. 24:17); "You [leaders] shall not ill-treat any widow or orphan" (Exod. 22:21). Does widowhood as such merit pity, or are the biblical injunctions contingent upon actual need? This question was also debated in the Mishnah (edited by the third century CE): "A pledge may not be taken from a widow, whether she be rich or poor."[40] Halakhic debate continued over centuries, with historical studies showing that there have always been wealthy widows, who by their lifestyle challenged the biblical injunction to show compassion for any widow as such.[41] Tension persisted between the biblical image of widows and the lifestyle of actual widows. This can be seen in the commentary by Rabbi Jacob ben Isaac Ashkenazi of Janów (1550–1624) in his *Tzena urena*. Thought to have been first printed in the late sixteenth century, this Yiddish work is a compilation of commentaries and midrashim on the weekly Torah and haftarah portions. Perused by men and women alike, the work gained immense popularity in the Ashkenazic world from the seventeenth century onwards.

Scholars of Yiddish literature have suggested that the work attained such widespread popularity, inter alia, thanks to the relevance of the homilies to readers' lives.[42] On the words "any widow" (Exod. 22:21), the book states the following:

> You shall not illtreat any widow whatsoever. Even if a widow is extremely wealthy it is forbidden to grieve her, since widows weep copiously and their tears do not flow in vain. For this reason a widow must not be grieved *with taxes*, even if she is wealthy. For without a husband her money is of no value to her. Jeremiah indeed compared Jerusalem to a widow, "She that was great among nations / Is become like a widow... she weeps in the night."[43] This teaches us that even though she is rich, enjoying all manner of luxury—and could forget all about her husband—at night she cannot forget him.[44]

The author of *Tzena urena* did not invent these ideas; he took them from Jewish tradition and incorporated them into his work. However, as Chone Shmeruk has shown, he exercised selective editing of his sources, choosing commentaries for their relevance to his readers' lives. These selections were chosen to promulgate his own views.[45] The duality and tension discussed previously are structured in the homily: a wealthy widow who enjoys luxury can forget all about her husband, but even rich widows weep in bed at night.

In fact, throughout the period under discussion, wealthy widows were subject to community taxes. Glikl could afford to "forget all about her husband," since he had ensured her financial security after his death.[46] Precisely because there were wealthy widows in actual fact, the author of *Tzena urena* wished to instill the (apparently not self-evident) understanding that widowhood is misery.

Naturally, not all widows in Glikl's circle (or elsewhere) were wealthy. The discrepancy between outward appearances of actual widows and deep-seated stereotypes instilled over centuries by halakhic and ethical literature found practical as well as psychological expression. Widows were made to acknowledge inferiority due to not having a husband in a society that extolled marriage and privileged men in the public and private spheres. On the other hand, in practice, widows were often expected to display independence and fortitude, thereby sparing the community the burden of supporting them. The twofold significance for the widow herself was that widowhood, despite its hardships, could offer opportunities.

A WIDOW'S FINANCES: HALAKHAH AND REALITY

Many female scholars have studied the connection between women's financial circumstances and their family situations and noted that discussing each of these separately is problematic.[47] Historical research shows two kinds of economic results for a new widow: immediate worsening of her financial situation or, conversely, increased financial independence as a result of inheriting the estate.[48] These two positions form the basis for our discussion of the financial state of widows in society. After her husband's death, a woman's financial situation depended on several factors: property she brought to the marriage, her ability to realize assets to which she is entitled by her marriage contract, her late husband's will, and her own ability to independently earn a living. Since Jews considered themselves subject to the halakhah in these matters as well, let us first look at the financial aspects of widowhood in Jewish law.

A WIDOW'S CLAIM TO HER LATE HUSBAND'S ESTATE IN HALAKHAH

In biblical law, a wife does not inherit her husband's property. However, historical developments led to rabbinic enactments in inheritance law that established the property a wife would receive when her husband died. This improvement in the financial situation of widows entitled a widow to the following kinds of property.[49]

The first was property she brought to the marriage, that is, the dowry, divided into "property of iron sheep" (*nikhsei tzon barzel*) and "property of plucking" (*nikhsei melog*). The value of "property of iron sheep" is estimated on the wedding day; the husband is liable for their loss of value and damage; and, upon the husband's death, the wife is entitled to the value of this property as estimated on the wedding day. "Property of plucking" refers to property in which the principal belonged to the wife, yet the husband was not liable for any damage or loss of value and had usufruct.[50] Dowry was an extremely important element in marriage agreements in the early modern age, and it could include chattel as well as real estate. These assets were itemized in detail in prenuptial betrothal agreements.[51]

The second type of property comprised gifts made with explicit provision that the woman could use them as she wished. This category included property received from her husband during their married life.

The third was the ketubah, the marriage contract. The ketubah sets out the husband's obligations and the couple's financial arrangements.[52] These were all dependent upon the bride's legal status; the basic ketubah amount (*ikar ketubah*) for a widow was generally half that of a maiden. The husband could supplement this with additional monies (*tosefet ketubah*), regarded as being as binding as the basic ketubah.[53] In addition to property she brought to the marriage at the time of the wedding, the widow was entitled to collect her ketubah and to maintenance monies from the estate. While the right to collect the ketubah comes into effect with marriage, it can only be realized when the marriage ends.

In Talmudic times, a woman could collect the amount of her ketubah from real estate only, not movable property.[54] Enactments in geonic times changed this so that a widow was entitled to collect the ketubah from any kind of property in her late husband's estate.[55] The actual figure of the basic ketubah is not given in the Talmud, but in Ashkenaz in later generations, it was very high indeed.[56] Such a high figure was prohibitive for most families and was not actually paid. The purpose of naming such high figures was apparently to give the woman more protection through her control of much of her husband's estate after his death.

The halakhah determines that the widow's claim had priority over any other debts the husband owed. The entire estate was, in effect, mortgaged to the payment of the widow's ketubah. In the event that the estate was insufficient for payment of the ketubah, the widow could, in certain cases, collect from his debtors.[57] If the ketubah amount was greater than half the value of the estate, however, the heirs were entitled to settle with the widow for only half the estate and keep the rest for themselves.[58] Over time, the absolute priority of the widow's claim lessened. The *Shulhan arukh* says that in the event that the deceased left landed property, the order of settlement follows the order in which the debts were incurred. In other words, if the ketubah came first—the widow collected first. If the debt was incurred first—that creditor collected before the widow. In the event that the deceased left only movable property, the ketubah could be claimed only after the creditor collected, even if the debt was incurred after the ketubah.[59]

In addition, there was maintenance (*mezonot*, lit. "food"); even if a wife did not inherit her husband's property, she was entitled to maintenance from his estate as long as she had not claimed her ketubah. The maintenance amount was designed to allow the widow to keep up the lifestyle she enjoyed during her married life. It included living accommodations, clothing, and the use of household items as in her husband's lifetime.[60]

According to Talmudic law, the heirs could require the widow to swear that she had not taken any of the ketubah money, either during her husband's lifetime or immediately after his death, in whole or in part, or anything else from the estate. This "ketubah oath" (or "widow's oath") would take place before the actual settlement of the ketubah claim.[61]

One of the most significant halakhic developments with respect to the widow's financial entitlements was the enactment attributed to Rabenu Tam (twelfth century): if a woman dies within twelve months of marriage without having borne children, her husband must return the dowry in full to her parents.[62] In the following century, it became common practice whenever one spouse died within two years of marriage that all property brought to the marriage by that spouse would revert to the respective parents.[63] Rabbi Moshe Isserles (mid-sixteenth century) gives this as the halakhic basis for Ashkenazic practice in his time in situations in which either spouse died.[64] Another rabbinic enactment was passed by the Council of the Land of Lithuania, 1761, in Słuck, in its final session. The council deemed the enactment necessary "at this time in this place": if one spouse died within three years of marriage, the entire dowry (in the event of the death of the wife) or the monies the husband brought to the marriage (in the event of the death of the husband) would revert to the respective parents or their heirs. Should one spouse die after three years but before five years of marriage, half the relevant amount would be returned to the respective parents unless the couple had children.[65] An interesting reaction to this enactment was made by the decisor Rabbi Avraham Tzvi Hirsch Eisenstadt (Poland and Belarus, 1813–1868).[66] According to him, though the Słuck enactment was entered in the community record book of Hrodna (Grodno), where he resided, and this enactment was followed by the community, it was not accepted by dayanim from other places who were not present at the council of Słuck. He added that in most places, a compromise was generally reached.[67]

THE WIFE, THE ESTATE, THE COMMUNITY

Glikl explicitly mentions that before her husband's death, he provided for the future—financial security for her and their children.[68] The memoir tells of less fortunate widows who were left destitute following the husband's demise. From her grandmother, Glikl learned that after the death of Glikl's grandfather, his wife and daughters were left penniless, forced to sleep on bare floors of wood and stone as they moved wearily from one dwelling to another.[69] By contrast, when Glikl's own father died, Glikl's husband and brother-in-law waived their share in the inheritance in favor of her mother, even assisting the widow in managing the property of the deceased.[70]

This last example demonstrates the importance played by the widow's social support system, especially that of the immediate family. These descriptions lead us to the ways in which the widows' financial situation was determined and the procedures they used to enact (or not) their rights to their property. Naturally, the couple's financial situation before the husband's demise plays a role in the widow's situation.

The following case from Prague demonstrates how ingenious maneuvering between legal systems could extricate a widow from her plight.[71] On Wednesday, July 18, 1759, a certain Jacob appeared before the rabbinic court of Prague with a complaint against his wife, Hannah.[72] Jacob claimed that Hannah had approached the non-Jewish local authorities, and, armed with her marriage contract as a legal document, she subjected his property as lien without his knowledge. This move precluded his selling without first settling her claim. Jacob wanted the beit din to order his wife to have the attachment rescinded on the grounds that she can only make a claim on her ketubah after his death. For her part, Hannah stated that she had learned that her husband was planning to sell part of his house to his sister in exchange for some derelict property. Hannah became anxious lest no funds be available in the future for her ketubah and therefore created the lien on her husband's property. According to the Prague record book, once a property was registered with the authorities under an individual's name, it could not be changed, even if another individual held a promissory note signed prior to the registration of the property. To protect her rights, Hannah needed the property registered under her own name.

The beit din in this case was forced to maneuver between Jewish law and that of the local authorities. As mentioned previously, in Jewish law, if the estate of the deceased is insufficient for payment of both the ketubah and other debts, the ketubah payment has priority. The beit din, well-versed in local regulations, knew that if Hannah cancelled the lien, and Jacob sold the house, she stood to lose her rights. Once the buyer registered the property in his own name before Jacob's death, her ketubah document would be worthless. The beit din urged Jacob to protect his wife's rights in their joint property by stipulating that the buyer commit to uphold Hannah's rights on the property. Lacking such an agreement, said the beit din, Jacob could not compel his wife to cancel the attachment.[73]

From this we can appreciate the extent to which a widow's fate depended on her familiarity with the rules governing social and economic life. She had to exploit this knowledge when necessary. The resourceful Hannah succeeded in securing her future by getting the beit din to acknowledge that the non-Jewish jurisdiction gave her an advantage. Once again, we see that intra-Jewish life did not take place in a vacuum. Long before community institutions lost much of their authority, individuals —including widows—could find ways to manage their affairs well beyond the scope of the community. However, widows less resourceful than Hannah, rich and poor alike, did lose funds that were rightfully theirs.[74]

Hannah understandably placed great importance on subjecting her husband's property to ensure her future, as the way in which the inheritance was divided between the widow, the heirs, and the debtors (if any) had a crucial impact on the widow's ability to live independently.

DIVIDING THE ESTATE

Many contemporary documents record the accepted ways of disposing of a person's estate after their death. As in non-Jewish society, following a death,[75] Jewish community organizations or local authorities would take a detailed inventory to ensure repayment of outstanding debts.[76] A bequest to the community served as added incentive for taking inventory down to the last item.[77] The probate process is described in the records of the Nikolsburg (Mikulov) community in Moravia (1708–1760):

> Immediately following the demise of any member of our community, it is the duty of the shamash of the synagogue and the

shamash of the beit din to go together promptly to the home of the deceased. They must take thorough inventory of the estate, down to the last item. Then they sign the document with the official seal of a community dignitary and a seal of one of the dayanim, none of whom have anything personal to gain from the estate, may God protect them. After the week of mourning, when heirs or creditors show up to make their claims, the aforementioned officials read out the inventory—land, goods, cash, valuables, household articles—nothing whatsoever was taken. Then the officials decide how much is available for settling the widow's ketubah, for the heirs, and for repaying creditors.[78] All this—to ensure peaceful settlement.[79]

As we know, community regulations reflect an ideal rather than actual practice. This is what makes the personal testimony of the Altona shamash so invaluable.[80] In his records from 1767–1792,[81] he describes how he was sent to homes in the community to take inventory of the property of the deceased, usually accompanied by another shamash.[82] His records have been cross-referenced with dates of death and other personal details on gravestones. The findings show that the inventory of the estate usually took place very soon after the person's death. For instance, the estate of Avraham Warburg went to probate at the close of the Sabbath, July 8, 1769,[83] the very day he died.[84] The estate of Yosefe Levi was inventoried on December 19, 1769,[85] the day of his death.[86] From the moment of inventory, no one was allowed access to the items until the estate was finalized and distributed in accordance with Jewish law.[87]

Some testators named an executor in the will; in some places in Germany, Jews were required to name a Christian executor in addition to a Jewish one of their choice, to protect the interests of the orphans.[88] When the deceased had failed to name an executor, community officials appointed one, sometimes in consultation with the family. Such was the case of Avraham Bacharach of Altona, who died in February of 1764: "For the widow of Rabbi Avraham ben Yosef Bacharach, mother of the orphans, we have named as executors R. Zanvil Hahn and R. Avraham ben Small Glickstadt,[89] with the approval of the relatives. The abovementioned shall supervise the payment of the widow's claim after she swears the widow's oath as is our custom; alternatively, a compromise will be reached in the interest of securing maintenance for the orphans, to ensure their livelihood."[90]

The executors were charged with dividing the estate, ensuring payment of the ketubah following the widow's oath,[91] protecting the rights of the children, and settling any of the deceased's outstanding debts.[92] They were required to guarantee they would divide the estate in accordance with Jewish law and to protect the rights of the heirs.[93]

Widows sometimes withheld items they considered their own property, refusing to allow them to be inventoried. This could lead to disputes between widow and heirs.[94] The legal proceedings often went against the interests of the widow, who, upon her husband's death, was not allowed to keep any item of his for herself, even things she had used freely prior to his death. This is what befell the widow of Yitzhak Halevi Horowitz, rabbi of Altona, who died on May 4, 1767.[95] Some four months after the events,[96] the shamash noted that on said date, he was sent by the community to the executor: "I was supposed to report the matter of a small silver goblet — the rabbi's wife wants her son to have it. She requests that said goblet remain with the executor for the time being."[97]

It transpired that several weeks later, the widow's financial affairs had not yet been settled, and many of her personal belongings were still held by the executor five months after her husband's death. By September 29, 1767, she had not yet received her ketubah money.[98]

On August 9, 1767, the rabbi's widow did receive financial aid of one hundred reichstaler from the community,[99] for the purpose of returning with her children to Brody, from which she originally came,[100] and for another trip from Brody to Altona. The widow also received a promise from community lay leaders that they would send to her new residence an annual stipend for the support of herself and her children for three years. This raises the issue of the financial implications of a husband's occupation for his wife upon his death. Widows of rabbis and other community functionaries who were considered "in sacred service" often received financial aid from the community after the husband's death. This aid was contracted between community officials and the hired functionaries.[101] Given that these positions were generally filled by men,[102] widows could not take over the husband's position,[103] unlike widows of merchants, for example, who often carried on running the family business after the husband's death.[104]

Prolonged negotiations between Rabbi Horowitz's widow and the executors of his estate continued even after she left the community.[105] Perhaps in order to spare their wives such unpleasantness, some testators stipulated in the will that the widow be exempt from the process of probate and division of the estate, or at least that the process be delayed until she might wish to remarry. As we shall see, the widow's remarriage could be potentially detrimental to the interests of the orphans of her first marriage. Some testators therefore willed their property outright to the wife, instructing that an executor be appointed only if she should remarry.[106] This was done, for instance, by Shlomo Elbe of Altona, as we learn from the community record book for 1764: "We have seen the will of the deceased . . . and he has left everything to his wife, until she chooses to remarry. In such an event she must appoint an executor and submit a faithful inventory.[107] She must also swear that she will hide nothing away from them—then, before the beit din, she will be paid her ketubah. The remainder will go to his orphan daughter."[108]

A testator wishing to spare his wife the entire probate process would explicitly bequeath the entire estate, or a part thereof, to his wife as an outright gift.[109] One such case was that of Aaron Umrich Gomperz, Glikl's great-grandson, who died on April 12, 1769. In his will, drawn up in Hamburg on November 24, 1768, Gomperz, after making several bequests to members of his family, dictated as follows:[110] "The remainder of my property, consisting of gold and silver, precious stones, promissory notes, household articles, clothing, jewelry, and movable property —everything I own with no exception whatsoever—is owned by my wife, Freba daughter of the late *parnas* and leader Yosefe Gottingen. All is hers as outright gift forever. From one hour before my death, it all belongs to my wife."[111]

Alternatively, a testator would name his wife executrix of the estate. This was the case with Gedalya Warburg, whose estate was probated in the Altona beit din on February 7, 1799.[112] After Warburg's death, his widow, Zipporah, divided the lands he owned in Altona among his children with the approval of the beit din.[113]

Division of the estate typically began following the week of mourning. As mentioned, payment of the widow's ketubah had priority over outstanding debts owed by the deceased. This principle became restricted through enactments and regulations,[114] and it was not always upheld.[115] In certain communities, restrictions were placed on this principle, as in Moravia in 1650. These enactments addressed cases in which the estate was insufficient to cover all debts owed by the deceased:

We have seen fit to enact the following fair and decent amendment, namely, that when he married this woman, if he owned houses, land, fields, orchards—her ketubah claim has priority (from the real estate) up to 400 gold pieces and 200 gold pieces for a widow,[116] also such garments as she brought to the marriage. Charity takes priority, by selling seats in the synagogue (in the men's or women's section)—priority even over the widow's ketubah. If he [the deceased] owns no land or acquired land after their wedding, she collects up to one hundred gold pieces, whether maiden or widow, and she shall also take all her clothes—with that her claim is fully settled.[117]

It emerges that the ketubah of a widow (in the present case: 400 gold pieces for a maiden at her marriage or 200 for a widow) was not always paid in full.[118] The widow depended for payment on whatever property her husband owned at the time of their marriage. According to this enactment, properties acquired by the husband during their married life were not included in the widow's entitlement to his estate as payment of her ketubah. As a result, joint property, acquired by the couple together during their married life, passed down to his heirs or went to his creditors—not to the widow—even if she was a partner in its acquisition or manufacture. Certain community interests apparently also took priority over the widow's claim: seats in synagogue—an asset of financial and social value—were the first assets to be realized by the community upon the death of a member, for the purposes of charity.[119] This is noteworthy, as we know from numerous documents that a seat in the synagogue could be rented out or mortgaged as collateral, which was often an important source of income for a widow. For example, on May 19, 1765, the widow of Rabbi Guggenheim of Offenbach rented out the synagogue seat that had belonged to her husband for the sum of six gold pieces a year for two years;[120] on January 22, 1775, Shainele, the widow of Yosefe Buchsbaum, mortgaged the seat he had owned in the synagogue for ten reichstaler, the sum she needed to pay doctors' bills.[121] The same was done by Tipkhe, widow of Herz Katz, on December 10, 1775, and again on August 10, 1777,[122] because she owed money to the community. Tzerli the widow of Zanvil Lancom did likewise on July 19, 1778, for the same reason.[123]

A widow's financial situation, then, derived primarily from her late husband's estate and her own ability to collect her ketubah. Moshe Rosman cites several examples of Jewish women in Poland whose husbands' estates did not suffice to pay off their debts; the widows experienced worsening of their financial situation as a result.[124] One of these was Rachel, the wife of Aaron Kushner. Given his outstanding debt of fifty gold pieces to the community of Winnica (Vinnytsia), she was forced by lay leaders to sell her house. Her appeal to the Polish authorities to prevent this was unsuccessful.[125] Disputes between widows and heirs or widows and other creditors are reflected in beit din records from Frankfurt, Altona, Kraków, Prague, and Metz, as well as in questions addressed to decisors throughout the Ashkenazic world. They are mentioned also in the few extant memoirs.[126] Testimonies to such disputes can be found in nearly all extant beit din records and in many community records. A few examples will suffice.

On January 19, 1783, the beit din of Altona heard the dispute between Esther, the widow of Lekish, and Shimshon Preger, a business partner of her late husband. Preger owed Leksh over one thousand reichstaler, but Leksh's widow and his sons could not collect the debt. The beit din initially ruled that Preger must pay his debt with no further delay, but then a compromise was reached enabling payment in four installments over a year and a half. The settlement explicitly mentions that Preger would indemnify the widow and orphans for any damages resulting from any business conducted by the partnership.[127]

The estate of Rabbi Jacob Emden (also known as Yaavetz; Altona, 1697–1776) was lengthily disputed by his widow, Tzviya Rachel, and the heirs and executors.[128] Tzviya Rachel was Emden's niece and his third wife. At their marriage in 1740, she brought him a dowry of 200 silver pieces.[129] In his memoir, Emden notes that contrary to his brother's promise to give her clothing and personal items, she entered the marriage without said property, and her husband had to give her clothes that had belonged to his previous wife.[130] During their married life, his financial situation greatly improved, and he died a rich man, leaving books, Torah scrolls, cash, and real estate.[131] In his memoir, Emden is very candid about the bitter disputes between his children from his first two wives and Tzviya, mother of six of his children:[132] "All the while that my daughters from my previous wives were still living at home with me, I had less peace than before, for my many sins. I now comprehended why our sages wrote of the verse, 'Your sons and daughters shall be delivered to another people' [Deut. 28:32] — this refers to a father's new wife. There is no cure for it! I was mistaken in thinking that when I married my brother's young daughter, she would obey me and treat my daughters and myself respectfully. But she was worse than her predecessor in this — endless quarrelling and strife, for as long as she remained in the house."[133]

After Emden's death, it emerged that his third wife had disputes with some of her stepsons, too. Zalman, Rabbi Emden's son from his first marriage, left his father's house when he was eleven years old and eventually settled in Brody.[134] He claimed that the executors of Rabbi Emden's estate gave the widow funds not lawfully hers. Emden junior wanted the non-Jewish courts to adjudicate; however (according to the beit din record book), the non-Jewish authorities instructed him "to obey Israelite law."[135] On May 31, 1784, the beit din of Altona ruled that the widow be paid the full amount of her ketubah, 300 dukats; until then, she would receive a monthly allowance equivalent to ten reichstaler, retroactive from her husband's death, for expenses, including maintenance for a maid. An additional sum would be paid to her for rent of living accommodations and upkeep of a maid following the sale of Emden's house.[136] Execution of the beit din's decision and payment of the ketubah would be put off until such time as the details of the ruling were made known to Meir, Jacob Emden's eldest son and head of the rabbinic court in another town. Meir, in due course, chose not to appeal the beit din's decision.[137] On March 19, 1786, Tzviya Rachel swore the requisite oath and, on September 7, 1787, signed the document declaring that her ketubah had been paid in full, including additional amounts and maintenance covering the period from Emden's death to that date.[138]

As in the Emden family, in disputes of this kind, the widow could find herself in protracted financial uncertainty. Eleven years and more passed from Emden's death to the actual settlement of his widow's financial affairs. In the interim, she received funds from the executors, but her financial situation was entirely dependent upon them. It seems that Emden's estate was not sufficient to provide a livelihood for his widow for an extended period of time, for in 1797 the community committee decided to grant her the sum of 100 schock as a temporary measure.[139] In 1800, it was decided to grant her an annual stipend of 200 schock, out of which she had to undertake to repay 100 to communal organizations for the rent on the apartment in which she was then living.[140]

The story of the Emden family was not unusual. Remarriage of widows and widowers was extremely common within this society, meaning that often the widow was not the mother of the children of the deceased, or was the biological mother of some but not all of them. Tensions ran high between the widow and children when the time came to divide up the estate. It is likely that widows who did not receive financial aid (thanks to the status of the late husband) suffered financially more than did Emden's widow.

WIDOWS AND COMMUNAL FEES

The financial structure of Jewish communities at this time was based largely on membership fees. The basic taxes were the householder tax and the asset value tax. Other taxes, permanent or temporary, were added, depending on the demands of local authorities and on the internal needs of the community.[141] Once every three or four years, the Jews were required to assemble for a tax assessment based on the declaration of assets by all householders. The relative tax payable by each householder to the state and community was determined based on this assessment. Most community enactments included a 50 percent discounted tax rate for widows.[142] This practice, common in non-Jewish society as well,[143] indicates that widows usually lived in worse financial circumstances than did male householders. In reality, things were not always as suggested in the enactments: while community tax lists show that in many communities, widows did pay much less than male householders,[144] there are also records of negotiations between financial officers of the community and widows over payment of taxes. In Kleve, a regulation from 1750 required widows to pay, in addition to half the householder tax, the full value of their total taxable assets, although in reality many widows were exempted.[145]

Already in the mid-seventeenth century, voices were heard opposing exemption of widows from full payment of communal fees and taxes. In some cases, concerted efforts were made to collect fees specifically from widows.[146] Feelings could run high over widows' exemption. Here is an example from Moravia in 1648: "Widows and orphans shall pay only half the amount paid by other householders as determined by taxation assessment. . . . If, however, a certain widow has the business acumen of a man, and is successful in her business affairs, additional tax may be placed on her, provided she does not pay the entire amount as do other householders.... A widow shall pay only half the capital tax to the community and state."[147]

In this regulation, a distinction is made between ordinary widows and widows who were successful businesswomen. Higher taxes were imposed on the latter. Similar regulations with differential taxation of widows depending on their financial situation and ability can be found in Bamberg in the late seventeenth century.[148]

Community record books from Hamburg, Altona, and Wandsbek show that this issue provoked constant debate, with regulations changing frequently. In 1686, orphans and widows were required to pay half the asset value tax and half the householder tax.[149] The 1726 version (in a note apparently copied from an older version) differentiated between widows and orphans who inherited substantial property and those who were left without. The former had to pay the full amount (half by the widow and half by the orphans). Widows left without any income paid only half the assets' value tax.[150] A regulation of March 20, 1757, reflects taxation-policy change with regard to widows and orphans who ran the business inherited from the deceased and showed a good profit.[151] We do not know if there was real change in the occupations of widows and orphans or merely in the way they were perceived. Glikl's memoirs show that half a century earlier, some widows in these communities did maintain a thriving business, a fact supported by studies dealing with other places in central and eastern Europe at the time. Therefore, it is unclear whether the updated regulation reflected a tangible change in widows' occupations, a change in the community's internal power structure, or some other factors that extant sources do not show.

It should be noted that a member of a community was liable for community taxes even after moving elsewhere.[152] If a widow remarried and wanted to move to another community, she first had to pay outstanding taxes. Such was the case of Bela, the widow of Meir Oppenheim of Offenbach; in 1773, she had to pay accrued community taxes of 400 reichstaler before she could move to Mainz.[153]

COMMUNITY AID FOR WIDOWS

Some widows required ad hoc or permanent financial aid from the community. Charity records show that recipients of regular financial aid generally included widows. Widows also received ad hoc assistance.

In 1731, for example, Altona extended financial aid to a widow for the marriage of her daughter.[154] In addition, the widow of Shmuel the Shamash received financial aid in the amount of four marks.[155] In 1740, expenditure of a monthly stipend in the amount of one reichstaler was recorded in the same community for the widow of Eli Cohen.[156]

A common reason for extending financial aid to widows was the marriage of one of their children.[157] Despite this, many widows had to appeal to wealthy Jews for support. During this period, vagrancy became widespread. Beggars were considered a threat, especially in Jewish society, and had to obtain a begging permit from community officials. The communities of AHW granted such begging permits to widows.[158]

JEWISH WIDOWS IN THE LABOR MARKET

In this period, many married women were active partners in their husband's businesses, as the husbands usually could not earn enough on their own.[159] Wives of merchants typically managed the business when their husbands were away on short or long business trips.[160] Some of these women continued to run the business after the husband's death,[161] while others were forced to find other livelihoods. A wife's partnership in the business could affect the outcome of future arguments between the widow and the deceased's heirs or executors. The case of Gutrad, the widow of Tevely Lisser, involved a dispute with the executors of her husband's estate. The case came before the beit din of Altona on March 26, 1792, a fortnight after his death.[162] The executors claimed that if the ketubah were paid in full, there would be insufficient funds left over to support the orphans. The court replied as follows: "Whereas it is well-known that this woman was a businesswoman in her husband's lifetime, turning a good profit; and whereas it is well-known that he wished his widow to have all his property—the entire estate, including household articles, goods, and chattels, liabilities, gold and silver and precious stones—all is hereby declared her property, in entirety and forever, to manage and control as she sees fit, without being held accountable to anyone. She owns it all outright."[163] Gutrad died less than four years later, and the dowry record she left to her daughters implies that she succeeded in gaining a respectable livelihood as a widow.[164]

Some widows pursued traditionally female occupations, such as midwife or ritual bath attendant.[165] Whether they chose these occupations upon being widowed or had worked in them beforehand is hard to establish. Some widows went into domestic service, and we can assume most did so due to the onset of financial difficulties upon entering widowhood. In autumn 1687, in Hildesheim, Saxony, Rabbi Eliakim Getz composed a responsum: Community leaders were demanding that a certain widower fire his widow maidservant since they suspected him of having sexual relations with her. The widower claimed it was common practice in his community for a widower to employ a widow as maid.[166]

Eighteenth-century census data on Jewish populations in Prussia and other data indicate that widows engaged in various occupations throughout the region under discussion.[167] Moshe Rosman has shown that Jewish women in Poland, including widows, were moneylenders, innkeepers, peddlers, saleswomen in shops, and rent collectors.[168] Gershon Hundert found that there were five widows among a group of Jewish grocery store owners in Tarnów who were accused of opening on a Christian holiday.[169] Among eighteen widows listed in the Halberstadt census of 1737, there was one cook, one nurse, five teachers, one moneylender, and one widow who cared for mothers in the first six weeks after giving birth. Among the forty-two Jews in the Halle census of 1750, there were two widows, both in the secondhand garment trade, who provided a living for their children.[170] Of the five widows registered in Königsberg that same year, one was a moneylender, one had a warehouse for goods and textiles, one traded in tobacco products and accessories, and two engaged in commerce (unspecified).[171] Five years later, in 1755, beer brewing was listed as yet another occupation.[172] Two of the ten widows in the Norden census of 1765 were ritual slaughterers,[173] as were two of the five widows in the census of Essen that same year. Community records of Zülz for December 31, 1794, note a woman resuming her occupation as butcher, perhaps following her husband's death:[174]

> The widow Yetele has appeared before us today and agreed to a compromise; seeing that she is an impoverished widow, we were compassionate. She is now resuming her occupation as butcher for our community, in partnership with another woman . . . she has until next Purim, when we will know if she has acted appropriately without dispute between them concerning butchery. Nor should our community officials have to trouble themselves with matters of ritual slaughter and butchery. If disputes do arise in the abattoir

during the specified time span, she will not be permitted to continue in this occupation.[175]

We find testimony of widows' occupations in many sources, yet not all working widows managed to scrape together a decent living. Based on real estate transactions in Poland, Rosman concluded that widows often had to sell their houses to provide for dependents.[176] Even for those who did make a living, he says, quality of life was worse in widowhood as compared to their married life. Many working widows were poor, as can be learned from census records of the property they owned and the value of their taxable assets. The situation of Jewish widows was like that of non-Jewish widows in early modern Germany. Sheilagh Ogilvie has shown that women generally did most of the housework, and many worked outside the home as well. Women generally earned less than men, their financial situation was worse, and many depended on charitable institutions.[177] As for Jewish widows, in 1720, the widow Perle Issa of Trebbin had a household of four;[178] despite her business in the textile trade, records designate her as destitute. The widow of Gavriel Simon of Bielitz (Bielsko), a wool merchant, lived in penury with six other people in the house, one of them her widowed daughter, despite having been in a business partnership with her son-in-law.[179] Such partnership between a widow and her children or sons-in-law was quite common, sometimes extending to sharing a residence.

LIVING CONDITIONS OF WIDOWS[180]

The non-Jewish authorities in most places under discussion required Jews to have a residence permit (*Schutzbrief*, lit. "letter of protection") to live in a town and be affiliated with its Jewish community. While some Jews in these areas held such permits, others did not. Whether or not an individual had a permit had far-reaching implications with regard to living conditions.[181] Ownership of real estate could differ significantly: in Prussia, for instance, Jews were generally permitted to buy houses, while in other places they were not. For widows, too, living conditions varied depending on legal jurisdiction and personal finances. Changing one's place of residence typically occurred upon a woman's being widowed, either because she remarried or because she lost the right to her husband's residence permit or transferred it to her sons or sons-in-law.[182]

The changed financial circumstances of a widow could also motivate a move to a different city. Non-Jewish authorities usually preferred granting residency rights to persons of sound financial means who could pay taxes. For this reason, the authorities did not always allow the transfer of residency rights from a deceased man to his widow.[183] Altered financial circumstances seem to have been the underlying motive for the recently widowed Yechig's sale of her house. The widow of Elia Balin of Worms, in 1684, made the sale of her house conditional on the buyer's agreement that her sons be allowed to buy it back from him within three years of the sale.[184]

The data we have about living conditions of widows are compiled from various sources that were not originally intended for that purpose. Nevertheless, they allow for the identification of certain patterns, which, in turn, demonstrate the range of options available to them.[185] One possibility was independent living: Glikl's mother lived in a small house of her own and even employed a maid.[186] Independent accommodations, alone or with unmarried children or servants, is known throughout the period. Marburg census data of 1657–1800 list ten widows as householders; nine of them had their children living with them.[187] In 1754 in Wesel, Sara, age fifty-two, the widow of Shimon Samuel, lived with her seven children. She managed her own household and ran a business.[188] In 1720, the widow of Yaakov Moses of Potsdam owned two houses, one of which she occupied with five other people.[189]

Another option was living with married children in their home or in the widow's own home. When she became widowed, Glikl's grandmother had no property of her own. She went to live first with her daughter Gluck, then with her daughter Ulke, and finally with her daughter Beyle, Glikl's mother.[190] Other recently widowed women, apparently not many,[191] likewise went to live with a married child, by choice or by necessity, sometimes with a daughter who was herself a widow. In 1765, the widow of Yosef Kalman lived in a house with her mother and her two children in Aurich.[192] In 1784 in Hagenau, Alsace, the elderly widow Anna Moch lived with her daughter and son-in-law.[193] Betrothal conditions occasionally included a provision that the bride's widowed mother was entitled to live with the couple, or, if she lived in her own house, they would provide her meals. We read the following in the betrothal of Meir Ganz and Frumit, June 1, 1802: "Meir hereby agrees that his mother-in-law Mrs. Breyne is proprietor and mistress of her house and all articles therein... making explicit provision that if they quarrel and cannot live together, said Meir will give his mother-in-law whatever household articles she requires and a weekly sum in accordance with the decision of the beit din."[194]

Some widows returned to living with their parents: On becoming widowed, a woman might move back in with her parents, for financial reasons, emotional support, or to care for a solitary parent. Ethel Levi of Herlisheim, Alsace,[195] lived with her two children in her father's house in 1784. The daughter of Gavriel Simon lived with her mother in Bielitz/ Bielsko in 1720.[196]

A widow could also live in the home of her in-laws or have them live with her: Adel, widow of Meir Avraham Levi, had her father-in-law living in her house in Königsberg in 1750;[197] the records do not show whether this arrangement predated her husband's death.

Living with other relatives was also possible. In 1784, a widow by the name of Göllen was living in her brother's house in Bischoffsheim in Alsace.[198] And, in some cases, a widow was a maid living with strangers or relatives, for instance, Lisette and Shenil in Hagenau, 1784.[199]

This range of options underscores once again how important family support networks were for a widow's future prospects. Such networks had a decisive impact financially and in choosing where she and her children would live.[200] Glikl hints at family tension underlying her grandmother's living arrangements as the widow left the home of one daughter and moved in with another: "Now, after my maternal grandmother had been there for some time — there were perhaps too many visits from her orphan grandchildren, or perhaps some other misunderstanding such as arises between parents and children — the poor woman moved with her orphan daughter to my aunt Ulke's."[201]

Tensions of this kind were perhaps the reason why widows felt the need to secure their rights in legally binding agreements signed in the beit din.

REMARRIAGE

Shaul Stampfer has found that in the first half of the nineteenth century, the rate of remarriage among Jews was higher than among Christians. Remarrying improved a widow's financial situation and gave her children better chances of survival.[202] Since the publication of Stampfer's article in 1988, few studies have addressed the subject of Jewish remarriage in the region and period under discussion.[203] Many have noted the methodological problems entailed in researching remarriage rates in historical populations, problems which apply to the place and time under discussion as well.[204] We do not have sufficient demographic data to establish statistical patterns of behavior among widows and widowers in Jewish society. Nevertheless, a broad picture emerges from the sources.

IDEOLOGICAL HERITAGE AND ACTUAL BEHAVIOR

Jewish tradition has always placed high value on marriage and offspring.[205] This had decisive implications for young widows who had not yet borne a child, and perhaps also for older widows. Given that second and third marriages were common in Ashkenazic Jewry in this period,[206] let us review several points of Jewish law concerning the remarriage of a widow.

Biblical and Talmudic law permit remarriage of a widow. Indeed, the Talmud assumes that a widow wants to remarry.[207] Remarriage is permitted ninety "complete" days after the husband's death, excluding the actual day of death and the day of the new marriage (= ninety-two days).[208] Another limiting factor for remarriage was a wife's obligation to her husband to nurse their children. The duration of this obligation was much debated in the Talmud and in halakhic literature, with most authorities putting it at twenty-four months. Hence, a woman who is widowed within two years of giving birth may not yet remarry (the Talmudic term is "a woman who is nursing the child of another man").[209]

Although remarriage is permitted, the Talmud expresses ambivalence about the remarriage of widows,[210] especially in the case of "a killer wife" (*katlanit*)—a widow who has buried two or more husbands. On the assumption that their deaths were somehow connected to some flaw in the wife or in her behavior, the rabbis deemed it wiser not to marry "a killer wife."[211] In practice, it seems that Jews in most communities did not refrain from marrying widows.[212] The *Shulhan arukh* ruling follows the opinion of Rabi in Tractate Yevamot: a woman who has already buried two husbands is indeed "a killer wife."[213] Yet, in the sixteenth century, Rabbi Moshe Isserles glossed this to apply only in cases of natural death, that is, not death in unusual circumstances. Leniency without censure was the general attitude to this law in his own society, he notes.[214]

Interesting evidence showing that a widow's remarriage was not seen as contravening Jewish law can be seen on gravestone inscriptions of women who married more than once. These inscriptions sometimes bear the names of both husbands. The inscription for Leible (died August 14, 1752), the wife of Rabbi Yaakov Hacohen of Frankfurt, bears the name of Popers, her second husband, as well as that of her first husband.[215] Likewise, the gravestone inscription of Egla Leidesdorf, the widow of Rabbi Akiva Wertheimer, rabbi of Altona from 1823 to 1838, bears also the name of her first husband.[216] This is perhaps because Egla was married to Rabbi Wertheimer for only a few years, as his previous wife and mother of his ten children died seven years before his own death.[217]

Yet ambivalence about marrying a widow persisted. In his memoirs, Rabbi Jacob Emden tells of his father, Rabbi Tzvi Ashkenazi ("Hakham Tzvi"; Třebíč (Trebitsch), 1660–Lvov, 1718), who refused an offer of marriage with a prospective bride from Prague because she was a widow.[218] Jacob Emden himself confesses that he was reluctant to marry his second wife because she was a widow.[219] It seems that life's exigencies clashed at times with the perception of a widow as a "killer wife."[220]

Historical research shows that in preindustrial Europe, many women chose not to remarry.[221] Sheilagh Ogilvie asserts that many non-Jewish widows in the Wildberg region were willing to pay a heavy price and take risks in order to remarry. At the same time, she adds, many withstood the social pressure to remarry.[222] Tamar Salmon-Mack observes that the desire to remarry was very strong among Jewish widows in Poland in the relevant period, adding, however, that not all of them actually did so.[223] Glikl's descriptions of widows accord with findings that merchants' widows in early modern Germany were less than eager to remarry.[224] In her account, some widows had reasons for ambivalence about remarrying, though they were rooted in other considerations than men's concerns about the "killer wife." Glikl describes her sister-in-law Yente, widowed at a young age, as refusing to remarry for some years because she was "an energetic young woman";[225] we may surmise that this independent-minded young woman saw no reason to subject herself to a man as head of the household. Glikl is even more forthright in supporting her own mother's decision not to remarry: "When my father died, may his memory be a blessing, my mother, may she live long, was forty-four years old. She had opportunities for many good matches, and could have remarried and had great wealth again. But the dear good soul never wanted that, preferring instead to remain a widow. She used the little she had left over, poor thing, for her own livelihood, to provide for herself and live in a small house of her own, retaining her housekeeper, living a comfortable, secure life."[226]

In Glikl's view, this is the desired model of widowhood: "If God punishes a woman and she loses her first husband, God forbid, may the good Lord give her this thought too. How pleasant is this dear woman's life, how many good deeds she does with what little she has, how patient, no matter what God, blessed be He, causes to befall her — so much can be written on this subject. She remained thus in her dignified widowhood."[227]

Glikl's admiration for a widow's not remarrying reflects her understanding that this decision derived from the widow's desire for freedom or from her faithfulness to the memory of her late husband. True, Glikl was writing after she herself had entered a dismal second marriage, yet she was not alone in praising a widow's decision not to remarry. Rabbi Jacob Emden similarly is full of praise for the widows in his family who made that same decision: his grandmother Nehama, after being freed from her agunah status upon valid testimony that her husband was dead, nevertheless refused to remarry. His mother, widowed at age forty-one, would not be consoled for the death of his father and turned down many offers of marriage. His sister Nehama (named for that same grandmother), a childless widow, nevertheless refused to remarry.[228] Granted, these accounts could very well be idealizations. Yet the writers were clearly in favor of widows' not remarrying, despite widespread practice — even in their own families.[229]

CHILDREN FROM PREVIOUS MARRIAGES[230]

When a mother of small children was widowed, remarriage included ensuring the welfare of her children. Despite unwillingness on the part of the beit din to appoint a woman as guardian of her own children,[231] there were, in fact, quite a number of such cases. This happened primarily when the testator stipulated explicitly that his wife be appointed the children's guardian, usually in joint guardianship with a male relative or friend of the family. The Metz beit din, for instance, was averse to appointing a woman as executrix for the estate or as guardian for the children. The beit din had to do so anyway, as it was answerable to the

French judicial system, which did recognize women in these functions. Since more and more Jewish women were turning to the civil courts to get guardianship over their children, the beit din did occasionally appoint a woman in this capacity.[232]

In addition, Jewish widows were required to ensure the future of the children by signing a prenuptial agreement with the prospective husband. At times, the right to claim the ketubah was made conditional on securing the children's welfare in advance, as part of the second marriage. Such was the case of Shprinze, whose husband, Wolf Minden, died, leaving four young orphans. The beit din record book of Altona's entry for March 17, 1797, reads as follows: "The betrothal agreement conditions explicitly state that the widow is not permitted to remarry unless beit din and guardians are satisfied that the new husband has undertaken liability — before the wedding — for all the widow's obligations."[233]

That same year, Feigel, the widow of Shmuel, undertook a similar obligation towards her daughter before the beit din of Kraków:

> Feigel, widow of the late Rabbi Shmuel, has undertaken, with solemn vow, according to our holy Torah, and of her own free will, under no duress, to support her daughter Zlaty from her late husband — to provide food and clothing for her orphan daughter from her own pocket until the girl reaches the age of fifteen. The aforementioned widow further expressly undertakes, in the event of her remarriage during that time, to ensure that her intended, before the wedding, takes her obligation upon himself. He will maintain the girl Zlaty until she reaches the age of fifteen — as above; feed and clothe her as a daughter of his own flesh and blood.[234]

These cases, culled from legal documents, perhaps create the impression that, were it not for the intervention of the beit din, a widow-mother would not try to secure the future of her children, but I doubt this is true. Such prenuptial agreements probably gave legal expression to the concern felt by the mother herself over the welfare of her children upon her remarriage. We may assume that the legal documents tend to express the common interest of the parties involved: the mother, the family of the late husband, and the community that did not want to be burdened with caring for orphans. However, there were probably also cases where tension arose between a mother and her children or between the widow and the family of her late husband, stemming from the widow's remarriage. Prenuptial agreements of this kind should be understood in this context. Rabbi Zvi Hirsch Kaidanover (d. 1712), in his work of ethical teachings, *Kav hayashar*,[235] attests to the underlying emotions in some of these family disputes:

> A wife takes her late husband's money for her ketubah, then after his death she marries another man and gives him all the money. His sons go barefoot, in tattered rags; they profit not at all from their father's wealth. Meanwhile, they see their mother eating and drinking with another man, taking pleasure with her second husband, while the orphans of her first husband sit betwixt stove and hob, gazing, observing, seeing their mother sitting there enjoying choice meats and wines and other delicacies. Would that they receive leftovers from her meals. "Oy, Oy," comes the sons' sigh from the heart, over all this. They tell each other, "All this wealth and money was our father's — yet we are not able to retrieve any of it."[236]

Kaidanover depicts a mother's indifference to her children's fate as she denies them any share in their father's estate in order to better enjoy herself in the company of her new husband. This harsh criticism, almost satire, smacks of misogyny. Nevertheless, it seems there were grounds for his description. The sources tell of widows abandoning their children, whether to devote themselves to a new husband or for other reasons. The community record book of Altona contains an entry for financial aid for the orphans of Shmuel Rothschild, whose children went to live with their uncle after their mother left town in secret.[237] Similarly, the grandson of Ephraim Barbira of Altona was brought up in the home of his grandfather after his father's death, after his mother went to Amsterdam for reasons not made clear.[238] These cases make us aware of the role of marriage patterns in inheritance disputes between widow and heirs — and sometimes even the widow's own children. Some scholars have suggested that a rich or childless widow had better chances of remarrying. This might have influenced widows when it came to distribution of the estate, even where their own children were concerned. In 1780, the decisor Rabbi Yedidyah Tiah Weil (Prague, 1721–Karlsruhe, 1805) penned a responsum in answer to a question about payment of a widow's ketubah. He writes that disputes were frequent: widows robbed their children, while rabbis preferred not to get involved.[239]

This rabbi rendered judgment in rabbinic court; his responsa served as a guide for other decisors in adjudicating inheritance disputes. Given his evident deep hostility towards widows, it must have found expression also in his treatment of the actual widows who came before him in the beit din.

The previous cases suggest that the family of the late husband also had an interest in the widow's remarriage, since in that event they would no longer have to feed the children of the deceased.[240] Litigation by widows concerning the orphans against the family of the late husband was common.[241] One example was the agreement between the widow of Izak Dehan and the brother of the deceased. Nine years after his death, an agreement was reached, to wit, the brother-in-law, Aaron Dehan, would give the widow money for the support of his brother's daughter until she reached the age of fourteen. Should the widow remarry, the brother-in-law would be exempt from paying child support. In that event, the widow agreed to bear responsibility for her daughter's care.[242] Financial considerations on the part of the late husband's family and their concern for his fatherless children at times spurred them to influence the widow not to remarry and to keep the estate in the family. In other cases, however, the interests of the late husband's family exerted pressure in the opposite direction.

A widow weighing remarriage no doubt took into account pressure exerted on her by the family of her late husband, but this was not the only factor. Glikl received many proposals of marriage, she recounts, but as long as she was financially secure, she never considered remarrying. Only when her financial situation deteriorated did she eventually remarry, not wanting to be a burden to her children.[243]

PRACTICAL HALAKHIC LIMITATIONS

While financial considerations seemed to have played a major role for a widowed mother in arriving at a decision whether to remarry, there were halakhic considerations, too. To what extent did the halakhic principle "nursing the child of another man" exert any real influence?

Responsa literature of the time abounds with cases of widowed mothers who sought to remarry before a child was two years old because their babies had died in the meanwhile, or because the mother was not nursing, or for some other reason.[244] Hiring a wet nurse, popular in non-Jewish society, particularly in the middle and upper classes, was less common in Jewish circles.[245] Some Jewish families did hire a wet nurse, for instance, when the mother died in childbirth or shortly afterwards.[246] In order to obtain permission to remarry during the two-year period following childbirth, a widow had to appeal to a decisor and explain her request, in person or by proxy. The halakhic issue of "a woman nursing the child of another man" affords a glimpse into the world of these women — their considerations and the difficulties they faced. It also clarifies the approaches and opinions of decisors on the importance of remarriage for young widows.

A widow who wanted to remarry is discussed at length in *Hakham Tzvi* by Rabbi Tzvi Ashkenazi (1707).[247] Hendele, the daughter of Yosef Stathagen of Altona, was widowed while pregnant with her eighth child. She gave birth shortly after the death of her husband. By then the doctors had pronounced her milk "poisonous";[248] they blamed the milk for the death of her first three children while they were still nursing. Four other children who did not nurse survived. Following this, Hendele hired a wetnurse for her newborn infant. Before the child had reached the age of two, Hendele found she wanted to remarry. Hakham Tzvi described the circumstances leading to her decision: "This woman was about to marry a certain widower, since her husband left her penniless. It is known, she cannot provide for herself and her children unless she marries this man. This widower cannot wait 24 months, so if she is not permitted to marry within 24 months — the betrothal will be called off."[249]

Poverty was the deciding factor in her decision to remarry; at least that is how the story was presented to the rabbi. Hakham Tzvi, Rabbi of Altona at the time, seems to have accepted the widow's position, for he granted her permission to remarry. The case sparked controversy among decisors. Rabbi Abraham Broda (Prague, Metz, and Frankfurt, c. 1640–1717)[250] did not grant Hendele permission to remarry. He went so far as to decree that whoever did marry her would be excommunicated.[251] Eventually, enough decisors were found in Altona itself who agreed with the position of Hakham Tzvi. Even after permission was granted, Hakham Tzvi was anxious not to let popular opinion weaken the resolve of the prospective bridegroom.[252]

We have no personal details about the widower who wanted to marry Hendele. Yet the previous description demonstrates the extent to which a widow's remarriage was not only a personal matter between herself and her intended bridegroom but affected the community and often involved power struggles among rabbis as well. When there was some doubt about whether the widow was allowed to remarry, the prospective husband may have been vulnerable to threats of excommunication and had to come armed with explicit permission from a rabbi. In this case, concern that the threat of excommunication issued by a rabbi from Prague would be deemed strong enough to change the prospective bridegroom's mind about marrying Hendele and supporting her children necessitated the public display of authority, wherein Hakham Tzvi convened a prestigious beit din to declare the marriage kosher. Hakham Tzvi himself was apparently not at all certain that the beit din's ruling would assuage the anxiety of the prospective husband. The rabbi made sure to announce that the prospective husband, if he still failed to marry Hendele, risked divine retribution.

We have no way to determine the extent to which this incident reflected the stance of men who wished to marry widows; it may reflect only the personal values of the Hakham Tzvi. As spiritual leader, he wished to compel his community to act in accordance with halakhah, and indeed depicted them as doing so. At the very least, this case shows that, in at least in some cases, widows wanting to remarry depended on rabbinical approval and influence. We can trace a change over the relevant period: in the early part, community institutions exerted greater influence, and excommunication was a graver threat; in the latter part, their power waned, and individuals had greater room to act independently rather than in accordance with the community's wishes.[253]

WIDOWHOOD: HOW LONG DID IT LAST?

The average duration of the state of widowhood is a function of marriage patterns in a given society, among other things. Age difference between spouses, age at marriage, and patterns of remarriage are some of the factors that may predict, to some extent, both the chance of becoming widowed and the potential duration of widowhood. We should add to this list religious views and restrictions as well as random individual events impacting life expectancy (such as accidents, unnatural deaths, and illnesses). While the present study does not include systematic processing of all such data, several examples will be presented and placed in broader context.

The age at first marriage in Ashkenazic Jewry, including in Germany and Poland, has been much researched, though the full picture is by no means clear.[254] Contrary to prevailing opinion until a few decades ago, it now appears that Jewish society hardly differed in this respect from that of its non-Jewish neighbors. Marrying at a very young age — under eighteen years old for men and under sixteen for women — was common only among a small minority of the economic and rabbinical elite.[255]

For other strata of the Jewish population, age of marriage seems to have risen gradually during the eighteenth and nineteenth centuries. According to the data presented by Liberles, marriage age for Jewish women in Germany in the second half of the eighteenth century was 22–24, while the majority of Jewish men married in the second half of their twenties.[256] Recent scholarship has uncovered other, regional trends among Ashkenazic Jewry.[257] Broadly speaking, however, age difference between husband and wife at first marriage in Jewish communities in the Ashkenazic world remained relatively constant: In Metz, 1740–1789, men married at age 23–29, and women married at age 17–24; in Berlin, 1759–1813, the disparity of the average age of marriage for men and women was 3.5 years. In localities in Germany bordering Poland, where Jews had a greater cultural affinity with Poland than with western Europe in the early nineteenth century, the median marriage age from 1815 to 1839 was 22 for women and 26 for men.[258] In Vilna, 1837–1851, the median was 18.5–19 years of age for women and 19.8–23.4 years for men.[259] It thus appears that age difference between men and women in a first marriage was in the range of 4–10 years at most, and usually about 4 years. This figure did not predict chances of widowhood for women since, at that time, female life expectancy was not yet significantly higher than that of males.

Remarriage patterns were another contributing factor in the duration of widowhood. Remarriage was common; many women remarried following a brief widowhood, while others, like Tzviya Rachel, the second wife of Rabbi Jacob Emden, mentioned previously, were married for the first time at a young age to an older widower.[260] However, many women remained widows for many years. Tzviya Rachel, also Emden's niece, was many years younger than her husband. He died in 1776, she on December 4, 1803.[261] In other words, she remained a widow for twenty-seven years. Esther, the widow of Lekish, was litigating her late husband's estate in January 1783,[262] and she remained a widow for eighteen years, until her death in October 1801. The database of gravestone inscriptions from Jewish cemeteries in Germany contains examples of women who remained widowed for many years: Yetcha, the widow of Leib Weiler of Bingen, died in 1731, fifteen years after her husband;[263] Sarah Merla, the widow of Aharon Eshklas of Bonn, died in 1825, forty-three years after her husband;[264] and Rechele, the widow of Leib Reiss of Frankfurt, died in 1791, thirteen years after her husband.[265]

We began the book with this discussion of widows because all of the agunot awaiting halitzah were widows and because some of the agunot in other categories of iggun shared the widow's fate in certain respects.

Our discussion in this chapter also highlights the role of gender. There were many Jewish widowers, but men did not have to face many of the difficulties that widows did; the concepts of "killer wife" and "a woman who is nursing the child of another man" and their impact on remarriage were pertinent to women only. This could explain findings showing that, in Poland, the relative number of widows was higher than that of widowers;[266] it appears that widowers found it easier to remarry than did widows. In economic terms as well, gender played a part when one lost a spouse: Jewish inheritance law was different for men and women, and many Jewish men engaged in "masculine" occupations (Torah teacher, rabbi, judge on the rabbinic court), meaning the widow could not carry on in her husband's occupation. All this made circumstances more difficult for widows, at least some of them.

Let us now turn to those widows who, in addition to losing a husband, had to await the halitzah ceremony before they could remarry.

2 : YIBUM AND HALITZAH
The Halakhic Basis for Freeing an Agunah Awaiting Halitzah

In the summer of 1829, a widow who wished to remarry consulted Rabbi Shlomo Kluger (1785–1869) in Brody, Galicia.[1] In his responsum (1830, published by his son in 1864), Kluger writes:

> It happened in our community, some fifty years ago. A man came, a widower by the name of Reb David, and married here. The woman gave birth to a boy, Reb Hirsch Itzik. This Itzik in turn married Haya Rachel. Then Reb David died, without any other children, none except for Reb Hirsch Itzik. In due course this son of his, Reb Hirsch Itzik, died childless, too. After some time, his wife, Haya Rachel, wished to remarry. She had never heard her husband mention a brother, nor had she ever heard from anyone else that he had a brother. But her mother-in-law—mother of her husband, Reb Hirsch Itzik, wife of Reb David—raised objections. She recalled that her husband, R. David, when he came from afar and married her, had a son of tender age, a boy of about ten. After their marriage, the boy's father beat him cruelly, until he ran away to the holy community of Brisk, to the esteemed Reb Hirsch, father of said Reb David. A letter from the boy would come every so often for his father, Reb David. For 22 years prior to Reb David's death, nothing had been heard from him until now.[2]

Taking the case of Haya Rachel as a starting point for a discussion of halitzah for agunot, we begin with a brief overview of relevant halakhic terms and principles. We are referring to a widow who is classified as an agunah solely because her late husband had a brother. The ensuing complexities played out in the decisions and priorities of decisors, the widow, the brother-in-law, and any other parties involved. Following this discussion, we can turn to widows who needed halitzah and were therefore included in the category of agunah for various periods of time. The halakhic background is important, as it enables us to understand the decisors' various considerations and will clarify the halakhic game and its impact on the lives of the men and women in question.

YIBUM AND HALITZAH: KEY CONCEPTS

The biblical source for *yibum* (levirate marriage) and halitzah (the ceremony releasing a man from the obligation to perform levirate marriage), as mentioned previously, is Deut. 25:5–10:

> When brothers dwell together and one of them dies and leaves no offspring, the wife of the deceased shall not become that of another party, outside the family. Her husband's brother shall unite with her: he shall take her as his wife and perform the *levir*'s duty. The first child that she bears shall be accounted to the dead brother, that his name may not be blotted out in Israel. But if that party does not want to take his brother's widow [to wife], his brother's widow shall appear before the elders in the gate and declare, "My husband's brother refuses to establish a name in Israel for his brother; he will not perform the duty of a levir." The elders of his town shall then summon him and talk to him. If he insists, saying, "I do not want to take her," his brother's widow shall go up to him in the presence of the elders, pull the sandal off his foot, spit in his face, and make this declaration: Thus shall be done to the man who will not build up his brother's house! And he shall go in Israel by the name of "the family of the unsandaled one."

Biblical laws of forbidden sexual relations prohibit a man from marrying the widow of his deceased brother.[3] Any marriage between them is invalid, and the punishment is *karet*, or "extirpation" (being cut off from the community). Yet, the prohibition is nullified by the requirement of levirate marriage in the circumstances described. The straightforward meaning of the verses suggests that levirate marriage (yibum) is a positive commandment, a good solution for preserving a man's name if he dies childless. Although the widow is not supposed to marry out of the clan, the will of the surviving brother — the levir — is decisive, impacting the fate of his sister-in-law. If he so wishes, he may marry his widowed sister-in-law to preserve the name of his late brother. If the surviving brother refuses to marry her, a ritual called halitzah is performed to release the widow from any bond with her brother-in-law and his family.

To obtain her release, the widow must in the first instance approach the elders and inform them that her brother-in-law refuses to marry her. Next, the elders summon the levir for clarification. Upon his declaration of refusal, the ritual proceeds. The widow removes her brother-in-law's sandal and spits at him. He is then publicly declared a refuser of levirate marriage.

The Mishnah restricted yibum by classifying certain cases as exempt from the requirement.[4] Based on the inclusive approach of the Talmud, the rabbis ruled that if the deceased had a child of either sex, or living grandchildren or greatgrandchildren, the widow was not subject to the requirements of yibum or halitzah.[5] Also, the Talmud deemed halitzah preferable to yibum in certain cases, for example, due to an age discrepancy between brother- and sister-in-law.[6] Qualifications applied for a pregnant woman and for a woman who had given birth prior to the husband's death, but the infant did not survive. If, after the husband's death, the widow gives birth to his child, she is exempt from yibum. If a son predeceased his father, however, and the latter then died without any living issue, the widow was subject to yibum.[7] Further restrictions and qualifications apply to a brother-in-law who is unable to perform the ritual due to a physical condition. A minor under thirteen years of age and one day may not perform the ritual;[8] the widow must wait until he attains his majority.

YIBUM OR HALITZAH?

The laws of yibum and halitzah developed over generations amid much debate.[9] The Mishnah asks whether yibum is always preferable to halitzah, or whether the decision should be left to the parties themselves. Mishnah Bekhorot 1:7 emphasizes the criterion of intent in making the decision: Did the brother-in-law wish to observe the commandment for its intended purpose? If he was suspected of ulterior motives, halitzah was deemed preferable. From historical sources, we learn that a brother-in-law often wanted to marry his brother's widow for her deceased husband's property. After a lengthy debate, Ashkenazic Jewry stopped levirate marriage and preferred halitzah.[10]

THE WIDOW REFUSES LEVIRATE MARRIAGE

The Bible depicts the widow as a passive party in levirate marriage. In practice, however, widows sometimes refused to go through with it. Responsa literature deals with questions such as, Can a widow be coerced into levirate marriage? Is she "rebellious" if she refuses?[11] Refusal could entail loss of financial rights. In the twelfth century, as Avraham Grossman has shown, Ashkenazic rabbis were in favor of coercing a widow into levirate marriage. This position often led to extortion by the brother-in-law. In the relevant period, however, halitzah had become established as the preferred method in Ashkenaz, and so coercion was no longer an issue. Another influential factor was Rabenu Gershom's enactment against polygamy, which became binding in Ashkenaz in the twelfth century.[12] A crucial implication of the enactment was that a married brother-in-law could not perform the levirate marriage, thus solving the problem for women whose levirs were married.

In numerous cases, however, the brother-in-law refused to perform the ritual of halitzah. The widow thereupon became an agunah, since she could not remarry unless halitzah was performed, and he could not be forced to perform it; coercion of an unwilling party was thought to invalidate the ritual.[13] The opinion of the famous Jewish commentator Rashi (1040–1105) — namely, that the unwilling brother-in-law could be coerced into going through with halitzah — was not accepted by contemporary decisors.[14] His grandson Rabenu Tam (1100–1171)[15] came up with an unusual interpretation of a position presented in the Talmud, with two radical applications. First, it is permissible to coerce an unwilling brother-in-law into undergoing the ritual of halitzah (with some exceptions). Second, levirate marriage should be forbidden, even when both parties want it. The latter conclusion incurred opposition, and it seems to contradict accepted practice in his time. This approach was vigorously debated in subsequent generations, and it seems that for many years, no categorical approach was implemented in Ashkenaz. Jacob Katz is of the opinion that it was Rabenu Tam's method that ultimately decided Ashkenazic practice.[16]

HALITZAH AND THE "APOSTATE" (*Mumar*) BROTHER-IN-LAW

The designated brother-in-law sometimes turned out to be a convert from Judaism to Christianity (Hebr. *mumar*, equivalent to the English "apostate").[17] In that case, his hostility toward Judaism could mean that he refused to take part in the ritual. As a result, the widow would remain forever an agunah. Halakhic debate raged for generations, with rabbinic enactments attempting to prevent this scenario. Rabbi Israel Bruna (Germany, 1400–1480)[18] suggested that a bridegroom declare that the marriage would be null and void retroactively in the event that his wife should need levirate marriage with a convert to Christianity. Conditional marriage of this kind raises thorny halakhic issues, as we shall see later, but the enactment was nevertheless accepted by most Ashkenazic decisors, and it was practiced in some places.[19]

THE HALITZAH RITUAL

Oral law, as interpreted by the rabbis, elucidated and explicated the biblical ceremony in Deuteronomy 25, in which the sister-in-law pulled off her brother-in-law's shoe, spat in his face, and declared that he "will not build up his brother's house" (25:9).[20] It explained the details of the ceremony in what ultimately became known as *Seder halitzah* (order of halitzah), the text of which appears in several halakhic works. *Shulkhan arukh*, which at this time was becoming the halakhic authority in Ashkenaz,[21] sets out the ceremony in fifty-seven paragraphs.[22]

The ritual is performed in public, before dayanim and an audience. The specific site for the ceremony must be publicized in advance; it may not be performed at night or on the Sabbath or Festivals; participants must apprehend its significance; and it must be performed with meticulous attention to detail and with the use of specific accessories. All undergo preparation: The beit din verifies the particulars (age and life circumstances) of the parties, for which the latter must supply proof. On the appointed day the widow fasts, refrains from unnecessary speech, and may not clean her teeth with a toothpick. On the preceding evening, the brother-in-law washes his foot and clips his toenails. All parties must be able to read the text aloud.

The ceremony itself comprises several stages: (1) Once identity has been verified, and there is nothing to prevent the ritual from taking place, the dayanim examine the halitzah shoe to be removed and inspect the man's right foot for cleanliness. The man puts on the halitzah shoe, winding the straps around his shin as the halakhah directs. (2) Wearing the halitzah shoe, he paces out a distance of four cubits, observed by the judges. (3) The judges explain to the parties the significance of the ceremony. Then the judge recites the verses to be said aloud by each of them.[23] (4) The man leans against a wall, his foot firmly planted on the ground. Halakhah states explicitly that he is not allowed to aid the widow in removing his shoe. (5) The widow approaches him, undoes the straps of his shoe as she raises his foot with her left hand, removes the shoe, and flings it to the ground. (6) She spits in the direction of his face in such a way that the judges see the saliva leave her mouth. (7) The widow pronounces the words, "Thus shall be done to the man who will not build up his brother's house! And he shall go in Israel by the name of 'the family of the unsandaled one'" (Deut. 25:9–10). All present repeat thrice after her, "the family of the unsandaled one." (8) The man returns the shoe to the tribunal. The dayanim proclaim, "May the daughters of Israel never need either halitzah or yibum."

With the conclusion of the ceremony, the bond between sister- and brother-in-law is severed. Any deviation from the details of the ritual can invalidate it, with implications for the fate of agunot.[24] Later, I will discuss the practical implications of each of the theatrical ceremonial details for society at the time.

As noted, all women who needed halitzah were widows. Becoming a widow involved practical and emotional changes, many of which were addressed by the halakhah. However, the widow who required halitzah was also subject to other halakhot, and over time, the rabbis formulated enactments aimed at alleviating some of these issues. We now turn to a description of these laws and enactments.

LEGAL STATUS OF A WIDOW REQUIRED TO PERFORM HALITZAH

A widow does not require halitzah immediately upon her husband's death; her bond with her late husband continues for ninety-two days.

During this time, she is not permitted to remarry and is entitled to maintenance monies from the estate.[25] After this waiting period, she no longer has any legal bond whatsoever with her late husband. Henceforth, any obstacle to her remarriage stems from her legal ties with her brother-in-law. This status does not entitle the widow to any maintenance from the brother-in-law as long as he has not refused halitzah. Nor is she entitled to maintenance monies if he was a minor (in which case she must wait for his majority). So, after ninety-two days, the widow is not entitled to collect any maintenance at all, either from her late husband's estate or from the brother-in-law who has not yet performed halitzah. Should the brother-in-law refuse to undergo the ceremony without satisfying the court with a valid reason, he is obligated to pay her maintenance for the duration of his refusal.[26] Once the ceremony has been performed, the widow is entitled to claim her ketubah from her late husband's estate.

COST OF HALITZAH

The halakhah that regulated the widow's legal and financial status was a frequent source of acrimonious conflict between the widow and her designated brother-in-law. Writings of different decisors reflect the fact that a brother-in-law's refusal to perform halitzah was not infrequently a means to extort funds from the widow. Katz and Grossman discuss many cases in which difficulties had to be overcome before halitzah could take place. In the course of the thirteenth and fourteenth centuries, three enactments were passed in the communities of Speyer, Worms, and Mainz (the three major Jewish communities on the Rhine) to resolve financial disputes involving halitzah.[27] In 1381, halitzah without remuneration, as well as coercing the levir to perform halitzah without renumeration, was actually presented as a positive commandment of biblical law: "We have seen several women become agunot because of brothers-in-law who demand unlawful payment. This is a transgression of the positive commandment of halitzah: 'His brother's widow shall go up to him in the presence of the elders, pull the sandal off his foot' [Deut. 25:9]. It is also a transgression of the commandment not to steal.... The Torah says halitzah without payment. It is said of positive commandments that one is to be beaten until he declares 'I agree' or unto death [Ketubot 86b]."[28]

Yet, less than a century later, Rabbi Israel Isserlein (Germany, 1390–1460) wrote as follows:

Reuven died childless. His wife needed [halitzah from] his brothers Shimon, Levi and Yehudah. Shimon presented himself for halitzah, demanding division of assets between them, in accordance with the enactment of the communities. Said the widow: "I do not wish to perform the halitzah ceremony or to marry any of you. I will remain an agunah." Replied Shimon: "That is because you do not want to share the property with me." Replied the widow: "So be it, let that be my intention." Levi and Yehudah now said to Shimon: "If you perform halitzah and share the property with her, you must share your portion with us, even though you are the eldest brother." Said the brothers to the widow: "Sister-in-law, we hear you have much property coming to you by provisions of your ketubah. That property was ours, and you must share your ketubah property with us." Says she: "If I perform the ceremony with one of you, I shall share the property with you all, be it much or little." What should be the legal decision in this case?[29]

In this dispute involving a widow and her three brothers-in-law (here called by the biblical pseudonyms standard in responsa), the eldest wants to perform halitzah. The widow refuses, preferring to remain an agunah. The brother-in-law suspects financial motives, which she duly confirms. Since the widow held property whose value exceeded that of her ketubah, the brothers wanted to coerce her into agreeing to halitzah so they could get their hands on her property. Isserlein's responsum shows that communities varied in actual practice regarding division of assets among the widow and the brothers of the deceased.[30] Relevant factors were the widow's age and finances, as well as the husband's family situation.

In this context, one important historical development was Rabbi Moshe Isserles's gloss on the *Shulkhan arukh*'s statement that any widow required to perform halitzah was entitled to claim her ketubah. Isserles observed that although the brother-in-law cannot be coerced into performing the ceremony, this must not delay the widow's right to claim her ketubah. She is allowed to claim the ketubah as if the ceremony had actually taken place. However, Isserles goes on to say that enactments allow for the widow and the brother-in-law to reach a compromise for sharing the estate, even if half the total value of the estate is insufficient for covering the amount of her ketubah. On top of that, all monies the widow spent during her married life are to be deducted from her share of the inheritance. If no compromise could be reached, she would have to swear the waiver oath. Neither the other brothers nor their father has any share in the half that goes to the husband's heirs.[31]

This underscores the financial aspect of halitzah. The danger that a recalcitrant brother-in-law would render the widow an agunah gave rise to an enactment that actually restricted her original rights. Now she had to waive her rights to monies rightfully hers in favor of the brother-in-law. The enactments decreed that widow and brothers-in-law divide the estate among themselves, even if the value of half the estate did not equal the value of the ketubah. On top of that, they deducted from her portion monies she spent during her married life! Clearly, despite the intention of the enactment to encourage brothers-in-law to perform the ceremony, this rule became a source of financial dispute between widow and brother(s)-in-law. Isserles suggests another solution, namely, reaching a financial compromise even when the widow is in possession of a writ of halitzah signed by the brothers — unless the writ states explicitly that they would perform the ceremony without remuneration.

A writ of halitzah was a document issued by the beit din attesting that a halitzah ceremony had been performed (and, by implication, that the widow was free to remarry). These sorts of writs, mentioned already in the Jerusalem and Babylonian Talmuds, had been in use for centuries.[32] The writ was devised to prevent the widow from remaining an agunah for the duration of any disputes with her brothers-in-law. In the writ, also known as "a writ of halitzah from the brothers" or, more commonly, a "writ of obligation to perform halitzah," the brothers of a bridegroom undertake, as part of the betrothal agreement, an obligation to his bride: should the husband die childless and his wife require halitzah, the brothers would perform the ceremony.[33] This was the writ that Isserles referenced. His writings, however, show that even in situations in which a writ promised future halitzah, when the time came, negotiations were frequently needed to agree on the price. This could be avoided only if the writ named a specific sum or stated that the ceremony must be performed without remuneration.[34]

In Ashkenazic Jewry in this period, it was common practice to ensure halitzah immediately following the obligatory waiting period of three months, and without remuneration. Among the many extant writs of halitzah is the one signed by the brothers of Yechiel Michl of Warburg in 1763 for their sister-in-law Jutta daughter of Reuven.[35] The writ ensured, at least theoretically, that the widow would not be subjected to extortion by her brothers-in-law, nor would she have to wait a long time for the ceremony as long as she went to wherever the brother-in-law happened to be to perform halitzah. If the brothers could not sign the writ — whether because they were not present or because the brother was a minor — the bridegroom's family would give the bride a security document promising that in due course the brothers would sign the writ of obligation to perform halitzah.[36] Alternatively, this obligation was specified in the betrothal agreement signed by representatives of bridegroom and bride. In certain places, part of the monies given by bride to bridegroom upon marriage were designated as a loan until such time as she received a signed writ of obligation to perform halitzah.[37]

We have just introduced the halakhic principles underlying rulings by decisors who were called upon to resolve issues of women in need of halitzah. We will next ask how, and to what extent, these principles were put into actual practice.

3 : THE HALITZAH TRAP

A case from Prague is instructive as to the procedures in store for a childless widow. On June 4, 1770, Libba, widow of Haim Otitz, appeared before the beit din in Prague to request permission to remarry. The beit din launched an investigation to find out if the deceased had any brothers. Inquiries were sent out to the community of Otitz. Eventually the beit din reached the conclusion that the deceased had had no brother.[1]

Obviously, the rabbinic court was seeking to determine if the widow was required to undergo the halitzah ceremony. We do not know how long the investigation lasted, but for its duration, Libba could not remarry. However, from her case, we become aware of a halakhic option that could have helped many women avoid the obligation of halitzah: "The woman Libba testified before us that her husband Haim told her he had had a brother, who went away and died. Libba did not rely on what he said. She would not marry him unless the marriage was contingent upon this. And so it was, he married her, publicly declaring that it was on condition [that he no longer has a live brother]. The officiating rabbi was the late Rabbi Mendel Bomsil. . . . A witness testified before us that this was so: that the late Rabbi Mendel Bomsil had performed a conditional marriage. The other witnesses are no longer alive."[2]

Lacking any proof that her husband's brother was dead, Libba insisted on conditional remarriage, on the assumption that this would exempt her from the obligation of halitzah should she ever need it.[3] In conditional marriage, the bridegroom declares at the marriage that, should certain circumstances arise, the marriage would be retroactively null and void. The marriage is valid as long as these circumstances do not arise. In the present case, Libba demanded that if her husband were to die childless, which would oblige her to undergo halitzah, their marriage would become null and void retroactively.[4] This halakhic solution was rejected by most Ashkenazic decisors,[5] but in this case, the officiating rabbi allowed the bridegroom to make this condition in public. It seems that Rabbi Mendel Bomsil was one of the few rabbis who enacted this policy.

The record notes that Rabbi Yechezkel Landau (Opatów, Poland, 1713–Prague, 1793),[6] a leading rabbinic authority of his generation, endeavored to verify that the officiating rabbi had indeed performed conditional marriage. This might suggest that not many were willing to perform such a marriage. Rabbi Landau's ruling shows that he had no evidence that the officiating rabbi had performed a conditional marriage in this specific case (although he had in other cases).[7] However, concluded Landau, without any real evidence that the deceased had ever had a brother, his widow was not obligated to undergo halitzah; she was free to remarry. Landau added that this case would prove instructive for other decisors.[8]

Jewish society was certainly aware that the obligation of levirate marriage threatened to render the widow an agunah, and efforts were made to protect these women. Another halakhic instrument for avoiding levirate marriage was the writ of halitzah, discussed in chapter 2. It was a commitment on the part of the husband's brothers, undertaken before or after the actual marriage ceremony, to perform halitzah, should it become necessary. This obtained also for marriage with a widow.[9] If a bridegroom could not provide this writ, the prospective match was liable to be called off. A case in point is recorded by Rabbi Jacob Reischer (Prague, 1670–Metz, 1733).[10] His responsum shows that no coercion was used to make the brothers provide a guarantee of future halitzah: "A young bachelor wanted to marry, but no one would marry him, since it is now our custom not to marry a man who has a brother unless he has obtained from him [his brother] a writ of halitzah without remuneration. This young bachelor has no such writ, since his brother refuses to sign it, despite being a bachelor himself in need of the same writ. He does not wish to marry; sinning, he makes others sin, too. Unless the beit din has the authority to compel him to provide the writ without remuneration, he will demand much in the way of dowry monies before agreeing to sign a halitzah writ."[11]

Yet signed guarantees of future halitzah were not always observed, despite the superstition that the spirit of the deceased would not rest until his brother had performed the ceremony.[12]

THE ESTATE OF THE DECEASED WHOSE WIFE REQUIRES HALITZAH

Some time after the death of Seligman Mayeh, there appeared a certain Yozel Merchingen to represent one of the heirs before the beit din of

Metz,[13] headed by Rabbi Aryeh Leib Ginzburg (d. 1785).[14] Mayeh had died childless, but he had two heirs.[15] One, a woman called Nentche, represented by Merchingen, lived not far from the community of Halberstadt; a second heir (anonymous) lived in Metz or its environs. Having located Nentche, the beit din notified her of the bequest. Merchingen, a dayan himself, was sent to collect it on her behalf. The case is instructive as to the settlement of the estate of a childless man whose widow requires halitzah.

In accordance with the procedure accepted by many contemporary communities, Mayeh's estate was sealed off immediately following his death. His widow received maintenance from the estate from the time of her husband's death to the time of halitzah, which was performed on time (i.e., ninety-two days after her husband died).[16] The widow was entitled to the amount of her ketubah and the additional amount stated therein, in accordance with her husband's last will and testament. Since, according to halakhah, the widow's entitlements in the estate preempted all other claims, it was necessary to pay her claim in full before deducting any other sum of money. To this end, the property of the deceased, consisting of household articles and movable items, was sold off. Unfortunately, the proceeds of the sale did not cover the widow's ketubah claim. There were also unpaid debts owed by the deceased to the Metz community and to another community. The estate also included promissory notes from non-Jews due for repayment. In order to make up the shortfall of the widow's entitlements, her settlement included promissory notes due for repayment. Other notes were deposited with a third party for collection so that the debts would not go unpaid. The beit din had to divide up the estate between Nentche and the other heir since both had the same degree of family relationship to the deceased. The second heir demanded payment in promissory notes due for repayment. The beit din persuaded him to buy out Nentche's share of promissory notes. This was done after the beit din deducted the debts of the deceased and court fees. The remaining total of 710 livres was deposited with Merchingen so that he could give it to the heir Nentche,[17] but not until she provided him with a note confirming that she had received all to which she was entitled from the estate and that she thus renounced any further claims to it. The settlement was approved by the beit din on February 9, 1780.

The levir in this case lived in the vicinity and was located without difficulty. Division of the estate therefore proceeded without delaying halitzah procedures. However, things did not always go so smoothly.

TRACING THE BROTHER-IN-LAW AND VERIFYING HIS IDENTITY

Let us recall the widow Haya Rachel of Brody, whose mother-in-law claimed that her deceased son had had a brother. In making that claim, she in effect rendered her daughter-in-law an agunah. Once again, we see the strong impact that patterns of family life had on the ability to confirm an individual's identity. The Jews in the region lived for the most part in small towns or villages with a small Jewish population. Young people frequently found a match in a distant community due to a lack of potential local partners. Moreover, middle- and upper-class parents preferred to marry off their children to a family similar to their own.[18] Glikl recounts how, in Hamburg, she made matches for her children with families in Frankfurt and Berlin and in other countries (Amsterdam and Metz). Jacob Emden of Altona similarly describes matchmaking for his children in distant places: his son Meir married the daughter of a wealthy man of Lissa; his son Meshulam Zalman made a match in Brody; his daughters married men from elsewhere in Poland.[19] When these couples married and set up house, at least one spouse ended up living far from his or her original family. Frequent travel for study or work was common, with Jews typically travelling from city to city and often from country to country. Travelers did not always maintain continuous contact with their families. As a result, it could be difficult to trace and identify a family member when the need arose. This could be devastating for widows awaiting halitzah, as can be inferred from a responsum by Rabbi Gershon Ashkenazi (Kraków, Nikolsburg, 1615–Vienna, Metz, 1693):

> A certain woman lived with her husband for barely two months before he died, about a year and a half ago. He died childless, and had two brothers — the elder, in Poland, goes from one yeshiva to another, as young Jews do. The younger (he has attained his majority) lives in this country. After concerted inquiry, we discovered that, last summer, the elder brother was studying at the community of Tishevitz [Tyszowce]. A relative said in his name that if the widow were to deposit a large sum of money with a third party,[20] he would

agree to come and perform halitzah. In any case, he left that place, and his whereabouts are unknown.[21]

The questioner states that the widow had been married only two months. Her brother-in-law was drifting from yeshiva to yeshiva, as young Jewish men were wont to do, either following a teacher or learning style or in search of a livelihood or spouse. In the second half of the seventeenth century, young Jewish men, mainly from eastern Europe, migrated westward, fleeing persecutions or other events. The same route was well travelled also in the eighteenth century due to changes in religious and intellectual trends. In the nineteenth century, as yeshivot in Lithuania and Hungary gained prestige, the number of young men migrating in the opposite direction—from western Europe eastward—grew.[22] Many of them drifted for years, on foot, getting an occasional ride on a wagon,[23] while the more affluent could afford to travel by carriage or boat.[24] The mail coach became a regular means of transportation in the mid-seventeenth century, and the duration and route of a journey could now be known in advance.[25] Throughout this period, however, travel still carried "the presumption of danger" (*hezkat sakanah*)—this was the term that contemporary rabbis used to describe the situation and, as we will see, this had halakhic implications[26]—due to weather conditions, natural disasters, highway robbery, and various other menaces. Responsa literature of the time is replete with reports of travelers who were drowned, robbed, or murdered.[27] It is easy to see why inquiries into the whereabouts of an individual—such as a brother-in-law needed for halitzah "who departed from there, and it is not known where he went" —could prove a lengthy process. Perhaps this explains why the question was put to Rabbi Gershon Ashkenazi only a year and a half after the woman was widowed.

Means for establishing an individual's identity were scant. One could easily assume a false identity or simply disappear. Therefore, multiple proofs were needed to confirm identity when a traveler arrived from afar. Widow Haya Rachel's mother-in-law claimed that her husband, David, had come to Brody from Brest (in Lithuania—now Belarus) fifty years earlier as a widower with a son. When the case came before Rabbi Kluger, he was faced with the task of tracking down the missing brother-in-law, who supposedly had run away from his father to live with his grandfather in Brest. Kluger, having duly written to Brest, received a reply from Rabbi Aryeh Leib Katzenellenbogen (d. 1840) with details of his meticulous investigation:

> I received your holy letter. We conducted an investigation but did not locate any well-known person by the name of Reb Tzvi with a son Reb David at the time that you wrote, only this: For thirty-odd years, there was someone called Tevele, and he was called up to the Torah by the name of Reb David ben Tzvi, but he has left this place and we do not know what became of him. That man was a member of the Ross family, a relative of Rabbi Zalman Perles of your community. That individual married a local woman, a relative of the late Rabbi David who was called David Temtzis and was a close friend of Rabbi Zalman Perles. Now Reb David Tevele has a son in our community named Reb Tzvi after his grandfather, but other than these we found no one at all named Tzvi with a son called David. I am writing all this after a thorough investigation.[28]

We see that identifying the brother-in-law was a matter of intricate investigation. Members of the community were asked to dredge up, from memory, details of former acquaintances — sometimes going back thirty years — to ascertain the name the man used for being called up to the Torah, the identity of his parents, and other particulars of family history.

Even when the widow's luck held out and her brother-in-law was found, the road to halitzah could still be bumpy. Halakhah prescribes that "the *yevamah* [widow awaiting halitzah] always follows the *yavam* [brother-in-law],", that is, that halitzah is done wherever the brother-in-law may be.[29] As a result, a widow might have to travel great distances in pursuit of a distant brother-in-law. The sister-in-law of Matityahu Aptiker of Altona traveled from Amsterdam for halitzah.[30] Grona of Brest sought out her brother-in-law in Altona in 1792. Travel was both perilous and costly. If the widow was reluctant to travel, the brother-in-law might agree to come to her — in return for travel expenses. Thus, the widow of Eli bar Aberle and her father undertook on April 10, 1799, to defray travel expenses for her brother-in-law in the amount of thirty schock,[31] as well as all other expenses he might incur relating to the trip.[32] That same year, Hannah, widow of Yaakov bar Manis, was issued a written receipt for her advance payment to a community official. The widow's payment was for any expenses incurred by her brother-in-law David so that he would come and do halitzah for her.[33]

WHEN DOES HALITZAH TAKE PLACE?

Halitzah without remuneration, as specified in the writs, should take place right after the obligatory three-month waiting period from the husband's death. This indeed happened in many cases. The Altona shamash was present at several halitzah ceremonies; according to the shamash notebook, Reuven Heckscher performed halitzah on July 12, 1781, for his sister-in-law, the widow of his brother Meir (d. April 10, 1781). Leib Wagner underwent the ceremony on September 1, 1773, for his sister-in-law, the widow of his brother Meir (d. May 10, 1773).[34] In both cases, the ceremony took place at the time specified in standard halitzah writs. According to the Wagners' gravestone, Meir died "an old man, full of years." His wife Bayla was apparently elderly when halitzah was performed; she did not remarry and died on April 21, 1791. We may conclude that the ceremony was sometimes performed even when the widow had no intention or possibility of remarrying. The reason for this is that the widow could claim her ketubah from the estate only after halitzah had been performed.

Some women grew impatient waiting for halitzah. Rabbi Yosef Steinhardt (Germany and Alsace, 1700–1776) replied to a question addressed to him by the head of the rabbinic court in Schnaittach. The question concerned a widow who, without waiting the requisite three months, went to the town where her brother-in-law resided and performed the halitzah ceremony with him. She lied about the date of her husband's death so as to speed up proceedings.[35] Upon her return, the local rabbi wanted her to undergo the ceremony again at the prescribed time — with a different brother-in-law, who lived at a great distance. The questioner describes the widow as destitute, without funds for travel. Meanwhile, she became engaged to be married, possibly explaining why she found it necessary to lie about the date of her husband's demise. Both questioner and respondent in this case validated the ceremony after the fact. Pending agreement of a third rabbi, wrote Steinhardt, she would not have to repeat the ceremony.

COST OF HALITZAH

After her travels, sometimes after much investigation, the widow reached the place where her brother-in-law was. Even then, there was no certainty that the ceremony would take place as planned. In 1696, Hakham

Tzvi replied to a question by Rabbi Shlomo Ayllón (1660–c. 1728), then head of the rabbinic court of the Portuguese congregation in London.[36] The story went as follows:

> Reuven married Dina, Shimon's widow. Her dowry brought him two thousand livres.[37] He gave her an additional thousand livres, and in her ketubah, he wrote, "three thousand." It came to pass that Reuven died childless—no more life in Israel. Dina was left with four brothers-in-law. The eldest of them went to France and became an idolater [converted], leaving Dina with the remaining three brothers. The youngest is married, and of the other two it is said that they married non-Jewish women and eat forbidden foods and suchlike. Some time later, the three brothers came to Dina, saying: "If you please, do not seek to become executrix of the estate of your husband, our brother Reuven. By the law of the land, the widow inherits half her husband's estate. Declare before witnesses that you have no wish to manage the deceased's property." For her part, she was unwilling to let them be executors of her husband's estate. A dispute ensued. Finally, a compromise was reached, to wit: the brothers would pay the amount of her ketubah, and one of them would perform halitzah.... This they undertook, that they obligated themselves with a writ of obligation drawn up by a scribe called a "public notary."[38] About three months later, they paid her entire ketubah as promised. And when the 91 days and more following Reuven's death passed, Dina wrote to the three brothers requesting that they complete that to which they had obligated themselves. They returned that they would not, since it was the eldest, who was in France, who properly should perform halitzah—Dina should wait for him to come from there. She claims that since the eldest is not there, the eldest of the rest should perform halitzah.
>
> The question asked of the rabbi is: which of the brothers should perform the ceremony? The questioner notes that the brothers' refusal is intended to force Dina to pay them exorbitant sums of money. They resorted to non-Jewish courts to litigate, maligning her at every opportunity. They say that they wished to marry her, but Dina refused to marry any of them, saying she was twice widowed already; as a "killer wife," she would not remarry. Also, be-

cause the eldest—the apostate in France—was a Gentile in every sense, a worshipper of idols, and a spendthrift to boot. No amount of money would satisfy him. One of the remaining three brothers had a wife and children. Dina refused to live in a den of vipers,[39] etc. The three brothers also claimed that since Dina had been a widow when she married their brother Reuven, she did not deserve any additional monies [stipulated in the ketubah].[40]

The previous case highlights many details connected to our topic, but before analyzing it in detail, two comments are to be noted. The first touches on the different attitudes of the Ashkenazic and Sephardic traditions to the question of whether to prioritize yibum over halitzah in situations in which both were possible. The Sephardic tradition and its implications will not be addressed in this book. The decision to analyze this case here, though the questioner should be placed within the Sephardic tradition, is based on the following two considerations. First, the question was directed to Hakham Tzvi, who was a rabbinic authority over members of the Ashkenazic community.[41] Second, as Howard Adelman has shown, even though Ashkenazic halakhic authorities tended to prefer halitzah, and Sephardic authorities yibum, in the seventeenth century, we nevertheless find decisions running counter to these trends. Intense controversy raged among Ashenazic and Sephardic sages over the question of yibum versus halitzah. The actual decision on the part of rabbis and the parties was based on social and personal considerations as well as halakhic ones.[42] Therefore, a discussion of this case may shed light on aspects not given expression in internal Ashkenzic decisors' deliberations.

The second comment relates to the issue, first raised in the introduction to this book, regarding the utility of responsa as historical sources. Both questioner and responder carefully composed their parts of the responsum, and the case histories include many details about Jewish life at the time of their writing. Historians and halakhic scholars are also aware that the rabbi answering the question in each case constructed a narrative that reveals his own worldview. Historians must both mine information from these sources and put them in context by comparing them with other contemporary extant sources. In our case, the widow Dina had the misfortune to marry into a family of several assimilated brothers.[43] The eldest, the preferred candidate for halitzah, went to France and converted to Christianity. Two other brothers married non-Jewish women and led a lifestyle in opposition to the requirements of halakhah. In mentioning these details at the very outset, the questioner is perhaps explaining why the assimilated brothers did not demand that Dina adhere to a halakhic principle (i.e., a widow does not inherit her husband's estate but claims her ketubah instead). The assimilated brothers chose to try to persuade her to relinquish the rights she enjoyed under non-Jewish jurisdiction (i.e., a widow inherits half the estate). It seems they considered the law of the land more favorable than Jewish law to the widow's interests. Dina eventually acquiesced and agreed to settle the dispute according to Jewish law and to claim her ketubah—in return for receiving a promise from the brothers that one of them would perform halitzah when the time came. The agreement was notarized by a public notary,[44] not signed at a beit din. The brothers duly paid out the amount of the ketubah. When, in turn, Dina requested from the brothers that they fulfill their obligation to perform halitzah, the brothers procrastinated and ultimately left her an agunah. The questioner ascribes to the parties arguments of a halakhic nature, raising three claims: first, the brothers demanded that Dina wait for the eldest brother—the one halakhah viewed as most appropriate for halitzah—to arrive from France; second, they claimed that they preferred yibum to halitzah; and third, they denied she had a right to collect the additional sum stipulated in the ketubah because she had been a widow at the time of her marriage to their brother. To this, Dina retorted that she did not want to marry any of them. She gave three reasons: her status as "killer wife," the eldest brother's being a convert to Christianity and a profligate to boot, and the third brother's being married with children. The questioner offered explanations given for the brothers' conduct: rumor had it that they wanted to cause Dina financial loss by forcing her to appeal to non-Jewish courts to enforce the agreement. The dispute extended to their refusal to pay the additional amount stipulated in the ketubah after her ketubah was paid.

We have no way of determining whether the story is based on an actual case or whether the author changed the facts in order to convey his views on certain fundamental issues. In any case, let us focus on several aspects of this case. Most striking is the legal proficiency demonstrated by the brothers and their willingness to exploit every means at their disposal to gain an advantage. Second, the questioner is aware of differences in inheritance law in the relevant localities; both Dina and the brothers,

The Halitzah Trap

in his view, could exploit legal differences to improve their respective positions. Finally, the questioner believed that Dina's cause would be better served in non-Jewish courts. This is why the brothers wanted to negotiate a compromise and why Dina wanted to appeal to non-Jewish courts if they remained recalcitrant.

Were brothers-in-law who were required to perform halitzah fully aware of their legal status? Did they exploit it to keep the widow an agunah? Was the woman in a better position in Jewish or non-Jewish court? Did brothers-in-law and widows maneuver among different legal systems to gain an advantage?

The sources that we have are not sufficient to answer all these questions, and other sources that might answer them have not been investigated. Yet several cases offer a partial answer. In the summer of 1792, the widow Grona travelled the long distance from Brest to Altona, in northwest Germany—over one thousand kilometers. She was seeking the family of her late husband, Zalman Peusner, and particularly his brother so that he could free her with a proper halitzah ceremony. On reaching Altona, she discovered that her late husband's brother lived in Lübeck, not far from there. Her father-in-law, Hirsch, to whom she had turned for assistance in finding her brother-in-law, was demanding a large sum of money in return for the halitzah ceremony. On July 29, 1792, the two of them petitioned the beit din headed by the chief rabbi of the community, Rabbi Raphael Cohen (in office 1776–1799).[45] The beit din issued its decision that very day after agreement was reached by the parties. The widow was to deposit a sum of money, in cash, with the beit din. The money would remain on deposit until her father-in-law arranged for his younger son to perform halitzah. Following the ceremony, the money would go to the father-in-law, and he would renounce any further claim on the widow.[46]

These matters teach us a good lesson about the relationship between legal documentation and actual implementation: The widow was in possession of a writ confirming that the brother would perform halitzah without remuneration. Yet, as in so many cases, the writ did not protect her rights, and she was subjected to extortion. The beit din in this case supported the husband's family; they demanded that the widow deposit cash with the beit din. The money would go to the father-in-law only after the ceremony had taken place. The duration of the marriage is not recorded; the sum the widow was required to deposit might have been related to property the husband had brought to the marriage. Another possibility is that the husband's family was entitled to that same amount because the value of the estate exceeded the value of the ketubah. Yet another possibility is that the beit din applied a literal interpretation to the writ: the ceremony itself would be performed without remuneration, but there was nothing to prevent other members of the family from demanding recompense (in the form of inheritance or other funds).[47] (This restrictive interpretation reappears in another entry in the beit din records.) The first decision did not put an end to the dispute. Eight days later, the widow petitioned the beit din once again, complaining that her father-in-law was not upholding his end of the bargain. She wanted the beit din to enforce its decision:

> Concerning the compromise reached in this beit din on Monday, 10 Av, between the parties Hirsch Peusner and Grona, widow of Zalman, son of Reb Hirsch. The aforementioned widow has approached us with much complaint, requesting that the compromise be enforced. She claims that Reb Hirsch refuses to uphold the compromise. Reb Hirsch appeared before us and declared that his son wants an additional 30 *adumim* [currency] from the widow. We, the undersigned beit din, rule that Reb Hirsch is obligated to make his younger son perform halitzah without remuneration, with no further claim, according to the writ [of halitzah]. If he refuses, he will be coerced. If he ignores this warning he will be punished by immediate excommunication.... If he persists in ignoring this, too, he will be liable for all expenses incurred by the widow due to his refusal. This ruling—firm and resolute—is hereby handed down by the beit din of Altona on Monday, 18 Av.[48]

It emerges that the objection of the beit din was not directed against payment for halitzah as such but only against the demand for direct payment to the brother-in-law himself. In fact, the beit din supported the father-in-law's claim for travel expenses to bring his son from Lübeck to Altona. However, when the brother-in-law tried to extort more money from the widow, the beit din objected vigorously and threatened him with severe sanctions. The sources do not explain why the widow did not travel to Lübeck for a ceremony without remuneration or why she preferred to deposit a large sum of money in return for the halitzah. Again, these funds were perhaps due to the family of her late husband anyway, or, perhaps, she realized that her father-in-law's involvement would be necessary to persuade his son to perform halitzah—and was willing to pay accordingly. Neither does the court record make clear if the threatened sanctions were against the father or his son. Finally, the record does not indicate if or when the ceremony ever took place. It is clear at any rate that the beit din had a decisive role in interpreting the writ of halitzah— the legal document intended to protect the woman—and implementing it. We learn, too, that the beit din had sanctions at their disposal to compel halitzah, should they choose to use them. I found no record of any actual excommunication in such cases, in this beit din or any other, and we cannot determine whether this particular sanction was ever used for this purpose.

Hirsch Peusner's son was not the only one to refuse his widowed sister-in-law halitzah, thus rendering her an agunah. Before we look at additional cases, let us briefly review the legal status of women during this time period. The widow Grona was present at the sessions of the beit din, where she represented herself. While not unique, this was certainly not always the case. Men too used legal representation.[49] There is some disagreement among scholars as to implications of the representation of women by men (in German, *Kriegsvögte*) during the early modern period in governmental institutions in general, and in courts of law in particular. David W. Sabean has claimed that representation of this kind was part of the more general exercise of male authority over females (*Geschlechtsvormundschaft*), intended as protection. In contrast, Ogilvie claims that men often exploited women by this arrangement without safeguarding their interests. There is agreement that throughout this period women did represent themselves in courts of law, but opportunity to do so was not always forthcoming.[50] Rabbinic courts differed in this respect, with regional differences. Extant beit din records are mainly from the second half of the eighteenth and early nineteenth centuries, a period of great change in relations between Jews and their non-Jewish surroundings. With all due caution in using sources to learn of earlier periods, we can say that in Frankfurt, AHW, Fürth, Prague, and Metz, women usually represented themselves before the beit din. When they were represented by legal counsel, it was not because they were denied the option of representing themselves.[51] In Prague, in November 1755, a woman called Ella represented her husband Shmuel before the beit din in a dispute he had with his business partner.[52] In Fürth, in 1816, two women were represented before the beit din by a man called Shlomo Fegerscheim;[53] I could find no record of any family connection between him and these women. Both cases involved a brother- and sister-in-law dispute over the estate of the deceased husband/brother, one of which also involved halitzah. In Offenbach and Warburg, women were usually represented by legal counsel. These smaller communities lacked their own beit din, with the local rabbi often acting as decisor.[54] Here, too, women could represent themselves, and they did so in a few cases. It is difficult to determine what considerations were at work when a woman had to decide if she would represent herself or engage legal counsel. Personal as well as financial considerations surely played a major part.[55]

Let us return to cases of levirs who took advantage of their position to gain benefit from delaying the halitzah. On April 3, 1740, Lippman Wenig appeared before officials of the Offenbach community, acting for his sister Brendl, widow of Leib Berl. Wenig demanded that Yosefe Perl perform unremunerated halitzah for Brendl, as set out in the writ of halitzah. Yosefe, agreeing in principle, demanded that the widow sign a waiver to the effect that she was willing to collect her ketubah in goods and property rather than in ready cash. Lippman objected, arguing that "he didn't want his sister to get into all that." Yosefe retorted that he would act in accordance with the decision of the leaders of the nearby community of Frankfurt.[56]

On November 6, 1772, there came before Rabbi Shmuel Steg of Warburg a man called Moshe acting for his sister Beyle, the widow of Shimon. He demanded that her late husband's brother perform halitzah and settle her financial affairs.[57] The widow's brother-in-law Mordechai needed to perform the ceremony immediately without remuneration, as stipulated in the writ in Beyle's possession. Now that the requisite waiting period of three months was over, he demanded that Mordechai pay the widow's ketubah in the amount of 720 reichstaler and add another 1,000 reichstaler, as set out in the late husband's will. The will, exhibited as evidence in court, further stated that the widow be allowed to continue to live in the marital home for the rest of her life. Mordechai, unmarried and childless, wanted to marry his sister-in-law rather than perform halitzah. Moshe testified that Beyle was not interested in marrying her brother-in-law; Mordechai responded that the signature on the writ of halitzah was not his own. Rabbi Steg, unimpressed, ruled that he must perform the ceremony and settle the widow's financial affairs within eight days. On November 9, 1772, the parties came again before the beit din, having come to an agreement. Accordingly, the beit din ruled that the brother-in-law would perform halitzah at a date to be determined by the head of the beit din. If he refused, he would be fined. The beit din further ruled that Mordechai would inherit his late brother's seat in the synagogue and fifty reichstaler with no further delay and another fifty within a year. We do not know the value of the estate or if it sufficed to pay the ketubah, so it is difficult to determine who benefited from the beit din's decision. Each of the parties had to pay a court fee of twenty-three reichstaler.

On October 11, 1815, an event was recorded in the Fürth beit din register,[58] presenting the perspective of at least some of the brothers-in-law who were obligated to perform halitzah (*yevamim*).

R. Meir son of Mendel Ullmann thought he could put off halitzah for his brother Moshe's widow until after the financial settlement. The beit din accepted his position in part, ruling that the estate be divided among the heirs in accordance with the will, except for 600 gold pieces to be deposited as security until the dispute between Meir and the widow Edele could be resolved. The rest of the property would go to the widow with no further delay, ruled the beit din. Two months later, on December 3, 1815, Meir and a man called Shlomo Fegerscheim, representing Edele, came before the beit din; this was the same aforementioned individual who represented two women in the beit din of Fürth.[59] It seems that the widow and her brother-in-law reached a compromise as to the disputed amount. Edele claimed that on the day of the compromise, she could not find the security writ that had been in her possession since her wedding day. She therefore agreed to the compromise. When the writ turned up, she claimed that the compromise was cancelled because it stated explicitly that Meir would perform halitzah without remuneration. His signature was affixed to the document. If he failed to meet this obligation, she wanted no halitzah at all. Meir replied that the widow held a pledge he had entrusted to his late brother. His brother had told him he could have his pledge back for nothing, even if he did not repay his debt of thirty-six gold pieces. Two witnesses confirmed this. He further claimed a share in the widow's income from her late husband's business from the time of his death to the date of halitzah. To the claim that he had promised to perform the ceremony without remuneration, Meir replied that Edele was not actually named in the writ as his late brother's wife. Dayanim

Zalman Ber, Lippman Bereu, and Judah Leib Halberstadt ruled on December 6, 1815: they rejected Meir's claim that his signature on the writ was not binding. The widow's demand that Meir perform halitzah without remuneration was also rejected. She was instructed to return his pledge for a reduced amount. Meir was required to swear to confirm its value.[60] The sources do not reveal if halitzah ever took place or if Edele remained steadfast in her refusal to pay for it. It should be noted that the brother-in-law designated for halitzah was not permitted to marry either until after the ceremony. With such a strong case, the widow Edele might very well have achieved her goal.

While extant sources do not allow for a more detailed picture, we certainly see that in all the previous cases, the designated brother-in-law was well aware of the widow's dependence on him. He was equally aware that he could exploit his advantage in their financial negotiations. To this end, diverse means were employed: the son of Hirsch Peusner explicitly demanded payment for halitzah, forcing the widow to appeal to the court again and again. Applying to the beit din involved time and expense since it convened at set times and litigants were liable for part of the salary of the dayanim.[61] Peusner's strategy was to make things even harder for the widow. Yosefe Perl demanded that his case be heard in distant Frankfurt, which further delayed proceedings. Mordechai Fokselheim tried to evade his obligation by claiming he was interested in marrying his widowed sister-in-law and by denying his signature on the writ. The twofold argument led to protracted litigation.

Enactments from the Middle Ages designed to restrict the brother-in-law's ability to extort funds from the widow failed to eradicate this behavior.[62] Women awaiting halitzah were an easy target for extortion. This often held up payment of the ketubah and remarriage. At the same time, affluent women like Edele could forgo halitzah altogether rather than pay for it. This probably diminished the brother-in-law's negotiating power.

In the cases discussed, we do not discern any unease on the part of the beit din at a widow's having to pay for her freedom. Despite the means at its disposal for coercing a recalcitrant brother-in-law, the beit din did not always come to the woman's aid. At times this meant she would be liable for an exorbitant expenditure of time and money. We cannot determine who benefited from the beit din's actions in each case since extant records do not include final outcomes. The records give the impression that Jewish courts tried to attain halitzah through compromise between widows and brothers-in-law, the latter inevitably trying to extract funds from their sister-in-law. In some cases, the beit din did not allow the family of the deceased to draw funds from the estate until halitzah had been performed. This was the case on November 4, 1779, following the death of Wolf son of Meir of Hamburg, presumably a wealthy man.[63] His father wanted to draw 500 reichstaler from the estate prior to financial settlement and halitzah. The beit din, rejecting this demand, ordered the brother of the deceased first to perform halitzah.[64]

It seems clear from these cases why some men specified in the will the exact amount to be paid for halitzah. This was done by Yosefe Mentzir of Altona in 1784 and by Yeshayah Levi, also of Altona, in 1798.[65] Each of them left instructions to pay the brother-in-law one hundred schock in exchange for halitzah. The latter explicitly left the rest of his estate in its entirety to his wife. In practice, a widow was sometimes able to claim her ketubah and settle her financial affairs prior to halitzah. Rabbi Nathan Maas,[66] head of the rabbinic court in Frankfurt, received the following complaint, dated March 9, 1770, from Eliezer Innsbruck of Neuwied: "I cannot comprehend why some people consider that my sister-in-law should receive her ketubah money prior to halitzah. Does it say anywhere at all that the poskim allow this? I have already written to community leaders saying that I will perform halitzah if an agreement with me is reached first, concerning her ketubah. . . . all the more so, since she has no promissory note from me."[67]

The beit din was aware that the writer was willing to perform halitzah; nevertheless, it ruled that her ketubah had to be paid first. I have not found a response to this letter, and so we cannot tell whether or not this ruling was actually implemented. In any case, the writer threatens to send out notices to all Jewish communities and make public this "infamous, unprecedented decision." His threat implies that this was an unusual ruling.[68]

COST OF THE CEREMONY

In addition to the widow's other expenses, the parties had to pay a court fee to the dayanim and the head of the court for officiating at the halitzah ceremony. Rabbi Moshe Isserles, glossing the *Shulkhan Arukh*, ruled that dayanim may not exact a fee for halitzah since the obligation is founded in biblical law.[69] His opinion notwithstanding, rabbis and dayanim did, in fact, collect a fee for this religious service. Fees of dayanim and other court fees were recorded in contracts between communities and the rabbis they hired. In many cases, we know the exact amounts paid.[70] In a contract of Meshulam Zalman Neumark, rabbi of the Three Communities (AHW), dated July 30, 1685, halitzah fees were determined by the value of the ketubah. For a widow whose ketubah was less than 600 reichstaler, the head of the rabbinic court received 6 reichstaler. For every additional one hundred reichstaler of ketubah value, the head of the rabbinic court received half a reichstaler. One third of this went to pay the other dayanim. For a widow who could not claim her ketubah or whose ketubah had no real monetary value, the community would defray expenses in the amount of 4 reichstaler, payable to the head of the rabbinic court. In Wallerstein, the community contracted with Rabbi Itzik Kahana Rappaport on December 17, 1763. His fee for officiating at a halitzah was 5 reichstaler, of which he was to pay the dayanim their due. The contract with Rabbi Horowitz in the Three Communities in 1765 specifies a fee of 6 reichstaler for widows with a ketubah valued at up to 300 reichstaler; for every additional 100 reichstaler, another half a reichstaler was charged. Here, too, the head of the rabbinic court was to pay the other dayanim out of that fee.[71] As mentioned in this book's introduction, payment to rabbis and dayanim for their services was a significant component of their salary. The ruling of Rabbi Isserles provoked occasional controversy with respect to fees for officiating at halitzah. In reply to a question by the head of the rabbinic court in Paks, Hungary, on taking payment for halitzah, Rabbi Yechezkel Landau replied: "Concerning your question: Do I take a fee for performing halitzah? God forbid! This has never happened and will never happen. Neither do I allow the other two dayanim serving with me to take as much as a single coin. As for the two additional [judges],[72] I do not object. Sometimes the latter give up something of theirs to the former, and I turn a blind eye. But, for my part, I take nothing at all, neither at start nor at finish."[73]

Tensions stemming from demand by rabbis for payment might explain why Jewish courts did not always hasten to convene for a halitzah ceremony. Altona beit din records deemed it necessary to note the work schedule upon appointment of new dayanim in 1764. If a get or halitzah was planned, the beit din was to convene without delay.[74]

Some women found it difficult to meet ceremony and travel expenses, and communal financial aid was sometimes available. On May 16, 1765, financial officers of the Altona community instructed the charity *gabbai* (community charity treasurer) to help the widow of Nahshon Levi pay her halitzah expenses.[75] On August 14, 1803, officers of the same community decided to extend financial aid to a widow from another community who was en route to London for halitzah.[76]

PITFALLS ON THE ROAD TO HALITZAH

Many halitzah ceremonies were performed during the period under discussion,[77] but very few records provide a detailed description of the ritual itself. A woman's transition from legal bond with her brother-in-law to freedom to remarry whomever she chose was,[78] for halakhic authorities, a process necessitating meticulous attention to detail. Inquiries were sent to decisors concerning the visual acuity of the officiating dayanim or the type of shoe to be used.[79] Rabbi Yehezkel Landau wrote in 1783 that on first arriving in Prague twenty-eight years earlier, he changed the type of shoe used for the ceremony. When he came to Jampol (Yampil), he refrained from introducing a similar change.[80] Other queries pertain to physical conditions that could prevent the brother-in-law from performing the ceremony.[81] Rabbis were asked about the validity of writs of halitzah,[82] or about the writ, issued by the beit din, that confirmed that the ceremony took place. Details of the ceremony occasioned halakhic dispute. Rabbi Yehezkel Landau recounts that Rabbi Zalman Emrich, who served with him on the beit din in Prague, wished to renew the custom of the widow's lifting the man's foot as she removes his shoe. Landau himself opposed restoring the custom. Controversy ensued, as can be learned from Landau's lengthy responsum in his *Noda biYehudah*,[83] to which Emrich duly replied that some places practiced the custom he supported.[84]

DELAYS DUE TO INVESTIGATIONS

Disagreements among dayanim often delayed the ceremony or raised doubts as to its validity. If a halitzah ceremony was invalidated, the widow was considered an agunah. Brothers-in-law sometimes took advantage of the importance attached to procedural accuracy in order to have the ceremony invalidated after the fact.

Confirming the identity of the parties constituted the first step of the process. Doubts about identity could arise even when the parties had arrived and were already present. This happened to Gittel, as recorded by Rabbi Yehezkel Landau, then rabbi of Jampol:

> A woman by the name of Gittel, wife of Haim son of Rabbi Tzvi, requested that I arrange the halitzah ceremony for her with her husband's brother. I consented, and wrote to him to come to us, since in his town there is no beit din. He came, and I started checking all the things that should be investigated on the day prior to the halitzah. When I asked about her husband's death, it turned out there was no clear testimony, just a "rumor" saying that there are some witnesses in Basel who testify he was killed. I told the woman to go there; an announcement would be made there calling for all witnesses to his death to come forward and testify before a beit din of three. The testimonies would be sent to me.[85]

Gittel duly brought back valid testimony (taken down by the beit din of Bazalia, April 1750, some thirty kilometers from there). The man had been killed at the end of the month of Tishrei in the year 1745, four years earlier. Gittel did not produce this testimony until the decisor demanded it. We do not know if, prior to approaching Landau, Gittel thought she would not be able to get halitzah or if she chose not to seek it. After approaching Landau, she would have to wait several months for halitzah. On July 10, 1750, over three months after she first approached him,[86] Landau penned a lengthy responsum in favor of freeing her from agunah status. His agreement was conditional on getting the support of two other dayanim from his community and of a prominent decisor from Brody.[87] This precondition, not unusual among decisors, further delayed the widow's release from her marriage, as will be discussed at length. We know nothing more of Gittel.

DELAYS CAUSED BY A BROTHER-IN-LAW EXPLOITING HIS HALAKHIC EXPERTISE

A brother-in-law well-versed in halakhah could exploit his knowledge to procrastinate and postpone the halitzah process for financial gain. Here is Landau writing in 1788 to Rabbi Shmuel Hayim of Kobersdorf (some 67 kilometers south of Vienna):

A man performed halitzah for his sister-in-law. Before the ceremony, he was seen to have full use of both legs. His right shoe was removed, as is required by Torah law. Then the widow made a match, and the betrothal agreement became public knowledge. The man claimed that his performance of the ceremony was invalid, saying he was in fact lame but had not said so at the time. He performed the ceremony fraudulently, knowing that the two parties, i.e., he and his sister-and-law who underwent halitzah, should divide up the estate of the deceased. He said the widow had declared that the deceased left no assets. Therefore, he too acted deceitfully by performing an invalid ceremony. He did this thinking that after her betrothal became known, and people knew the amount of her dowry, he would declare to the beit din that the halitzah was invalid. At that point, she would need to repeat the ceremony and would be obliged to share her assets with him.[88]

The local rabbi, fearing the ceremony was indeed invalid, wrote to Landau for advice. Landau replied: "If we believe him, she will have to repeat halitzah with all the brothers. It is a bad business. If this man had his way, no daughter of Abraham would ever have halitzah with peace of mind. The brother-in-law, after the ceremony, would pretend to be lame and drag his foot, invalidating the whole thing."[89]

Landau perceived that other men might follow suit, which would undermine women's confidence in the entire halakhic process of halitzah. He therefore pronounced the ceremony valid despite the brother-in-law's confession to fraudulent behavior. Similar cases show that men succeeded at times in delaying the remarriage of widows: as long as halakhic disagreements persisted, the widow was not allowed to remarry.[90] In fact, other family members of the deceased, men and women alike, often tried to prevent the widow from remarrying. The institution of halitzah was certainly regarded by men and women as useful for their own financial gain. From the gender perspective, the more halakhic knowledge one possessed, the more advantageous it could be for financial gain. Those in rabbinic circles were no doubt more familiar with the halitzah ritual than those who did not have much to do with halakhah. Women naturally had less access to such knowledge and did not always have funds at hand to enlist halakhic experts and were therefore often at a disadvantage.

THE COMMUNITY AND THE AGUNAH AWAITING HALITZAH

Not only those with a personal interest sought to exploit the agunah. Rabbi Jacob Reischer was asked if it was permissible to deny a widow halitzah as a means of exerting pressure on her father. The man had offended the community, which then asked if they could withhold halitzah from his daughter until he complies with the congregation and the beit din.[91]

Withholding communal religious services as a disciplinary measure against wayward members was not new. Denying members community burial services, circumcision, and use of the ritual bath and not counting a man for the prayer quorum were all frequently used.[92] It should be noted that in this attempt to add halitzah to this list, it was the widow's father who was the offender here, not herself. This question reflects the perception that women were under the guardianship of the men in their family (the father or the husband). Reischer responded that a woman leaves her father's guardianship upon her marriage and therefore should not be used as a hostage. Reischer also noted that the proposed course of action also would harm the brother-in-law, an innocent party; he would not be permitted to marry either until the ceremony was performed.

Halitzah could be a cause of community dispute. The writings of Rabbi Jacob Emden of Altona describe such an incident that occurred there, and in which he himself was involved. On February 25, 1739, the beit din of Altona heard testimony by Yehiel son of Shlomo Zalman about the death of his uncle Ephraim. Ephraim, who had converted to Christianity several years before, was sole brother-in-law of Haya, a young widow of the community who required halitzah.[93] Haya was engaged at the time and, based on this testimony, requested permission to marry. According to Emden, Rabbi Yehezkel Katzenellenbogen (Lithuania and Germany, d. 1749)[94] sought Emden's opinion. After reviewing the case, Emden ruled that the testimony was insufficient for freeing her from agunah status.[95] Emden claimed that Katzenellenbogen initially accepted his opinion but then relented under pressure from the families of the prospective bride and groom, ruling that the widow-agunah could remarry.[96] Emden was thwarted by community leaders in his attempts to publish his own refusal of permission for the widow to remarry.[97] She remarried on the strength of Katzenellenbogen's permission. The couple remained childless; Emden saw in this a vindication of his position.[98]

Just as widowhood was marked visually by special garments, so, too, was release from widowhood: a regulation in the Fürth community book of customs states that a widow shall remove her garments of mourning immediately following the halitzah ceremony.[99]

Part Two

Dead Men, Chained Women

4 : BITTERLY SHE WAILS
Agunot in Times of Persecution and War

War, massacres, and expulsions made iggun a very real danger for many women in Ashkenaz during this period. Other contributing factors were increased mobility, either voluntary or not; expanding transnational and transcontinental commercial opportunities; and improved transportation. Religious and spiritual trends, such as conversion, secularization, the Sabbatean movement, and the Jewish Enlightenment and Hasidism, all increased a woman's risk of becoming an agunah.

Our period begins in 1648, the end of the Thirty Years' War in the Holy Roman Empire. Jews lived in territories of conflict, including principalities of Germany, Bohemia, Sweden, Denmark, and other areas in central Europe. Populations suffered where battles were fought during the prolonged conflict in places such as northern Germany, Thuringia, and Bavaria.[1] The fate of the Jews depended largely on the individual ruler of the specific territory where they resided.[2] In that year in Ukraine, the Khmelnytsky Cossack uprisings, known in Jewish historiography as *Gezerot tah-tat*, or "Evil Decrees of 1648–1649," broke out. These events led to a series of wars lasting nearly two decades.[3] Historians differ as to the impact of the war on the Jews, the extent of destruction, and the speed of restoration.[4] All agree that killings and massacres of Jews took place on a large scale. The Jews had no time to estimate the extent of the horrors or to record the precise death toll. Other Jews were taken captive or converted to Christianity; yet others managed to flee.[5] Whereas refugees from western and central Europe fled eastward during the Thirty Years' War (this migration continued throughout the seventeenth century), in the massacres of the 1648–1649 uprising, many Jews fled westward—to Amsterdam, Hungary, Romania, Bohemia, and Moravia.[6] In the turmoil, families perished or split up; survivors often never knew what had become of their loved ones.[7]

There are several extant accounts of the 1648–1649 massacres, written soon after the events by Jews,[8] or by non-Jewish victims, or by perpetrators.[9] Several of the Jewish sources state explicitly that the massacres and destruction left many Jewish women in the state of iggun. Thus Meir ben Samuel of Szczebrzeszyn, in his *Tzok Haitim* (*Difficulty of the Times*), published as early as 1650, states: "Many prominent, respectable women remained widowed after the husband's death; many of these were agunot who knew nothing of their husband's death, believing in fact that they were being held captive, and that they themselves would remain agunot for the rest of their lives."[10]

Being highly emotional, these testimonies cannot be considered reliable; nevertheless, they are of great historical value as primary sources. Despite the (possibly) imprecise figures and impressionistic nature, studies have corroborated the events described on the basis of non-Jewish sources.[11]

Proof of the acuteness of the agunah problem can be found, for example, in the records of the Council of Four Lands, which was the autonomous Jewish corporate body active in Poland between the middle of the sixteenth and the middle of the eighteenth century. Representatives from the four lands, that is, Great Poland, Little Poland, Polish or Red Russia, and Volhynia, met once or twice a year, and they engaged in legislative, administrative, judicial, spiritual, and cultural activities related to Jewish life in Poland.

Records from this council in 1650 mention that a rabbinic assembly in Lublin had issued enactments concerning agunot,[12] although we have neither the exact texts nor the exact date when they were issued. We have further proof in responsa by rabbinic decisors who were asked to rule in cases concerning women who became agunot in the events of 1648–1649.[13] Although all these works are by men, they document some testimonies by women as part of the halakhic discussion. Due to the special halakhic nature of the agunah problem, for example, women's testimony was admissible for the purpose of freeing an agunah, and conversations between woman and the decisors were occasionally documented as well.

We do not know how many agunot appealed to decisors during the 1648–1649 massacres, nor do we know the ratio of women who were granted their request to women who remained agunot. Thus, we would do well to reexamine Salmon-Mack's claim that after the immense trauma, the rabbis of Poland were prepared to make every effort to solve the problems of agunot whose husbands died in the war.[14] Responsa volumes contain only a fraction of the rabbinic rulings, and they were edited in accordance with the public image the rabbi or compiler sought to project. Cost of publication was another practical consideration at work. Extant responsa dealing with agunot in 1648–1649 contain no small number of replies granting the agunah permission to remarry, but they also contain several instances where the decisor wrote that he did not dare free her. Therefore, the claim by Salmon-Mack that the enactments passed by the rabbinical council concerning agunot solved in a single sweep a cluster of pervasive problems that arose from the persecutions is no more than wishful thinking.[15]

Were decisors as eager to document their refusals to permit an agunah to remarry as they were to publicize their consent? We will return to this question presently.

SARAH AND LEAH: WAR AGUNOT

The responsa *Tzemach tzedek* by Rabbi Menahem Mendel Krochmal (Kraków, 1600–Nikolsburg, 1661) presents a case that is indicative of the fate of the agunot, the underlying value system of the rabbis they consulted, the discourse during the massacres, and its impact on the lives of these women. Menahem Mendel Krochmal fled the pogroms and instability of Kraków, settling in Moravia (in today's Czech Republic). After holding the position of rabbi in several local congregations, he was appointed rabbi of the city of Nikolsburg. A prominent decisor, he corresponded with many contemporary leading halakhic authorities. Krochmal's treatment of agunah cases in the 1648–1649 uprising was described by Yitzhak Zeev Kahana as follows: "Much effort was made by Rabbi Menahem Mendel to alleviate the suffering of agunot who fled to Moravia in the years *tah-tat* [1648–1649] as they came knocking at his door. He sought to release them from the bonds of iggun."[16]

One of the several agunah cases in Krochmal's volume of responsa is that of Sarah, who consulted him in 1653, accompanied by her sister. Sarah wanted to be freed from her status of iggun.[17] She recounted how she herself had seen her husband killed in the pogrom of Polonne (Polonnoye) in the district of Volhynia in Ukraine. The region was hard hit by the Cossack uprising; the Jewish community of Polonnoye was attacked and completely destroyed in the summer of 1648.[18] Like many others—sometimes following directives from Jewish leaders—Sarah and her sister escaped. Krochmal writes: "A woman came before me, by the name of Sarah daughter of Rabbi Mordechai of Nova Chortoriya,[19] weeping and wailing over her husband, Rabbi Yoel, who died during the decree [the massacres] in the holy community of Polonnoye. He was slaughtered before her very eyes, hers and those of her sister, Zlata, who is here with her now. She requested that I look into her case and grant her permission to remarry. I refused, saying: 'How can she be permitted to remarry, given that he was killed in war?'"[20]

One cannot help but register the drama of the scene as depicted by the rabbi, but first, let us note that Krochmal's account was included in a halakhic compilation intended to instruct his colleagues. Reading his account, they could follow the considerations at work in his decision-making process. As such, and as was mentioned in the introduction, we should not regard his description solely as documenting reality. Rather, it expresses the writer-rabbi's attitude toward his subject, as he stresses elements he considers most salient to his halakhic ruling. Recent studies have demonstrated that responsa literature played an important part in constructing the public image of the decisor for his readership. Krochmal, one of the most prominent rabbis of his time, was no doubt aware of this.[21] Sarah's role in their dialogue is mediated by Krochmal, who articulates her written words. We have no way of knowing if these were her exact words or if she said more than he recorded.

Despite the aforementioned considerations, there are good reasons to regard Krochmal's description as reasonably reliable. First, the author of a responsum had to describe the circumstances in which testimony was given and quote it verbatim so that other rabbis might correctly understand his halakhic process. Many responsa concerning agunot include appendices containing verbatim transcripts of beit din testimony. The decisor would often copy these testimonies into his own responsum, as it is likely that Krochmal did in this case.[22] Second, in the halakhic process of granting an agunah permission to remarry, much significance is attached to the content of testimonies that the beit din accepted as grounds for its decision to release the agunah from her marriage or to not release her, and the motives of the witnesses are equally significant for reaching a decision. In this kind of responsum, then, halakhic significance inheres in every detail pertaining to the identity of the witnesses and to the impression they made on the decisor. Hence, whether the dialogue is represented exactly as conducted or whether it was edited, we may take the description as reasonably reflecting the reality of the world in which the decisor and the agunot lived.

Let us return to Sarah. The city of Polonnoye was destroyed in the summer of 1648. It is not known how long Sarah wandered or when she reached Moravia.[23] Several sources tell of the plight of the fleeing refugees: roads were perilous, with constant danger of robbery, rape, and murder.[24] Those who had a horse and cart used them wherever possible; others made their way on foot, often carrying small children. The refugees were constantly on the move for fear of pursuit by the mob, snatching moments of rest wherever they could.[25] By the time Sarah reached Rabbi Krochmal in the summer of 1653, she had already been through severe ordeals, as he noted in his description. We do not know why she approached him at that particular time: perhaps she had not had a spare moment beforehand to consider her legal plight, or perhaps she was considering marrying again. Nor do we know if she consulted other rabbis before Krochmal. Be that as it may, the time factor was crucial: The more time that had elapsed after her husband's death or disappearance, the slimmer the chances of finding witnesses who could reliably recall events in detail.

Krochmal reports that his grounds for refusal to grant Sarah's request for permission to remarry were that her husband had died in war. Krochmal's approach was not unusual, based on a case reported thirty years later by the decisor David Oppenheim (Worms, 1664–Prague, 1736).[26] Oppenheim wrote about Leah, a woman whose husband was killed in the Austrian conquest of Budapest in 1686:

> Leah daughter of Yitzhak of Budapest, widow of Yonah [lit., "dove"] son of Aaron of Budapest, came to me, weeping and wailing bitterly. She had been living as a lonely widow for several years, a shackled agunah, and the dove found no rest for her soul, as he was killed on a day of battle. . . . And many people told her of his death honestly, but their testimonies cannot be put together into one testimony, though all agree that his was a strange and unusual death. And this poor woman almost fell apart, pleading before decisors to find a solution to her problem and free her from iggun, and some scholars have already dealt with her case.[27]

We learn that Leah approached Oppenheim armed with information about the circumstances of her husband's death. Yet this information, gleaned from different individuals, was not presented in such a way that would enable her freedom, and she remained an agunah for a long time. The account suggests that the testimonies she provided were from writings of the late rabbi of Hungary, with no indication as to his own evaluation of the credibility or relative weight of the evidence. Nor is it clear if it was the late rabbi who heard the testimonies in a beit din or if Leah herself gave them to him.

It emerges that, prior to his death, the rabbi of Hungary did receive testimonies obtained in the beit din from the following people: Matityahu son of Israel, about whom the beit din wrote that "his testimony in general and in its particulars is sound and credible; he saw Yonah lying dead on the ground," and David son of Eliyahu, about whom the beit din wrote that his testimony "indicated clearly that he too had seen Yonah, husband of the said Leah, lying dead on the ground." Another witness, Avraham son of Shimon, heard someone saying that a certain gentile woman said explicitly that she had seen Yonah killed.

We do not know if the beit din was negligent in failing to record all the details reported by the witnesses; we do know that the beit din was satisfied as to their credibility. However, to Oppenheim, these testimonies seemed insufficient grounds for freeing the agunah. He duly appointed a new beit din. He heard witnesses himself and ultimately permitted Leah to remarry several years after her husband had been killed.

Why did the first beit din — while acknowledging the credibility of witnesses saying they had seen her husband dead — nevertheless not release Leah? Oppenheim makes it clear that he started handling her case only after previous appeals on her part to other rabbis. He writes that she knocked at his door night and day, requesting him to free her. Oppenheim chooses to inform his readers that Leah approached several rabbis, himself included, again and again before finally getting permission to remarry. Krochmal, too, noted that he initially rejected Sarah's request. We may infer that an agunah needed fortitude and staying power in her attempt to convince a decisor to release her from her marriage.

We left Sarah standing before the decisor. Krochmal's initial refusal to take her case, on the grounds that her husband died in war, was based on the halakhic principle that a woman's testimony that her husband was killed in war is inadmissible.[28] Krochmal was acting as was expected of him. Yet Sarah was accompanied by her sister, so Krochmal could have heard the sister's testimony: a woman's testimony is admissible in agunah cases, even when the case involves death in wartime, if she pronounces, "he died; I buried him." The testimony by a woman can then be used to release the agunah. Halakhically, then, Krochmal could have heard the sister's testimony before dismissing Sarah's case, yet he chose to not do so.

At this point, gender relations in the agunah-decisor interaction come to the fore. Halakhic proficiency in this period, as mentioned in the introduction, belonged essentially to men; women had extremely limited Torah and halakhic learning.[29] The encounter between agunah and decisor almost inevitably involved a woman lacking the relevant halakhic background confronting a knowledgeable man. Sarah put forth her best arguments, but she did not know enough Jewish law to turn them to her advantage. Had she known at the start that there were no clear-cut halakhic grounds for his refusal, she presumably would have tried to persuade him to reconsider. Her unfamiliarity with the ins and outs of Jewish law limited her control over her own situation.

But, as Krochmal reported, Sarah did not give up: "And then she raised her voice in weeping: Why did her cry go unheeded, given that she knew for certain that her husband was dead?! And why should she be suspected of taking lightly the prohibition against a married woman's remarrying?!" Sarah's frustration is clearly evident, and the decisor gave her no chance to express her pain. He refused to even consider her case. We feel keenly her indignation as she is faced with the gap between the information in her possession, on the one hand, and the rabbi's indifference, on the other. As far as the agunah was concerned, Krochmal was impugning her probity and her commitment to halakhah. She insisted that her husband was dead and was clearly aware of the grave prohibition against a married woman remarrying while her husband was still alive.

Clearly, an agunah's chances of being released from the shackles of her marriage depended in large measure not only on her halakhic proficiency but also on her personality. A less assertive woman than Sarah might have been intimidated by Krochmal's initial refusal or assumed that his argument reflected an unassailable halakhic position. A less adamant agunah might have been dissuaded, might have relinquished hope and resigned herself to remaining an agunah forever. But Sarah remained undaunted. Krochmal was softened somewhat, if not entirely, by her counterargument. He decided to put her to the test:

To test her, I said, "This matter is not new; the same thing happened to several other people who came to this country as war refugees. They remarried based on their own testimonies that they had seen their wives killed, and afterwards, it was discovered that the women were still alive." At this, Sarah and her sister chorused in unison that the cases were entirely different! For a married man it is easy to marry another woman; if later his first wife turns out to be still alive, he may simply divorce one of them, and he will have met his obligation. But for a woman it is not so — her punishment is much more severe. It would be an aberration, never to be undone.

The test case advanced by Krochmal is surprising. The implications of error for a man who remarries in this situation are much less severe than for a woman. The decisor could have cited cases in which a woman was released from her marriage to a missing husband on the basis of her own declaration that he was dead — then he showed up. Surely such a case would have made her sufficiently fearful of a similar tragic outcome. So why did he choose a reverse-gender example?

Perhaps he was using this example to determine whether Sarah was aware of the difference between a man remarrying based on the erroneous assumption that his spouse was dead and a woman doing so. Halakhically, if a woman remarries on the assumption that her husband is no longer alive, and afterwards it emerges that he was alive at the time of her remarriage, she is prohibited to both men. By contrast, when the genders are reversed, the repercussions of a man's second marriage are much less severe. If it is discovered that his first wife was still alive at the time of his remarriage, he may simply choose which of the women to divorce, remaining married to the other. His children from the other woman are not considered mamzerim and instead are full members of the Jewish community.

Sarah was well aware of this halakhic difference and knew something else as well. She noted that it would be "easier" for a man to remarry, not that it would be "permissible" for him to do so. It would appear that her assessment of her own situation as an agunah was based on her practical experience. Many families split up during the persecutions and massacres in Ukraine; among the refugees were men who did not know what had become of their wives. Krochmal and other rabbis replied on several occasions to appeals from men seeking to remarry after their wives had disappeared or had been taken captive. According to halakhah, a married woman who has been in captivity may not return to her husband, for fear she became impure (that she was violated) in captivity. In medieval Ashkenaz, however, a man could not remarry without divorcing his first wife who had been taken captive or had converted.[30] From the statement by Rabbi Moshe Isserles, who ruled that "in the time of the decrees [massacres]" such a wife may return to her husband, we learn that the halakhic approach was unchanged in his time.[31] Yet following the massacres of 1648–1649, some leading halakhic authorities permitted a man to remarry even if his wife had not returned and he had not divorced her in accordance with Jewish law.

In fact, Krochmal himself was involved in a case of a refugee from the Ukraine pogroms who settled in the community of Hoiesov (Hoiieschau). His wife "had been taken captive by Kedarites [= Tatars]"— no one knew what had befallen her. He received permission to remarry from two of the greatest halakhic authorities of that time: Rabbi David son of Samuel Halevi Segal (Poland, 1586–1667),[32] on a visit to Moravia, and Rabbi Gershon Ashkenazi (Poland, 1620–Metz, 1693), Krochmal's son-in-law. The permission to remarry gave rise to controversy among leading rabbis in the region; Krochmal opposed the decision and demanded that the husband divorce his captive wife before remarrying. In the same community where this took place, a beit din convened to hear Sarah's testimony on September 16, 1653.[33]

If the husband in question was a *cohen* (of priestly lineage), he found it easier to obtain permission to remarry since the strict halakhot regarding a cohen and whom he could marry meant that his first wife would not be permitted to go back to him in any case.[34] It appears that men who wished to remarry after the massacres were able to do so with relative ease, even without furnishing proof that their wives were no longer alive. They did not wait for formal permission, as they could cite weighty halakhic authorities in support of their request.

On her journey from Ukraine to Moravia, Sarah might have also encountered non-Jewish women whose situation was similar to her own. From them she could have learned that a different future was in store for them. Along with Jews fleeing the massacres were refugees of other ethnicities.[35] On their escape routes, they often found themselves passing through the principalities of Germany. In Christian canon law, a marriage could be dissolved if a person was absent from home for more than seven years and their whereabouts were unknown. The remaining spouse was then free to remarry on the assumption that the missing spouse was dead.[36] After the Reformation, Protestant law shortened the waiting period to five years in some places; sometimes even a single year sufficed.[37] Encountering such widowed non-Jewish refugees may have intensified Sarah's frustration, leading her to insist that Krochmal permit her to remarry.

Sarah's persistence paid off. "I was filled with compassion for her," reports the rabbi. "I decided forthwith to look into the matter of her status with respect to remarriage."[38] Krochmal exhibited some compassion *only after Sarah passed his test* by countering his initial refusal. Eventually, relying solely on the testimonies of Sarah and her sister, Krochmal granted her permission to remarry. But her troubles were not over. Krochmal insisted on obtaining affirmation of his decision by Rabbi Aharon Shimon Shapira (Prague, 1600–1680), rabbi of Prague (apparently Sarah's place of residence).[39]

The question of whether a sole decisor might free an agunah remained a matter of halakhic controversy throughout the ages. Insisting on a second decisor's approval, as in Sarah's case, presented yet another formidable obstacle for the agunah, since she was now forced to wait even longer until the decision came into effect.

The sources do not tell us if Sarah ever remarried.

AGUNOT IN THE POGROMS OF 1648–1649: IMAGE AND REALITY

Kiddush Hashem, or "sanctification of God's Name,"[40] refers to Jews choosing martyrdom or unbearable hardship rather than giving up their religion. Among the stories of heroism that were seared into Jewish consciousness by the pogroms in this period, the courage of agunot was not left out. One such story was preserved in a source that was written a hundred years after the fact.

Rabbi Yaakov Emden, author of responsa *Shaar Ephraim*, tells the story of one particular agunah, his own grandmother Nehama, daughter of Rabbi Ephraim Hacohen (Lithuania, 1616–Hungary, 1678). At a young age, Nehama married Emden's grandfather, Rabbi Yaakov Ashkenazi (father of the Hakham Tzvi). When pogroms devastated Ukraine, she went to stay with her parents. As her husband fled Ukraine, he came across a mob:

> When they encountered this pious man, the warden of captives ordered him to kneel down and extend his neck for the sword, which he did. He stretched out his neck to be slaughtered, to sanctify the Name of God by death. When he was on his knees, waiting for the death blow, already nearly dead of fright, an Angel of God touched him, for into the heart of the wicked one God put compassion for the boy of such tender age. Instead of striking his victim's neck with the sharp blade as he intended, the wicked one dealt a blow with the flat of the sword, saying scornfully, "Rise, away with you, you dog!" In this manner, by a miracle, he was spared death by the sword. Afterwards he hid among the dead during an entire day for fear of being discovered.[41]

Emden's grandfather survived, according to his grandson, by eating weeds and whatever else he could find. But witnesses to the event comprehended something quite different: "Then, as he was lying among those holy dead, some other Jews hiding there saw everything my grandfather did: How he fell to the ground as the wicked ones sought to kill him. They were sure his head had been cut off as he knelt for the slaughter. When they saw the sword on his neck, they were certain he could not live. He fell over from the blow administered with the flat of the sword. The blow turned out not to be fatal, but those watching from afar were frightened to death.[42] They thought his head had been cut off and fallen to the ground."[43]

These survivors reported what they thought they had seen: a soldier killing Jacob Ashkenazi. Reaching Moravia, they testified, "We saw with our own eyes how he knelt to receive the blow, and then his head was cut off." Relying on their testimony, continues Emden, the Gaon Rabbi Joshua Heschel of Kraków (1595–1663)[44] freed the man's wife, Nehama, from the state of iggun and permitted her to remarry.[45] This permission, based on the imagination of the witnesses, could have led to disastrous results: "But his wife, a most beautiful young woman, could not be consoled for the loss of the husband of her youth. The pious woman insisted on remaining pure, to produce a magnificent line of descendants... and, indeed, half a year later, the 'dead man' returned,[46] and it was a sign and a wonder for Israel."[47]

Emden's story has a happy ending: Yaakov and Nehama enjoyed a long marriage. They went to live in the land of Israel, where Nehama died when Emden's grandfather was over seventy years old.[48]

But the story of the man who returned from the dead, continues Emden, sobered the rabbi. From then on, no agunah in that generation of massacres and turmoil was granted his permission to remarry, even with two valid witnesses — for there were very many agunot in those terrible times. He had permitted a married woman to remarry! He could not risk such a mistake again. In this way the verse came to pass for Emden, "No harm befalls the righteous."[49]

If someone of Rabbi Heschel's stature had indeed adopted the stance that Emden ascribes to him, the matter would have been influential in the dialogue over freeing agunot in his time. Yet, I found no record of such influence in sources that were composed in either Heschel's or the subsequent generation. Nor did I find any corroboration of Emden's story in any other source.[50] As a result, we may feel free to speculate that Emden, who included this information in the context of his autobiographical composition, may have described events in the way that he did to glorify his own family background and lineage. Emden's father, the Hakham Tzvi, was born in 1658, only ten years after the events Emden describes. Emden himself was born in 1698, fifty years after the outbreak of the uprising. In fact, he never knew his grandfather and grandmother at all. Yet we should not disparage this family tradition, since, for Emden's readers, two points were exemplified by the story of the miracle that befell the grandfather who was willing to sanctify God's Name by death and the pious grandmother who chose to wait indefinitely for her missing husband. First, halakhic decision-making concerning an agunah is fraught with danger and pitfalls. The decisor is liable to make mistakes even in ostensibly straightforward cases. For Emden, this was not merely theoretical; rather, his autobiography describes a case in which he himself feared freeing an agunah who required halitzah. His fears proved justified when the "dead" husband returned one day. It is significant that Emden's published responsa do not include any cases of his freeing agunot.[51] Second, according to Emden, an agunah would do well to forgo remarriage altogether since there was always a chance that her husband was still alive. Emden's ambivalence about remarriage once the agunah received permission is clearly evident in his account. His grandmother Nehama, an agunah who refused to remarry even after she was granted permission, was, in Emden's view, an exemplary model of piety and virtue. Her act was comparable to the men's act of martyrdom, of sanctifying God's Name by death. His own sister Nehama, named after their grandmother, also became an agunah when her husband was killed in the forest. Following in their grandmother's footsteps, she refused to remarry—a decision much lauded by Emden.[52]

We may conjecture as to Emden's motive in constructing this family myth. In his *Megillat sefer*, Emden writes that he learned European languages and read about "deceitful, cunning strategies" employed by gentiles.[53] This might refer, inter alia, to the work by Jean-Baptiste de Rocoles on imposters throughout history (published in Amsterdam in 1683 and in Germany, in German translation, in 1761).[54] The work was subsequently reprinted in several editions. Two consecutive chapters in that work tell of Shabtai Tzvi, the "false Messiah," and of the imposter who pretended to be Martin Guerre. The imposter lived with Guerre's wife for many years until the real Martin Guerre reappeared. Emden, a fierce opponent of Sabbateanism, could have become acquainted with the story of Martin Guerre in this form. As a result, he was afraid of the disastrous consequences of permitting an agunah to remarry, especially if she could lie to her neighbors about the identity of the man she called her husband.

It is difficult to assess the reaction of Emden's readers to the myth he created. After all, he was one of the leading halakhic authorities of his generation and afterwards. His views had theoretical as well as practical implications.

We have no data relating to the number of agunot that turned to decisors following the massacres of 1648–1649 or to the percentage of those freed relative to those who were not. The cases of Sarah and Leah demonstrate that even when the agunah actually had information that could free her from her marriage—and even when permission was ultimately granted—the road to attaining it was strewn with obstacles, not least of which was the stringency of decisors. This is not to say that no agunah was ever granted permission to remarry during the persecutions of 1648–1649. We know of several agunot who were granted such permission in these persecutions and in other wartime situations.[55] But the cases we have looked at here, as well as others,[56] suggest that the decisors' claims that they did their utmost to end women's agunah status should be revisited.

5 : TWO TALES OF MURDER

Glikl describes matter-of-factly the danger in store for Jewish men as they went about their daily routine in the mid-seventeenth century, during her childhood: "Early in the morning, straight from the synagogue, these wretches would go into the city, and toward nightfall, as the gates were about to close, they would return to Altona; the poor things often risked their lives on leaving the city because of persecution by worthless thugs, until every woman, poor thing, gave thanks to God when her husband returned home safely."[1]

Glikl was born in Hamburg in 1645. In April 1648, after the expulsion of the Jews from Hamburg, the family moved to Altona, returning to Hamburg about a decade later.[2] Like many Jewish communities at the time, the Altona community numbered only a few hundred families.[3] Altona was no more than a quarter of an hour's walk from Hamburg, but Jewish men who traversed this route regularly to earn a living in the city were in constant mortal danger. For this reason, every married woman was permanently at risk of becoming an agunah. (Altona and Hamburg, despite their physical proximity, were also in different legal jurisdictions in this period, a fact whose relevance we will examine later.) In the late 1680s, two murders took place in Hamburg, and they were documented in two autobiographical accounts: Glikl's memoirs and the account by Shmuel Heckscher.[4] This rare case of two accounts of the same events affords a double perspective — a woman's and a man's. As they offer a rare glimpse into the fate of agunot in late seventeenth-century Germany, we will look at them at some length.[5]

Heckscher penned his impressions of events he witnessed as notes he wrote in a volume entitled *Tzemah David*, which he had in his possession. His notes were published in David Kaufmann's edition of Glikl's memoirs.[6] Heckscher seems to have recorded his impressions no more than a few years after the events, while Glikl's reminiscences were written many years later. For this reason, some scholars consider the former more reliable.[7] I tend to differ, based on the analysis presented in the following section.

TWO NARRATORS, TWO NARRATIVES

On October 14, 1683,[8] Avraham Zimla Metz, a Jew who had come to live in Altona several years before, disappeared. According to Glikl, the once-wealthy man lost most of his money when he came to live in Altona after remarrying following the death of his first wife. A moneychanger, his occupation necessitated much dashing about and spending long hours in taverns owned by non-Jews.[9] When he failed to come home one evening, Sarah, his wife, went around to his friends looking for him. The man could not be found, and his fate remained unknown for a long time. Sarah was left an agunah.[10] Over four years later, a second man disappeared. This time it was a young man by the name of Aaron,[11] married and a father of four, another moneychanger. This man's wife (her name is not mentioned) was equally unsuccessful in tracing his whereabouts. News of his disappearance spread. A few days later, following a concerted investigation by members of the community, it was discovered that he had been murdered. The killer was apprehended. He confessed, and Aaron's body was found. The killer was suspected of being implicated also in the disappearance of Avraham Metz. Under interrogation, the man confessed to that murder as well. The body of Metz was found, and Sarah was released from being an agunah. The murderer was executed.

While this sequence of events appears in each of the two accounts, the stories differ as to the roles ascribed to the participants and in the details each source chose to emphasize. Together they illuminate varied aspects of Jewish society, particularly its attitudes toward the agunah.

Both accounts, taking the traditional view, ascribe to divine providence the role of engineering events and averting disaster for the Jews. Heckscher wrote down his notes on the blank pages of a book a few years after the events. We do not know why he chose that particular time or that particular book. By his own account, he had nearly fallen victim to the same murderer; his primary motive in writing was to offer thanks to God for his deliverance.[12] By contrast, in Glikl's rendition, gratitude to God is mentioned only at the end, not as a focus, and it does not constitute her primary motivation for writing.

Another marked difference is the role of the narrator and, consequently, the sequence of events. Heckscher, as participant-narrator, is a key player in the affairs he describes. His firsthand report includes what he himself said and did. Glikl is a passive observer, not at the center of events. Glikl begins with the disappearance of the first murdered man and his wife's plight. Heckscher mentions him only at the very end, since he chose to tell the sequence of events only from the point at which he became personally involved; for him the discovery of the body of Avraham Metz concluded the affair.

In Glikl's memoirs, the murders come right after the story of how she and her sons were nearly swindled. Her motivation for placing the murders at that particular point appears to be associative rather than chronological: The men who disappeared had fallen prey to a swindler, who turned out to be a murderer, too. Glikl and her sons were similarly nearly swindled by a man who sent her a forged letter ostensibly from her youngest son, Yosef.[13]

Glikl frequently ponders the character of this or that individual, questioning human ability to ascertain the true nature and identity of another. Chava Turniansky has observed that Glikl rarely describes physical appearance, being interested rather in inner qualities, in what a person says and does, not in outward mien.[14] The elusiveness of a person's real character crops up several times in the memoir. Never certain of the other's real motive, we are ever vulnerable to deceit and ruin.[15] Her own experience of being deceived by appearances is related in the wrenching story of her second marriage. At age fifty-four, her son-in-law suggested she marry the widower Hertz Levi. This is how Glikl describes the circumstances leading up to her unfortunate second marriage: "Just then I received a letter from my son-in-law, Moshe of Metz, may he live long... in which he mentions that Reb Hertz Levy was now a widower, and what a respected, learned, wealthy man he was, and what a household he maintained. In short, he praised the man highly, as indeed he was, to all appearances. *Man sees only what is visible, the Lord sees into the heart.*"[16]

Anxiety over possible discrepancy between a person's outward appearance and actual intent is not unique to Glikl. Such a concern would seem to be universal, even trivial. However, in this period, there was real danger of one's encountering an individual living under an assumed identity. Maria Boes has claimed that sumptuary laws were enforced by the authorities in the seventeenth century in an attempt to curtail crime and the use of a false identity.[17] In their study on women passing themselves off as men in seventeenth- and eighteenth-century Europe, Rudolf M. Dekker and Lotte C. van de Pol have shown how common it was to assume a false identity. The phenomenon was widespread in Hamburg, as in other port cities.[18] Society, both Jewish and non-Jewish, regulated itself by emphasizing the significance of social class, gender, and ethnicity through apparel, division of public and private spaces, and access to positions of power and influence.[19] Women, particularly women of low socioeconomic status, impersonated men in order to overcome gender restrictions.[20] Many women found a disguise useful at some point; disguised as a soldier or sailor, a woman could take advantage of the army or navy to travel or to change her identity. Scholars note that the roots of this practice lay in earlier times, and it became widespread both in reality and in the collective consciousness from the late sixteenth century on.

Let us return to Glikl. In Hamburg, a bustling seaport thronged with travelers passing through from many countries, it was not easy to confirm an individual's true identity. The fact that Glikl associated her anecdote about agunot with a forged letter provides a clue to understanding contemporary concern with penetrating outward appearances. The question of whether truth and reality could be discovered by observation rather than solely by predetermined religious belief characterizes this period of the profound, all-pervasive influence of the Scientific Revolution.[21] As we have seen, some problems of agunah status relate to establishing an individual's identity and ascertaining the circumstances of his life and death. Iggun is related to the fact that a man might disappear and change identities or that a woman might give false testimony about her husband or about her own legal status. Attitudes towards agunot were shaped by constant monitoring of the threat to the social order embodied by the elusiveness of personal identity.

When the disappearance of Avraham Metz became known, the community was thrown into turmoil: "The woman became anguished. Some say he ran away from her after she quarreled with him. This went on for three years, I believe, while people said whatever they liked, many speaking ill of this martyr, may God avenge his death, things I will not repeat in writing. But our human weakness is such that we often speak of things we have not actually seen, alas."[22]

Glikl employs the present tense to report the gossip about the agunah, attributing it to human weakness ("some say," "we often speak"), suggesting a characteristic response in cases where a community is faced with a person's disappearance, not an exceptional response that happened in this particular case. In other words, Glikl's narrative documents the fact that a person's disappearance would naturally give rise to a slew of speculation and rumor. Given the danger Jews faced every day — the Jews had to return to Altona at nightfall when the city gates were shut for the night; they were unsure that they would return alive[23] — it might be assumed that murder would jump to their minds. However, this is not how Glikl describes it. She reports two other theories: Avraham Metz's wife's behavior was the cause of her husband's disappearance, or else his own blameworthy conduct was. The possibility of murder is not even raised among the speculations circulated after his disappearance, though this turned out to be what happened in this case. Iggun was such a threatening concept because it exposed fundamental human vulnerability: a man could be murdered, and his wife could become an agunah. Pointing the accusing finger at the agunah or her husband created the illusion that only one guilty of bad behavior risked this terrible fate. A quarrelsome wife risks ending up with a missing husband, as in the Yiddish saying *Heynt a shlumper, morgn an agunah* ("Today a slattern, tomorrow — an agunah").[24] In this view, a man's disappearance could be explained by his bad behavior. Good behavior, accordingly, should provide protection. We see how important speculation and rumor were in preserving social order, inculcating awareness of the need for couples to conduct themselves properly.

Speculation also had a bearing on the social status of involved parties and how they were perceived. When a husband disappeared, leaving his wife behind as an agunah, it was she (and her children) who paid the price in loss of social status and future prospects. This fact underscores the importance of gender on social life, especially that of agunot.

Jews as well as non-Jews in Altona and Hamburg were involved in exposing the identity of the murderer. While Heckscher focuses on his own story, Glikl tells at length of the women involved. We learn what an agunah's life was actually like: "In this manner, Sarah was left stranded, a grass widow, poor thing, for more than three years, with her poor fatherless children, forced to let people gossip about her husband, may God avenge his death, and pass judgment on him as they pleased."[25]

Writing several years after the events, Glikl's sympathies clearly lie with the agunah, a relative of hers.[26] We know that the communities of Hamburg and Altona were both small in the period under discussion, and therefore, it is safe to assume that their residents knew each other.[27] How, then, are we to understand Heckscher's silence regarding the agunot? A mere question of interest? Or is this gender-related: Were these two authors exposed to different social phenomena given their respective genders? Did the gossip and rumors fail to reach Heckscher's ears?

Sociological studies attribute to gossip both universal and context-specific functions.[28] Some scholars have claimed that in the early modern age, women employed gossip to cope with their inferiority in personal and public life.[29] In fact, the German term *Weibergeschwätz* — "women's gossip"— attributes a certain kind of discourse to women. However, in what follows, I wish to discuss the pivotal role of gossip and rumor for men and women alike in community life. In this period, gossip was a means of social regulation by the authorities. In some places in Germany, directives encouraged people to report the unusual behavior of their neighbors, and a rumor was often enough to involve the authorities and get a person convicted of a crime.[30] Any slur on one's reputation could very well be disastrous in Jewish society as well.[31] Contemporary responsa and beit din records document litigation by men and women who sought to clear their names after ill-wishers spread slander or made scurrilous attacks on them in public. Rabbi Moshe Shimshon Bacharach (d. 1670), head of the rabbinic court of Worms, decreed excommunication for anyone spreading gossip about a certain couple in the community of Neckarsulm. They had fallen victim to what he considered slander about their alleged laxity in observance of *niddah* (ritual purity) laws.[32] In the 1670s, Raphael son of Kalman of Altona was fined by lay leaders of the community. The reason: Nehemiah son of Ephraim lodged a complaint claiming that said Raphael had accused him in public of stealing.[33] In 1756, an announcement was made on the Sabbath in the synagogues of Fürth: a fine would be imposed on anyone slandering a certain cantor of the community by linking him with a certain "decent" woman.[34]

In such cases, gossipmongers were questioned and the parties investigated to establish whether there was any truth in the rumors. If the rumors proved false, sanctions were imposed against the scandalmongers. The influence of gossip was certainly strong enough to alter one's status in the community, and an agunah could be particularly vulnerable.

Glikl recounts how Sarah was forced to endure gossip without any means of defending herself and her missing husband's good name.[35] She and her fatherless children had to lead a lonely existence, helpless in the face of malicious gossip and censorious neighbors.

There is no reason to suppose that Heckscher was unaware of the rumors surrounding the disappearance of Avraham Metz. At the same time, Glikl, herself a widow, might have been more keenly aware of the harm such gossip could wreak on the agunah's life. Even if she obtained permission to remarry, the scandal reduced her chances of finding a good match. Anyone contemplating marriage with a widow or widower took into account conduct in the first marriage. Rumors that a woman's husband deserted her because she was quarrelsome meant she could not expect a good match.

Gossip was also often the means for tracing the whereabouts of a missing husband. Consequently, gossip helped free agunot from their marriage. Glikl describes the day after the disappearance of Aaron, the second man:

> In the morning the news spread everywhere. One said he had been seen here, another said something else. At noon people met at the Bourse and talked about it, whereupon Reb Zanvl son of Reb Meir Heckscher said: "A certain maidservant came to my house yesterday—she had some gold—wanting to know if I had six or seven hundred reichstaler, and if so I should go with her because there was a foreigner at her house with many objects of gold and precious stones to sell. Since I had no money, I didn't go with her." Now, there was another man there by the name of Lipman,[36] who asked what the maidservant looked like and what she had been wearing. Said Reb Zanvl: "She was dressed in such-and-such fashion." Said this Lipman: "I know that maidservant and I also know who she works for. I don't particularly trust the gentleman she works for." Talking in this manner they left the Bourse and went home.[37]

In Heckscher's account, he himself went to the Bourse to urge people to conduct inquiries everywhere they could to uncover whatever deception was afoot in the hope that their efforts would lead them to some clue.[38] The Bourse, in addition to being a place for commerce, served as a social meeting place where conversation could help establish the truth. It would seem that the line between mere rumor and actual investigation was not always clear.[39] It emerges from Heckscher's account that this very conversation revealed the link between the maid's employer and Aaron's disappearance. This in turn led to the hunch that the same man was implicated in the disappearance of Avraham Metz—which turned out to be true.

The two accounts—by Heckscher and by Glikl—shed light on an agunah's dependence on the sociolegal status of the Jews in the community to which she belonged. As noted, the authorities in some places in Germany elicited information from the public and used it to maintain social order. In an effort to curb crime, the authorities encouraged people to report on others. And yet both Heckscher and Glikl tell of hostility shown by the non-Jewish authorities to the Jews who were requesting an investigation. Reporting suspicion of murder to the authorities was extremely dangerous, according to Glikl. The official in charge of Jewish affairs in Altona even warned the Jews: if their suspicions proved false, all their property would be seized.[40] The authorities were not always keen to investigate crimes against Jews; perhaps this is why the circumstances surrounding the disappearance of Avraham Metz remained unknown for so long. These matters reveal an additional obstacle facing agunot who had to provide evidence that would enable them to remarry in accordance with Jewish law: The interest of the agunah could be perceived as endangering the entire community.

WOMEN'S SOCIAL NETWORKS

In both accounts, it was a woman, a member of the community, who solved the mystery and discovered the murderer's identity. This, in turn, enabled the release of the agunah from the marriage. In both accounts, Heckscher and Lipman formed suspicions as to the identity of the killer after their conversation in the Bourse. But without any proof there could be no hope for the agunah, as Glikl observes: "The matter had nearly been forgotten, as is the way of the world: Even a weightier matter of much greater importance, if nothing further is done about it — is doomed to oblivion. The grass widow and her orphans however still grieved."[41]

The men formed a well-founded suspicion, but in fact it was Rivkah, Lipman's wife, who insisted on taking steps to discover the murderer's identity.[42] The "world" described by Glikl was presumably a masculine one, indifferent to the plight of the agunah and well aware of the risk of incurring the wrath of the non-Jewish authorities. Women were keenly aware of the agunah's living in limbo. The murderer's identity was ultimately discovered through the maidservant's confession. Heckscher reports that he and Lipman had already surmised that the maid knew of her master's implication in the murders. They went to the suspect's house; not finding him at home, they tried to elicit information from the maid but did not succeed.[43]

A few days after they first began to suspect the killer, the Jews succeeded in getting the authorities to declare Aaron missing. A reward was offered to anyone providing information leading to him. When the murderer tried to flee the city, Rivkah summoned the police, and the man was arrested and searched.[44] Nothing incriminating was found, and he denied any connection to the killings, even under interrogation by every possible method.[45] The Jews despaired of ever arriving at the truth. At this point, Rivkah put her acquaintance with the maid to good use:

> As soon as she reached the field separating Hamburg from Altona, she encountered the maidservant who worked for the murderer. Rivkah knew her well—she was the same one who had approached Jews wanting them to accompany her to the murderer's house if they had six or seven reichstaler. So Rivkah says to the maidservant: "It's lucky for you and for your master and his wife that you ran into me. Your master and his wife have both been arrested in Altona because of the murder they committed, and they have confessed everything. It remains only for you to confess too. Once that's done, the boat is waiting to take you and your master and his wife away from here, because all we Jews want is to know for sure that Avraham is dead so that his wife can remarry. We don't want anything else of you," as she went on and on telling the maidservant.[46]

The ruse was successful; the maidservant confessed. She had been her master's accomplice in planning and carrying out the murder. Rivkah persuaded the maid to accompany her to the home of the investigating official. There the maid repeated her confession, this time specifying where the body was buried.

Rivkah, an exceptionally intelligent woman, in Glikl's opinion, was successful thanks to personal acquaintance with the gentile maid. Jews and gentiles would meet in private and public spaces and conducted varied reciprocal relations.[47] Men tended to meet in public places for business, while women met for traditionally "female" pursuits. Rudolph Dekker termed these informal women's networks "mum-culture." In certain respects, these networks proved stronger than those formed by men.

When faced with external threat, he suggests, women's social ties were faster in mobilizing the community to action.[48] Although his remarks pertain to non-Jewish society in Holland, he stresses that such activity is well-known in other countries as well. This accords with the findings of Claudia Ulbrich on non-Jewish women in eighteenth-century Alsace who worked as domestics for Jews on the Sabbath. These maids became familiar with Jewish customs, which made them agents for disseminating information in social networks across the religious divide.[49] In Glikl's memoirs, the maid says she confessed because she trusted Rivkah and did not consider her a threat.[50] Thanks to their intimate acquaintance, the maid saw in Rivkah a confidante.

In Glikl's description, Rivkah presented herself to the maid as acting on behalf of the dead man's wife. The maid was moved by this to confess. It seems that the maid regarded herself and Rivkah as sisters-in-arms, at least insofar as the fate of a third woman was concerned. In some cases, then, female solidarity prevailed over ethnic or religious divides. Jewish and gentile women sometimes regarded themselves as sharing a common fate, needing to protect themselves from the same dangers as they helped each other in "women's affairs." For agunot, these connections could be invaluable, opening up channels of communication that were inaccessible to men. Gender roles and female solidarity thus played a crucial role in determining the fate of agunot.

SHE'S ABOUT TO MAKE HERSELF COMPLETELY CRAZY

The enterprising Rivkah was one of many women who acted in uniquely female modes under the strict gender-role division of the time.[51] Rivkah's husband, Lipman, in response to his wife's insistence — "We will have no rest or peace until we find out!" — called her "crazy," for "even if it's true, what can we do? This is Hamburg; we must not breathe a word of it."[52] Keeping silent was the only reasonable reaction in his view. Glikl herself, as narrator, associates being "crazy" with Rivkah's behavior: she frantically rushes to and fro, cannot keep still: "The poor woman could not sleep at all, and she was driving everyone in the house crazy."[53] She could not sleep at night in her obsession to find the murderer, so much so that her husband feared that "she'd end up making herself completely crazy."[54]

Nathalie Zemon Davis demonstrated several decades ago that women were associated with madness and believed to possess an inherent rebellious streak. They thus were perceived as a threat to rational social order. These views were prevalent in Europe for centuries, supported by supposedly scientific theories which drew on the ancient belief in humors and of the womb as a site of madness.[55] These ideas took hold in Jewish society as well, for instance, in the writings of the Jewish physician Tobias Cohen of Metz (1652–1729). Cohen, one of the first Jews to study medicine at the University of Frankfurt-an-der-Oder, believed the female reproductive system was a source of madness and imbalance.[56] Zemon Davis and others have shown how these notions operated on several social and ideational levels. On the one hand, it deepened women's obedience, since women did not want to be labelled as mad. On the other hand, such notions opened up modes of action for Jewish women that were closed to them in the hegemonic social order.[57] Some scholars pointed to another implication: These ideas rendered women not always responsible for their actions. In this way, they escaped punishment, whereas a man in a similar situation would have been severely punished. Dekker has claimed that men urged women to perform acts of rebellion in situations in which, had men acted that way, they would have been seriously endangered. The assumption was that the authorities would show more leniency to women.[58] Lipman's labelling of his wife as "crazy" can now be seen not as mere scorn but also as a realization that under the guise of madness, she could accomplish what men could not.

The maid, after confessing to the murder, specified where the body was buried. As the killer continued to deny everything, the official warned the Jews: "The President said: 'I cannot help you anymore. If I have the murderer tortured based on his maidservant's testimony — and he bears up under torture and refuses to confess — where will this game lead? You must handle it yourselves, stand on your rights in Hamburg. Get permission from the authorities immediately, without delay, to search for the dead man in the murderer's house. Once you find the corpse in accordance with the maidservant's confession, let me handle it from there.'"[59]

Hamburg and Altona were under different legal jurisdictions at the time. Hamburg was an independent seaport city administered by a council, while Altona was administered by an official ("president") of the Danish crown.[60] The Jews had to maneuver between these powers.[61] Investigations of a death by unusual circumstances generally would be handled by local authorities.⁶² The fact that Altona's president told the Jews to investigate on their own makes it clear that the authorities did not always cooperate with requests by the Jewish community for official investigations. In this case, the Jews of Altona did appeal to the Hamburg authorities. Gendarmes were authorized to assist the Jews in searching for the murderer. Glikl says:

> They summoned all the councilmen and showed them the corpse where it had been found—according to the maidservant's statement. The council wrote it down in a protocol and issued an affidavit. The corpse was then put in a cart and taken to Altona. There was a huge crowd of sailors and craftsmen, indescribable, maybe one hundred thousand people, yet no one uttered a single derogatory word. True enough, this was an evil crowd; even when things are peaceful they stir up trouble and hatred of Jews, yet this time they all dispersed quietly. The next day, the distinguished leaders of the community took the affidavit and brought it to the President in Altona, who held both the murderer and justice in his hands. Moreover, at that time, the Jews preferred that the case be tried in Altona. Once again, the President presented his arguments to the murderer, confronted him, and revealed what had happened, and he confessed to everything. The widow also got back some of her husband's money that was found, may God avenge his death. The murderer was remanded into custody pending trial.⁶³

From Glikl's account, it emerges that the Jews needed a permit from local officials to bury the dead man. Once it was granted, they could take the body to the Jewish cemetery in Altona. In the two cases reported by Glikl, the Jews were the first to find the dead men. When the corpse had been identified in accordance with Jewish law, the two women were duly freed from agunah status and permitted to remarry: "Sarah, his wife, gave some identifying marks on his body from which it could be established that she need not remain a grass widow; this was duly established, and she was permitted to remarry."⁶⁴

Rivkah's initiative and cunning strategy of nearly going mad proved successful: the two Altona murders were solved, the bodies found, and the agunot released.

6 : IDENTIFYING THE DEAD IN THE INTEREST OF FREEING THE AGUNAH AND TAKING REVENGE

Jews were keenly aware of how important it was to identify a corpse in accordance with halakhah in order to free the dead man's wife from her status as an agunah.[1] The Jewish burial society (*hevra kadisha*) was in charge of identifying the dead in accordance with halakhic requirements and also of all burial arrangements. The burial society record book of Schwersenz (Swarzędz) reports a drowning in 1678:

> His cheeks were bearded with mud so that his face could not be seen for the dirt. He drowned in the early morning of Friday, 9 Nissan, and was not found until Tuesday, 11 Iyyar [about a month later]. He was taken straight to the cemetery, to the place where the dead are purified for burial, still wearing all his clothes, and the small leather skullcap on his head. Learned men of the yeshiva supervised and examined in order to decide what should be done. We examined the body to make sure there were no traces of blood on the clothes. No blood was found on his clothes. Then they stripped off his shirt. Face and body were found to be greatly bloated. As is the custom, we washed him with strips of linen sheets dipped in cold water, lest God forbid we remove the skin. We continued until gradually his face was cleansed of mud and dirt. Then some sharp-eyed people recognized him. Next, we purified him as we do for all the dead, with wine and the whites of eggs.[2]

From this entry we learn that the corpse of a Jew could be properly identified if it was found in a place that had people who were knowledgeable about halakhic requirements. When non-Jews discovered the body, things became more difficult for the agunah. In 1765, Rabbi Yehezkel Landau ruled in the case of an agunah that anyone discovering a body must report it immediately to the non-Jewish authorities.[3]

If a corpse was discovered by a non-Jew, or if its discovery became known by means of the testimony of a non-Jew, it was more difficult to release the dead man's wife from the marriage. This is because testimony given by a non-Jew about finding a body was admissible only under the category of "speaking innocently" (*mesiah lefi tumo*). The ramifications can be seen in the following question addressed by Rabbi Israel Segal, head of the rabbinic court in Brod, to Rabbi David Oppenheim, rabbi of Prague.[4] A murder took place in 1690 in a village near Freistadt. It happened when Shlomo, a resident of the town, was taking a solitary walk to the home of a non-Jew at the latter's invitation. The non-Jew said he had gold to sell and warned Shlomo not to tell anyone where he was going. Shlomo told no one except his wife. When Shlomo failed to come home, his wife, accompanied by her brother-in-law, set out to the home of the non-Jew to look for her husband. The man would reveal nothing. The Jews appealed to the local nobleman, requesting that he question the murderer so that they could bury the body, and "for revenge," and "to [later] marry off his wife."[5] They promised the nobleman money in return for conducting an investigation. The murderer was questioned, he confessed, and showed them where the body was buried. Accompanied by local authorities, the Jews went to the indicated spot, where they found the body of the murdered man. He was clothed as he had been before his death, but the face was unrecognizable due to the condition of the corpse.

The questioner emphasized that he wished to free the agunah, since he knew for certain that the missing man had been murdered and buried.[6] Seeking Oppenheim's affirmation of his position, the questioner wrote that there was really no need for all this, since he knew for certain that the man was killed and buried. However, as per protocol, he also outlined the halakhic difficulties the case entailed. Did the murderer's confession fit into the category of "speaking innocently"? The killer did not specify the name of the dead man's father or of the town where he lived, as required by halakhah—did this invalidate his testimony?

At first, Oppenheim refused to free the agunah from her marriage. He reprimanded the rabbi for not adequately questioning the wife, which might have facilitated identification without recourse to the murderer's testimony, as identifying physical marks could have sufficed. He determined that this was not a case of "speaking innocently," since the confession was part of an investigation conducted by a non-Jew for remuneration. The rabbi was instructed to question the agunah again. Only after further correspondence did Oppenheim agree to free the wife from her status of iggun,[7] based on information that had not been obtained by non-Jews in their investigations.

The halakhic catch is nicely illustrated in these historical circumstances.[8] Non-Jewish authorities were necessarily involved in murder investigations, including identification of the body; this meant that evidence obtained from them could not be used, since it did not fall into the halakhic category of "speaking innocently." This explains why members of the Jewish community considered it their duty to become involved in identifying and burying a Jew whose body had been found by non-Jews. This happened in 1768, when a rumor reached Altona that a Jew had been killed. The shamash documented the event:

> Today, on Wednesday, 15 Shevat,[9] rumor reached us that a man had been killed on the road from Boizenburg.[10] It was Avraham son of R. Yaakov Hazan of Mannheim. Our community leader, R. Yehiel, sent word of the bad tidings to R. Hirsch,[11] since R. Avraham had been killed near Boizenberg. Indeed, it is the duty of our community to conduct a thorough investigation. That is, first to question the boy Lazer, who is staying with Reuven Berlin, and ask if all this is true, since he said he saw it happen. Reuven Berlin will tell us if Lazer is trustworthy. If so, it is the duty of our community to send someone from here to Boizenberg to see what is to be done; since it is a case of *eglah arufah*,[12] then it is our own responsibility. *The business leaves us with a possible agunah, besides other problems.* For this reason, one of us must be sent there to investigate because the body might be left [unburied] in Boizenburg until a report arrives from Mecklenburg.[13] In any case, one of us must go there at the community's expense.[14]

Records show that Jewish communities defrayed expenses for investigation and burial in cases of missing men. This happened in 1735, when Yosef son of Naphtali Hertz of Offenbach died on his way to Köln (Cologne). A Jew from nearby Deutz bribed a local official to obtain permission to give the dead man a Jewish burial.[15] Generally, however, it was the family of the murdered man that bore burial expenses. Records of the communities of AHW, for instance, show that the community would defray these costs only rarely, on account of financial difficulties — for instance, if several children in the same family died one right after the other. Agunot often had to bear burial expenses themselves,[16] which must have added to the financial strain of coping with the husband's absence.[17] Bureaucracy could make it difficult to bury the dead in accordance with halakhic requirements. In the previous case, for instance, the Jews realized burial would be delayed until documents could be obtained from Mecklenburg. Such delay contravened the halakhic prohibition against postponing burial. Furthermore, delay made it more difficult to identify the body within the prescribed halakhic timeframe.

PRICE OF REVENGE

In the previous case, the community's motive as they were galvanized into action was to hasten the release of the agunah from her marriage. The "other problems" in the description might allude to the desire for revenge. Some contemporary sources show that revenge for the murder of a Jew motivated communities to investigate and identify the victim in at least several cases.

Glikl recounts how her husband's brother was killed when he and two companions were accosted by robbers. "Although they [the community] made every effort on every level to seek revenge, it was all to no avail; there was no revenge."[18] Glikl ascribes the motive of revenge also to Rivkah's investigation of the murder of Aharon the moneychanger in Altona: "She would not calm down until vengeance was served."[19] The nature of the desire for revenge comes to the fore in the following entry in the record book of the Council of the Four Lands: "Even on those occasions when we knew we would not be able to exact revenge on the murderers, we assigned avengers nevertheless, to track them down and bring them to justice, to make known far and wide that Jewish blood is not worthless [*hefker*]."[20] In an attempt to prevent further killing of Jews, then, Jewish communities made concerted efforts to bring killers of Jews to justice and ensure they received due punishment. By doing so, they hoped to instill the belief that justice had been done and order restored. However, it was not always clear whose duty it was to actually take revenge. Rabbi Menahem Mendel Krochmal was asked the following questions about a murder: "Regarding one who was killed while travelling, and the identity of the murderer is known: We can take revenge if one of the victim's relatives demands that the killer be brought to justice.

May we compel the relative to pursue the killer and bring him to justice? Can we compel him to bear the expenses for such operations, if he is well-to-do? How much money can we compel him to spend? Who is considered a 'relative' for this purpose?"[21]

Murder inquiries necessitated negotiations with non-Jewish authorities, at no small expense; community leaders did not always consider it their duty to bear this expense. From this question, it emerges that an appeal by the victim's family to the authorities could lead to an official investigation, yet it seems the family was reluctant to lodge a formal complaint. Krochmal was asked to determine the degree of family relationship to the dead man that would obligate relatives to pursue the killer. In other words, the community wanted the family to bear the cost of revenge. Krochmal ruled that community leaders had the right to compel relatives of the murdered man to demand vengeance. He limited the cost the family was required to bear to standard expenses; they were not liable for additional costs, such as bribing officials.

Salmon-Mack has shown that in Poland-Lithuania, the financial situation of the victim's family was a factor in determining who would defray the expenses of bringing a murderer to justice. In fact, pressure was often exerted on the wife to fund the investigation as an obligation to her dead husband.[22] Charging the widow with the responsibility for funding a murder investigation and related expenses certainly added to her financial burden.

The question posed to Rabbi David Oppenheim regarding the woman whose husband, Shlomo, was murdered and his body found with the help of non-Jewish authorities serves as a model for examining the treatment of agunot. The questioner was already in possession of the facts he needed for positive identification of the body as the missing man. Despite this, he appealed to a higher halakhic authority, seeking affirmation before giving the agunah permission to remarry. Oppenheim at first refused the request and even reprimanded the questioner. Oppenheim acted similarly in the case of the agunah Leah (see chapter 4, "Sarah and Leah: War Agunot"), whose husband was killed by the Austrians during the conquest of Budapest in 1686. There, too, he initially refused but subsequently obtained sufficient proof to satisfy halakhic requirements. Ultimately, he did free the widows from their agunah status.

A recurring pattern emerges: A decisor is asked to free a woman from agunah status. A local rabbi would not give the agunah permission to remarry on his own authority; instead, he would recommend approval of the woman's request, then send the testimonies he had collected to a senior decisor for confirmation. Usually, the latter initially rejected the application. I will return to analyze this pattern further after discussion of a few other matters.

7 : "NOTHING OF HIM WAS EVER FOUND SAVE A SHOE AND BELT"
Freeing an Agunah When the Corpse Is Missing

The homes of the wealthy differed vastly from those of the poor in the German cultural expanse, with palaces on one hand and veritable sties on the other. Until the nineteenth century, most houses in Poland were made of wood;[1] fires culminating in loss of life were a regular occurrence, and often nothing at all remained of the victims.[2] Similarly, death by drowning meant that there was often no body to be recovered or that a body resurfaced unrecognizable. Drowning was a common cause of death, whether in the course of routine activity in proximity to rivers or other bodies of water or while travelling.[3] A good-luck charm (*segulah*) for finding a drowned person, as described by Yosef Hahn Neurlingen (1570–1637), dating apparently to the early seventeenth century, expresses the helplessness felt in these situations:[4] "a good-luck charm for finding a person who drowned and cannot be found: If you toss a wooden bowl upon the waters and let it float, the spot where it settles is where the drowned one is. I heard that a man called Meir was found in the river in this fashion.... If this is true, it is a *segulah* and a wonderful thing for freeing the wife of the drowned man, so that she need not remain an agunah."[5]

As discussed earlier in this part, people often died away from home while travelling or visiting another community for business or study. They were considered missing persons by their family and the community; without a body to identify, the wife of the missing man was an agunah. She could receive permission to remarry only on the strength of circumstantial evidence or witnesses to the man's death. If a Jew witnessed a fellow Jew's death, he was highly aware of the importance of giving testimony for the purpose of freeing agunot. Jews knew how necessary it was to document precisely all the circumstances of death. When a Jew died away from home, the local Jewish organizations were usually meticulous about taking testimony from any witnesses as required by halakhah. Circumstances of death were also documented in community record books. The shamash of Altona describes the drowning of a visitor to the community, Tevely of Koblenz, on February 8, 1779. The shamash explains how the man was identified and records the sums paid to the authorities in exchange for permission to handle burial arrangements. Three days later, he recorded the death of another visitor, Nathan of Göddern.[6] On April 24, 1800, the beit din of Heidingsfeld heard evidence of two young men from Galicia. They wished to document the circumstances of the death of their friend Israel son of Peretz, from a small town in Poland, who had died a year earlier in a military hospital near Wurzburg.[7] An entry in the record book of the community of Austerlitz (1814, during the Napoleonic Wars) states explicitly that details of the deaths of two Galician Jews were taken down in the local hospital in order to prevent their wives from becoming agunot.[8]

The importance of such documentation for agunot can also be ascertained from the following letter, sent by Rabbi Elazar Fleckeles (Prague, 1754–1826) and Rabbi Shmuel Landau (Prague, d. 1834) to the rabbi of Forchheim in Bavaria, on May 11, 1808:

> A woman of our community, one Fromit daughter of the late Reb Hirsch, wife of Michael Leib, wept before us, saying that according to a letter she possesses, sent by a man called Yudah Katz of Brandeis to his brother, a certain visitor, Michl Bodeshein by name, died and was buried there on 13 Shevat 5469 [February 11, 1808]. We do not know if the man is this woman's husband. It could be that his name in German was Michl Bodeshein. Begging a thousand pardons, since this concerns an agunah, would you kindly notify us if it is true that this Michl Bodeshein died in your community on said date? What name was he generally known by? By what name— his and his father's—was he called up to the Torah? Before dying, did he mention a wife here in Prague? If so, did he give her name? Did he mention his daughter? etc., etc. Any identifying marks, any books or travel documents he may have had with him, anything that could assist in freeing the agunah—please apprise us of any evidence heard by the beit din as required. Signed respectfully, [illegible], rabbis of Prague.[9]

Such a request was not unusual. On June 25, 1789, the beit din of Prague granted permission to a woman called Perdil to remarry, based on a letter

—received nine years earlier—reporting the death of her husband.[10] The same beit din freed Esther daughter of Meir Austerlitz from her marriage on the basis of a letter from a rabbi in Poland which reported the death of her husband there.[11]

WITNESSES AND TESTIMONY

The stories of two agunot, Edele of Nikolsburg and Hinde of Ostrog, are reported several times in eighteenth-century responsa literature, by the rabbis who handled their cases.[12] From the case descriptions in the writings of the decisors, we can elicit much information about the fate of these two women and of other agunot who found themselves in similar circumstances.

Rabbi David Oppenheim signed his ruling permitting the agunah Edele to remarry on July 16, 1692. The rabbi based his opinion on three detailed testimonies by two witnesses recorded over about one year (1691–1692).[13] The responsum concerning Hinde contains testimonies by seven different individuals as heard by the beit din in 1782, over five years after she became an agunah. Rabbi Meir Margaliot (rabbi of Ostrog, 1777–1790) refused at first to free Hinde from her agunah status. Following his refusal, missives were sent off to decisors in Poland and elsewhere. Over the course of the correspondence, Margaliot revisited his position and subsequently penned a lengthy responsum freeing the agunah. Let us examine the identities of the numerous witnesses and the content of their testimonies in order to appreciate the halakhic requirements and their practical implications for the agunah.

"Testimony" has become, in recent decades, a key term in a number of academic disciplines. Aspects of testimony come into sharp focus with respect to epistemological function, in relation to "truth," judicial process, and political and social discourse.[14] Two concepts are particularly relevant to our discussion: testimony as narrative and discrete cultures of testimony.

For our purposes, we use the term "narrative" as defined by Shulamit Almog: "Verbal representation of a sequence of events and facts embodying an incident relevant to the legal proceedings."[15] The place of narrative in testimony and in the judicial process has been extensively researched in the context of research on the links between law and literature, which has developed a great deal in recent years.[16] Narrative plays a significant part in decisions made by witnesses and judges alike, affecting the relevance of the details of events to the judicial process; the hierarchy between the details included in the testimony and in the judges' decisions; and — in light of these — the order in which events are presented, the choice to emphasize this or that detail, and the language and style used in the proceedings. Thus, as several scholars have shown, contrary to the notion that the judicial procedure reflects an actual reality, in any particular case, it is the narrational decisions of witnesses and judges that shape multiple representations of any sequence of events, rather than the actual events.[17]

Louise Bethlehem pointed to the existence of "cultures of testimony," which work to standardize patterns of witness presentation — whether consciously or unconsciously — through institutionalized techniques or social mechanisms.[18] Standardization is a function of the desired effect on the target audience (reader or hearer) or relates to other social processes. "Cultures of testimony" is used here to designate official or social aspects of testimony, that is, means by which an individual learns what testimony is, the rules and practices associated with giving testimony, and socially recognized imagery and implicit messages associated with witnesses and testimony.

HALAKHAH, LAW, BATEI DIN, AND NON-JEWISH COURTS

To better understand the significance of the procedure of collecting testimony for the agunah, we turn first, in more detail, to the workings of the beit din. The beit din was one of the most important communal institutions of Jewish society at this time and, as previously mentioned, was charged with hearing testimony in agunah cases.

Michael Mann, Kenneth Stow, and others have recently observed that from the sixteenth century onward, courts of law were a powerful instrument used by the premodern state to deepen their control over individuals.[19] The task of government was acknowledged to be control of the lives of individuals through a uniform system of courts of law. This, in turn, heightened the awareness of individuals as to the activity of the judicial system. This process had consequences for Jewish society as well. Extant beit din records show that Jews also grew more conscious of judicial institutions. While these records have not yet been sufficiently studied, extant research has revealed the following details.

Proceedings of the rabbinic courts by and large followed the format of the non-Jewish courts in the same region.[20] Demarcation of Jewish or non-Jewish jurisdiction was not always clear-cut. As a result, throughout this period Jews tended more and more to maneuver among jurisdictions to gain an advantage. Consequently, the authority of the beit din waned in some areas.[21] As mentioned in the introduction, Jewish courts were dispersed throughout Ashkenaz, and one beit din typically served several communities. The rabbi of the city headed the court, assisted by the other elected judges (dayanim). The beit din met regularly, usually twice a week, generally in a room next to the synagogue or in the rabbi's home.[22]

As it still does today, beit din work in the period under discussion focused on collecting testimony. Dayanim questioned witnesses and, if they needed additional guidance, sometimes called upon an expert witness in a given profession. The Altona beit din record book mentions physicians' serving as expert witnesses in Berlin in connection to the health of a certain woman who had a dispute with her husband.[23] Most testimony in the beit din, including for freeing an agunah, was given in the local Yiddish vernacular,[24] though it was written down in Hebrew by the judges.[25] This seems to prove that witnesses were not compelled to testify in an unfamiliar language; rather, they could speak freely in their own idiom. Yet we should not conclude that giving evidence was a spontaneous act. It was preceded by the following ritual: the head of the rabbinic court would caution the witness to conceal nothing and testify only to what he knew to be true. The formula prescribed by halakhah for warning witnesses was the same in agunah and other cases.[26] Additional warning was sometimes needed, as for the testimony about the death of Edele's husband. The judge's report reads as follows: "We cautioned him: It is no small matter to free a married woman so that she is free to marry anyone she chooses — based on your word! Only if you are absolutely certain that it was indeed Hirschel Shahor."[27]

The procedure itself impressed upon witnesses the heavy responsibility of testifying for an agunah. They had to realize the potentially grave consequences of their testimony.

WITNESSES FOR THE AGUNAH EDELE OF NIKOLSBURG

Sometime before 1691, Hirschel Shahor, husband of young Edele, went abroad, and all contact with him was lost. For some time, Edele "did not know what had befallen him."[28] His travel companions then returned to Nikolsburg and testified: They were on a ship, and Hirschel fell overboard. The body was spotted two weeks later but could not be recovered. It took over a year and a half until Edele was granted permission to remarry.

The case notes of Rabbi David Oppenheim include three testimonies by two witnesses. No explanation is provided as to why the first witness testified twice: on January 24, 1691, and a year later, when emissaries were sent by the beit din to hear his evidence again, on January 22, 1692. But the circumstances in which the second witness testified are documented. After hearing Berl, the first witness, Oppenheim asked to hear a second witness. This man could not come to the beit din, so emissaries were sent to him: "We the undersigned set out on a mission, as instructed by the great beit din.... We left Nikolsburg, as instructed by the esteemed and revered head of our rabbinic court and chief rabbi of our land and of all Moravia, Rabbi David Oppenheim. We were sent to hear testimony of a certain [illegible]. Suffering from a leg injury, he could not come to our beit din."[29]

We see how complicated the process of hearing evidence for the agunah could be. Jews were generally well aware of the crucial role of witnesses for freeing an agunah, but witnesses could not always present themselves to the beit din at the appointed time. In this case, despite the distance, Oppenheim instructed judges to travel to the home of the witness.[30] Other rabbis did not always act in this way; we may assume that people who witnessed an event did not always come forward to testify.

What did the witnesses choose to relate? What were their narrative choices? What could their testimony teach us about the ways in which information regarding missing persons was collected? Berl's first testimony (1691) includes the following:

> We were on the river Morava.[31] When the Sabbath ended, we were moored by the bank. Hirschel Shahor of our community was with us. He drank a few flasks of wine, then went to a corner and stretched out, taking off all his clothes except for his shirt. He lit a

candle, stuck it on the deck, and walked to the edge of the ship's deck to relieve himself into the water. He fell overboard, for our many sins. The water made a kind of gurgling sound. "Hirschel, Hirschel!" we shouted, but there was no answer. We descended into the ship's cabin; Hirschel was not there. His clothes were lying in a heap, except for the shirt. The candle was still burning. That's how we knew Hirschel had fallen overboard. They moved the ship, and the next one over, too, in order to search the river all over—but we found nothing. A fortnight later, we were returning home by the same route. The downstream current was strong as we sailed upstream. The current had carried him not far from where he had fallen in. He was stuck fast in a tree. He was leaning out of the water, with his shirt still on him. The water had pushed the shirt up around his shoulders as he leaned back into the tree, but his entire head was out of the water. The fish had started to nibble the tip of his nose. His beard had fallen out and so, too, the hair at his temples; only wisps remained on his head. I recognized him at once as Hirschel. I promised the ship's crew money to haul him out of the water. I accompanied them, and we worked for over two hours. We did everything we could, but we couldn't reach him. The water wasn't deep enough [for the ship], and no smaller boat was available. That's why we couldn't get to him.[32]

Berl chose to relate numerous details that were calculated to convince the judges that he knew Hirschel well, that the latter was indeed dead, and that his body had been identified. Berl recounted that Hirschel consumed a large quantity of wine before lying down for the night. This provided a reasonable explanation for Hirschel's losing his balance and falling overboard. Berl described in detail what Hirschel was wearing before he fell, emphasizing that the body was clothed in the very shirt Hirschel had been wearing before his disappearance. He dwelt at length on the direction the ship was heading and the pull of the current; this explained how the body became lodged in a tree-trunk in the stream where it was found. This detailed account was subsequently corroborated by the second witness. Even with all that, Berl's testimony clearly raised halakhic problems. He had not actually seen Hirschel fall overboard; he had only heard a sound and drawn his conclusion based on circumstantial evidence. The report that Hirschel drank wine that evening strengthened the assumption that the missing man had indeed fallen overboard. Yet doubts lingered. Berl could have used his imagination to fill in the gaps with unfounded details. Another halakhic problem was that Berl reported seeing the body two weeks after Hirschel's disappearance, while halakhah allows witnesses to testify to a death no more than three days after the person's disappearance. Hirschel's face was unrecognizable ("The fish had started to nibble the tip of his nose"); this too went against the halakhic requirement that "one may testify [that a man died] only if he can testify about seeing the face with the nose intact."[33] Finally, Berl admitted he had not been able to recover the body, so it could not be confirmed that it was Hirschel.

The beit din asked Berl to testify a second time. They were concerned that he had misidentified the body; at that distance, he could not even be sure the man was dead. In his second testimony, Berl repeated the details of his story. He added that he had tried to retrieve the body to bury it. He stopped only when he felt himself in danger of drowning, too: "I swear under oath. I was a mere two or three paces from him. I could see that he was definitely dead. I absolutely recognized him. And fish had started nibbling the tip of his nose, and his hair had fallen out in the water, and he still had some of his beard. I observed him for about half an hour. I knew without any doubt that it was Hirschel Shahor."[34]

The second witness, another member of their community, happened to be travelling on the same river when he ran into Berl. Berl requested his assistance in recovering the body. This second witness confirmed that the dead man was Hirschel Shahor and that the body was stuck fast midstream in the river in such a way that it could not be retrieved.

It appears that the beit din was satisfied with the accounts of the two witnesses. It helped that both hailed from Nikolsburg and were known to the dayanim. Oppenheim, at any rate, was convinced that Hirschel had drowned. He composed a lengthy treatment of the case, ending by freeing Edele from her agunah status despite the difficulties. This case teaches us that the decisor could avail himself of various means to overcome seemingly insurmountable halakhic obstacles. And, indeed, at the end of the responsum, Oppenheim appended a sentence that testifies to his anxiety that others would oppose the ruling: "lest this beit din be called over-lenient in respect to freeing agunot,[35] we see fit to issue this call for two additional rabbis to read the above."[36]

Oppenheim's anxiety that freeing a number of agunot within a short time would give him a reputation as a lenient decisor shows the atmosphere in which he was operating: the decisor was expected to not be overly lenient regarding agunot. Aside from this, we learn that a decisor was not concerned solely with the specific agunah; rather, he was thinking how other rabbis would perceive his decision.

A similar case is discussed by the young Yechezkel Landau. Rabbi Landau refused to give his permission for an agunah to remarry, despite permission from two other rabbis.[37] If a rabbi gained a reputation for leniency, other rabbis might be reluctant to give their permission. In fact, many were reluctant to do so.

HINDE OF OSTROG

During the Sukkot holiday of 5537 (September–October 1776), a fire broke out in Ostrog (Ostroh).[38] A boy of fourteen perished: Menahem Mendel, son of the head of the rabbinic court in Działoszyn.[39] Two years previously, Menahem had married Hinde, the only daughter of Rabbi Shmuel Shmelke Hacohen, community dignitary and son of a prominent rabbinical family, an extremely wealthy man. Hinde was left an agunah at a very young age. Her family made every effort, at considerable expense, to obtain information that would make it possible to free her from her status as an agunah. Eventually, she was freed some five years after the disappearance of her husband.

WITNESSES FOR THE AGUNAH HINDE

The witnesses had not actually seen Menahem die. Rabbi Meir Margaliot, who wrote up the case, included transcripts of the testimonies of seven witnesses heard by the beit din of Ostrog; there was also one written testimony. This was five years after the fire; presumably, earlier attempts had been made to bring the witnesses to the beit din in order to free the agunah. An aunt of Hinde's seems to have been the driving force for producing these witnesses, as may be gathered from the list of their names. They included, besides the aunt, also the widow of "Hanagid Mordechai,"[40] who owned a store next to the aunt's store; the aunt's sister-in-law; "Rabbi Shaul," the son of "Rabbi Meir";[41] Hannah the wife of Rabbi Lazar, who may have been a friend of the family; Mindl, wife of Itzik Hacohen, who lived close to where the fire was; and "Eli the leader [*Harosh*]."[42]

The list suggests that the beit din heard men and women as witnesses, as the halakhah demands in the case of freeing agunot. Was there practical significance to the witnesses' identities? Did witnesses who belonged to a specific communal stratum have an advantage over others? The list of witnesses in this case does not enable us to answer these questions with any certainty. Although four of the witnesses bear the honorifics of community leaders, it is possible that they were the ones who testified because the agunah herself belonged to that communal stratum. Nevertheless, it should be noted that we know that during the period in which Hinde's case occurred, in many Jewish communities, lay leaders were gradually restricting the authority of the beit din while claiming a more active role for themselves in the processes of the reception of the beit din's decisions.[43] It should also be noted that in such cases, the decisor's decision was based, among other things, on his own impressions of witness credibility. Hence it seems obvious that an agunah with witnesses coming from the community leadership had better chances of success than one whose witnesses had lower social positions.

TESTIMONY FOR THE AGUNAH HINDE

The multiple testimonies collected over the prolonged endeavors to free Hinde from her marriage describe the behavior of Jews and non-Jews after the youth's disappearance. Given the number and detailed nature of the testimonies, I will not quote them verbatim. Instead, I will present the progression of the issues that arises from them, the witnesses' narrative choices that are worthy of our notice, and my conclusions that are relevant to our subject.

The first witness was Bayla, the aunt of the agunah (her father's sister). Having been cautioned by the beit din, as is the custom, Bayla recounted conversations that were her basis for stating that Menahem Mendel was no longer alive. "The old apostate woman, the judge's wife, used to come into my shop," testified Bayla. The old woman owned the shop; she rented it out to Bayla and came there often. When rumor that Menahem Mendel had been seen alive reached the old landlady, she said "of her own accord, without being asked," that "the son-in-law of Rabbi Shmelke is not of this world, and may her hand be cut off if it proved otherwise."

Bayla and her landlady had several such conversations. In the first year after the youth's disappearance, the old woman said there was as much chance of finding his bones as of "laying straw down on a swamp." A similar conversation took place after the agunah's father received a letter from the rabbi of Dubno, which made him take his daughter there. Rumor had it that Shmelke's son-in-law had converted to Christianity and gone to Dubno. The old landlady instructed Bayla to reprimand anyone spreading this rumor since Shmelke was spending money in vain efforts to find his son-in-law.

Bayla's evidence should be analyzed on the assumption that her words were calculated to influence the decisor. For us, reading the transcripts 250 years later, it is possible to differentiate factual reality as known to the decisor from witness narrative choices intended to convince the listener of the veracity of the evidence. Although the distinction is not always clear-cut, the attempt to assign each detail in the case to the appropriate category may shed light on important aspects of the case.

Rumor: Rumors abounded about the missing husband, and, given the circumstances of the aunt's conversations with the apostate woman, it seems that these persisted for quite some time. At first, it was said that Hinde's husband had run away and his body was in the marshes area. A letter received by the agunah's family some four years after the event unleashed a fresh spate of rumor.[44] For the first time, it was suggested that Menahem Mendel had converted to Christianity. This bolsters the claim that rumor was an inevitable part of iggun cases. Bayla's testimony sought both to lay the rumors to rest and at the same time to exploit them for freeing the agunah. This case also shows the expanses through which such rumors spread. As with Rivkah in Glikl's memoirs, networks of Jewish women with their non-Jewish acquaintances were here put to work for gathering information that could be turned to personal advantage.

Halakhic proficiency of witnesses: Evidence obtained from a non-Jew is admissible only if he was "speaking innocently." Bayla's remark about the convert landlady—she offered information without being asked for it—suggests that Bayla was familiar with the halakhic requirements on this point. As in Sarah's case, discussed previously, witnesses' halakhic proficiency again proves important, as well as their ability to present their testimony in a way that reflects this proficiency. Bayla's rabbinic family background no doubt prepared her for formulating points in her favor. In early modernity, there was increasing awareness of the minutiae of the different legal systems, a result of the dissemination of legal texts and of the development of legal bureaucracy.[45] The witness called "Eli the leader" clearly also came well prepared: "I went to see the apostate now called Anthony Shofet, whom I consider a good friend. I drew him into conversation: 'I came to consult you in these difficult times. I want to go into business.' In this fashion, I arrived at the matter in hand. I said to him: 'I met Rabbi Shmelke on my way here; he wants to send me to Paris and pay me for going on his behalf. He has heard from his son-in-law. I could make a good profit.' To which the apostate replied: 'Don't you go even one step! You think he's alive, but I swear to you that he is no longer of this world. In the fire he ran past the bridge and remained there in the marshes.'"[46]

Eli "led his friend into conversation" to elicit information from him; this formulation makes it clear that this witness, too, was well-versed in halakhah.[47]

JEWS IN NON-JEWISH SURROUNDINGS

To lend credence to her statement that Menahem Mendel was no longer alive, Bayla cited conversations with someone who had converted from Judaism to Christianity. Presumably the landlady, as a convert herself, would have known for certain if the youth had converted to Christianity. In this way, Bayla hoped to convince the decisor that rumors to the effect that Menahem Mendel had converted were groundless. Possibly, Bayla thought the non-Jews would know what had befallen the youth.

All other witnesses also cited non-Jews or converts from Judaism as sources of information. "Shaul the learned" testified that a year after Menahem Mendel's disappearance, a certain non-Jew showed him some human bones in the marshes, of a size commensurate with the missing youth. The fourth witness, a woman called Hannah, testified that the gentile astrologer she consulted said "he is no longer in the world." Likewise, the witness Mindl testified that two non-Jewish women, guests of hers, were heard saying to each other that the Jews were making a big fuss for nothing; the boy was no longer in this world.

Evidently, in Ostrog, Jews were friendly with converts to Christianity. Rabbi Margaliot raised no objection to this friendly relationship, implying that positive relations between the two were self-evident. In eighteenth-century Poland, converts from Judaism were few.[48] Yet, it was in Ostrog that Bishop Franciszek Kostrzewski staged Jewish-Christian public disputes in an effort to convert the city's Jews.[49] Therefore, we can surmise that the relations between Jews and converts that are evident from this case are not representative of Polish society in general. However, even if the picture of friendship with converts in the present case was unusual, it was nevertheless possible. For the agunah, the affinity between Jews and converts was of special import. According to two of the witnesses in the case, the non-Jews who knew the boy's location feared revealing this information to their Jewish neighbors lest they be implicated in the murder. It would appear that converts acted as a conduit for passing to the Jewish community information obtained from non-Jews. Margaliot hints that information that non-Jews preferred to conceal was obtained from converts. Giving his reasons for accepting Bayla's testimony, he writes: "When a gentile questions another gentile, this information is to be considered 'speaking innocently.' The same holds for an apostate woman speaking to a gentile, when she has been fully assimilated among them for many years—she has been married for many years to a gentile husband and has children by him. Her son-in-law is a priest. She is fully assimilated, like one born and bred. Consequently, the gentiles would not suspect her of investigating on behalf of the Jews."

Margaliot is assuming that, normally, non-Jews would suspect converts of collusion with the Jews; only a convert who has been assimilated for many years had a chance of gaining the trust of the gentiles. At times, then, ties between Jews and non-Jews played an important part in collecting the necessary material for freeing an agunah. Willingness on the part of converts to assist Jews may have derived from their familiarity with aspects of halakhah and could provide the Jews with crucial information.

This hypothesis contradicts the attitude of converts to iggun as hitherto presented. According to Elisheva Carlebach, in her comprehensive study of converts from Judaism in Germany, Jewish society and the church both required the convert to give his Jewish wife a get before he could marry a Christian woman. It was the converts to Christianity themselves who refused to take part in any Jewish ritual, including divorce.[50] While Carlebach does not refer specifically to the role of converts from Judaism in obtaining information about missing husbands, she does note ties between Jews and converts in Germany.[51] However, based on her research, it is hard to imagine converts in Germany actively

"*Nothing of Him Was Ever Found...*"   : : : 121

assisting an agunah as did the converts in the case history by Margaliot. This dissimilarity might be explained by different conversion patterns in Germany as compared to Poland. In Germany, converts tended to come from the upper classes and sought to assimilate into non-Jewish society; in Poland, converts came predominately from the lower classes.[52] Conversion in Germany, while not free of economic and other considerations, was frequently accompanied by deep ideological conviction. In Poland, by contrast, many Jews were motivated to convert by a desire to escape economic hardship, not necessarily by any deep-seated religious belief.[53] The proverb "A Jew who converts to Christianity deserves to drown" exemplifies the pervasive hostility of non-Jewish Poles toward Jewish converts to Christianity.[54] And, thus, in Poland Jews maintained ties with converts, since many converts, failing to assimilate into Polish society, were reluctant to sever all ties with their previous community. Also, as Yehezkel Fram has shown, the Jewish community did not always relinquish hope that the convert would one day return to the fold.[55] We have here an example of local differences among Jewish communities affecting agunot.[56]

THE GENTILE ASTROLOGER WOMAN AND THE RABBI

The testimonies in favor of freeing the young Hinde from her status as an agunah underscore her family's helplessness. It also enables an understanding of what was considered a reliable source of information at the time. The witness Hannah cited an astrologer; and she was not the only one. The witness Raisa elicited information from a female convert by telling her that many astrologers and sorcerers were saying that Menahem Mendel was still alive.[57] These two testimonies are surprising, since consulting a soothsayer would seem to contravene halakhah.[58] However, Jewish society, including rabbis, had considered astrology accepted practice for centuries. Yehoshua Trachtenberg notes the widespread belief that every individual has a star and astral bodies govern human life and events.[59] Maimonides was the exception in prohibiting use of information obtained by consulting an astrologer, says Trachtenburg.

In this respect, the Jews were no different from their gentile neighbors. Europe in the sixteenth century was still in the grip of "astrology fever,"[60] though, by the eighteenth century, astrology was no longer considered a scientific or legitimate religious practice, and it became associated with the uneducated masses.[61] Hannah and Raisa both testified before the beit din that they had consulted an astrologer. Rabbi Margaliot rejected the evidence obtained by astrology but did include it in his responsum.[62] Perhaps he did so in order to impress upon his readers the gulf between popular practice and his own position.

"SHE WAS NEVER PROVED NOT A VIRGIN ALL THE TIME SHE LIVED WITH HER HUSBAND"
Additional Strategies for Resolving the Agunah Problem

Margaliot's responsum, comprising twenty-eight printed pages, explicates his reasons for permitting the agunah to remarry. He addresses the status of testimony obtained from a female convert who was supposedly knowledgeable about the Jewish religion. Could she be classified as "speaking innocently"? She had not mentioned the dead man's father by name or the name of his town. Was the identification positive despite this omission? Could the marshes where the bones were found be considered "a body of water without end"? In several places, Margaliot crosschecks testimony of different witnesses for contradictions. His doubts on some halakhic points are understandable given the particulars of the case. Yet, some of his arguments seem contrived. He invokes the oft-repeated formula, "should there be anyone who doubts anything of what we have written here..."

Margaliot's responsum is not dated; we do not know who found his decision controversial. Other sources that mention Hinde's case emphasize completely other halakhic considerations, which shows that, before Margaliot released Hinde, her family must have appealed to other halakhic authorities for help. In a question to Rabbi Raphael Hacohen, then rabbi of the Three Communities (AHW), we read:

> Concerning a case in the holy community of Ostrog: On the Sabbath of Sukkot, devouring flames leapt up. In the turmoil, we lost the marvelous, smart, young Rabbi Menahem Mendel son of Rabbi Aharon Hacohen, that was the head of the rabbinic court in Działoszyn. His wife was left alone, an agunah, the only daughter of her esteemed father, Rabbi Shmelke Hacohen. Nothing at all has been heard of him, nothing was ever found, only a shoe and

a belt. We do not know what befell him: is he alive or dead, or a captive? Much money has already been spent looking for him — all in vain. The missing youth was only twelve-and-a-half years old when he married, and about fourteen-and-a-half years old when he disappeared. According to the wife's mother and the neighbors, she remained a virgin during the whole time she was living with her husband. The agunah herself claims she is still a virgin. She declares that she was never penetrated, as she had no interest in such a thing, and one time only he lay on top of her and had only touched that place, when someone rapped on the door. Startled, he leapt up. Here ends the question I received from two esteemed rabbis of Brody.[63]

These details shed new light on events as described by Margaliot based on the testimonies he heard. We now learn of a different approach on the part of the agunah's family, one that does not rely on the circumstances of her husband's death. The family and local rabbis appealed to other decisors, requesting an annulment of the marriage. The marriage was never consummated, they claimed, due to the tender age of both spouses.

Hacohen's responsum is undated, and we do not know if it preceded Margaliot's or came afterwards. In any case, it reveals additional strategies for resolving the agunah problem. Naturally, this course of action was open only to those who were knowledgeable about halakhic requirements for annulling a marriage. Halakhic proficiency proves once again to be advantageous to the agunah. Also importantly, an agunah, failing to get the desired response from the local rabbi, could turn to other, perhaps more distant, halakhic authorities. Rabbi Margaliot as local rabbi initially refused Hinde's request. Ultimately, he acceded, basing his decision solely on testimonies heard by the beit din in Ostrog in 1782. Why did he not employ the strategy of annulment? Did he not have access to the material consulted by Hacohen? Or did he have a fundamental resistance to this approach? Obviously, the way in which events and details were presented to him greatly influenced his decision. Since the agunah was a member of his community, Margaliot did not hear about the case via letters; he could question witnesses and form his own impression of their credibility. Raphael Hacohen, by contrast, learned of the case through a letter he received from another rabbi. It seems doubtful that he even knew of the testimonies used by Margaliot, those which eventually earned Hinde her freedom, as Hacohen never mentioned them. Another possibility is that Hacohen's responsum predates the first testimonies heard by Margaliot.

This becomes more likely in light of the responsum by Rabbi Yehezkel Landau. Landau received no fewer than three questions from fellow decisors about the Hinde case. His first responsum is dated September 13, 1781.[64] Landau's son offered an extensive critique of his father's responsum, to which his father duly replied. On September 25, 1783, Landau once again addressed the case.[65] In his first reply, his summary of events is quite similar to that of Hacohen's:

> Concerning the wretched young woman, of the highest and noblest of families, who these many years is shackled in chains as agunah. According to the evidence, this is what occurred: The woman was betrothed to a youth and married him. According to testimony given in his hometown, the marriage took place six months and more before his thirteenth birthday. He lived with his wife in her father's house until he reached the age of fourteen and a few months. At that point, the husband was lost, or fell in among gentiles, or wandered far away. Nothing has been heard of him to this day. The woman says her husband never came near her at all, as she would not let him. Only once did she give in, mortified that she could not prove she married as a virgin. He lay on top of her and almost touched that place, when someone knocked at the door of the room where the couple lay together, and, from fear caused by the knock, he jumped away from her. All this happened when he was not yet thirteen years old, since this was the summer after the wedding.[66]

Two years later, Landau was approached again by rabbis from Brody, who recounted the story of the fire: "Concerning an agunah about whose husband nothing is known, except that at the time of the great fire, when the flames were already devouring the corner of the roof, he went up to the attic to rescue his property. Nothing is known of his leaving. After searching, bones were found there. They consulted physicians, who said there was no doubt they were human bones. They added that no one could live if these bones were missing from his body."[67]

Landau, indeed, refused at that time to free the agunah, based on the accounts contained in the two questions he received. Nothing in his reply suggests that he realized it was the very same case. Subsequently, he did find out — Hinde ultimately married Landau's grandson.

"PENDING AGREEMENT OF TEN RABBIS OF OUR GENERATION": DECISORS AS COLLEAGUES

We may conclude that the agunah, or someone acting on her behalf, presented more than one narrative in an attempt to influence the ruling. This might explain the advantage of an appeal to halakhic authorities in a distant place; they knew only what they read in letters. Appellants could include or emphasize such material as they thought might influence the decisor in their favor. Conversely, they could eliminate or downplay anything they feared might work against the agunah's interest. However, appealing to a distant decisor could be a double-edged sword.

Raphael Hacohen noted that the rabbis of Brody (some 130 kilometers' distance from Ostrog) wrote to him about Hinde while he was residing in Hamburg (some 1400 kilometers' distance from Ostrog). From his words, we learn that Ostrog's local rabbi was reluctant to encroach on the turf of a colleague; he preferred to stay out of the whole affair.[68]

Raphael Hacohen was apparently in no hurry to reply to the Brody rabbis, not wanting to seem disrespectful of the Ostrog rabbi, Meir Margaliot. Only after the Ostrog rabbis themselves appealed to him, making it clear that Margaliot would not give a decision, did Raphael Hacohen agree to take on the case. After much halakhic debate, he agreed to grant the agunah permission to remarry, by retroactively annulling her marriage to a minor. However, in his concluding remarks, he made his agreement conditional upon support by ten other decisors. The obvious implication is that if the ten were not forthcoming, his own permission would be revoked.[69]

Clearly, rabbis in distant places were reluctant to take on an agunah's case unless they could be certain the local rabbis were aware that they had been approached. In some cases, the appeal to distant decisors became a bone of contention. Raphael Hacohen's condition — that his decision must be upheld by ten other rabbis — underscores the agunah's vulnerability in the welter of rabbinical struggles for prestige and territorial control. Ultimately, Hinde was released from her agunah status. Her second marriage was to Yudl Landau, grandson of Rabbi Yehezkel

Landau. After some time, some evidence arrived that enabled releasing her, but Landau's *Noda biYehudah* does not specify the nature of that evidence.

The methodological challenges involved in this case remind historians that we must exercise great caution in forming conclusions based on responsa literature. Cross-referencing different sources leads to the conclusion that descriptions in responsa literature are partial and usually reflect the decisor's specific point of view. At times, responsa reflect the interests of the questioners, not necessarily those of the agunah.

Hinde's case appears in the volume on rabbis of Ostrog by Menachem Mendel Bieber, printed over one hundred years after the events. Biber describes the youth-husband as a saintly prodigy held in awe by Jews and Christians alike. He even relates that the youth was hailed as the "Messiah of the Jews." Jealousy was the motive for killing him, in this account.[70] The author does not say how this conclusion was reached. Far from an accurate description, his anecdote is, rather, a lesson in the formation of myths around vanished men. Nothing is told of the life of the teenage widow.

8 : THE AGUNAH WIFE OF LEMLI WIMPE OF METZ

In July 1727, one Lember Levi of Metz, also known as Lemli Wimpe, set out for Paris on business.[1] He expected to return home before the New Year to spend the High Holidays with his family. Sadly, he was murdered on the return journey.

CASE NOTES IN RESPONSA LITERATURE AND COMMUNITY RECORD BOOKS

Several rabbis described the circumstances leading up to the iggun of Lemli's wife.[2] The Metz community memory book also reports the case.[3] Rabbi Jacob Reischer, rabbi of Metz, recounts as follows: "In the month of Tammuz [June–July], 1727, a certain householder from our holy community of Metz, by the name of Lemli Wimpe Halevi, set out by mail coach for Paris on business. He intended to return home for the New Year, as he had promised his wife and family. He had also sent out letters to this effect. Specifically, in his last letter, the month before Rosh Hashanah, he repeated that he would be back for the holiday, as his business had gone well. He wasn't sure if he would be returning from Paris by mail coach or in a driven wagon in the company of other Jews who were also in Paris."[4]

According to Reischer's description, Lemli kept in touch with his family while he was away, and they knew his expected date of return. For his trip back to Metz, some 330 kilometers' distance, he decided not to take the mail coach but to travel with a gentile coachman he knew from previous trips.[5]

Lemli had a choice of travelling home from Paris with fellow Jews or with a gentile coachman. Travel required permits and sometimes negotiations over price.[6] Lemli's decision to travel with the gentile coachman sealed his fate. Rosh Hashanah Eve came and went, and Lemli had not returned home. On the second day of the holiday, an official notice came from the judiciary bureau of Châlons:[7] "Last Wednesday, at about eight or nine o'clock in the morning, a coach and three horses were found in the woods near Congy. A Jew was lying on the ground nearby, dead, by the name of Lember Levi, with all his clothes, linens, and papers. In the middle of the pathway lay the body of the murdered coachman, by the name of Gran Joseph."[8]

A letter subsequently received by Lemli's widow informed her that the local authorities had conducted an investigation into the murder. They heard evidence from three local villagers: "Early Wednesday morning, they were on their way to their day's work in the fields or the woods. Near the village, they encountered three armed gentiles on horseback. The villagers heard the gentiles saying among themselves: 'That so-and-so promised he would be leaving the inn very early in the morning, but he isn't here. And now we have to wait for him?' The villagers paid no attention to this and went on their way toward the city. About an hour later, they heard a scream and a shot. Terrified, they hid in the woods."

Following their investigation, the local authorities were able to positively identify the murder victims. The families were notified. However, identification procedures as carried out by the non-Jewish authorities made it worse for the agunah, since they prevented the identification by halakhic procedure. Further details were communicated by the authorities to the community of Metz: The bodies were left lying on the ground until the following Thursday. After noon, the judiciary officials arrived to inspect the bodies. The coachman was buried in a cemetery on Thursday afternoon; the Jew was buried in a nearby valley. His personal effects — clothes, letters addressed to him by name stating that others owed him money, and holy books — all were deposited with the court to protect the rights of his wife and heirs.

In this account, the two bodies were left on the ground where they were found until the authorities could come identify them, twenty-four hours later. The widow was concerned that identification of the body failed to adhere to halakhic requirements:

> At the close of the holiday of Rosh Hashanah, Lemli's widow dispatched two householders from here who knew her husband Lemli well. They had travelled with him several times in the past, and would look for distinguishing marks on his body, such as were known to all: He was bald, and the little finger of his left hand was al-

ways crooked while the others were straight. The two men reached the town where he had been buried on Friday, 4 Tishrei [September 19, 1727]. And they disinterred the body. Since it was impossible to bring him here, he was buried in the garden of a dignitary.

Lemli's widow arranged for his body to be identified only on Friday, September 19, 1727, nine days after the murder. As previously mentioned, halakhah requires identification of a body within three days after death. On their way back home, the two emissaries stopped by the courthouse of Châlons to collect Lemli's personal effects. All were marked with his and his wife's initials.[9] His name and signature were inscribed in his books, and on letters of others confirming their debt to him.

The widow's emissaries returned to Metz on September 22, 1727, and they gave their evidence before the local beit din that very day. They testified that the face was disfigured beyond recognition, but they identified Lemli by the marks on his body: his baldness and the crooked little finger of the left hand.

The Metz memory (*yahrzeit*) book entry notes that Lemli's wife, and apparently the rest of the community, were satisfied that the murdered man was indeed Lemli Wimpe. The entry said: "May God safeguard the soul of holy Lemli son of Menahem Wimpen Halevi, for he was upright and honest all his days, kind to all, especially the poor. In business affairs he was honest, in prayers devout. On the High Holy Days, on his way home from Paris, he was murdered along with his coachman, right in the middle of the road, near the village of Congy, which belongs to the son of the lord President [illegible][10] who did him the kindness of burying him on his land. That is his burial place. His wife and children gave charity for him."[11]

It emerges that Lemli's widow, the family, and residents of Metz, Jews and non-Jews alike, all accepted the veracity of the details told them by the authorities and the emissaries. However, on January 21, 1728, about four months later, Rabbi Reischer of Metz decided the information was too scanty to enable him to free the widow unless leading rabbis gave their permission as well.[12]

AGUNOT AND RABBINICAL POWER STRUGGLES

As common in discussions about agunot, the decisor's ruling comprised several parts. First, he enumerated possible doubts regarding the possibility of freeing Lemli's wife from her agunah status: The witnesses had not actually seen the man die; hearing a sound, they inferred he had been shot. This discredited their testimony for purposes of identification. He also discounted the authorities' account, since their motive was to assure the public that the killers had been apprehended; in Reischer's opinion, they could therefore not be classified as "speaking innocently." He rejected the identification of the dead man by his clothes and books, since Lemli could have lent them to someone else. As for the unique feature of his crooked little finger, this was not an unmistakable distinguishing feature. Imposing halakhic categories on reality conflicted, in this case, with what reasonable people took to be true. Reischer instructed Lemli's sons not to recite the Kaddish for their father nor to observe ritual mourning until such time as a beit din and leading scholars freed the agunah.[13]

In his ruling, Reischer seems preoccupied less with the question of whether Lemli Wimpe was dead than with determining who wielded the authority to decide. As Jay Berkovitz has shown, in Metz, there was ongoing conflict between lay leadership and halakhic authorities. This conflict is perhaps reflected in Reischer's responsum.[14] However, Reischer was actually in favor of appointing dayanim who were not ordained rabbis, so this reason seems insufficient. For Reischer, the category of "agunah" related not to external reality but to the halakhic system. The system was designed to determine whether it could be proven that a man was dead. We are struck once again by the discrepancy between the widow and her family's perception of circumstances and that of the decisor. While the widow and her family were concerned with Lemli's fate, and while, once they received sufficient information, they accepted his death as a fait accompli, the decisor was concerned with the ability to determine, based on halakhic categories, whether Lemli could be pronounced dead.

Reischer apparently did take into account the general belief that Lemli was dead. After he raised all the doubts, based on the opinions of the strict authorities, that Lemli could be identified, he proceeded to undermine the objections he had raised and refute them, citing more lenient halakhic views. For instance, that of the Mabit (Moshe ben Yosef di Trani, Safed, sixteenth century): If a man goes missing while he is travelling, and then a body is found on his very route, it can be assumed that he is indeed the missing person. He noted that there are decisors who say that one does not usually lend one's prayer shawl or phylacteries to another, and therefore we can assume that the dead person did not lend them to another. As for the dead man's crooked finger, Reischer also cites the Maharam of Lublin, who claims that any aberration in a man's limb constitutes a distinguishing feature. The way was now clear for Reischer to free the agunah from her status. Indeed, Reischer even reveals that he admits that there is sufficient halakhic precedent to free the agunah. Further, Reischer claims that he is aware of sufficient halakhic precedents to do just that. After all that, however, Reischer still refused to assume sole responsibility for freeing her. In addition, he stipulated a waiting period of one year before the agunah could get married again.

Controversy persisted over whether an agunah could be freed on the authority of a sole decisor. Rivash (Isaac ben Sheshet, fourteenth century) held that the rabbi handling the case should consult "all rabbis of the region," while Rabbi Moshe Lima was of the opinion that permission granted by a single rabbi sufficed. Reischer chose the stricter approach. His caution—the widow had to wait a year and obtain permission from two other rabbis—was typical. Reischer consulted at least two other decisors about this case: Yehezkel Katzenellenbogen of Altona and David Oppenheim of Prague. The latter, on February 11, 1728, granted the agunah permission to remarry, leaving in place the requirement of waiting another year.[15] Katzenellenbogen, in his reply of February 13, 1728, evinces discomfort at making the agunah wait another year, given the firm evidence of her husband's demise.[16]

IGGUN AND CUSTOMS OF MOURNING

The decisors' responsa reveal other halakhic issues relevant to the agunah and her family. Reischer instructed Lemli's sons not to recite the Mourner's Kaddish or observe ritual mourning. In this, he was following the view of Rabbi Moshe Isserles: mourning must not be observed until the agunah is free of the marriage.[17] Whether the family obeyed or not, entries in the community record books show that they did observe the custom of giving charity in memory of the deceased. It is important to note that decisors in other localities acted differently. For example, Rabbi Katzenellenbogen in Altona permitted a missing man's family to recite the Mourner's Kaddish in a prayer quorum (*minyan*) at their home, since general opinion was that the man was dead.[18] Allowing the family to recite Kaddish made their mourning public knowledge.

In Altona, one could not usually convene a prayer quorum in a private home. Anyone wishing to do so needed permission from the local rabbi. Neglecting to obtain permission meant incurring a reprimand by the community's shamash.[19] When prayers were held in a family home, the entire community knew the reason and knew, too, that the act had the official stamp of approval. In the present case, then, Katzenellenbogen's permit publicized the family's mourning, openly defying the prevailing custom in cases of agunot. According to Jacob Emden, Katzenellenbogen dispensed permits for home prayer services to flaunt his authority.[20] Perhaps in the present case as well, in addition to his sensitivity to the mourners' emotional needs, his permission reflects tensions between himself and certain other community authorities.

9 : DEATH OF A MERCHANT
Gutta and Avraham Heckscher of Hamburg

Avraham Marcus Heckscher was born in Altona on April 26, 1745, to Mordechai son of Shmuel Zanvil Heckscher and Rachel Falk.[1] His wife, Gutta (Gutchie), daughter of Levin Mariboe of Copenhagen, was two years his junior. The couple had at least seven children, born from 1763 onward.

The Heckschers were one of the oldest, most prestigious families in the Three Communities (AHW). Several members of the family are mentioned in extant community documents.[2] It is therefore not surprising that details of the lives of Avraham and Gutta Heckscher can be reconstructed from documentary evidence.

Avraham Heckscher was a merchant who dealt in commodities such as clothing, clocks, gold, and precious stones.[3] At trade fairs in the Hamburg vicinity, which he attended regularly, he offered his goods for sale. He also travelled to fairs in more distant cities. The sources do not tell us anything about Gutta's involvement in her husband's business, but we know that in 1779 she was a moneylender and pawnbroker.[4] A comprehensive picture of Heckscher's finances and business affairs emerges both from the correspondence addressed by Heckscher to the Hamburg municipal council—in which Heckscher presented the chronology of his dispute with his business partner, Hyman Samuel Behrend[5]—and from entries in the Altona Court books.[6]

A lengthy chain of events unfolds in these letters (April–September 1790). Heckscher left goods worth 5,600 marks, a considerable sum at that time, with his partner. The partner was supposed to sell the goods at the fairs of Lüneburg, Stade, Wismar, and Rostock. Heckscher sent a man by the name of Marcus Magnus to accompany the goods.[7] The original plan was for Behrend and Marcus to return to Hamburg after the Rostock fair, but Marcus fell ill and they stayed on in Lübeck. He died there shortly afterwards. Heckscher, fearing his goods would be lost, followed the two men to Lübeck, where he approached the authorities to have his property restored to him. The authorities, for their part, commandeered the goods in Behrend's possession. Financial dispute between the partners ensued. To resolve it, Heckscher wanted to litigate in the Lübeck courts. Behrend claimed he was not subject to Lübeck jurisdiction but would litigate in Altona before the rabbi. Heckscher refused: Jewish judges knew nothing of the law, he said, and the beit din accepted only documents in Hebrew or Yiddish.[8] Ultimately, he was forced to litigate in the beit din of Altona. His case was heard in two sessions at least.[9] We do not know how the dispute was resolved, but Heckscher apparently continued in his occupation as a merchant in the following years. In the winter of 1795, he attended the Leipzig fair[10]—but never came home.

The beit din of the Three Communities began hearings on distribution of Heckscher's estate on January 14, 1796. On the day of the hearing, he was still missing, presumed dead. His wife still had not received permission from the beit din to remarry.[11] Retelling the story several years later, one source claimed that Heckscher had allegedly been murdered by a Frenchman from whom Heckscher had stolen a diamond. In this version, the Frenchman pursued Heckscher to Leipzig, beat him to death, and took the diamond off the corpse, then escaped to America.[12] Other sources date the events to October 1, 1795, adding that Heckscher was buried in the cemetery of Halle, some forty kilometers from Leipzig.[13]

The facts of Heckscher's murder emerge only from secondary sources. By contrast, beit din records paint a vivid picture of the lawsuit, the fate of his wife and children, and the financial implications of his murder. At the time of Heckscher's death, his wife was forty-eight years old. The couple had seven children: Mordechai, Shaynche, Galda, Haike, Brendl, Esther, and Leib. Mordechai, the eldest, about thirty-two years old at the time, was by then married to Eva daughter of Yaakov Moshe Shlesinger.[14] Shaynche was married to Itzk Laminitz. Galda, Haike, and Brendl were unmarried. Esther, born 1779, and Leib, born 1783, were still adolescents. While the legal sources do not report anything of the family's emotional state after the murder or of their financial worries, copious extant documentation reveals financial and legal details. It is a rare opportunity to trace events stage by stage, observing how beit din proceedings impacted the financial situation of a recent agunah.

Since some of Heckscher's children were minors at the time of his death, the beit din appointed two guardians for the estate: Moshe Frankl and Joshua Feivush Cohen.[15] After conducting an inventory, they reported to the beit din.[16] The value of the household utensils, goods, movable property, and outstanding debts owed to the deceased totaled 8,144 schock and 12 schilling banco. His house was valued by professional surveyors at 13,000 schock. Since it was mortgaged for 8,000 schock, its liquid value was 5,000 schock only. All in all, the guardians reported property totaling 13,144 schock, 12 schillings. The deceased owed debts totaling 23,456 schock, 14 schillings; that is, his debts exceeded the value of his assets. The guardians, with the eldest son, Mordechai, therefore petitioned the beit din (January 20, 1796) to transfer management of the estate to Mordechai. The beit din, satisfied that the wife and grown daughters had no objection, duly transferred all assets and liabilities of the estate to Mordechai.[17]

Mordechai also obligated himself to provide for all the needs of his widowed mother for the rest of her life. In return, Gutta waived all claim to the estate, including payment of her ketubah.[18]

Mordechai Heckscher had additional liabilities: His married sister Shaynche had given her husband power of attorney to waive her right to "half a male heir's portion" in the estate.[19] She was in possession of a writ attesting to this right, given to her by her father. Mordechai obligated himself to provide financially for all his unmarried sisters and younger brother Leib until they married, and to pay for their weddings.[20]

Probate continued as, on June 16, 1796, the guardians requested that Mordechai be compelled to report additional property he had received from Leipzig, which had not been inventoried. The beit din instructed Mordechai to transfer to them all the property he had received, regardless of his other claims, despite the agreement signed in the beit din in January of that year. The beit din, on the guardians' request, wrote to the authorities in Leipzig asking them to forward any remaining property belonging to the estate. The property was to be sent directly to the guardians or the beit din—not to other creditors or to Mordechai.[21]

In December 1796, the remaining property arrived at the beit din.[22] It was inventoried and valuated at 27,091 schock plus assorted goods in the amount of 2,576 schock in Mordechai's possession. The revaluated estate now totaled 29,667 schock.[23] This last shipment seems to have reignited the dispute. On January 16, 1797, Gutta Heckscher's legal representative sued her son Mordechai for part of the estate, her earlier waiver notwithstanding.[24] The representative exhibited in court the original signed betrothal agreement. The following figures are given in the documents as grounds for Gutta's claim:

Dowry after deduction of one-tenth for tithing: 7,500 schock
Additional monies added to the basic ketubah: 2,500 schock
Melog property [lit. "property of plucking"]: 6,000 schock
Total: 16,000 schock

Itzk Laminitz, Shaynche's husband, also claimed 6,000 schock of the estate, despite the waiver he and his wife had signed. The beit din recalculated again, and two days later the new distribution of the estate was recorded. Once again, the beit din ruled that the estate in its entirety would pass to Mordechai as sole executor. Mordechai obligated himself to give his mother (still an agunah at the time) 1,300 schock per annum for life. The record states explicitly that this responsibility would endure even in the event of Mordechai's death, in which case it would pass to his heirs.

Finally, provisions were made for Avraham Heckscher's daughters, signed, interestingly, by his wife and all their grown children, male and female.

In order to generalize from this case to the financial status of other agunot, several points, some of which were touched on previously, should be clarified. A man's sudden disappearance meant immediate involvement of the authorities to administer the estate and care for any children. This fact presumably had a different impact on agunot from different social strata. Coping was easier for an agunah who had worked with her husband in the family business or who had family members who could negotiate with the authorities on her behalf. It has been claimed that women's financial independence gradually diminished over the course of the eighteenth century with the growing tendency in civil courts to not appoint women as guardians of an estate or of property.[25] Given the same tendency in rabbinic courts,[26] there was nothing unusual in the beit din's decision to put Gutta's eldest son in charge of the family finances. Women without an adult son capable of assuming legal responsibilities were probably more vulnerable to seeing the family properties administered by strangers, and, with the loss of their husbands, these women lost their financial independence, too. Yet the beit din documents state explicitly that management of the estate was transferred to Mordechai Heckscher only after the agreement of the wife and other female dependents. And we cannot rule out the possibility that the beit din took into account possible appeals by one of the female members of the family to non-Jewish courts.[27]

In the Heckscher case, it made financial sense to transfer management of the estate to the eldest son. Mordechai Heckscher, with his business partner, Salomon Heine, established a successful bank in Hamburg in 1797, shortly after his father's death.[28] However, Gutta's repeated attempts to claim additional monies from Mordechai underscore her financial dependence on her son. If other contemporary rabbinic courts handled such cases in a similar manner, it is obvious that a widow's relationship with her son could decide her financial fate.

Could an agunah claim her ketubah before she was free? The issue sparked much halakhic controversy. The beit din divided up the estate before Gutta was free to remarry, citing her ketubah and betrothal conditions. Perhaps the decision was made in compliance with local law. Alternatively, the dayanim might have recognized that in this case, the halakhic requirement to postpone distribution of the estate was impractical for reasons unconnected to halakhah that are not detailed in the sources.

Despite Heckscher's preference for litigation in non-Jewish courts, I found no mention of any member of his family's pursuing this avenue in the matter of the estate. If Gutta ever sought to be freed from her status as an agunah, there is no mention of it in beit din records, though they do contain documents freeing other agunot of that time.[29] We know only that Gutta died at a ripe old age in 1824 without having remarried.[30]

Part Three
Troubled Marriages

10 : SCENES FROM MARRIAGES IN CONFLICT

In May–June 1773 in Prague, Rabbi Yechezkel Landau issued a responsum to a question put to him by Rabbi Yitzhak Hacohen, head of the rabbinic court in the community of Leipnik,[1] concerning an agunah:

> The woman Blimele daughter of Moshe has been an agunah now for upwards of nine years from her husband Yeshayah son of Leible Leshni of Leipnik. Husband and wife had quarreled before this; indeed, they had already appeared for judgment before the rabbi of the holy community of Nove Mesto,[2] so that she could obtain a get from her husband. Her husband had deposited pledges as guarantee that he would give her the get, but the rabbi returned the pledges. After this, Yeshayah stole something and fled to distant parts. She never saw him again, and she has remained an agunah ever since.[3]

Unlike agunot we have discussed previously, Blimele remained an agunah for many years not because her husband had been killed but, rather, because he had absconded without granting her a Jewish divorce. Blimele and Yeshayah had already appeared before the beit din to end their marriage; Yeshayah even deposited pledges as security, to be returned to him upon his delivering the get. But before he could do so, the rabbi returned his pledges for some unexplained reason. Meanwhile Yeshayah stole something and ran away, leaving his wife an agunah. We learn from the testimonies included in the responsum that this same Yeshayah was absent for no fewer than six years before being apprehended in the town of Rytschef, Germany.[4] There he was hanged with three other criminals on July 6, 1770.[5] Witnesses testified that Yeshayah, before being hanged, expressly requested of them that they inform his wife of his fate. But these testimonies, recorded only three years later, failed in Landau's opinion to provide sufficient information for him to free Blimele from her status of agunah.

Responsa literature and other sources cite additional cases of men who chose to abandon their wives and render them agunot.[6] Some of these men drifted for years. The wife initially might support these travels, only to end up not knowing what had befallen her husband. There were also crooks who deliberately married and left their wives as agunot with the intent of gaining some profit, leaving their "chained" wives behind to evade punishment. Unlike those men who disappeared due to circumstances beyond their control, the men in the present section chose deliberately to make their wives agunot.

I am claiming that abandonment is a choice. This claim draws upon the notion that an individual in a given culture acquires what the sociologist Pierre Bourdieu called "a feel for the game."[7] Culture is like a game, and people who live in a specific community inherit knowledge of the rules of the game—the set of all possible types of behavior in the framework of life in that culture, along with their significance and implications—and, consciously or unconsciously, people internalize the consequences of playing by the rules. An individual can choose to obey or to flout these rules, fully aware of the risk of incurring whatever sanctions society imposes on those who breach its conventions. Deviant behavior may actually be a deliberate strategy, like when a basketball player deliberately commits a foul on the court so as to stop the clock and gain more training time with his coach. In other words, culture instills in the individual not only a set of rules but also a system of knowledge deriving from these rules and relating to them. The assumption is that a man in the culture would acquire knowledge about the concept of iggun and be aware of its consequences for both himself and his wife.

To fully appreciate the implications of choosing to desert a wife and make her an agunah—rather than give her a get—we must look at the nature of marital conflict in the relevant period. According to extant sources, conflict was common and stemmed from various reasons. It should be emphasized that discussing marital conflict in relation to agunot does not imply that men left their wives because of problems in their relationship. We reject the logic of the old saw: if a man leaves his wife, she must have done something to cause it.[8] I do not find this convincing. Men abandoned their wives in all sorts of circumstances, for all kinds of reasons. A man could become embroiled in trouble unrelated to his family life or be driven inwardly to roam and wander. It may be assumed that underlying the decision to abandon a wife was the knowledge that society did not exact a heavy price for this behavior. Obviously, abandonment did sometimes take place amid severe marital difficulties. To evaluate the role of marital conflict among the contributing factors in cases of a man deserting his wife, we should examine the nature of such conflicts as well as the alternatives available in such circumstances.

THE IDEAL JEWISH FAMILY

As late as the second half of the nineteenth century, much of Jewish society still adhered to the traditional way of life, with living conditions largely unchanged for two hundred years.[9] Living quarters were typically cramped, shared with servants, distant relatives, and neighbors.[10] Earning a living was hard, and many subsisted in penury.[11] Frequent pregnancies and high infant and child mortality rates exacerbated difficulties.[12] Marriage age among the social elite was often very low;[13] marriage patterns meant newlyweds had to cope with emotional stress and tensions as they were forced to live far from their parents in new familial surroundings.[14] Most people in these societies adhered to their parents' way of life, yet there were signs of permissiveness, assimilation, and religious conversion. Later, ideologies of Enlightenment, Haskalah, and Hasidism opened up new vistas for the individual. Technological innovations such as printing and advances in public transport offered information about distant places and new ways of reaching them. These changes impacted family life and societal notions of family.

Jacob Katz wrote on the traditional Jewish nuclear family that there was "tremendous pressure to marry" and "no positive social value to remaining single."[15] While this portrayal of Jewish society as founded upon a stable family unit has subsequently met with criticism, it does not differ essentially from the work of contemporaries of Katz.[16] Non-Jewish European society has often been described as consisting of patriarchal family units around an axis of a couple living together in a stable, monogamous marriage, ending only with the death of one of them.[17]

While Katz did not deny the existence of marital conflict or divorce among Jews, he considered attitudes towards divorce as follows:

Nor would one generally break up a marriage, except in cases of clear and absolute failure: total sexual dysfunction, adultery (especially on the part of the wife), barrenness, or radical incompatibility (as displayed in constant, open, quarrelling), etc. People had not been raised ideologically to expect happiness, and the absence of romantic satisfaction in a marriage would not lead to divorce. There were, moreover, tremendous hardships involved in divorce. The husband had to consider the economic cost.... Women, on the other hand, knew that divorce would leave them with a much-reduced status. The divorcée's chances of remarrying were slim, especially if she had been the cause of the divorce, whether because she had produced no children or because she was suspected of adultery, or because she was obviously argumentative. Independence was in no way an advantage to a woman in this society. Only a widow with children to raise could be seen as in effect substituting for her husband and could thus maintain the economic and social status of the family as occurred in the case of Glikl Hamel. But it was doubtful that a young divorcée could find a viable economic role for herself; there was certainly no independent role for her. Of necessity, she was forced, therefore, to seek refuge in the house of others by returning to her parents or relatives, or for the lower classes, by taking a job as a household domestic. For these reasons, divorce was generally rejected as a quick solution for a family tension.[18]

To explain why, in his view, Jewish couples hardly divorced, Katz links social and economic factors that acted as a brake preventing divorce to the notion that individuals did not expect happiness in marriage. In his view, couples rejected divorce due to those factors and chose other coping strategies. As will be shown, several factors mentioned by Katz did frequently play a role in a husband's decision to avoid divorce. In such cases, the wife became an agunah even though divorce might have proved better for her. Several decades ago, scholars suggested that the family as depicted by Katz is an idealized version: cases of divorce were by no means rare in Jewish society,[19] though less common in some places than others.[20] It is also important to notice that Katz used the terms "end a marriage" and "divorce" as though they were interchangeable, but they are not.

As many scholars have shown, and as will be seen later, contemporary sources show that marital conflicts were not rare, and couples in conflict who went to the rabbi sometimes separated without formal divorce.[21] Examination of several cases of marital conflict makes one suspect that the statement by Katz that couples generally preferred to preserve their marriage, even at a heavy price, should be revisited.

Traditional Jewish society regarded marriage as one of the most important lifecycle events. For men, marriage was the sole legitimate framework for observing the commandment of procreation. For women, marriage was a primary goal in its own right. We can certainly assume that marital problems brought a sense of failure, alongside the pain and sadness.

According to Yemima Hovav, in her extensive study of images of women in rabbinic literature, the prevailing concept of matrimony was a clear-cut hierarchy. Works by men for men portrayed women whose sole role was "helpmeet"[22]—to help her husband fulfill his destiny. Yet, writings by women and for women stressed the husband's dependency on his wife and extolled women for their strength. In all the sources cited by Hovav, the prevailing view sees a good wife as obedient, doing her husband's bidding. Hovav further notes that in these writings, the wife is responsible for the couple's relationship, for better or for worse. The husband is required to cleave to "a good woman"; these images were internalized by both genders.[23]

But not everybody always follows the "best path." In this period, there were certainly those who rebelled against societal conventions. The focus in this section on marital conflict does not mean that marital relations in this period were always fraught; they were not. Sources indicate that many couples enjoyed a long life of amicable partnership.[24] Yet I reject the claim made by Katz, Liberles, and others that depictions of marital strife necessitating external intervention represent extreme, atypical cases, exceptions to the rule.[25] There are good reasons for believing that marital crisis was less infrequent than is commonly thought. However, it is not my intention to present quantitative statistical data or to analyze chronological developments and processes that shaped the nature of marital relations in Jewish society in the period under discussion. Instead, I will present models that illuminate the range of possibilities available to couples in crisis in this period. In other words, what follows is not a comprehensive structural analysis but, rather, an anatomy of individual incidents.

MARITAL CONFLICT IN BETROTHAL CONTRACTS

Prenuptial agreements (betrothal contracts, or *shetarot tenaim*) stating steps to be taken in the event of marital quarrel were already common in the German cultural space in the late eighteenth century;[26] so, quarrels between spouses were evidently common. This can be learned from a case that came before Rabbi Yechezkel Landau and from the prenuptial agreement signed by Shmuel Zanvil son of Isaac of Harburg and Henele daughter of Joseph Segal of Leutershausen on April 19, 1787. The text of the agreement is identical to that in *Nahalat shivah*:[27] "If, God forbid, the esteemed Zanvil should do unto his wife [Henele] anything that is intolerable to her, and she has to petition the beit din, he shall immediately give her ten gold pieces for her maintenance and will continue to do so monthly, for the duration of their quarrel. Likewise, he shall give her the clothes and jewelry belonging to her. He shall appear with her before the beit din within a fortnight of her petition. Once they have come to an understanding, Henele will return to her husband's house, and she shall return whatever monies remain to her, including all the clothes and jewelry, to their original place."[28]

It is not known when clauses of this kind became standard in prenuptial agreements. Yet, the very reference to marital tension ending in judgment in front of a beit din, in the framework of an official document signed by members of a couple before their marriage, shows that such tensions were in the realm of possibility and that people in this period saw the need to contend with them in a controlled manner. Because similar provisions appear in betrothal contracts from many communities, it is appropriate for us to pay attention to a few details in the wording of the contract: (1) The document refers only to conduct the wife finds intolerable, not vice versa. (2) The evaluation of behavior is subjective, not absolute—the document does not detail specific intolerable acts, leaving the definition to the wife. (3) It is assumed that certain cases will require adjudication and that the rabbinical court has the authority to decide matters of marital conflict. (4) It is assumed that it is the wife who will need legal recourse; the document does not require a wife to appear in court at her husband's demand. (5) The husband is required to appear before the court within a fortnight of the wife's complaint.

This document ostensibly protects the wife from intolerable behavior at the hands of her husband. However, since the beit din is designated as the arbitrator, any practical implications clearly depend on the court's approach to marital conflict in general and to complaints by women in particular. Documents of this kind reveal very little about the couple's dynamics after marriage or the actual implementation of the betrothal contract. In order to explore actual social reality, we must turn to other sources.

The following case came before Rabbi Shmuel Kojdanow (Kraków, 1614?–1676),[29] rabbi of congregations in Poland, Austria, Moravia, Germany, and Lithuania. A question was posed to him by the head of the rabbinic court in Wurzburg, Germany:

> Reuven and his wife lived together amicably and normally for eight years, without quarrel. Recently the wife rebelled against her husband. She committed two grave misdeeds: She left his house without telling him and returned to her father's house. Furthermore, she took with her whatever she wanted of her husband's property. Reuven, on coming home, cried out, "Woe is me, my wife! My money!" He wanted her back, for she was the wife of his youth. He demanded the dayan compel her to return to her husband. Now, the woman stood up in court and declared she could not live with this man, because when she was married to him, he had an epileptic fit — four or five times. She could not bear to live with him with this defect. She is repulsed by him, cannot eat in his company, certainly cannot be intimate with him. She says she would rather remain bereft in lonely misery until her hair turns white, if the law of Israel does not let her have a get.
>
> The husband freely admitted his defect, but said the doctors told him there was a cure, as he was still young. Furthermore, his wife and her family all knew of his condition and accepted it. He wished to bring witnesses to this effect but has not yet done so. In fact, the man said he had been bonded to [supposed to marry] a different woman before marrying this woman. That bond ended due to his condition — the whole world knew the reason why the first bond had ended.
>
> She claims bitterly that she knew nothing of it — if her father and relatives knew, they never told her. She is willing to swear to that effect.[30]

This couple lived amicably for eight years, until the wife grew "rebellious" and left home without warning, taking with her whatever she liked. The husband petitioned the court to compel her to return, to live with him as his wife. For her part, she claimed that she did not know of his epilepsy when they married. She stated that the condition made it impossible for her to live with him and be intimate with him. She wanted a divorce—if Jewish law did not allow it, she would rather remain an agunah without a get for the rest of her life than live with him.

We have no way of knowing if the details given here accord with what actually happened. The description most likely reflects the way the questioner fitted known details into halakhic structures, rather than the way the parties presented their case. In any case, we must ask ourselves: To what extent is this case representative? Did women initiate dissolution of marriage out of disappointment? Did this happen only if the marriage turned out to be "transaction based on error" (*mekah ta'ut*)? What were their chances of success? Did men, too, seek to end a marriage? How active were rabbinic courts in such cases? Which of the options implemented by the couple in this specific case—leaving home, turning to the court to compel the wife to return—were available to couples in similar situations, and what were the implications of the respective choices? What was the actual implication of choosing to remain "bereft in lonely misery"?

Extant sources do not allow for conclusive answers. For the first half of the period under discussion, we have to depend mainly on volumes of rabbinic writings, whose shortcomings have been widely discussed; for the second half, we also have archival materials, such as letters and beit din records. Our analyses may lead to conclusions that are biased, given the restricted sources. However, these sources shed light on important aspects of married life, including circumstances that might have led a man to desert his wife and make her an agunah.

Throughout the period under discussion, personal status and family life were matters of public interest. Societal reaction to marital disputes was influenced by Jewish law, at least for most of the relevant period, by ideas and norms coming from Jewish and non-Jewish society, and by economic factors.

HALAKHIC DIVORCE

As we have seen so far, rabbinic authorities handled both marriage and divorce for most of the period.[31] There were some rabbinic enactments that gradually eroded the authority of the beit din in certain places.[32] That being the case, most matters of personal status were still handled by Jewish courts, even after the mid-nineteenth century. As we have seen, many betrothal contracts stipulated that any dispute be adjudicated in a Jewish court, and, indeed, they were.[33]

While Christian canon law forbade divorce, as did other legal systems throughout Ashkenaz at the time, Jewish law recognized the possibility of dissolving a marriage by a get—a legal document with which a man divorces his wife. This is based on the biblical law in Deut. 24:1–2, according to which only the husband has the right to initiate a divorce. The precise circumstances under which a man might exercise this right were much debated throughout Jewish history. The medieval rabbinic enactment known as *Herem derabenu Gershom* restricted the husband's right by decreeing that the divorce would come into effect only if the wife received the get of her own free will.[34]

Dissolving a marriage through divorce had monetary consequences. Halakhah says that the husband is required to return the woman's property and pay her the basic amount and (if applicable) the additional amount required by her ketubah and her dowry. Being poor does not exempt a husband from this obligation. The settlement also includes child support and provisions for custody. Halakhah obligates only the father to pay child support, and again, being poor does not exempt him. According to the halakhah, children under six of either gender would be better off living with their mother. At age six, boys go to live with the father, and girls remain with the mother.

Halakhah does not require either party to be to blame for the divorce. Jewish marriage is effected only by mutual consent, and halakhah makes it possible to dissolve a marriage by such consent as well. Yet, in reality, sometimes only one party wants a divorce. According to halakhah, when one spouse turns to the beit din in order to compel the other to agree to divorce, the beit din can determine only whether the husband or wife should give/receive the get. It cannot coerce them into doing so. The get must be given freely by the husband; otherwise, it is a "get by coercion," which is invalid.[35] The wife also must receive the get of her own free will. Unless these legal conditions are met, the couple are still married to each other and may not marry anyone else.

When one spouse petitions the beit din to rule that a get must be granted, it is the beit din's role to investigate both sides' claims and determine whether there is halakhic justification for granting the request. According to the fundamental halakhic principle, a man and woman, upon entering into marriage, undertake certain obligations, and if they fail to meet these without sufficient justification, they are considered "rebellious." Halakhah specifies several grounds for divorce: some are objective, while others, which concern the conduct of the other spouse, are subjective.[36] In this regard, too, husband and wife are not equal.

A woman is entitled to petition the beit din to compel her husband to give her a get if she can prove objective circumstances precluding her from engaging in sexual relations with him. The halakhic term for a woman's physical revulsion towards her husband, to the point at which she cannot engage in sexual relations with him, is *ma'is alai*. This category covers contagious disease, disgust due to bad odor, claims of impotence (which means she is denied her right to sexual relations), or his being unable to sire a child. If the beit din finds the wife's claims genuine, she would be entitled to payment of her ketubah. But if she claimed the ketubah together with the get, she was suspected of having financial motives.[37]

In addition, the following conduct on the part of the husband could constitute grounds for the beit din to compel him to divorce his wife: (1) He denies her right to sexual relations (meaning that he refuses to engage in sexual relations with her, which violates the halakhic requirement of *onah*);[38] whether the couple are cohabiting or he has abandoned her, she is entitled to seek that he be compelled to give her a get and the additional monies as per the ketubah. (2) He refuses to give her money for maintenance, entitling her to demand both financial support until the get is delivered and the get itself. And, yet, decisors throughout the ages have debated whether a husband can be obligated to give a get when he is financially unable to support his wife (if he is ill or out of work, etc.). (3) The husband's behavior is "not in accordance with the law," a term subject to broad interpretation. Basically, it refers to circumstances in which the husband beats his wife, abuses her verbally, forbids her to see her family, betrays his wife and cohabits with another woman, or entraps her into transgressing halakhah and demands that she behave not in accordance with halakhah. A wife must prove habitual behavior, not an isolated incident. Finally, the husband must be seen to be unrepentant of his bad behavior.

In all the above, if the beit din rules that the husband must divorce his wife, the wife is entitled to payment of her ketubah and maintenance until the get arrives. This obtains even if she has left home before being halakhically divorced.

Similarly, if a husband has proved his wife's bad behavior, he is entitled to demand that his wife accept a get. For a husband demanding divorce, we must distinguish between objective circumstances and his subjective view of his wife's conduct. A husband who proves he cannot cohabit with his wife or engage in sexual relations with her due to her physical impairment may request that she be compelled to receive the get. Alternatively, he may obtain permission from one hundred rabbis to marry another woman. The same holds true should he prove he has lived with her for ten years without her giving birth. The latter exemplifies the essential difference between the situation of husband and wife: halakhically, a man may be married to two women at the same time. For a woman, this is obviously not possible.

Similarly, a man who proves there is a flaw in his wife's conduct may demand that she be compelled to accept the get. Two categories should be distinguished: First, "transgressing against the Law of Moses," which means a wife sets out deliberately to entrap her husband into flouting halakhah (for example, serving nonkosher food or having intercourse with him while she is menstruating). The second is "transgressing against Judaic law," meaning immodest behavior, a broad category covering insults and disrespect towards her husband. Another category of conduct, *maaseh kiur*, or "act of ugliness,"[39] enables a husband to demand a divorce if the court rules that such acts are proof of her adultery. It should be stressed that whenever there is conclusive proof of the wife's adultery,[40] her husband is forbidden to continue to have sexual relations with her. He is obligated to divorce her and she is obligated to accept the get, even against her will.

Besides the legal consequences and change of personal status, being compelled to accept a get also had monetary implications. If a husband proved that his wife transgressed against the Law of Moses or of the Jews or has committed "an act of ugliness," she forfeits her ketubah monies.

As noted, even in situations in which the beit din compels one of the two sides to give or receive the get, the divorce would still not come into effect until both parties act of their own free will. It was not within the power of the beit din to coerce them into acting. The wife's situation, in this regard, is worse than that of her husband: If a woman maintained that she did not receive the get of her own free will, this usually had no effect on the husband's legal status. On the other hand, if the husband claimed after the fact that he did not give the get of his own free will, the get is considered "coerced," and the woman remains his wife nonetheless. If, meanwhile, she has remarried, the latter marriage is invalid — and any children born of it are mamzerim. Consequently, there was a rabbinic enactment decreeing that the beit din must receive from the husband, in advance, a legal declaration (like a modern affidavit) overriding any prior statements to the effect that he was coerced into giving the get.

The divorce goes into effect once the get has been written and delivered to the woman.[41] The get document, following a standard text, specifies the names and other designations of the husband and wife, the names of their fathers, and the date and place where the get was drawn up. The husband instructs the scribe to write the get on his behalf, and the beit din supervises to prevent any errors that would invalidate the document.[42] Once the get is drawn up and signed by two witnesses, the husband delivers it into his wife's hands, also in the presence of two witnesses.

Delivery of the get need not take place in the presence of both parties. It may be delivered via an agent who is appointed in the presence of a beit din. A document of proxy appointment specifies the names of the divorcing husband and divorced wife. As long as the get has not actually been delivered to the wife, the husband may cancel it. Only after the woman receives the get in the presence of two witnesses is she formally divorced.

The previous brief overview of divorce in Jewish law makes clear the degree to which a couple embroiled in marital strife — when one of them wants a divorce and the other does not — is dependent on the beit din. In addition, we see how important it is for the spouses to be able to prove the facts that they cite as grounds for the divorce. The details of the divorce ritual underscore the possibility of error and manipulation by the divorcing couple or by others: the witnesses, agents, and rabbinic court judges.

What was the practical significance of theoretical halakhah for Jewish society? It is likely that contemporary Jews were aware that divorce was a halakhically viable option. But did they see any advantage in opting for divorce? Was divorce really possible, or did social and institutional obstacles block the way?

Katz's sweeping statement notwithstanding, it is difficult to make conclusive observations that would hold true across all Jewish communities. Despite communal institutions and shared values across the Jewish world, the decision whether to divorce or not was also driven by personal and socioeconomic constraints. I concur with Joel Harrington's critique: our ability to discern personal and behavioral diversity in history has been blurred by historians who award too much weight to institutions and laws.[43] Katz's statement seems to me typical of the bias awarding too much weight to legal and rabbinic sources. The cases presented here will help us better understand the forces at work in the decision to dissolve a troubled union, as well as the available alternatives.

JEWS IN THEIR SURROUNDINGS

Jewish attitudes to married life and marital conflict were not influenced solely by halakhic considerations and prevailing views in Jewish society. Jews were not isolated unto themselves; they were influenced also by ideas current in non-Jewish society and by its institutions. Recently it has been suggested that from the end of the eighteenth century, Jews began turning more and more to non-Jewish courts to resolve conflicts, including family affairs.[44] Therefore, a brief overview of the issues of marital conflict—divorced men, divorced women, and "problematic" spouses—in non-Jewish society will enable us to consider the implications of the choice whether to litigate in Jewish or non-Jewish courts (or to just run away).

In her *Disorderly Women*, Wiltenburg examines images of rebellious women and female power in the street literature of early modern Germany and England. This genre had a steadily growing, varied target audience. She found that serene married life was thought to be the destiny of a select few, namely, men lucky enough to find a good woman. Marital conflict was seen in terms of female rebellion against male authority —a wife's refusal to succumb to the "correct" order of things, in which a woman must obey her husband-ruler. Women were portrayed as overbearing, seeking their freedom, and the patriarchal "correct order" was seen as opposing the inherent rebellious nature of women. Many such

German works complained of women neglecting their household duties and frittering away their time in frivolous gossip. They also describe women as screaming when their husbands beat them, with the intention of drawing the neighbors' attention.[45] A Polish preacher observed that a woman has no need for a head of her own; her husband's head is enough, as a two-headed creature is a monstrosity.[46]

As to the husband, German street literature assumes a good husband to be the absolute ruler in his home, who does not fear his wife. In fact, men rarely controlled the household. In this genre, a man assumed he had the right to strike his wife if she failed to act as she should, while women are depicted as rejecting this assumption. Marriage in these works, according to Wiltenburg, is a hierarchy of power relations. While many such works describe the power of women to shape the marriage—for better and, mainly, for worse—their primary message is that a man must exercise great power to sustain the marital union.

Canon law courts, despite their ban on divorce, could, in specific circumstances, grant couples a special dispensation to divorce, though not to remarry. Disputes between husband and wife naturally arose everywhere. Even where canon law reigned—and especially where its reign was not absolute—couples inevitably found ways to separate even without formal divorce.[47] The option of divorce was one of the most significant changes to family life brought by the Reformation of the sixteenth century, and yet, divorce did not become widespread all at once. Luther and Calvin both decreed that only infidelity and (within certain boundaries) abandonment, not marital incompatibility or cruelty, constituted grounds for divorce. And so, during the seventeenth century, formal divorce was still rare in the Protestant world.[48]

In the course of the eighteenth century, under the influence of the Enlightenment, divorce came to be seen in certain circles as an expression of individual liberty and as consistent with human nature.[49] Yet public opinion in Germany and Poland was not moved by the new spirit of the age,[50] and, as we will see, the influences of that spirit on the justice system remained minor for a long time.

ECONOMIC IMPLICATIONS

As already mentioned, Jacob Katz claimed that economic implications were one of the considerations that kept couples from divorcing. It's worth paying attention to Katz's wording: "Men," he claimed, "had to consider the economic cost. . . . The original Talmudic purpose of the Ktuba [sic], 'that it not appear easy in his eyes to divorce her,' was still in force in this period."[51] Katz is somewhat vaguer as to the economic motivation of women; his claims are based mainly on the assumption that "it was doubtful that a young divorcee could find a viable economic role for herself; there was certainly no independent role for her."[52]

The basis for Katz's claim is clear: according to Jewish law, a man who divorces his wife must return her dowry and pay her ketubah. But in order to validate the claim that this prevented men from divorcing, we should ask whether these halakhic requirements were actually enforced. As for women, Katz seems to overstate the case on several counts. First, women played a much more active role in economic life than Katz assumed.[53] Second, if men avoided divorce for the reason Katz claimed, surely this would have been an incentive for women to seek divorce! To fully understand the economic implications of the alternatives available to estranged couples, let us look at beit din rulings on financial disputes and at their ability to enforce these rulings.

VIOLATION OF THE LAW OF MOSES AND LAW OF YEHUDIT (JUDAIC LAW)

A marital dispute came before the beit din of Rabbi Meir Eisenstadt (Poland, 1670–Austria, 1774).[54] The details appear in a letter from an anonymous rabbi to Eisenstadt and in the latter's reply.[55] The source of the dispute seems to have been the woman's deviation from the demands of halakhah, which forbids married couples from having sexual relations while the woman is menstruating and for a week after. At the end, it also requires a woman to purify herself from her niddah state by immersing in a ritual bath (mikveh). In this case, the husband asked to divorce his wife, claiming that she had had sexual relations with him more than once while she was niddah and had concealed her status from him.[56] Questioned by the beit din, the woman confessed that she had done just that. She thus was found guilty of "transgressing the Law of Moses." Upon the husband's solemn oath of ignorance about her state at the time, he would be entitled to divorce her without paying her ketubah. Before the divorce could be effected, the wife—who apparently did not want a divorce—"went somewhere else," effectively delaying delivery of the get.

The husband appealed to the beit din, which ruled that he had the right to divorce her by using an agent to deliver the get. He was even permitted to marry another woman should his wife refuse to receive the get. This ruling was widely publicized (on the wife's initiative or by other parties). The same anonymous rabbi wrote again to Eisenstadt, taking issue with his decision on several counts. Eisenstadt's reply affords a glimpse into the dynamics of the couple's relationship and also reveals something of the workings of the beit din headed by Eisenstadt:

> She entrapped him several times: She had intercourse with him when she was a niddah, concealing her state from her husband by saying she was pregnant. When, afterwards, her husband examined her wrap, it was quite clear that she was still bleeding copiously with her regular period. She gave the wrap to the gentile laundress, beseeching her not to reveal to whom it belonged. All this she confessed to the beit din. She did it, she said, out of childishness, not knowing it was a severe transgression. We duly cautioned her as to the severity of this transgression: "As is well known, if a woman leads her husband astray in this, he divorces her without paying her ketubah, and the Almighty punishes her as well." About three months later, she resumed her misdeed, repeating this same transgression as though it was permissible behavior. Several women testified that they saw her wearing the white garment and saw her wrap at the gentile laundress, stained with menstrual blood.[57] The laundress innocently told them that the woman had requested that she not tell anyone whose wrap it was. Moreover, this woman neglected to go to the ritual bath for three months, telling the woman attendant that she was pregnant.[58] We consider this "a woman whose female neighbors know she is menstruating."[59] On being questioned a second time, the woman again confessed to having sexual relations with her husband while she was niddah but claimed her husband knew of it.[60]

This detailed description paints an interesting picture of the intimate life of a married couple during our period of study. We learn that conjugal intimacy was a matter whose details were exposed to the general community through various means. The niddah ritual, for example, which we are accustomed to seeing as a private matter, was a practice that, in this period, made public details of conjugal intimacy. The rabbinic court, for its part, utilized information possessed by members of the community on the conjugal intimacy of others. The ritual bath turns out to have been a site of communal supervision of marital life. The women questioned about the wife's conduct, including the gentile laundress, cooperated with the rabbinic court and implicated the woman.

In this period, the majority of Jewish society adhered to a traditional lifestyle; those who chose to deviate from it in private life were vulnerable to exploitation of their private information by the estranged spouse. In this case, the husband claimed that the wife had decided to have conjugal relations with him while she was niddah, and the wife claimed that he knew this. We obviously have no way of ascertaining the truth, yet it was the woman who paid the price for deviating from the norm. To avoid facing any adverse consequences, the husband was required merely to swear that he did not know his wife was niddah when they engaged in sexual relations. The beit din accepted his version and not hers — and his wife lost her ketubah.

This raises the question: What role does gender play in this incident? Was it mere chance that the beit din accepted the husband's version and rejected the wife's? Or were women generally perceived as less credible? As we have previously mentioned, in halakhah, a woman is generally not considered a valid witness. But in certain matters pertaining to women, a woman's testimony is admissible. However, here, as in other cases, we do not know from their rulings what the dayanim were thinking. The question will have to remain unanswered for the present.

From the actions of the laundress, the neighbors, and the rest of the witnesses, the couple's relationship seems to have been subject to incessant manipulation by neighbors and acquaintances. Husband and wife, in their turn, manipulated the others as well.

According to Eisenstadt's description, despite the severity of the events, the beit din was in no hurry to allow the husband to divorce his wife. Instead, the court gave the wife several warnings before deciding that the husband could divorce her. We cannot know the nature of the dynamic between the husband and wife or what spurred the husband to petition the beit din at that particular time. We do not even know if he sought immediate divorce or merely wanted the beit din to get his wife to mend her ways. Be that as it may, the beit din, with Eisenstadt at its head, did not rule immediately that the husband could divorce his wife, choosing instead to warn the wife about the severity of her actions and to question witnesses before accepting the husband's account and ruling on the matter. This indicates that divorce was not a facile option in the eyes of the rabbinic court.

ESCAPING THE FATE OF A BATTERED WOMAN

The following source was published by Robert Liberles in the context of an extensive study of Jewish family life in Germany in the early modern age. It is a letter written in 1741 by a woman named Tzerlin to her uncle Moshe Segal of Halberstadt, and in it she recounts at length how her husband regularly abused and humiliated her.[61] The letter reveals a contemporary woman's expectations of married life and the personal and social implications of a foundering marriage. This document is unique in presenting a woman's point of view, and, in contrast to most sources used for historical study of married life, its writing is free of the stylistic constraints typical of legal and rabbinic sources.[62] Tzerlin tells a tale of woe in her own style, seeking her uncle's advice. Here is an excerpt:

> For, because of our many sins, I have an extremely bad life with my husband, may he be granted life, who doesn't value me as a woman, as if my righteous parents had, God forbid, shamed him and he received me like a penniless whore. It is impossible to be more downtrodden and rejected, not only by him, but by the members of his family, who would gladly poison me with a spoonful of water if they could. His mother whispers day and night in his ear and magnifies the conflict even more. All week long he doesn't eat at home even twice; whenever she cooks anything, she does not let him go home unless he eats with her first, while I and my poor children have nothing to eat all week except bread and butter because he does not buy us any meat except a bit only for the Sabbath, and I don't even have flour with which to prepare soup, and no beans or peas. But none of this would be important—there are many other poor people in this world whose lives are no better—if, together with this, I had peace at home, and if my husband lived with me harmoniously as benefits an honest man, I do not say like to a wife, but at least like to a human being.[63]

This section, only a brief one from her long letter, reflects Tzerlin's expectations of marriage. It seems that, in her eyes, life is either "good" or "bad"; a woman expects certain behaviors from her husband, while others cause her only misery and suffering.[64]

Tzerlin was not expecting luxury, only for her husband to appreciate her as a woman and to live with her in amicable partnership.[65] Her anger at her husband for treating her like "a penniless harlot" indicates the importance she attaches to the status she had when entering marriage and on what she viewed as the correlation between the money a bride brings to a marriage and her status within it. It has been well-documented in scholarly literature that a young woman's marriageability depended to a great extent on her parents' economic status or on her own ability to raise a dowry.[66] Yet, Tzerlin's words add emotional depth to what is already known: it was considered shameful for a man to marry a bride with no money, and she was perceived as a "harlot." We learn further from the letter that the husband squandered the meager property his wife brought to the marriage, leaving her and the children penniless and financially completely dependent on him.

Tzerlin wrote to her uncle in secret, imploring him to keep it confidential; she feared her husband would turn violent if he found out. Liberles is correct that the letter displays a number of typical elements that characterize battered women.[67] Tzerlin's husband and his family isolated her, an orphan, from her surroundings and warned her not to tell others how he treated her. Despite this, she somehow plucked up enough courage to tell her uncle of her husband's violent behavior. When her husband found out, he did severely beat her, saying, "You would shame me, make everything public knowledge? Here, now you know what a beating is and what hardship means. Until now it was nothing, now that you made it worse, I have nothing to lose. People know, you shamed me in public."[68] After her husband's perception that he had been humiliated, Tzerlin was forced to write to a certain woman in the community, retracting her accusations against her husband and pretending all was well.

Tzerlin's letter and her husband's speech quoted there show us that society expected a married couple to behave amicably and live together peacefully. If an individual was known to behave otherwise, it was enough to cause him public humiliation. Theoretically, this incident teaches that a spouse in distress could involve the community in the hope that shaming and peer pressure would have an improving effect. Yet, this letter also demonstrates the limits of this option: Tzerlin's cry for help failed, whether because her husband and his family isolated her or for other reasons connected to her personality, her life's circumstances, or the Jewish community in which she lived.

In one incident described in her letter, her husband threatens her: "I will hurt you so badly that you will run away, or maybe I shall run away myself and leave you sitting here an *aguna* [*sic*]."[69] His speech reflects the range of possibilities he saw available to him, including the link between marital conflict and the husband's choice to make his wife an agunah. There was certainly a real option for either spouse to desert the other, and the husband raised the possibility of both. But here we must pay attention to one important fact. The husband describes his wife's running away as a result of the pain he will cause her, while for himself, absconding had a purpose: to make her an agunah. Both parties are aware that the husband's fleeing would sentence his wife to become an agunah, while a wife would abandon her husband only as a last resort. Tzerlin's initiative in writing to her uncle is a sign of her hope that her relatives would come to her aid if they knew of her situation. That is, living in proximity to extended family was seen as a source of support for a couple. At the same time, if one spouse lived far away from extended family while the other lived near relatives, it put the spouse living far away at a disadvantage.

It is not known if Tzerlin's uncle ever replied to her letter, or if she ever left her husband or if he acted on his threat to flee and make her an agunah, or if the matter was ultimately decided upon by some beit din. Tzerlin's fate remains a mystery.

MARITAL DISPUTES IN RABBINIC COURTS

Tzerlin's letter raises the question of whether she knew anything of the activity of the beit din and if she had a chance of getting relief there. This in turn leads to a broader question: How did the beit din act when such troubled marriages came before them? Did it allow the couple to separate if they wished, or did it raise objections? Can we discern gender bias in beit din rulings which could have influenced the decisions of the individuals in marital crisis? Were there aspects of the beit din's activities that may have caused either party to prefer approaching them for assistance or, alternatively, to refrain from doing so and turn to other solutions, such as absconding?

The incidents from responsa literature that have been shown here,[70] and likewise additional incidents of marital disputes that appear in this genre, do not allow us to form conclusions about the activity of the beit din or dayanim due to the methodological problems discussed in the introduction. However, from the mid-eighteenth century onwards, we do have beit din records containing many descriptions of marital disputes, and these illuminate the workings of the beit din. Obtaining full answers to the previous questions would require systematic quantitative research that is beyond the scope of the current study. Nevertheless, an analysis of individual cases provides us with much information about the works of the beit din and may help in answering at least some of these questions. When we read beit din records, it is important to remember that, for the most part, the records do not contain complete protocols of all sessions or even full transcripts of everything said by the parties, witnesses, and judges. A beit din record usually includes the court's decision and a summary of the course of events that led the beit din to it. In many cases, the beit din's ruling also teaches us about the chain of events that preceded the beit din sessions. We must remember to exercise caution, since legal narratives are not straightforward descriptions of reality but, rather, the recorder's interpretation, and they reflect its rulings and presentation of events. It is precisely because of this that they provide us with an invaluable glimpse into the workings of the beit din.

NO PEACE WILL EVER COME OF DISPUTE: ROLES OF THE BEIT DIN IN DIVORCE SETTLEMENTS

Beit din records give the impression that once a couple resolved to divorce, the beit din raised no objection. This was the case of Mordechai son of Meir and Faygele daughter of Zanvil, whose dispute came before the beit din and lay leaders of Fürth on October 26, 1752.[71] It is not known how long the couple had been married when the dispute broke out, but we know that they had several children together. The beit din concluded "no peace would ever come of dispute," and the couple agreed to a financial settlement and divorce mediated by the beit din.[72] The property was divided between them, ensuring they and their children had sufficient living expenses and could pay off their shared debts to community organizations.[73] Interestingly, the beit din assumed that husband and wife would both wish to remarry in the near future. However, while the husband was required only to pay off his debts before entering into a new betrothal, the wife was ordered by temporary injunction to agree not to marry for ten years anyone of that same community. The background leading up to this step is not sufficiently set out in the court records, except for the remark "their quarrels were not of the normal kind . . . there is cause for concern on several counts."[74] The nature of these concerns is not elucidated.

Some fifty years later, Shlomo Zalman son of Eliyahu Segal and his wife Esther daughter of Moshe were divorced before the beit din of Kraków. The couple had one son. The reason for the divorce is set out in the beit din record for August 18, 1800: "The neighbors and everyone in our community knew that Shlomo Zalman and his wife Esther never had a single moment without quarrelling. Their shouting was heard day and night in Jews' Street and in all of Kraków."[75] Earlier intervention of the court and other mediators had had little effect. This time, they agreed on three arbitrators, who realized there was no hope of rapprochement.[76] Consequently, the beit din gave its approval for divorce. According to the divorce settlement, the entire cost of the proceedings would be defrayed by Esther; Shlomo did not have to pay anything at all. Their son, Shalom, would live with his father henceforth, while his mother would pay the boy's expenses—a weekly sum of two gold pieces—until he reached the age of fifteen. When the boy needed clothing and linen, both parents would share the expense equally.[77]

The ruling seems in the husband's favor, since it is the wife who has to bear all expenses of the get, as well as much of the expenditure for the maintenance of their son. The child was to live with his father. This impression is based on a twofold assumption, that women found it harder to earn a living and that mothers wanted their children to live with them. This assumption fails to take historical reality into account, as, indeed, the continuation of the document allows for a different interpretation. The court did not raise the possibility of the man's remarrying. Yet it is stated explicitly that the boy's mother, even if she remarried, would still be liable for the boy's maintenance—and if she fails to do so, her ex-husband may return their son to her care with no further obligation on his part.[78] This settlement seems surprising given that halakhah requires a father to support his children. Nor do the sources tell us whose initiative the settlement was or the financial standing of each parent. However, as we saw previously, remarriage entailed ensuring ongoing financial support for the children, and children could also impede entry into a new marriage or remain a bone of contention for the new couple. It is therefore likely that it was in Esther's interest for the child's father to have custody while she herself provided child support. This arrangement would make it easier for her to remarry. The rest of the settlement supports this interpretation, stating that, should the mother fail in her obligations to her son, the father would be able to return the child to his mother. The father would then be exempt from any financial obligation to his son.

We see that the beit din authorized the granting of a divorce when both spouses wanted it. In at least some of these cases, the beit din even approved settlements that did not fit within the traditional halakhic parameters for divorce.

BEIT DIN AS MEDIATOR AND ARBITRATOR

When Avraham son of David Shohet of Altona left his wife, the court, on July 28, 1768, blamed parental interference: "Avraham son of David Shohet must cohabit with his wife, according to the law of Israel. His wife must swear not to visit her mother or have her mother visit her. We have duly warned her that breach of this vow means she will be divorced without receiving payment of her ketubah. Avraham too is forbidden to visit his father or have his father visit him. If Avraham refuses to cohabit with his wife, he must pay her maintenance as determined by the beit din."[79]

The records do not state which spouse appealed to the court to help restore equilibrium in their home. Given that the husband might refuse to live with his wife, it seems likely that it was the wife who petitioned the court to bring him back to live with her. Be that as it may, the records state that the woman agreed to swear not to visit her mother or have her mother visit her on pain of losing her ketubah. Although the husband also had to undertake not to visit his father or have his father visit him, no penalty was imposed for breach of the commitment. Was it common practice for the court to distance one spouse from the original family? Were they less lenient with women, perhaps due to some ideal of married life?

The next case is also instructive with respect to views on a couple's proximity to their respective parents, especially in times of marital crisis. Strained domestic relations are reported in court records for the case of Bonfit son of Ber Frankfurt and his wife Dusil daughter of Yaakov son of Itzik.[80] Due to endless quarrelling, they appeared twice before the beit din in Altona between January and April 1769. After hearing their lengthy complaints and acrimonious accusations, the beit din, in order to restore peace in the home, told Bonfit to rent living quarters in Altona and live there with his wife:

> The rent would be paid by his wife's father, the aforementioned Yaakov. The living quarters should be in the house of an honest man who is not a member of Bonfit's or his wife's family. If no such apartment is available, he is to rent one in a Jewish quarter. Bonfit shall live there with his wife until after she gives birth, that is, four weeks after the delivery. After that he had a choice: To return to his home in Hamburg with his wife—during this time the two of them would conduct themselves amicably, pleasantly and lovingly, without quarreling—let them behave as proper sons and daughters of Israel. Yet, if, God forbid, they start fighting again, the neighbors will find out who started it. That will be the basis for applying the letter of the law. Bonfit, should he not wish his father- and mother-in-law to visit, has the right to oppose a visit of theirs. The exception: when his wife is giving birth, or if something happens to her, her mother is permitted to come to her. Bonfit can demand that his wife not visit her father's house . . . all this has been reached by compromise and mutual consent.[81]

On January 26, 1769, the divorce settlement was reached.

The source of tension was overinvolvement of the wife's parents in the couple's life. The disagreement seems to have been over where they would live before the birth of their child. Dusil wanted to move nearer to her parents in Altona, while Bonfit preferred to stay in Hamburg. The court ruled that the couple would move to Altona for four full weeks following the birth. They would occupy living quarters not owned by a relative of either of them. If no such apartment was available, they would find accommodations in a Jewish neighborhood, to be paid for by the wife's father. At the end of this period the husband would be permitted to return to Hamburg, and his wife would be obligated to go with him.[82] But this was not the end of it. On Thursday, June 1, 1769, the beit din of Altona described the marital situation as follows: "We the undersigned beit din heard the case of Yaakov son of Itzik. He was shouting and making accusations against his son-in-law Bonfit for abusing his wife, the former's daughter. We heard testimony of the husband beating his wife violently. He quarrels and fights with her. He ignores previous court orders to live with his wife or pay her maintenance.... He was excommunicated in synagogue but does not care. The court warned Bonfit that if he failed to provide an itemized expenditure for his wife and son, the court would be forced to rule in his absence."[83]

The record goes on to specify necessary guarantees from his mother-in-law or brother-in-law proving compliance with the ruling. Otherwise, the community would impose further sanctions.

The original petition was apparently made jointly by husband and wife (or at least in their presence) with the intention of reaching an agreement. By contrast, the second session took place at the instigation of the wife's father, Yaakov. Yaakov levelled harsh accusations of domestic violence at his son-in-law. Apparently, Bonfit's quarreling and violence continued after the birth of their son. Bonfit flouted the court's first ruling on correct marital conduct; it seems that the court did not make much of an impression on him. He refused to pay his wife her maintenance, did not appear before the court as ordered, and did not provide an itemized expenditure for upkeep of his wife and son. Despite sanctions (excommunication in the synagogue), he did not mend his ways. Dusil's belongings, including clothes and jewelry, were transferred at some point to a third party—a lay leader of the community. This was common procedure when the court recognized a petition by one spouse for the protection of their share of joint property. Only when Bonfit failed to provide an itemized expenditure as ordered did the court instruct that same lay leader to transfer Dusil's belongings to her father. The latter had to name guarantors to ensure the return of the belongings if instructed to do so. At this point, Bonfit was granted a month's extension to appear opposite his father-in-law before the beit din. If he refused, he would be declared "rebellious," with all due consequences.

THE BEIT DIN'S APPROACH TOWARD THE INVOLVEMENT OF THIRD PARTIES IN MARITAL CONFLICT

The previous cases show that a couple's family or wider social circle could intervene in their marital affairs. This in itself may have caused marital tension. To resolve conflicts caused by the interference of parents or neighbors, it was sometimes necessary for yet another party to become involved: the beit din. We have found that when a quarreling couple came before the beit din, the dayanim took a stand on the desired closeness of the spouses to their respective parents and family. This result was usually to the wife's disadvantage. In the first case, sanctions applied only to the wife if she went to her mother or invited her mother to her house. In the second case, the husband could keep his wife away from her parents, against her will, four weeks after giving birth. Rather than being random, these decisions reflect longstanding policy in the rabbinic court of Altona. The following story furnishes further proof.[84] On December 6, 1796, the beit din of Altona dealt with a dispute between a husband and wife, Pais son of Meir of Elmshorn and Rachel daughter of Israel.[85] According to the court records, the husband regularly denied his wife access to her belongings, until finally she ran away to her parents. The court mediated a settlement: The husband would leave his wife's belongings in her permanent possession, and his wife, for her part, undertook to never travel from home without informing him first. If she violated the agreement, she stood to lose her ketubah. In addition the wife's mother was not allowed to take her daughter back home with her without the daughter's husband's knowledge.[86]

In the case of Bonfit and Dusil, the court called upon neighbors to report any quarrel of theirs and who started it. As noted, halakhah does not require as grounds for divorce the blame of one spouse. Why then did the court seek information about their quarrels? Was this common practice or an ad hoc measure? Let us look at several additional cases for a possible answer.

On October 13, 1795, the beit din of Altona held several sessions in the case of Wolf Hollender and his wife, Hannah. The court appointed several individuals to inquire into the affairs of the couple and find out which of them instigated their fights.[87]

The court resorted to even more drastic measures in the case of Zanvil and Miriam Berlin, as seen in the entry for August 16, 1795:[88] the couple would live together, with a chaperone.

We seem to be looking at an underlying policy rather than ad hoc measures, at least in the beit din of Altona. What factors led to this policy?

Similar to the harnessing of gossip for regulating the community, interference by neighbors in a couple's married life was not the fruit of idle curiosity or prurience. Rather, third-party involvement was the product of deliberate policy aimed at maintaining social order. Remember, in some places in Germany at that time, decrees encouraged people to inform on their neighbors.[89] It is worth stressing that in this way, the authorities exercised control over the individual, not only in the public sphere, but also in family life. In this regard, the beit din was following the contemporary norm in Jewish institutions and non-Jewish civil society.

THE BEIT DIN AND MARITAL VIOLENCE

Despite Dusil's plight, neither she nor anyone arguing on her behalf appealed to the beit din to force her husband to give her a get, given his violent behavior towards her, and the beit din did not encourage the couple to divorce, either. Was this approach typical? Other cases in beit din records shed light on this question. In the beit din of Kraków, on January 1, 1798, Hinde daughter of Raphael complained about her husband, Sender son of Yosef. The record reads: "She does not want to cohabit with her husband, since he does not behave properly with her. He spends her dowry money. He struck her several times for no fault of hers."[90] Sender, for his part, claimed that he had not spent as much of his wife's money as alleged. In any case, he added, he spent it because it was hard for him to make a living. The beit din records do not state whether the wife sought a get or whether the husband wanted her to come back to live with him. The court ruled that "a husband cannot be coerced into giving a get" and "his wife [may not be coerced] to cohabit with him." The court's decision: they would live apart until after the upcoming Passover; then, "let justice pierce the mountain" (i.e., the strict interpretation of the law would apply).[91]

Despite the husband's violence, the beit din did not urge the couple to divorce. However, it allowed the wife to move out in order to distance herself from further abuse. Her husband was not allowed to compel her to leave her familiar surroundings.

A separation was not always considered a good solution, even in cases of severe physical abuse. The beit din records of Fürth at the end of the second decade of the nineteenth century tell of Yosef son of Lazer Shohet, who beat his wife, Henne. The case came before the beit din on Monday, August 18, 1817:

> Concerning the quarrel of R. Yosef the son of R. Lazer Shohet and his wife Henne. After stating their mutual complaints, the parties

signed a compromise: They would follow whatever the court should decide. We heard from the wife that on the eve of the holy Sabbath, her husband beat her violently and inflicted injuries. He admitted this shamelessly, adding that his eldest son was to blame for provoking quarrels between him and his wife. We rule that R. Yosef is given the choice—if he behaves decently—to cohabit with her at home, on condition that he distance his eldest son, cause of the strife, from home, before bringing his wife back. He must undertake never to strike her again, for it is an abomination in Israel. And if he refuses this, he is liable for payment of a week's upkeep for her; and if he does not give her [the money], she may borrow money from others, for which he will be liable. If he refuses still, let him divorce her with a get according to Jewish law, and pay the amount of her ketubah and the additional amount of 600 gold pieces.[92]

The facts were undisputed. Yet the beit din, after raising several possible courses of action, left the choice in the husband's hands. If he were unwilling to accept any of the options proposed by the court, he would have to divorce his wife and pay her the ketubah plus the additional amount of 600 gold pieces.

We do not know if the husband mended his ways following the court's intervention. We do know that the couple did not divorce since, two years later, Henne, now Yosef's widow, was claiming her late husband's estate in court.[93]

It may be concluded from these cases that the beit din would denounce a violent husband but would not urge divorce. The court did not even always permit the battered woman to distance herself from her husband. Despite the fact that domestic violence is halakhically valid grounds for divorce, these rulings were not without legal precedent. Rabbi Moshe Isserles (Rema), one of the most influential halakhic authorities of sixteenth-century Ashkenazic Jewry, ruled that though a man who beats his wife is considered a sinner and must be compelled to divorce her, in some cases he may not be coerced to do so. This opinion concurs with that of Rabbi Binyamin Ze'ev of Arta (Greece and Italy, c. 1475–1545), author of *Responsa Binyamin Zeev*, who had written that in certain circumstances, a man may be justified in striking his wife.[94]

In the court documents I read for this book, I did not find cases in which a woman was accused of committing physical violence against her husband. But, in several cases, the wife was accused by her husband of "improper conduct." One such case was that of Hertz Hamel and his wife Rivkah, in the beit din of Offenbach, on November 23, 1749.[95] The court was satisfied that "Rabbi Hertz of Hamel's wife Rivkah behaved improperly towards him from the day they married, with shameless arrogance, needling him over money, and his and his family's honor. She would curse her husband roundly." The court was convinced that Hertz had to bring his sister to live with them, as his wife did not run the household properly, while his sister was a most capable woman. It seems that his wife petitioned the court for an injunction to have the sister-in-law leave their home. The court found Hertz's description of his wife credible. The court nevertheless, out of moral obligation (*lifnim mi-shurat ha-din; ex gratia*), instructed him to remove his sister from the marital home. If Rivkah started cursing him or his parents again, Hertz could make her leave home for four weeks. During this time, he would pay her maintenance. Afterwards, she would return to her husband's house, and they would live together as man and wife. Should she once again curse him or his parents, she would be duly punished, as before. The court ruled, moreover, that Hertz was forbidden to go eat at his sister's. He had to take his meals with his wife: "Whatever he eats, she eats."[96]

Hertz reportedly beat his wife on several occasions. The court ordered him to stop and further ruled that Rivkah's behavior did not constitute grounds for divorcing her without payment of her ketubah. Should she claim that she can no longer bear his continued beatings, he would have to divorce her and pay the ketubah amount of 400 gold pieces. It appears that Rivkah was the spouse who petitioned the court for relief, though this is not stated explicitly. It seems too that at some point in the litigation, Hertz sought to divorce his wife without paying her ketubah. The court, while recognizing that Rivkah had behaved improperly, neither urged Hertz to divorce her nor made it easy for him to do so. It is clear that the court used its authority to impose a "balance of fear" in the home. The threat hanging over Hertz—if he beat her, he had to pay the full amount of her ketubah—was no doubt a strong deterrent working in Rivkah's favor. In any case, the description of the court's ruling makes it difficult to assess which of the spouses it favored.

DIVORCE IMPOSED BY THE BEIT DIN

On Thursday, December 28, 1797, the beit din of Kraków signed a decision on the foundering marriage of Yosef son of Zvi Hirsch and Friedl daughter of Yitzhak. The honorifics of the respective fathers imply that both families were of the social elite. The wife sought a divorce on grounds of revulsion from physical contact with her husband (*ma'is alai*). The husband wanted them to stay together. The court cited the principle that the husband could not be coerced into divorcing his wife, nor the wife coerced to live with her husband against her will.[97] Yet the court divided their joint property: Friedl got her clothes and jewelry, but she was forbidden to sell them. Yosef got the remaining property, to dispose of as he liked.[98] Yosef was not ordered to pay maintenance for the time they were not cohabiting. Yet the court took precautions to prevent Friedl's becoming an agunah: Yosef had to report to the head of the beit din if he left the district. If he wanted to leave for good, he would have to report every three months.[99]

Friedl is an example of a woman who became an agunah because her husband refused to divorce her in accordance with Jewish law. The details are instructive: (1) Despite Friedl's halakhically valid grounds for divorce, the court did not try to convince the husband to divorce her. (2) The court did nothing to alleviate Friedl's financial situation; she did not receive the maintenance to which she was entitled for the period when they lived separately. And (3) although the court required the husband to report his whereabouts in writing every three months if he left town, it is doubtful whether this was enforceable. The very fact that the beit din raised the possibility of his leaving town shows that this was a realistic option. In sum, Friedl was denied freedom and financial independence, while her husband was not subjected to any travel or financial restrictions.

Familiarity with legal procedures pertaining to one's own case is again seen to be significant. Friedl might have known about the specific grounds for divorce of physical revulsion (*ma'is alai*), conceivably through her family circle of learned rabbis. It is not known if she used that actual expression or if the court scribe cast her description in accepted halakhic terms.

Another case does suggest that parties studied legal terminology in order to better plead their case in court. For several months in the course of 1797, the beit din of Warburg heard a dispute between Shmuel son of Yaakov, the shamash, and his wife.[100] Her husband left home, and she was now claiming support and money to buy shoes. Shmuel, in order to avoid payment, requested that the court send a bailiff to their home to carry out an inventory. This having been duly executed, it was found that the food in the house was barely sufficient for his wife to live on until the upcoming Passover festival. Shmuel undertook to supply matzah, meat, utensils, and firewood in anticipation of the festival. He also sent her half a reichstaler to buy shoes. In return he demanded an injunction against his wife's selling any possessions that were in the house before the court reached its decision. Shortly before Passover, the court set a date for the hearing in the presence of both parties: April 27, 1797. The two duly showed up in court and were questioned. The following agreement was reached: (1) The husband would pay the wife a weekly allowance for as long as they lived separately, on his account.[101] (2) If she could no longer shelter in community facilities, he would pay the annual sum of one ducat towards her rent elsewhere.[102] (3) She was forbidden to sell any joint property without his consent. And (4) should she do so, the income would be deducted from her maintenance monies.[103]

The wife's financial situation worsened as a result of the marital conflict, and she was forced to live temporarily in a community facility. The settlement makes clear her long-term financial dependence on her husband, but it is not recorded if either of them considered this a disadvantage.

From Shmuel's request the next day that certain details be included in the court record, we learn of the wife's deviousness:[104]

> Yesterday in court, the husband asked [his wife]: "Why did you impugn my reputation by accusing me of having sexual relations with you before we were married?"
> She answered: "You said bad things about me, too."
> The husband said: "The things I said about you were true; the things you said about me were lies."
> The wife replied: "A certain woman whose name I cannot disclose urged me to go to [two men] and malign my husband. They would believe me. This would be to my advantage."

The court scribe noted that the quoted exchange would not be included in the official protocol without the wife's consent.[105]

The court then questioned the wife. She was not entirely innocent: Aided and counseled by a certain woman, whose name she refused to divulge, she fabricated the story of her husband's having sexual relations with her before their wedding. The intention was to blacken his name in the hope of gaining an advantage. It is likely that parties in other cases also consulted others and received advice about legal procedures and strategies to improve their legal position.

MARITAL CONFLICT IN NON-JEWISH COURTS

Obviously, non-Jewish courts handled cases of marital conflict as well. Scholars have suggested that in the last third of the eighteenth century, from which time we have beit din records, Jews increasingly litigated in non-Jewish courts to resolve conflicts, including family affairs. This raises the following questions: Which spouse enjoyed the advantage in a non-Jewish court? Did these courts operate according to different principles from those guiding Jewish courts? We do not have, as yet, a systematic comparison of different religious courts. However, isolated studies on local courts can point to some of their characteristics.[106]

In the area under discussion, marriage and divorce were handled by ecclesiastical courts, while civil courts dealt with crime and financial disputes over movable property or real estate.[107] However, some overlap ensued due to multiple jurisdictions and political change.[108]

David Frick has shown that divorce was a viable option in Vilnius in the seventeenth century.[109] Maria Bogucka is of the opinion that while the authorities frequently forced women to live with a violent husband,[110] from the late seventeenth century onwards, more and more women in Poland rebelled by deserting their husbands, especially poor women without joint property.

Sheilagh Ogilvie, studying marital crisis in German-speaking regions, looked at courts of law in the Black Forest region in Wurttemberg in 1646–1800. She examined 313 such cases and found that (1) about one-third of the couples whose claims made it to court separated before the hearing; (2) women initiated separation more than men; (3) in one-fourth of the cases, the wife blamed the husband for their financial difficulties, whereas in 9 percent of cases, the husband blamed the wife for these same difficulties; (4) a recurring factor was tension between one spouse and family members; (5) other frequent factors included verbal abuse by the husband and sexual problems of one spouse; 45 percent mentioned physical abuse by the husband, and 8 percent by the wife, nearly always as a reaction to the husband's initial violence.[111]

According to Ogilvie, when a woman appealed to the court, her situation did not usually improve as a result. In fact, it worsened. Financial decisions tended against women—sometimes they were even instructed to return property they had previously owned. The courts usually ordered the wife to obey her husband, "for her own benefit," even as they reprimanded the husband or ruled against him. Courts were lenient with wifebeaters, while wives who left home due to a violent husband were usually forced to return. Ogilvie's findings, along with those of others, show that in many areas in Germany, violence of a husband towards his wife was tolerated as long as he did not inflict visible injury. In some cases, wives were even beaten to death and their husbands left unpunished. In this period, women could not depend on getting relief in court.[112]

In conclusion, it is doubtful whether Jewish or non-Jewish women could expect any advantage in petitioning a civil court, at least for much of the relevant period. This doesn't mean that Jewish women never petitioned civil courts or that on occasion this may not have been to their advantage; however, it seems that they usually did not have reason to do so. Men, on the other hand, might have enjoyed an advantage in civil court, especially men who were in disfavor with the Jewish community or those of low social status.

This overview of available options for a spouse in marital conflict provides primarily a possible understanding of the basis for a husband's choice to abandon his wife, leaving her an agunah. We have found that, at least according to halakhah, such a choice may have offered a man an easy way out of marital crisis—a path he could pursue to avoid shame and financial loss. And, indeed, the sources do contain cases of men who chose this option: they absconded, leaving an agunah behind.

11 : "CONCERNING THE AGUNAH WHOSE HUSBAND LEFT FOR DISTANT PARTS"[1]

In his *Shirei Yehudah*, printed in Amsterdam in 1697, Yehudah Leib Minden (Zelechow, 1630–Altona, 1711)[2] implored his readers to hire only cantors and teachers (*melamdim*) who would bring their wives with them to live in the community:

> Some communities with financial means hire teachers and especially cantors who are unaccompanied by their wives. In this the communities are acting wrongly in the eyes of God—they shall be held accountable. They are the cause of so much trouble, so many temptations—it cannot even be put down on paper. Those men lead others astray. With a wife in a distant land, they conduct themselves here as bachelors. As our sages taught, "He who is without a wife is without Torah." They cannot study properly for worry over wife and children they left behind in distant lands. Like agunot and straw widows, they count the *omer* every day.[3] The verse of doom has come to pass: "In the morning you shall say, 'If only it were evening!' and in the evening you shall say, 'If only it were morning!'"[4] All this brings no end of terrible trouble and worry of the worst kind. For our many sins, we see with our own eyes how many of these depraved sinful teachers fall into evil ways. They desert their wives, abandon them, then send a get—many even marry again without bothering to divorce at all! Such a man simply abandons a loyal wife forever.

Minden goes on to say that twice a year, in Nissan and Tishrei, emissaries seek out these men in an effort to make them go back to their wives. He concludes by repeating his plea: hire only teachers and cantors who are accompanied by their wives.[5]

Minden, himself a cantor and poet, had travelled among Jewish communities before settling in Altona. He witnessed teachers and cantors straying from Jewish values.[6] Minden's reproach was directed less at the "sacred vessels"—the hired teachers and cantors working under punishing conditions—and mainly at community organizations, which he held responsible for the difficult work conditions. The hired educators and cantors had to work far from home, counting the days like agunot. Inevitably, this led to widespread infidelity and divorce.

Abandoned wives, men remarrying without divorcing, long-distance divorce—were these really so prevalent among teachers and cantors? Did the situation necessitate reform of hiring policy in Jewish communities? Did communities actually send emissaries to seek out missing husbands?

On November 3, 1869, Eliezer Lipman Silberman, editor of the Hebrew weekly *Hamagid* (published in Lyck [Ełk], eastern Prussia, though most of its readers were in the Russian Empire), complained that in the decade since he had first started printing personal notices by agunot looking for their missing husbands, the paper had been inundated with such appeals. The notices came from all over the Ashkenazic world, some seeking husbands who had gone missing many years earlier.[7]

Did the same trend continue during the nearly two hundred years separating the two writers? It was a time of profound social and intellectual change that reshaped Ashkenazic Jewry.[8] In early modern Europe, it was quite common for a man to leave his wife and children, so much so that in Germany it was "a plague."[9] Very little is known of the extent of this phenomenon in Jewish society, nor do we have sufficient data to assess the number of abandoned wives.[10] However, responsa literature and other sources do indicate that Jewish society was not free of this behavior. In cases of a husband's prolonged absence, most non-Jewish legal systems allowed (at least theoretically) dissolution of the marriage by a third party (court or civil official).[11] By contrast, in Jewish law, an abandoned wife cannot extricate herself from her predicament unless her husband willingly delivers a valid get or unless there is valid evidence of her husband's death. In what follows, we first consider the abandoning men: the social background, motives, and practical implications of their actions. Next, we turn to the women: the implications for them and the means available for dealing with the situation.

THE WANDERING JEW

"An agunah whose husband left her for distant parts" is one of the terms used in rabbinic literature to refer to an abandoned wife.[12] As has been discussed, travel, drifting from place to place, was a regular part of life for Jews throughout this period.[13] This raises the question: Were there criteria that determined the maximal length of time considered legitimate for travel? A wife finding herself alone for many years did not necessarily consider herself abandoned. Labelling a woman an agunah when her husband was away on a prolonged trip often resulted from her own self-perception. As long as she regarded her husband's absence as reasonable and did not seek to dissolve her marriage, she was considered a married woman for all intents and purposes. Once she sought to dissolve the marriage due to his absence, she was defined as an agunah. For certain groups of men, prolonged travel was a legitimate lifestyle; a survey of these groups can help us understand the women's position.

MERCHANTS

Many Jews were involved in commerce of all kinds in this period. This was due partly to restrictions on Jews' joining guilds of artisans and craftsmen and partly to increased use of promissory notes (*membrana*) in Poland and Germany.[14] A merchant would regularly attend trade fairs held in cities in Germany and Poland or travel further afield, to Holland, Russia, Denmark, Italy, France, England, and even India.[15] Merchants could be away for a few days at a time or several years. Rabbi David Oppenheim deals with the case of a merchant who travelled regularly on business for three or four months at a stretch, until the one time that he disappeared and never returned.[16] Rabbi Jacob Emden travelled extensively himself for many years, leaving his wife and children behind. He writes of Mordechai Hamburger, who traveled to India and remained there ten years, leaving behind a pregnant wife and nine children.[17] He returned eventually; we know nothing of the circumstances of his wife's life during his absence.

Other sources do afford a glimpse into the wife's experience during her husband's absence. Glikl frankly acknowledges that she did not like her husband traveling to trade fairs, because of the danger involved:[18] "and I certainly would have preferred arranging it so that my husband, of blessed memory, could stay at home."[19] Her husband continued to travel despite her anxiety, and she acknowledged that his trips were necessary. Rabbi Emden's wife preferred to stay at her father's house while her husband travelled to Lemberg in the summer of 1718, where he remained for nearly a year, though before departing, he asked her to join him.[20] A prayer of "supplication" for women in Yiddish (published in Offenbach, 1778) was intended for "the wife whose husband is away from home."[21] The prayer makes it clear that a wife whose husband was travelling had good reason to worry and pray for his safe return.[22] In fact, responsa literature contains many cases of women who became agunot when their merchant husbands went missing on a business trip. Some died abroad (killed or murdered) or fell ill and died.[23] Others chose to disappear and start anew somewhere else. Rabbi Yehudah Leib of Pfersee (1645–1705) deals with the following case: A few months after marrying a girl of fifteen, the husband went travelling among the villages to do business and disappeared. At first it was thought he had been killed, but it turned out that he had run off to a distant place.[24]

TEACHERS AND STUDENTS

Teaching and studying Torah in a distant yeshiva also necessitated prolonged absence from home.[25] What is the maximum permissible length of time for a Torah scholar to absent himself from home? Rabbinic literature through the ages has grappled with this question. Stories in the Talmud exemplify the heavy price exacted by studying Torah away from home.[26]

In Ashkenaz in this period, it was customary to hire teachers (melamdim) from distant places. For instance, many German-speaking communities would hire teachers from Poland and Lithuania.[27] Community regulations give the varying length of time a Torah scholar could be away from home: In 1623 the Council of the Land of Lithuania limited to two years the term of service for a Torah teacher, or anyone coming from another country to work in their communities. After two years, the man was required to furnish proof that his wife and her relatives had given permission for him to prolong his absence. Without this proof, he was subject to expulsion from the country. If he did not comply, he was liable for a large fine and excommunication in all Jewish communities of Lithuania and Russia. Even before the two years were up, the beit din had the authority to expel the man immediately.[28]

A similar regulation was passed in the community of Fürth in Germany on December 22, 1773. The background was apparently communal finances and restrictions on living permits. For a married man with children who came to the community to teach children or to study Torah, if his home was at a distance of up to eight furlongs (about thirty kilometers) from Fürth, he had to return home every six months, and if his home was further away, he could reside in Fürth for a period not exceeding three consecutive years.[29] However, cases discussed in responsa and other sources show that not all Jewish communities were as scrupulous about preventing teachers from being absent from their homes for lengthy periods.[30]

Another source explicitly linked the prolonged absence from home of married Torah teachers and students to their marital relations. Community leadership naturally wanted to keep families together. Rabbi Tzvi Hirsch Kaidanover, in his ethical work *Kav hayashar*, writes of "men who leave home and betray their wives, become teachers, then get into all kinds of dubious business deals to make money. And they certainly sin with regard to spilled seed. When they finally start out on the trip home, they are waylaid by highwaymen or robbers. And those men do not know that out of each drop of their wasted semen, one demon is created, and those demons appear in the form of robbers and steal all the man's money."[31]

The fact that accepting a teaching position could provide an escape route for men trying to leave home is seen in the case of Salomon Maimon (Lithuania, ~1753–Silesia, 1800), who abandoned his wife. Maimon claimed in his memoir that his father had betrothed him to the daughter of a woman who treated him cruelly. Tensions ran high between the young bridegroom and his mother-in-law. He reported that he was forced to leave home and find a position as teacher, returning home only for major festivals (more on Maimon in this chapter, under "Maskilim").[32]

Torah teachers also regularly took positions far from home, and responsa literature mentions several wives of Torah teachers who became agunot.[33] Married men would also travel to study Torah at distant yeshivot, leaving their families behind.[34] In 1756, Rabbi Yedidyah Tiah Weil (Wotitz/Votice, Bohemia) composed a responsum dealing with a student of his who vowed to travel to a distant yeshiva for three years: "And now his poor wife is weeping and wailing; she has no money to live on for herself and her daughter. He tells her that he has lands—she should sell them to live on, adding that his father-in-law promised him allowance for food for another two years. To which she replies that there is a lien on the land in her name as part of her marriage contract; her father declared bankruptcy because of it."[35]

Taken aback by his wife's reaction, the Torah student asked his rabbi if it was permissible to renege on his vow and cancel the study trip. Weil ruled that he could do so if, and only if, he had exhausted every other possible means of getting his father-in-law to support his wife and daughter during his absence. Only then would he be released from his vow. And even then, only on the condition that two other rabbis affirm Weil's opinion.

THE MILITARY

Jews who served in regional armies—chiefly as suppliers, sometimes as military personnel—were away from home for long stretches at a time.[36] In the seventeenth century it was still common for family members to accompany a soldier on his postings,[37] but rabbinic sources document cases of Jewish men in the military who left their wives behind. Such a case occasioned this responsum (undated) by Rabbi Menahem Mendel Krochmal:

> The lament of a young woman reached my ears. She married a bachelor. After the wedding, he went off with the army to a distant land, to supply provisions, and tarried there for five long years. She was forced to seek him out in foreign parts. When she found him, she wanted him to stay with her and travel no more—or divorce her. For she was sick with worry lest her husband be killed in war or die somewhere without witnesses, and she would remain an agunah forevermore. But the husband does not want to divorce her, for she was the wife of his youth and he found nothing wrong with her. However, he also did not want to stay home with her, for he was eager to go off to war and get rich, then return to his country and home, to live there with his wife. To prevent iggun, he is willing to do what is needed according to the rabbis, so that if he returns home within two years, he will be returning to his wife. This woman appeared before me in great distress, lamenting and weeping, seeking the authority of a beit din to grant her a remedy.[38]

This woman lived without her husband for five years, until at last she was forced to search for him. We have no information about the conditions of this woman's life during her wanderings in search of her husband. According to Krochmal, providence led her to her husband—which suggests he thought finding him was no easy task. As we will see, this assumption was justified. A mid-eighteenth-century letter-writing manual contains a model letter requesting financial aid written on behalf of a woman whose husband was attached to the military. The woman's fate is described as follows: "After much beseeching and imploring, the writer of this letter has acquiesced to write on the behalf of the poor woman, bereft and alone, mother of three small children. She was forced to divorce because her husband went off to war at the urging of his no-good companions. Before he left, she had to accept a divorce from him, lest he be killed and make her an agunah. The divorce cost her all she had, left her penniless with small children to feed."

The letter concludes with exhortations to fellow Jews to extend financial aid to this woman.[39]

How did such women, whose husbands roamed with armed forces, feel?

The abandoned wife in Krochmal's responsum did not perceive her situation as sufficient grounds for divorce, despite having been abandoned for five years. When she finally tracked down her husband, she asked that he stop travelling or grant her a divorce, because she feared becoming an agunah. He refused, claiming that if he left the military, he could not earn a living. At the beit din, he asked to be allowed to continue his travels with the army for two more years without divorcing his wife. At the end of two years, he promised, he would return home to her.

This case demonstrates how the halakhic category of iggun served the husband's interests, acting as a chastity belt,[40] allowing a Jewish husband to roam far and wide, confident in the knowledge that his wife was chained to their marriage. This arrangement was even more rigid in premodern times given the absence of contraceptives and the control exercised over female sexuality. A married woman who had a liaison with another man while her husband was away risked disastrous social and halakhic consequences. In these circumstances, the woman preferred a divorce. But halakhically it was the husband who decided whether to divorce—or to leave his wife an agunah forever. In this case, the husband's will took precedence over his wife's.

Krochmal's response was a maneuver designed to prevent lengthy iggun: the husband could divorce his wife before leaving on his next tour of duty. The couple would undertake before the beit din to marry each other a second time if the husband returned home within two years. To this effect, they made a solemn vow, on pain of excommunication, and also had to put up securities. This solution was not new: The Talmud tells of King David's warriors divorcing their wives before going off to battle.[41] Based on this opinion, three methods were developed to prevent iggun for a soldier's wife.[42] First, prior to leaving for war, the husband delivers a get to his wife, effective retroactively, in case he is killed in battle.[43] Second, the get comes into effect if the husband does not return from war for any other reason, such as being taken prisoner. Third, the husband gives his wife an unconditional get before he goes off to war; this way there was no danger whatsoever of the wife becoming an agunah.

The method of the unconditional get was enacted in the thirteenth century by the Tosafist Rabbi Yehiel of Paris.[44] It was designed not for men going off to war but for the critically ill. Cognizant of the halakhic complications involved in conditional divorce, Rabbi Yehiel ruled that a childless, deathly ill man could divorce his wife. That way, she would not have to undergo levirate marriage (yibum) or its alternative ceremony (halitzah). But since this divorce did not result from either side's wanting to get divorced but, rather, to prevent the wife from becoming an agunah, Yehiel required the divorcing couple, on pain of excommunication, to remarry each other should the husband recover from his illness.[45] Rabbi Moshe Isserles (RMA/Rama) cites this arrangement in his gloss on *Shulhan arukh* (under "some say," which typically denotes a minority opinion). Based on this, at least until the early seventeenth century, some communities allowed such divorces when the husband was critically ill. After the "Vienna affair,"[46] Meir ben Gedalyah (Maharam) of Lublin, one of the most prominent halakhic authorities of Poland, ruled with five other decisors that this type of get was henceforth invalid. A different opinion was held by Rabbi Joshua Falk Hacohen and sixteen other decisors. Krochmal was familiar with the opinion of the Maharam of Lublin and dealt with it in the context of his responsa. Although, Krochmal said, this solution should not be applied if a husband set out on a long journey for leisure,[47] its use was justified when, as in this case, there was real danger of iggun. This ruling was upheld by the head of the rabbinic court of Vienna and apparently by other rabbis as well. In the specific case in question, the husband did divorce his wife before setting out on his journey. When he failed to return after four years, she remarried, on the strength of the get he had given her before he left.

There were, in fact, men who divorced their wives before going away with the military.[48] In some places, this solution was also utilized by men setting out on a long journey for other reasons. The Kraków beit din records show that in the late eighteenth century, the beit din headed by Rabbi Yitzhak Halevi of Lvov (i.e., Lemberg, d. 1799) affirmed several divorce agreements that applied the enactment of Rabbi Yehiel of Paris to cases of men who left for long journeys. For instance, on the divorcing couple Feivel son of Aaron and Raizele daughter of Zvi Hirsch, he states: "If he returns within six years, they will marry each other again. If not, she is free to marry another. But if in the allotted time, this divorcée marries another man, she must pay a fine of thirty red coins [currency]. In no way does the fine cancel excommunication."[49]

The six known cases in the Kraków beit din record book show that a man could set out on a journey ensuring that his wife would not become an agunah, then resume his married life upon his return.[50] Despite this halakhic precedent, not all men who set out to war utilized this method. Responsa literature documents several cases of women who became agunot after their husbands were deployed with the military in distant places, either voluntarily or against their will.[51]

As a rule, Jews in Poland did not often serve in combat roles in the seventeenth and eighteenth centuries. Jewish sources mention the military mainly in connection with Jews who funded military expenditures through a tax or as suppliers. A few Jews did take active parts in military campaigns, mainly protecting areas where they lived. The picture changes in the late eighteenth century, when the Jews of Galicia had to supply a quota of soldiers to the army shortly after the region was annexed by the Austrian Empire in 1788. As of 1827, the Russian army started conscripting Jews.[52] Court Jews in the principalities of Germany were the main suppliers to local armies in the seventeenth and early eighteenth centuries.[53] German Jews served in the Prussian and Napoleonic armies mainly from the first decade of the nineteenth century.[54] In the early part of the relevant period, a small number of women became agunot due to a husband serving in the military of his own free will.[55] In the latter part of the period, the number of agunot increased as a result of compulsory military service.[56]

THE ITINERANT POOR

In his *Unwanted Child*, a study of abandoned children in Germany in the early modern age, Joel Harrington found that poverty was a leading factor for men abandoning their wives and children.[57] Maria Bogucka reached a similar conclusion with respect to Poland and the region.[58] Poverty was widespread in Jewish society in the Ashkenazic world; Jewish society, too, had to deal with impecunious absconding men,[59] some of whom had families.[60] Itinerant Jewish beggars were a common sight. Some of them had a permit to beg (*Bettelbrief*), issued by Jewish community leaders.[61] The permit usually stated where the beggar resided and why he had to leave his home. These permits, as well as cases recorded in responsa, show that beggars drifted great distances without their wives. A responsum by Krochmal dated 1656 addresses the case of a man from Lvov (Lemberg) who fled to Amsterdam because of money trouble. After marrying there, he returned sometime later, without his wife, wanting to divorce her.[62] Rabbi Meir Eisenstadt dealt in 1722 with a case of a man seeking refuge in a different community, again because of money trouble. He stayed away for a long time, leaving his wife an agunah.[63] An anonymous letter sent in November 1733 to Aharon Segal of Worms requests details concerning a man who absconded after falling into debt, leaving his wife penniless. He never returned home and died in the town of Westhofen.[64] Poverty was therefore one of the reasons husbands abandoned wives in Jewish society as well, as records show a connection between itinerant beggars and agunot.

In his work about itinerant beggars in eighteenth-century Germany, Otto Ulbricht uses the term "wandering newspapers."[65] In their wanderings, he says, these men consciously collected bits of invaluable information and anecdotes to spread wherever they went. Krochmal tells of an itinerant beggar who was of assistance in freeing an agunah. As he describes, an itinerant beggar was the emissary for delivering a get in Ludomir. The beggar was also charged with investigating rumors of the death of the brother-in-law designated to perform halitzah in Jaroslav.[66] At the fair, he found witnesses who testified before a beit din that the brother-in-law was dead. Thanks to this beggar, the agunah was freed.[67]

The beggar in the story had a twofold function: He was made a halakhic agent for delivery of a get to a woman whose husband had left for distant parts and wanted to divorce her—and, in addition, he was asked by Krochmal and his beit din to assist them in finding witnesses to the death of the brother-in-law of a different woman, who could then be freed from her agunah status. The common practice of appointing a beggar as emissary facilitated the search for missing persons, providing at the same time a source of income for these destitute men.[68] Jews were keenly aware of the ramifications of iggun; these spurred itinerant beggars to collect information about missing husbands for families eagerly awaiting news of their loved ones.

Along with the genuine information beggars passed on in a sincere effort to help, the less scrupulous could not resist the temptation to exploit the expectant families financially. In other cases, beggars supplied incorrect information, whether innocently or maliciously. Rabbi Haim Hacohen Rappaport (d. Lvov, 1771)[69] was asked by someone in the city of Glogow about an agunah called Beyle, whose husband had deserted her. Sometime later, reports reached her of his death. A poor man testified that Beyle's husband was already married when he had married her. The beggar had remonstrated with Beyle's husband for committing polygamy, at which the husband had bribed him to keep silent.[70] Rabbi Yehezkel Landau deals with the case of an itinerant "guest" who claimed to have information about a man who had gone missing many years earlier but refused to divulge the details before receiving payment.[71] Rabbi Moshe Sofer-Schreiber, the Hatam Sofer (Frankfurt, 1762–Pressburg [Bratislava], 1839),[72] dealt with an agunah whose husband was conscripted into the army. He was gone some thirty years. At some point a poor man came to town with partial information about the missing man, which set into motion a series of complications in the process of freeing the agunah.[73]

IMPOSTERS AND SCOUNDRELS

Ulbricht's study of survival strategies of itinerant beggars found that imposters were everywhere.[74] Jewish sources suggest a link between impersonating another and iggun. Establishing a person's true identity was extremely difficult, as was confirming information obtained from afar, and women became victims of married swindlers who passed themselves off as unmarried. Krochmal tells of an agunah whose husband betrayed her a month or two after the wedding. He left her, taking with him all his possessions and hers, too. For four years, she heard nothing from him. Then she found out he had married another woman in Poland—violating Rabbenu Gershom's ban on polygamy.[75] When the man was identified a few years later by someone visiting Poland, he relented and charged the visitor with delivering a get to his first wife, but the get contained errors and was ultimately pronounced invalid, leaving the woman an agunah. Many such stories appear in responsa literature and archival materials. Rabbi Aryeh Leibush Lifshitz (Jaroslav, 1767–Brzesko, 1846)[76] records a case of a woman from the community of Kalbisow whose husband left her an agunah for eight years.[77] During this time, he came to another community, likely Kłaj,[78] where he presented himself as a bachelor and married again.[79]

TWO LETTERS

Two letters from the estate of Rabbi Shmuel Steg of Warburg reveal how the widow Frieda daughter of Michl became an agunah. The year was 1792. The first letter was sent to rabbi Steg by a friend of the agunah to whom she had appealed for assistance in obtaining a get. The second letter was written by Frieda herself. This is another of the rare cases where we have two accounts of an agunah's story, one from a man's point of view, the other from a woman's. The second letter is also unique as a rare first-person account by an agunah. The two letters were first published in the Hebrew version of this book.[80] Readers may perhaps feel some of the excitement I felt when I found these rare testimonies after long months of trying to reconstruct the lives of women who lived centuries ago.

FIRST LETTER

The letter from Yaakov son of Mordechai Segal to Rabbi Shmuel Steg,[81] dated September 30, 1792, opens with customary salutations to a learned rabbi, copious titles and honorifics, and protestations of the writer's lack of learning. Yaakov introduces himself as an acquaintance of the agunah Frieda. Frieda asked him if he knew anything of her husband, who had left her six years previously and disappeared without a trace. Itzik Lansburg was originally from Prussia. She gave his last known whereabouts as Bomst (Babimost) in Poland, near Silesia.[82] After six years, she had received no more letters. She had been miserable ever since he left. Recently she heard a rumor that he was studying in Hannover. Yaakov felt obliged to tell the widow that he did, indeed, know this man. He had been a ritual slaughterer (*shohet*) in Barsinghausen, a village near Hannover. Meanwhile, he had left that place and was now living in the village of Leobendorf, teaching children. Yaakov ended his letter by asking the rabbi for assistance, and he enclosed her letter. It should be noted that according to Yaakov's description, Frieda's husband, Itzik Lansburg, had left "the wife of his youth," and Frieda herself lost all her happiness due to his desertion. This story is similar to those of other absconding husbands, but Frieda's own letter reveals some additional details, as we shall see in the next section.

SECOND LETTER

The agunah's own letter to Yaakov was sent from Frankfurt-an-der-Oder, dated September 3, 1792. She had seen a letter from Yaakov to his parents, saying he would like to help her. Apparently, the husband had told Yaakov that his wife was dead. Not only (she continues) did he spend all her money and sell her valuables and possessions, over 1,000 reichstaler; he also had 50 reichstaler belonging to her son from her first marriage, whose father had died. Itzik had vowed with a solemn oath to repay her whenever the son needed it for his own trade. "Two and a half years ago," she continues, "he came here demanding a divorce. I demanded my ketubah payment. It was clear he did not have the money to pay it. But now I see from your letter that he is a villain; he is saying 'I have no wife.' Now I want him to divorce me. As for my ketubah money — let him sign, with a solemn vow that he will repay it when he has the means. The same goes for the 50 reichstaler he owes me — to be duly paid as soon as possible." Frieda states that her letter is sent to her friend as a power of attorney and requests that he arrange the matter as soon as possible, warning that the husband might run away. She adds that she herself is poor and does not have the means to bear the expenses.

Frieda's letter reveals that she had been married before marrying Itzik Lonsburg and that she had a son from the previous marriage. She does not say why the first marriage ended, but at the time of the writing her first husband was no longer alive. It further emerges that her son stood to inherit a certain sum upon his coming of age. Frieda had owned property when she married Itzik, but he spent all her money, as well as her son's, and ended up penniless. At this point her husband left her, then reappeared wanting a divorce. Frieda refused, since in his desperate financial situation, he would never be able to pay the amount specified in her ketubah. The husband then absconded, leaving Frieda an agunah. For a long time, she heard nothing at all. It seems that as long as Frieda entertained hopes of her husband's finding the wherewithal to pay her ketubah, she preferred to stay married to him. Her attitude towards divorce changed only on learning from Yaakov that her husband was passing himself off as unmarried; on top of that, he was telling people that his wife was dead. It was then that she asked her acquaintance Yaakov to intercede on her behalf with Rabbi Steg to initiate the divorce proceedings. She also wanted her husband to confirm in writing that he would repay the monies she and her son were entitled to.

Frieda believed the rabbi had the authority to impose restrictions on Itzik's movements pending delivery of the get. Her acquaintance seems to have thought it wiser not to act hastily. Before writing to Rabbi Steg, Yaakov asked her, perhaps at the rabbi's suggestion, to go to the place where her husband was residing. Only when she refused, saying she could not afford the trip, did Yaakov write to Rabbi Steg for assistance, attaching her letter.

What sanctions did Frieda expect the rabbi to impose to prevent her husband from disappearing again? Tamar Salmon-Mack has claimed that absolute monarchies, such as Hungary, had mechanisms in place to track down missing husbands and arrest them.[83] Evidence (albeit from a later period) shows that government assistance for tracking down a missing person was sometimes forthcoming. However, it is more likely that any sanctions the rabbi could impose were confined to the Jewish community itself.

A comparison of the two letters shows that Yaakov did not use all the information in his possession. His selective narrative choices produced for Steg a commonplace picture of a man who was absent from his home for an extended period. Though Yaakov did mention Frieda's misery, he did not inform the rabbi of her husband's ill treatment of her—possibly because he knew the rabbi would be reading Frieda's own letter telling the rest of the story.

The sources do not reveal whether Steg took any steps upon receiving the letters, and there is no further evidence to show how things turned out. The rare documents testify to the importance of an agunah's ability to act on her own behalf and to the fact that rabbis often had to rule solely on the basis of letters, without meeting the agunot in person.

TWO AGUNOT, ONE HUSBAND

The following case was the cause of rabbinic controversy, as reported by Rabbi Yehezkel Landau, who decided it. At the center of our story are two agunot, seven hundred kilometers apart—one lived in Pinne (Pniewy),[84] in the province of Poznań, the other in Przemyśl, in the province of Lvov (Lemberg). Both women were abandoned wives. The woman from Pinne was an agunah for many years; we do not know how long the woman from Przemyśl was an agunah. Both women fell victim to swindlers. Landau's story is as follows:

 A man walks into a store owned by a bereft and forlorn agunah in Pinne, whose husband had left her many years earlier. The man engages her in conversation as if interested in buying something. He starts asking about her husband, and she says she has heard nothing from him. The man tells her that he has heard something about her husband. At this, the woman looks at his face more closely, and it seems to her that he is her husband. He departs, leaving her wondering. She consults the rabbi. They bring in the man, she recognizes him, and mentions distinctive physical marks on his body. And all the townspeople too recognize him as So-and-So the son of So-and-So from their town, her husband. At first the man denied everything, until they spoke with him and asked him to give her a get, and then he confessed that he was this woman's husband and divorced her. From there he left and presented himself as unmarried, and then he went to Przemyśl. There a certain agunah recognized him as her husband. And all the members of the local Jewish community recognized him as So-and-So the son of So-and-So from their town, the husband of the woman in Przemyśl. The man confessed that, in Pinne, he had divorced a woman who was not his wife, for money.

 And the rabbi of Przemyśl and his beit din wrote that the woman he divorced in Pinne should still be treated as a married woman because the man who had divorced her was definitely not her husband and was from the community of Przemyśl. And after that, members of the Jewish community of Pinne sent messengers to Przemyśl, and the messengers recognized the man as a native of their city, and husband of the woman in Pinne. Since then, both the Jews of Przemyśl and the Jews of Pinne have been claiming that he is from their city.[86]

 From Landau's responsum, it is not clear to which of the two women the man was actually married. Landau ruled that both were to be considered married women, meaning they could not remarry. Whoever he was, this consummate con man managed to engineer a win-win situation. Either way he got money: for giving information or for giving a divorce. No sooner had he divorced the woman of Pinne than she became his agunah, because the get was invalidated. If the woman of Przemyśl was his real wife, then he gave the woman in Pinne a get although she was never his wife. In Landau's account, the man received payment in return for delivering the get. We see how vulnerable agunot were to extortion by an imposter who could pass himself off as a long-lost husband. In this case, the woman from Pinne mentioned physical marks on his body, while members of both communities recognized him as their own. This just emphasizes the degree to which it was difficult to identify people who were absent for long periods of time.

The most famous case of an imposter passing himself off as a missing husband in non-Jewish society in the early modern period is the story of Martin Guerre. In sixteenth-century France, a man by the name of Arnaud du Tilh claimed he was Martin Guerre, the missing husband of Bertrande. This newcomer lived with her for several years until he was found out and eventually hanged. One of the judges published his case notes, and the case is now well-known in many languages.[87] The historian Natalie Zemon Davis, who conducted exhaustive research into the story, noted that in the absence of technological means for ascertaining a person's identity, people had to rely on memory. This made it easier for imposters, since those who remembered were prey to their own wishful thinking or to manipulation, whether in favor of the imposter or against him.[88]

BELATED IDENTIFICATION OR CUNNING DECEPTION?

It was a woman's credibility that was questioned in a case reported by Rabbi Shlomo Kluger in 1830.[89] The woman lived as a widow, claiming that her husband had died. She paid all the living expenses of her underage brother-in-law as she waited for him to grow up and perform the halitzah ceremony. One day, a man appeared in the town claiming to be her missing husband back from the wars. Tired of waiting, she agreed to a divorce. Kluger's halakhic discussion raises the suspicion that the woman, perhaps aided by an accomplice, had hired this very man to impersonate her husband as a way out of her predicament.[90] This scenario is no less plausible than that of the return of the long-lost husband. After all, both sides stood to gain from a divorce. This again demonstrates the great distress of women in these situations.

As to why she had not recognized him immediately, the woman explained that she had been married at a young age; many years had passed since then. We do not know if this is the truth, but we can certainly see why she thought the rabbi would accept this answer. Marriage at a tender age was at high risk of ending with the husband's deserting his wife and thus making her an agunah. Early marriage characterized the Jewish social elite but was common in other groups as well.[91] Young marriages are associated with marital difficulties; flight was one way of resolving them.[92] Yet the motley gallery of characters we have seen here is a reminder that men abdicated responsibility in all kinds of circumstances and ages.

CRIMINALS

That Jews were involved in criminal activity in this period is well-known,[93] but the connection of criminality to family life has hardly been explored. Jewish criminals did not differ much in their way of life from their fellow Jews. They were generally married men, many of them fathers, in typical Jewish occupations.[94] As opposed to their non-Jewish counterparts, notes Egmond, Jewish criminal gangs were made up of men only. Wives of criminals led normal lives, at least outwardly. The wife was not even always aware of her husband's activities, although the criminal's home was usually open to his cronies as a venue for conducting dubious business. Among the criminals were men who deserted their wives with the intention of returning home someday, while others disappeared for good. Emden tells of a man who joined a gang years after abandoning the wife he had married at a young age.[95] Criminal activity often created even worse circumstances than usual for agunot.

The agunah Blimele (see chapter 10), whose husband absconded after stealing, never saw him again.[96] Landau's language sets up the connection between the criminal act and absconding, leaving the wife as an agunah. Jewish criminals who left home and drifted relied on the geographical dispersion of Jewish communities; they used organized networks to glean information and took advantage of protection extended to them by communal institutions.[97] This organizational structure created a special risk of iggun for wives of Jewish criminals both because of the husband's prolonged absence and because he might be apprehended and jailed or executed far from home.[98] Under such circumstances, it was extremely difficult to obtain testimony about the fate of the men. As discussed in part 2 regarding husbands who were murdered while travelling, evidence from a non-Jewish court that a criminal had been executed was not admissible in a beit din. This, along with the halakhic difficulty of confirming death based on circumstantial evidence, raised many obstacles for a criminal's wife who wanted permission to remarry.

The case of Blimele and her husband, Yeshayah, is a good example of this. They were about to divorce when he stole something and absconded for fear of being caught. For the six years he was away, Blimele was an agunah. Then he was caught stealing again and sentenced to death by hanging. Three years later, Blimele requested permission to remarry based on the testimony of two witnesses. The first, Wolf, had been the couple's neighbor. He testified to being present at Yeshayah's hanging and said that two weeks later, he and several friends cut down the body from the gallows and gave the man a Jewish burial. The second witness, Avram son of Moshe Tiplitz, reported:

> There were four of us there with the abovementioned Wolf.[99] Then two more came. Together we travelled to Ritscheff during the persecutions. Then someone named Yeshayah stole something, and we were there when they took him and hanged him. My friend Wolf asked to speak with him, and then my friend told me that the man asked that his wife be told how he died. I watched as he was hanged. When he was dead, we left. He was tall, with a short yellow beard. I didn't know him; only my friend knew him. This was three or four days before [the fast of] 17 Tammuz, and three days after the hanging, we cut him down, four of us. We got 40 gold pieces in return for interceding with the authorities to give him a Jewish burial.[100]

In the quoted description, we find the typical stages of apprehending a criminal, sentencing, and execution. Public hangings of criminals were an ordinary event in some places in premodern Europe. The condemned man was usually granted an opportunity to speak before execution in order to enable him to confess.[101] This ostensibly made it easier to free the wife of a Jewish criminal from her marriage, compared to an agunah whose husband died in unknown circumstances. However, a closer look at the sources shows this is not always so. In the archive of the Mainz community, there is an affidavit of the local beit din, from March 10, 1808, concerning three Jews who had been apprehended in Wiesbaden and hanged six days beforehand.[102] The witnesses conversed with the condemned men to prepare them for repentance and death.[103] In that same conversation, they were told the men's names and their distinctive marks. One of the witnesses noted, "[the] hanged man, Moshe son of Nissan, told me the name of his town, but I've forgotten it. He said his wife's name was Keindele, now living in Galhausen.[104] She had a little girl called Haya Sarah, and the wife was pregnant when they parted. He asked me to report all this to the head of the beit din in the community of Galhausen, a relative of his wife's, so that if she gave birth to a boy, the son would be named Moshe, after his father."[105]

Information about the condemned man obtained prior to execution was invaluable for the agunah. Halakhically, if, prior to his death, a man says his name, his father's name, and the name of his town—these particulars are sufficient to confirm his identity. This is precisely what Moshe son of Nissan did before he was hanged. But the witness (known as "the Torah scholar") forgot the name of the town. This could derail the entire process of freeing the agunah, and yet, the witness did not bother to write down the details he heard from the condemned man. Moshe son of Nissan wanted the rabbi of his community notified of his death and requested that should his wife gave birth to a boy, his son would be named after him. This was confirmed by another witness. That he forgot the name of the town suggests that freeing the agunah was not a top priority for this witness; perpetuating the name of the dead father was. Support for this interpretation can be found in testimony by another witness. Hertz Hamel went to Weisbaden to handle the burial of the three hanged Jews.[106] On his arrival in Weisbaden after the hanging, Hamel did not notice any identifying marks on the bodies or the color of the men's hair; he added that it was nighttime.[107]

Testimonies about the hanging of criminals in far-off places underscore once again the difficulties entailed in correctly identifying an individual in accordance with Jewish law. Whether in one's lifetime or after death, the process of identification was open to errors of all kinds. Let us now revisit the case of Blimele.

Landau took on the case of the agunah Blimele in answer to a question by Rabbi Yitzhak Hacohen Lipnik in June 1773. The questioner took the view (in a responsum) that the Mishnah must be strictly upheld: witnesses must actually see the man expire for their testimony to be admissible.[108] This disqualifies Avram's testimony, who claimed to only have been present at the hanging.[109] The questioner, seeking a way to free the agunah, was assuming the noose broke Yeshayah's neck, and so there could be no doubt whatsoever that he was dead. Landau rejected this position; he also found contradictions in the testimonies as to time of burial. Landau refused to free Blimele from her marriage. Three months later, he composed a second responsum on the case, from which it emerges that Blimele was still an agunah at the end of that year.[110]

The testimonies reported here, as well as the decisors' discussions, show that testimony of a man's death was a double-edged sword for the agunah. On the one hand, without valid witnesses who could confirm the identity of her husband and his actual death, she could not obtain permission to remarry. Ostensibly, her interest would be to bring in as many witnesses as possible. On the other hand, the very multiplicity of testimonies could compromise her chances, since testimonies were based on memory, and witnesses often remembered things differently or described the same detail in different terms.

CONVERTS TO CHRISTIANITY

When a Jew converted to Christianity, there were repercussions for family life.[111] Jews chose to convert for a variety of reasons: War or persecutions,[112] a desire to assimilate into non-Jewish society, or a need to improve their quality of life.[113] Others converted to Christianity out of religious belief. It has been claimed that in Germany converts were generally of the social elite, while in Poland the poorer Jews converted to evade persecution.[114] However, responsa literature contains stories of German converts from lower classes as well.[115] If both spouses converted, their marriage had a chance. But if only one spouse converted, marital crisis was inevitable. Men initiated religious conversion more often than did women, and if a wife refused to convert with her husband, she was at his mercy; he could decide to grant her a divorce or not.[116] While Jewish law regarded a convert to Christianity as no longer Jewish in some respects, for divorce he was still considered a Jew. So unless the convert delivered a valid get, the wife remained a married woman.[117] Jewish and non-Jewish authorities tended to take the same position on the personal status of converts: both sides required the convert to divorce his wife before marrying a Christian woman.[118] Rabbi Gershon Ashkenazi tells of a convert who wanted the get to be conditional upon his receiving payment for it; the local rabbi refused. Non-Jewish authorities, when approached, supported the rabbinical position.[119] Given this, some converts to Christianity did agree to divorce in accordance with halakhah,[120] while others refused, either for mere convenience's sake or in defiance of being asked to take part in a ritual that had become meaningless for them. A refusal could make the wife of a convert an agunah for many years' time.

Rabbi Yehezkel Landau, in Prague, dealt with the case of Havah, an agunah in his community. Her husband had converted to Christianity in Hamburg, then married a non-Jewish woman there. Havah could not persuade him to give her a get and remained an agunah for many years. The man died in 1755, and only when witnesses to his death came forth was she permitted to remarry.[121] As in this case, converting to Christianity could involve moving to a different town, either because of military conscription or for other reasons.[122] In some cases, the convert would finally deliver the get;[123] in others, the wife had to make concerted efforts to locate him. Unlike deserting husbands who were affiliated with Jewish communities in their new hometown, converts to Christianity tended to shun Jewish society. This meant that attempts to find the missing husband with the aid of a distant Jewish community were doomed to failure. Rabbi Zvi Hirsch Zamosc (Poland and Germany, 1740–1807) discusses an agunah whose husband left her and subsequently converted to Christianity. He went to Kraków and married a non-Jewish woman without divorcing his first wife. Every time he came to a new town, he went under a different name. Only after his death, many years after he had deserted her, was his true identity established and the woman allowed to remarry.[124] Landau replied to a question from the rabbi of Aszód, Hungary, requesting permission for an agunah to remarry. She was a widow when she remarried, and her new husband deserted her, taking all her property with him. It transpired that he had converted to Christianity several years earlier.[125] Landau refused to free the agunah unless she could obtain a get.[126]

Once they had renounced Judaism, converts to Christianity were indignant at being asked to undergo a Jewish divorce. Elisheva Carlebach quotes Friedrich Wilhelm Taufenburg (original name: Avraham Oppenheim), who pointed out the absurdity of Christian authorities' collaborating with Jews to demand that a convert give his wife a get.[127] In the early nineteenth century, the practice of keeping wives "chained" in a marriage to a man who had renounced Judaism provoked harsh criticism within Jewish society as well. In the 1830s, the Galician *maskil* (supporter of the Jewish Enlightenment; pl., *maskilim*) Joseph Perl (Turnopol, 1773–1839)[128] wrote an essay attacking the halakhic principle of requiring the wife of a convert to obtain a get before she could remarry.[129] Addressed to the Austrian authorities in Lemberg (Lvov), the essay did not question the authority of rabbinic courts in matters of marriage and divorce. Rather, its thesis was that by requiring a person who had renounced Judaism to undergo a Jewish divorce, halakhah as it had developed in Ashkenaz contravened both biblical law and human reason. A convert, concluded Perl, should be exempt from the requirement of undergoing Jewish divorce before a rabbinic court. The Austrian censorship banned publication of Perl's essay, since it upheld the jurisdiction of the rabbinic courts over matters of marriage and divorce (despite restricting their authority in other matters).

HASIDIM

The rise of the Hasidic movement was one of the most important developments of Eastern European Jewry in the late eighteenth and early nineteenth centuries.[130] The impact made by Rabbi Israel ben Eliezer, known as the Baal Shem Tov (from 1736), and his disciples was the harbinger of the mass movement which would both inspire and provoke fierce debate as Hasidim battled with *mitnagdim* (lit., "opponents") for legitimacy within the Jewish world. Among other criticisms, Hasidism was accused of undermining the institution of marriage and making Jewish women worse off. The claim was that young men who joined the movement supposedly left their wives and children for lengthy sojourns at the rebbe's court, even during Sabbaths and holidays. As Perl, the maskil, wrote in 1816: "All day long the *hasid* sits around in the *kloyz* [small house of study] or with the tzaddik . . . while his wife and children have to live at the expense of strangers or subsist on stale bread, in shameful conditions."[131] In the late eighteenth century, a treatise entitled *Zot torat hakenaot* (lit., "Theory of Zealotry"), attributed to R. David of

Makov (Poland, d. 1814), accused Hasidism of luring men away from their wives. He claimed that the Hasidim deny their women the right to bear children (as in Mic. 2:9, "You drive the women of My people away / From their pleasant homes"). The women remained agunot, while the children grew up like sheep without a shepherd.[132] Given the fact that the work was written in a polemical context, it is difficult to evaluate the picture of family life the writer was describing.[133]

Scholarship continues to debate the effects of Hasidism on family life.[134] However, in the responsa literature, I have not found a single case of iggun that was attributed to the husband's joining the Hasidic movement or to his sojourn with the rebbe.[135] Obviously, this does not prove that no Hasid ever abandoned his wife; but even if some did leave a wife behind,[136] a lengthy absence from home was quite common among certain groups, and in this respect, Hasidim were not unusual.[137]

MASKILIM

The winds of change in Jewish society that began in the mid-eighteenth century with the European Enlightenment and the Jewish Haskalah (Enlightenment) occasionally led to family tension.[138] Some maskilim abandoned their wives, leaving them agunot, although the prevalence of this behavior is disputed.[139] Salomon Maimon left home, and his wife became an agunah for many years. His story is well-known,[140] but since it is pertinent to the subject at hand, we will revisit it here.

The autobiography of Salomon Maimon adopts an accusatory tone and is clearly a biased account, the author's self-portrayal as he wished his readers to perceive him, not an exact description of reality.[141] Composed at the end of the 1780s, the memoir was published in Berlin in 1792–1793. Maimon's intended readership comprised German-speaking Jews and Christians. He set out to tell of his personal metamorphosis in lifestyle and beliefs, from a Jew in a traditional Lithuanian community to an enlightened resident of Berlin.[142]

Maimon's memoir is unique in its detailed description of how he abandoned his wife and made her an agunah. Obviously, the writer's personality affects the chain of events; we cannot infer from this case the behavior of other maskilim.[143] However, the way in which Maimon chose to describe the circumstances surrounding the making of an agunah do shed light on iggun in the context of the Jewish way of life and show that a man's choice to leave his wife as an agunah may have been related to the ideological movements he joined. Maimon's personal story stemmed both from flaws in traditional Jewish society and from perceptions of love and marriage that he encountered on his journey.

Salomon Maimon, who would later become a distinguished philosopher, was born in 1753 in Lithuania. His keen powers of observation and critical faculties were directed from an early age against the Jewish society in which he lived. At age eleven, he was married off to Sarah, thanks to a ruse on the part of the bride's mother, whom Maimon characterizes as "a Xanthippa."[144] The early years of marriage were miserable: He quarreled often with his mother-in-law, who beat him regularly. This led to tension between himself and his wife, whom Maimon describes as caught between a rock and a hard place.[145]

When Maimon was fourteen, after being forced to undergo several treatments to ensure his proper sexual functioning, his first son was born,[146] followed by an unknown number of other children.[147] This is how he described his unfortunate situation in retrospect: "My life in Poland from my marriage to my emigration, which period embraces the springtime of my existence, was a series of manifold miseries with a want of all means for my development, and, necessarily connected with that, an aimless application of my strength, and the painful memories which I strive to stifle."[148]

Besides the misery and financial strain on a man who found it impossible to bear the burden of providing for a family,[149] the young Maimon was beset by doubts about the Jews. The state of the Jews was, for him, an outcome of both ignorance (the result of religion) and superstitions held by the Poles which affected the Jews. "All these causes," he said, "combined to hinder me in the course of my development, and to check the effect of my natural disposition."[150] In 1777, at age twenty-four, he set out for Germany to pursue his intellectual interests. Maimon left behind a wife and children, the oldest, David, ten years old. His silence on the issue of his children makes him no different from men of other socioeconomic or cultural backgrounds we have seen who did not regard a lengthy separation from wife and family as anything out of the ordinary. As dramatic as Maimon's trajectory from Poland to Germany was in his own eyes, it was in fact a well-trodden geographical and cultural path.[151] However, several descriptions in his book seem to imply that, with hindsight, no model of marital relationship in Jewish society suited his needs and aspirations.

Matrimony in traditional Jewish society enabled a husband to attend yeshiva without the need to earn a living for the duration of his Torah studies. This arrangement could appeal to a man hoping to escape domesticity. Maimon, who blamed his misery on his father's bad choice of a wife for him, could have divorced her and remarried, given his already considerable reputation as Torah scholar. He could have chosen a match that would have let him devote himself to his studies.[152] This, however, was merely theoretical, since in fact Maimon was bent on studying philosophy, which lacked the prestige of Torah study. No potential wife was likely to settle for this.

Maimon traveled to Königsberg, Poznań, and Amsterdam. He was briefly in Stettin (Stettiner) and lived in Frankfurt for two years before settling in Berlin. During his travels, he experienced both hardship and prosperity. His memoir, written frankly and in great detail, hardly mentions the family he left behind—whether because he simply didn't care or for other reasons, we do not know. We do know that he was not in touch with them for a long time and did not provide for his wife and family. He ignored them until forced to give them his attention.

Twice his wife issued an ultimatum: He must come home and live with her or divorce her and enable her to move on with her life. The first ultimatum was in 1784, some seven years after he left home, when he was in Hamburg:

> My wife had sent a Polish Jew in search of me, and he heard of my residence in Hamburg. Accordingly, he came and called on me at the gymnasium. He had been commissioned by my wife to demand that I should either return home without delay, or send through him a bill of divorce. I was unable to do either the one or the other. I was not inclined to divorce my wife without any cause; and to return at once to Poland, where I had not yet the slightest prospect of making a living or of leading a meaningful life, was to me, impossible. I presented all of this to the gentleman who had undertaken the commission, and added that it was my intention to leave the gymnasium soon and to go to Berlin, that my Berlin friends would, I hoped, give me both their advice and assistance in carrying out this intention.[153]

His memoir ponders ethical issues, but never in connection to the dilemma posed by his wife.[154] As Bluma Goldstein correctly observes,

Maimon employs narrative choices to conceal the grave implications of his behavior for his wife. He describes her only in passing, as a one-dimensional character.[155] While he expounds lengthily on his own musings, he is quite oblivious to her feelings and thoughts. Many Jewish customs are elaborated in the memoir for the reader's benefit, but not the halakhic implications of abandoning one's wife. Maimon conceals the bitter anguish he caused his wife and the fact that he denied her the right to continue with her life. Maimon, well-versed in the procedural details of Jewish marriage,[156] could have divorced his wife prior to leaving home, or afterwards, at her request, thereby severing his ties with the past. Instead, he chose to keep a foot in both camps specifically on the issue of his marriage by persistent refusal to grant his wife a get. On meeting the messenger sent by his wife, he did not inquire after his family. All his thoughts were for his own welfare and for proving he was in the right. Through a rhetorical device in the quoted passage involving the use of "can" and "want," he becomes the subject who "cannot" fulfil either of the two options.[157] The reader suspends judgment as Maimon presents his actions as necessitated by halakhah. Knowing that the husband must deliver the get of his own free will, Maimon emphasizes that he did not want to divorce his wife. A wife petitioning the beit din had to provide a reason for wanting a divorce; Maimon made it clear to his readers that he saw no reason to divorce his wife. The readers might have been convinced of his good faith, but the messenger was not. Despairing of eliciting agreement to a get, he consulted a rabbi.

Rabbi Raphael Hacohen of Hamburg was a fierce opponent of the Haskalah and more than once excommunicated Jews who refused to live in accordance with halakhah.[158] It is understandable that the emissary hoped that the rabbi could help him elicit a get in this case. In fact, Hacohen's authority extended only so far. Maimon claimed that as a student at the gymnasium, with its own disciplinary courts for students, he was not subject to the jurisdiction of the beit din.[159] The issue of multiple jurisdictions over the Jewish population, and the declining authority of the beit din, made it difficult to enforce halakhah; this often had implications for agunot. The rabbi could not compel Maimon to divorce his wife, but it seems that Maimon the maskil was eager for a confrontation and acceded to Rabbi Hacohen's summons to appear before the beit din in the matter of his divorce. Neither of them seem to have been unduly troubled by the plight of the agunah. Hacohen was shocked at the change in

Maimon's lifestyle and tried to persuade him to mend his ways. Maimon, for his part, took pains to belittle and mock the rabbi and Jewish praxis in general — then departed without delivering the get.

Some two years later, Sarah came to Breslau to see Maimon in person, accompanied by their eldest son. She demanded that he come back home with her to Poland — or give her a get. Although Maimon was "in great distress" himself at the time, still, her request seemed to him unreasonable: "I had now lived some years in Germany, had happily emancipated myself from the fetters of superstition and religious prejudice, had abandoned the base manner of life in which I had been brought up, and extended my knowledge in many directions. I could not, therefore, return to my former barbarous and miserable condition, deprive myself of all the advantages I had gained, and expose myself to rabbinical rage at the slightest deviation from the ceremonial law, or the utterance of liberal opinion."[160]

Even now he did not inform his wife immediately that he had no intention of acquiescing. He first claimed that he intended to raise a sum of money so as to go back with her and live together in Poland free of the censorious Jewish society. Sarah refused this idea and insisted on an immediate divorce. Although Maimon realized that this was the lesser of two evils, he continued nevertheless to heap obstacles in her path. He tried to persuade his eldest son to remain with him in Germany and change his way of life. Maimon paid his wife a sum of money but tried to delay her departure, saying they should travel together to Berlin to try to raise more funds. When she remonstrated with him, saying neither of them could ever be happy where the other chose to live, he had to agree. Still, he concealed it from her, since "it still made me sorry to lose a wife, for whom I had once entertained affection, and I could not let the affair be conducted in any spirit of levity. I told her, therefore, that I should consent to a divorce only if it were enjoined by the courts."[161]

Surprisingly, at this point, Maimon mentions his love for his wife; nowhere is this mentioned in the telling of the thirteen years they lived together before he left Poland. This narrative choice reflects the change the concept of love had undergone in his mind with his move to the west. Germany extolled reason but also saw the rise of sentimentalism, and its expression was encouraged in men as well as women.[162] Maimon's memoir reflects what Trepp has called a tendency to soul-searching and self-analysis of one's emotional relationships. She further claims that many men began at that time to identify themselves through emotions and their private life, as in the present case. In a letter to Goethe, Maimon, already living in Germany, wrote that he "was so enamored of philosophy and married it, without stopping to thing about how he would support himself—or it."[163] In Goethe's popular novel *The Sorrows of Young Werther*, published in 1774, the protagonist commits suicide because of unrequited love. Maimon's letter becomes clear: he presented himself to the great thinker who had grasped the power of love as one whose love of truth surpassed love for a woman.[164]

Despite this protestation, Maimon did have to contend with a woman's love. An episode in his memoir recounts trips to Holland where he engaged in philosophical discourse with a certain widow. He harbored no feelings for her, he writes, other than respect for her learning; nothing else about her attracted him. Besides, he adds, since he was still married, his only intention was to engage in philosophical discourse. But the woman fell in love with Maimon. He describes the events thus:

> It was during a conversation of this sort, that we fell upon the subject of love. I told her frankly, that I could not love a woman except for the sake of womanly excellences, such as beauty, grace, agreeableness, etc., and that any other excellences she might possess, such as talents of learning, could excite in me only esteem, but by no means love. The lady adduced against me arguments of *a priori*, as well as instances from experience, especially from French novels, and tried to correct my notions of love. I could not, however, be so easily convinced, and as the lady was carrying her airs to an absurd length, I rose and took my leave. She accompanied me to the very door, grasped me by the hand, and would not let me go. I asked her, somewhat sharply, "What's the matter with you, Madam?" With trembling voice and tearful eyes, she replied, "I love you." When I heard this iconic declaration of Love, I began to laugh immoderately, tore myself from her grasp and rushed away.[165]

Intellectual discourse on the nature of true love was typical of that period. Debates on love and its role in marriage were popular in literary circles, as well as in the expectations of young people at the time. For Maimon, married off at a very young age, love played no part in his marriage. In his travels he encountered a new kind of relationship between a man and a woman, based on intellectual and spiritual partnership. This model of love was much admired in Maimon's circle.[166] In part, it was based on the change in women's education: like the widow, a teacher of French and reader of French novels, wives and daughters in Maimon's circle were educated and took part in intellectual discourse.[167] Yet, Maimon presents himself as disliking this model. He makes it clear to his interlocutor (and to his readers): "Certainly, it is beauty alone that pleases me in a woman."[168] The very fact that he could say this to an educated woman, with whom he claims to have had a close relationship, reveals that the picture was much more complex than the way in which he chose to present it; he himself was clearly experiencing an inner conflict.

We note here that Maimon opened his description of this episode by saying that he was still married. Even many years after abandoning his home, his marriage still seemed to occupy a place in his thoughts. He reminisced about his wife, the extraordinary beauty; he must still indeed have harbored warm feelings towards her. Perhaps he saw no contradiction between his distance from his family and what, from afar, he sought to portray to himself as a feeling of love toward his wife—and thus he saw no need to divorce her. Perhaps his perception was based on the Talmudic model embodied by Rabbi Akiva and much extolled in Jewish tradition: Rabbi Akiva loved his wife despite his absence from home for twenty-four years. However, Maimon's attitude changed when his wife showed up in person: the chasm between them was suddenly unbridgeable. Nor did she seem beautiful anymore, but coarse, uneducated, and unrefined, yet sharp-witted and courageous. Until that moment, his marriage had connected him to his past life, and he had been reluctant to break with it. He realized now that the marriage was over.

Eventually he gave in to his wife's pleas and went with her to the beit din, though he insisted that the rabbis compel him to grant her a get. Maimon was determined to prove that there was nothing the rabbinic court could do to help the agunah. The rabbi remonstrated, but Maimon kept arguing until the rabbi grew infuriated. Once again, Maimon departed without divorcing his wife. But the recalcitrant Maimon could not withstand his wife in person. He finally gave in to her pleas, on the condition that the local rabbi not be present at the ceremony.[169]

"HE LEFT HER NO LIVELIHOOD OR CHILD SUPPORT": THE FATE OF AN ABANDONED WIFE

Abandoned wives had to cope with financial difficulties, even penury.[170] Rabbi Yosef of Romansweiler (Romanswiller), Alsace, recalled an agunah who appeared before his beit din on Wednesday, May 15, 1754: "Tzirl daughter of the late Gimpel, of Flapza,[171] is solitary, without her husband, known to all as Rabbi Yonatan Katz of Poznań. He married her in accordance with the law of Moses and Israel, and she has no child with him. These three years and more, he has been away in distant lands. He left her no livelihood, nor has he written so much as a single letter since he left. This lonely woman's investigations to learn his whereabouts have all come to naught. She has no choice but to hire herself out as a domestic servant, to keep body and soul together."[172]

It emerges that Tzirl approached the rabbinic court upon discovery that, before leaving home, her husband had deposited a large sum of money with a trustee. The trustee refused to hand the money over to her without the authorization of the beit din. Tzirl and the trustee appeared together before the tribunal; Tzirl was required to bring witnesses to confirm her identity and credibility. Satisfied that she was speaking truthfully, the dayan authorized the trustee to give the agunah her husband's money.

Like Tzirl, other agunot also worked as maidservants due to their financial straits. A 1728 letter to Rabbi David Oppenheim tells of another agunah who was forced to work as a servant for five years: "This miserable woman, Sartil daughter of Akiva, weeping bitterly, is striving to find a way out of her predicament. Several years ago, her husband, Moshe son of Avraham, betrayed her. As of the year 1723/24, she is a servant in the holy community of Prague."[173]

Domestic service provided the agunah with a livelihood of sorts. However, some people refused to hire an agunah so as not to encourage immodest conduct — or the birth of a mamzer.[174] This can explain the regulation forbidding the hiring of an agunah as a maidservant in AHW.[175] In Germany, Jewish women were in domestic service mainly in cities or large towns; more Jewish men than women were in domestic service in the smaller towns. The regulation further restricted livelihood options for women, whose chances of finding work were slim in any case. A manual which included formats of typical letters (published Grodno,

1797)[176] attests to the typical financial difficulties of agunot. The following formulation is suggested for a letter admonishing a husband for abandoning his wife and children and leaving them destitute: "I am astounded at your betrayal of your wife, the bride of your youth. You have discarded her; she can find no comfort these several years. The wretched woman waited for your return, hoping and praying—for naught. With no bread or water in the house, the destitute woman has no way of feeding your fatherless children. Should you have any complaint, why, then, free the mother and keep the children."[177]

The assumption is that the husband harbored resentment against his wife.[178] The reference to sending away a mother bird before collecting the eggs or fledglings from the nest makes a point: a husband who abandons wife harms his own children. For an agunah with children, life was harder financially. In premodern society, women who managed a household had to maneuver between caring for children and earning a living. Grim poverty was not unusual, and in extreme circumstances, a mother might even abandon her children. Harrington has shown that 75 percent of requests to place a child in an orphanage in Nürnberg were related to the father's disappearance or death.[179] Jewish sources also show a close connection between iggun and the financial hardship of caring for children. In responsa literature, the abandoned woman is often described as waiting in a home devoid of everything. David Oppenheim deals with an agunah-mother who testified, in the course of searching for her husband, that she and her children had no bread to eat.[180] In 1762, the community of Altona assisted the agunah Adel daughter of Avraham Halle, who could not meet the payments for her daughter's wedding.[181] A scribe in Lublin, Hillel Sapperstein, wrote a letter on behalf of Rabbi Meshulam Zalman Ashkenazi, adding a personal request, addressed to Rabbi Shmuel Segal Landau, for help. The scribe's son, a ritual slaughterer in Germany, had abandoned his wife and daughter several years earlier. His whereabouts were unknown. The daughter-in-law, Frumet daughter of Meir, and twelve-year-old granddaughter, Rivka, "have nothing, for I cannot afford to support them. Times are so hard, more so since my first wife died."[182] The letter illustrates the importance of family networks to agunot as they struggled to cope with daily life. Since his own son was responsible for the agunah's financial straits, Sapperstein felt obliged to assist his daughter-in-law and granddaughter, but in his own financial situation he could offer no help.

MEANWHILE, HIS WIFE HAD ADULTEROUS RELATIONS AND BECAME PREGNANT

Besides poverty, agunot also had to deal with prejudices casting them as a threat to the social order and to community morals.[183] Rabbi David Oppenheim gives a typical expression of this view. Two young agunot are obsessed with getting married, he writes, and therefore he determined that it was the decisor's duty to guard against moral degeneration, by which he meant the possibility they would engage in illicit sexual relations.[184] Perhaps he noted this in order to speed up the process of freeing them from their agunah status. But were there grounds for his anxiety? Before we answer this question, let us first look at several facts that arise from historical research and from sources used in this study.

Throughout the period under discussion, female sexuality was strictly regulated by both the Jewish community and the non-Jewish authorities.[185] The Jewish population included many single women, widows, and to a lesser degree divorcées, all living under constant suspicion of scheming to seduce men and thus being a threat to the community's moral standard.[186] Women of childbearing age added the risk of their bearing children who would become a burden on communal resources. Anxiety intensified with respect to agunot. An abandoned woman was considered doubly dangerous: as a woman who lived on her own, without a husband, she was the object of envy in the eyes of married women who were dissatisfied in their own marriages. Agunot were considered an object of male desire,[187] with the added danger of mamzerim, since an agunah who had sexual relations with anyone other than her husband was committing adultery according to halakhah.

Thus, as sexual permissiveness began to permeate some Jewish circles,[188] many communities made legal enactments to keep down the rate of out-of-wedlock pregnancy.[189] In Altona, for instance, in 1768, a midwife by the name of Friedche was excommunicated for refusing to divulge the name of a woman who had given birth to an illegitimate child.[190] In that same community in the mid-eighteenth century, children born out of wedlock were registered as such,[191] either for the purpose of reporting to the non-Jewish authorities, who sometimes requested this information, or for monitoring unwanted social elements.

Despite the harsh attitude of Jewish and non-Jewish authorities, pregnancy out of wedlock continued in Jewish society, albeit at a lower rate than in non-Jewish society.[192] Among the Jewish women who became pregnant by illicit sexual relations were married women as well. Unmarried mothers could sometimes keep the baby if the father acknowledged paternity or by covering up the circumstances of the child's birth.[193] Yet, in the matter of mamzerim, the community made sure that their status was not forgotten.[194] In the records of Rabbi Raphael Hacohen was registered the birth of "the mamzer Meir son of Avraham." The baby had been born to Mindel daughter of Hirsch, a married woman who gave birth to another man's child.[195] In 1798, the same beit din accused a married woman of carrying the child of another man.[196] The practical implications can be seen in a question sent to Rabbi Meshulam Zalman Hacohen, head of the rabbinic court in Fürth. The question, from the community of Detmold, concerned a reputed mamzer who had been born in 1773.[197] The rumor began when he was born seven years after his mother's husband had run off, leaving her an agunah. Twenty-nine years later, the rabbi of Lippa refused to allow him to marry until the rumor could be laid to rest. The man's elderly mother was thoroughly questioned.[198] She was obliged to furnish proof of the circumstances of the pregnancy and precise date of the birth.

The sources document cases of iggun lasting many years; some agunot presumably tired of waiting for their husbands and had sexual relations with other men. As long as neither party in an illicit affair had an interest in making it known, the affair tended to remain secret. Given the strict view of mamzerim, we might expect agunot to refrain from engaging in illicit sexual relations. Contemporary responsa literature has yielded only a few instances of agunot who became pregnant during the absence of the husband. Rabbi Avraham Natan Neta Meisels, head of the beit din of Vizhnitz in Lithuania in the 1730s,[199] mentions "a woman whose husband went off to a distant land and remained there several years, and, during that time, his wife had adulterous relations and became pregnant."[200] Rabbi Aryeh Leibush Lifshitz discusses a married woman who became pregnant while working as a maid far from the place where her husband lived.[201] When a certain agunah whose husband had been absent for many years gave birth when still married to him, the Hatam Sofer was asked his opinion.[202] Even though sparse documentation of such cases does not necessarily mean they were rare in reality, given the gravity of the laws regarding mamzerim in halakhah, we would expect to see more examples of questions about them in the responsa literature. We may, therefore, conclude that such cases were not widespread.

One way an agunah could deal with her predicament was to try to remarry before she was freed from her previous marriage. It should be noted that during most of the period in question, marriage required a license from the local rabbi. Communities and rabbis were generally strict about this.[203] But just as men wandered from place to place presenting themselves as unmarried, so, too, could women move to another town and remarry by pretending to be widowed, divorced, or a freed agunah. Hakham Tzvi was asked about a woman who was thought by all to be a widow, who married a certain man. The marriage was not consummated, for she told him that she was menstruating.[204] The day after the wedding, a letter arrived from a certain rabbi, saying that she was forbidden to marry since she was considered an agunah.[205]

Following the revelation that the woman had not been free to marry, the new husband wanted to divorce her. Hakham Tzvi ruled that her new husband was permitted to give her a get even against her will. A similar case was brought before Rabbi Mordechai Benet (Hungary, 1753–Bohemia, 1829): "Concerning a woman considered for several years to be a widow. She then married, at which point people started saying she had in fact been an agunah when she remarried—her first husband had left her and was forgotten. When all this came out, an explanation was demanded. The woman said she had obtained a license to remarry from the beit din, but this could not be confirmed. She consequently claimed that her son had misled her in telling her that the license from the beit din was in the hands of her uncle."[206]

According to the text, the first husband had already been sixty years old at the time of his disappearance, and the events described took place some twenty years afterwards. When all this became known, the woman fled the country. Her second husband petitioned the beit din to let him live with her as man and wife—or divorce her against her will, or marry another woman. He could not cohabit with his wife, ruled Benet, because when they married, she was already married to another. The man was allowed to divorce her against her will or marry another woman.

It stands to reason that other cases of an agunah's remarrying before being free of her previous marriage were never found out. This state of affairs certainly heightened suspicion of all agunot, in addition to the continued suspicion of their innocence.

APPOINTING AN EMISSARY TO
FIND THE MISSING HUSBAND

Salomon Maimon recounts how his wife, Sarah, sent an emissary to track him down. We know of this man only that he was a Polish Jew. It is likely that Sarah, or someone acting on her behalf, had to pay the emissary for his services. It is difficult to assess the amount, but responsa literature tells of women who lacked the funds to pay an emissary to look for the missing husband.[207] Rabbi Yehudah Leib of Pfersee dealt with the case of an agunah of a man who converted to Christianity. In her worsened financial circumstances, she could not afford to send an emissary to look for him.[208]

What resources did an emissary have at his disposal? Maimon's memoirs indicate that Sarah did not have any precise information as to his whereabouts, so the emissary had to rely on rumors.[209] This account accords with the observation made by Salmon-Mack that random searching was the most efficient way of finding a missing person in that period.[210] Randomness seems to have applied more to the earlier part of the period; by Maimon's time, there were already institutions in place that could help locate a missing husband. In the late eighteenth century, Hamburg—where the emissary found Maimon—was undergoing rapid population growth with the arrival of thousands of immigrants.[211] In 1787, the city had a population of over one hundred thousand, and the authorities had to take measures against unwanted social behavior resulting from rapid growth. One such measure was to record in the census, initiated in Hamburg in the early eighteenth century, details about strangers in the city who attached themselves to various groups. As in all premodern cities in Germany, foreigners did not enjoy the same rights as permanent residents, although they had to pay community and municipal taxes. This is one reason for the effort made by the authorities to collect information about strangers in town. We do not know if Sarah's emissary approached the authorities for assistance in finding Maimon. Had he done so, he might have learned that Maimon was residing at the Altona gymnasium, since Maimon would have needed a living permit to stay there.[212]

It would have taken the emissary several weeks to travel the hundreds of kilometers from Sarah's home in Nieśwież (Nyasvizh), Lithuania, to Hamburg. Tracking down a missing husband took time and money. Besides messengers sent by a wife,[213] messengers were also appointed by communities. The Council of Four Lands, as early as 1635, sent an emissary to search for men who had abandoned their wives. He was sent by a community near Ostrog and traveled as far as Bohemia.[214] Yehudah Leib Zelechow (Minden) mentions emissaries in his time who were sent out by communities twice a year for this purpose.[215]

However, finding the husband was not enough. For a wife to be released from her status as an agunah, the newly found husband had to agree to give her a get. Sarah's emissary failed to persuade Maimon to divorce her, so Sarah had to go see Maimon in person. Other agunot did the same.

WIVES SEEKING THEIR HUSBANDS

Sarah set out from Germany with her son, who was about twenty years old at the time. Other agunot who traveled in search of a missing husband were likewise accompanied by family members: fathers, mothers, or other relatives.[216] Some agunot travelled far and wide on their own, when there was no relative able or willing to accompany them. Rabbi Ephraim Zalman Margaliot (Brody, 1762–1828) writes of a young agunah who, several years after her husband left her, set out to look for him.[217] When she came to the town where he was living, he ran off again, and when he was finally found, he refused to divorce her. Rabbi Yosef Yoel Deutsch (Tarnopol/Ternopil, 1790–1853)[218] dealt with an agunah from Skała in Galicia who set off for the city of Belz in the wake of rumors of her husband's death there.[219] Wandering in search of a missing husband could be extremely dangerous. Vagrancy was common, despite regulations and laws for the protection of local residents.[220] Itinerant beggars were also a common sight. A beggar, as explained previously, needed a permit explaining why he had to beg for a living or risked arrest for vagrancy. Not owning a permit reduced the chances of getting financial assistance or temporary lodgings from the authorities. A woman wandering on her own was especially vulnerable. On top of that, such women were often suspected of prostitution or other illicit activities. The search sometimes culminated in tragedy for the agunah and her family, as in the case discussed by Rabbi Mordechai Ziskind Rottenberg of Lublin (d. 1690).[221] To modern eyes, what follows might seem extraordinary, but many details are well-grounded in reality:[222]

In a certain land, there lived a husband and wife. The man, a specialist physician, traveled extensively for his work. He left his wife for several years' time. After four or five years of this solitary existence as an agunah, with three children, she decided to go look for her beloved husband. She found him at last, in our community.[223] Now, when the man saw his wife and their three children, he was overcome by remorse, whereupon he took them in to live with him. This was at the end of the month of Elul [in the year 1686]. The wife's betrayal was discovered when she gave birth at the end of Tevet [around four months later], to a full-grown, well-formed infant. The husband was away from home at the time. As her shame became known, she began to fear her husband's anger. Pitiless, she killed her own infant in secret right after birth. She attempted to pass it off as a miscarriage, but there was a bleeding wound; it was obvious she had killed the baby. At first, she told the women that she had been impregnated by a Jew. Then she came to decisors to ask whether she could be permitted to remain with her husband, and to repent for her crime and for killing her baby, which she confessed. The beit din interrogated her, warning she must tell the truth. It was hinted she might be allowed to stay with her husband despite her crime. At this, she told us the whole story: Her father and mother had sent her, the agunah, to search for her missing husband. At Amsterdam they saw her off, entrusting her into the care of a travelling couple. The couple decided to remain in a town a short distance from Amsterdam. They entrusted her into the care of a gentile carter, saying, "Do not fear, you are a mother of three — the oldest a boy of eleven." So she travelled with this gentile carter. One night, they had to sleep in the forest. There they were attacked by soldiers, and she was raped. She became pregnant, and when the baby was born, she said it was eight months old and could not live. This was her entire story.[224]

The couple's story was sent to Rottenberg after they appealed to the beit din for permission to stay together, despite the fact that the wife was suspected of adultery during the husband's lengthy absence. This suspicion was based on the fact that the husband was absent for several years, and when she finally joined him, she gave birth to a viable child four months later. According to halakhah, if a wife has had sexual relations with another man, the husband and wife may no longer live together, even if they both want to. But an exception could be made if the woman had been raped.

The historical context of these events sheds light on aspects of iggun that have not yet been explored. The reality reflected in the description is as follows: A couple had been married for several years. They had three children. The husband was a physician. For reasons unknown, he, like many men at that time, left home and drifted off. After a few years, the wife, accompanied by her children, set out to search for him. She found him, they reunited, and resumed life together as man and wife. Some four months later, she gave birth to a full-grown baby. She killed the baby and at first tried to pass it off as a natural miscarriage. When questioned, she said that the baby's father was Jewish. She then approached halakhic authorities for permission to continue living with her husband and also confessed to killing the baby and asked them how she could repent. In the course of the beit din's investigation, the woman claimed that she had conceived after being raped while travelling to find her husband.

Rottenberg had to decide: Could he accept the woman's version (pregnancy by rape), or should he conclude that she had engaged in consensual sexual relations with another man before being reunited with her husband? The decisor based his ruling solely on halakhic precedent; we will look at the historical context. Was rape widespread in late seventeenth century? How was rape perceived at the time?

We have only partial knowledge of the incidence of rape in early modern times. It is likely that many rape incidents went unreported, as indeed is the case today, to protect the victims' reputation. Legal definitions of rape at the time, as well as assumptions about female sexuality, meant that sexual abuse often did not fall into the category of crime.[225] Maidservants were especially vulnerable to rape, and this included Jewish housemaids.[226] In wartime, the incidence of rape increased, though we have no statistics.[227] It is generally assumed that many incidents of rape took place in private homes, though cases of rape on main thoroughfares and side streets are documented in peace as well as wartime.[228]

It becomes clear why the agunah's parents feared for her to travel alone and why her travel companions sought to reassure her when they parted ways. Rape was a very real danger for a woman travelling alone. Rottenberg ruled, without having met the woman, that her story was not credible; he decided that consensual sexual relations had taken place.

This scenario is at odds with the high probability of rape for a woman travelling alone. Why did Rottenberg rule as he did? The answer seems to lie in perceptions of female sexuality at that time.

RAPE: REALITY AND PRESUPPOSITION

Rape, particularly while travelling, was the standard explanation women gave for pregnancy out of wedlock, to escape punishment.[229] This further supports the notion that in those historical circumstances, rape was a reasonable occurrence. However, this is where the underlying gender bias of legal definitions assumes practical implications. For centuries, a woman's body was considered the property of a man—her father or husband. Hence, rape was treated as damage to another man's property. Legal action failed to take into account emotional and physical harm to the victim. Although in the early modern age the issue of a woman's consent to sexual intercourse did enter the discourse in many legal systems, this generally did not improve the situation for rape victims. Widespread belief held that a woman conceived only if she had consented. Once a woman was known to be pregnant, there was no longer any question of rape: according to this logic, if she became pregnant, she must have consented.[230] As a result, men were found guilty of rape only infrequently, as the rapist's version was usually accepted over the victim's. Authorities treated rape victims harshly, and a woman was often suspected of cooperating with her rapist. Although the law did allow the death penalty for a convicted rapist, courts throughout Europe usually opted for more lenient sentences. Consequently, very few rapists were actually executed.[231]

Rottenberg's ruling can be explained by what the Nobel Prize winner Daniel Kahneman has termed "accessibility" in decision-making. According to this explanation, decisions are often made based on the difficulty or ease with which mental content comes to mind.[232] Kahneman has observed that judgments are frequently made based on perceptions that are more accessible than others to the decision-maker's mind. If an element is more accessible, it can be retrieved easily, and thus it will be considered more important than the alternatives. Researchers debate the list of factors that determine the extent of accessibility of mental content to the human mind. Kahneman underscores the linkage between the prominence of a specific detail and the extent of its accessibility. He also notes that different formulations of a single situation can render differing extents of accessibility to its different components.

Rottenberg presented his ruling as inevitable, predetermined by halakhic precedent. However, by applying the concept of availability, we see that his decision was also influenced by his views on the sexuality of women in general, and of lone women in particular—and by how the events were presented to him. As mentioned, an agunah was perceived as a potential seductress, and rape victims were accused of cooperating with the rapist. Therefore, we may surmise that the image of the agunah's willingly engaging in sexual relations was most easily accessible in the rabbi's mind, as it accorded with commonly held perceptions. Putting this possibility aside in favor of less prominent mental images would have required a concerted effort of consciousness on his part. Moreover, this was the foremost perception for whomever presented the case to him. While the agunah's version was already known, including her claim of rape, this claim appears only at the very end of the question; whereas the beginning already notes the pregnancy that resulted from her "loose morals." Hence, this image had already been planted in the rabbi's mind before he was even aware of the woman's claim of rape. Thus, in his final decision, the weightier image was that of loose moral conduct. In this analysis, agunot and adultery were linked in a self-fulfilling prophecy: decisions were influenced by images, and images were reinforced by decisions.

AGUNOT AND THEIR MURDERED INFANTS

The agunah in the previous case was accused of killing her newborn infant for fear her shame would become public. This account coheres with the information brought forth in the research. In the seventeenth and eighteenth centuries, infanticide by the mother was a familiar, much-discussed occurrence in non-Jewish society.[233] A few scholars who have researched this subject have drawn a typical profile of women accused of infanticide. Women who killed their babies or were accused of doing so tended to be poor; they were often maidservants whose unwanted pregnancies endangered their livelihoods and chances of marrying. Unmarried or married women of higher social class who committed infanticide were afraid their reputations would be ruined when the out-of-wedlock pregnancy was discovered. Infanticide was often preceded by attempts to terminate the pregnancy by various means or to hide it by going into domestic service elsewhere. Like the agunah in our story, these women usually maintained that they had lost the baby through a natural miscarriage. However, the ongoing involvement of others in one's private life, as well as the living conditions themselves, made it hard to hide the truth. Rublack has shown that from the seventeenth century to the end of the eighteenth, authorities in Germany adopted harsher measures against infanticide. Women who were found guilty were brutally tortured and then executed.[234]

Infanticide existed in Jewish society as well, though on a much smaller scale. Shimshi-Licht discusses several cases from the second half of the eighteenth century and rightly claims that the Jewish leadership in German-speaking regions were not unduly upset by the phenomenon.[235] Hence, the fact that one of the very few recorded cases of infanticide in responsa literature involves an agunah indicates that in the minds of contemporary Jews, the situation of iggun was associated with deep distress.[236]

ASSISTANCE FROM COMMUNITY LEADERS

Being an agunah in Poland from 1650 to 1800, says Salmon-Mack, was "the personal problem of the agunah."[237] Our study so far shows that this holds true for other parts of the Ashkenazic world as well. At the same time, in some cases, communities offered assistance. Archives have yielded letters written by lay leaders and rabbis to their counterparts in distant places, requesting assistance in searching for missing husbands. We have discussed several such letters and will now mention one more example.

In July of 1836, Rabbi Shmuel Yosef Halevi Landau, head of the beit din in Kempen (Kępno) in the province of Posen (Poznań), Prussia, sent a letter to Rabbi Avraham Bing of Würzburg and his community leaders. The letter concerned two young men from wealthy families, Shimshon Wolf Takles and Yeruham Fischel Wertheim. The two, both married men, went off in secret against their respective fathers' wishes, leaving their wives behind. They took all their possessions with them. Apparently, they went to a university town to study languages and medicine. "They acted secretly, foolishly, as young men do." The sender begs the recipient not to let the young men leave town and to notify him exactly where they are staying. If they could not be found, he wanted the Jewish community leaders to approach the police — discreetly — to ensure they did not budge.[238]

The fact that two young, moneyed men abandoned their wives and children was a sign of the times. Haskalah was spreading, and negatively affecting the community's ability to trace the whereabouts of any Jew. The sender assumes, because of the young men's affiliation with maskilim, that local community leaders would not know of their arrival in the city. He therefore requests assistance, not only through inquiries in the Jewish community, but by approaching non-Jewish authorities (the police) to find them and make sure they did not leave. It is worthy of note that the writer was concerned with the honor of the absconding men and repeated multiple times the necessity of keeping the investigation discreet. The request stemmed, perhaps, from the desire not to harm the two men. Perhaps, however, it also stems from the concern that if the men felt themselves slighted, they might not cooperate when found, which would reduce the agunah's chances of getting a divorce. The request also reflects the typical ambivalence of the times towards deserting husbands. A case in point was recorded by the Altona shamash. On July 7, 1768, he was instructed by that month's community lay leader to report to the head of the beit din. He had permission to proceed with the excommunication of Meir Ettigen for abandoning his wife and children.[239] While Altona community leaders considered implementing this punishment, presumably it was no longer efficacious once the deserting husband had left the community. And yet, the very fact that it was being considered indicates that someone thought it would have the desired effect. Given that, note that the actual decision was left to the rabbi. Other cases show that community leaders, when they did want someone excommunicated, did not leave the rabbi any say in the matter; instead, they would request that the rabbi issue the formal writ of excommunication. In the present case, the lay leader seems to have been ambivalent about excommunicating the deserting husband.

A GET SENT FROM A DISTANT COUNTRY

Halakhah permits a husband to divorce his wife without his presence by appointing an agent, before witnesses, who will deliver the get. The husband must furnish the agent with a writ of proxy for this purpose.[240]

Many men took advantage of this option to send the get by proxy, sometimes from great distances. On November 19, 1788, a get was delivered to Rachel Miriam of Hamburg by an emissary from her husband in Schwerin. In Elul (August–September) 1789, Rachel Faygele daughter of Rabbi Raphael Hacohen received a get from her husband by proxy.[241] Sending a get by proxy could free an agunah, but the practice could actually turn the woman into an agunah.

Writing and delivering a get is a matter of meticulous halakhic detail. The text, the names of the divorcing parties and of their fathers, and their place of residence, all must follow a precise format. Validity of a get sent from afar was frequently questioned, with decisors regularly invalidating the document. Several types of errors could invalidate a get. Rabbi Menahem Mendel Krochmal was asked by Rabbi Gershon Ashkenazi to rule on the validity of a get written in Fürth on May 11, 1656, and delivered to a woman by the name of Petshele daughter of Nathan. Ashkenazi questioned the validity of the document on the grounds that letters were missing in some words and the names of the signatory witnesses differed from those in the writ of proxy.[242] The get was valid, ruled Krochmal, but Ashkenazi was not convinced. He held up the delivery of the document and asked the local rabbi in Fürth for confirmation of the particulars. An entire year went by before the long-awaited reply was received and the get validated.

Gershon Ashkenazi himself was consulted about a get sent from afar. The husband had abandoned his wife right after their wedding. He had been missing some five years, during which time he had married another woman. A man who happened to recognize him had persuaded him to deliver a get to his wife. This time Ashkenazi validated the get, despite an error in the name of the wife's father. Possibly this was done in concession to the questioner's observation that it would be extremely difficult for him to obtain a new document from the husband since the latter had meanwhile gone off to war. Even so, Ashkenazi ruled that the get would only be delivered to the woman on the condition that three additional decisors approved it.[243]

Different linguistic customs in the place of origin of the get and its destination could also call the validity of the document into question. Going by the principle that divorce proceedings may differ depending on the relevant language,[244] several decisors would accept a get whose format differed from their own. Others, who regarded language differences as actual errors, refused to validate them. Many such cases are reported in the responsa literature of the time,[245] sometimes depending upon technological innovations that changed the ways in which a get could be delivered. Rabbi Chaim Halberstam (Tarnogród 1793–Sanz, 1876)[246] was asked by his son-in-law about a get received from a distant place. The agunah's father was known in his community as Netta. He was called up to the Torah by the name of Nathan Zvi or Netta Zvi or Nathan Netta Zvi. In the get, his name was given as "Nathan Netta Zvi known as Hirsch." In his own community, the man had never been known as Hirsch! The father himself said it had been a childhood nickname.[247]

Halberstam refused to validate the get, one reason being the manner of its delivery: by mail, with no address, only a name. Someone in a different city might very well bear the same name. Without an address or the name of the city, the document could be meant for someone else entirely — indeed, this had several times happened to him.[248]

Proxy delivery of a get also has strict rules. The emissary — whether appointed by the wife for receiving it or by the husband for sending it — must be appointed before witnesses. A get could be temporarily or permanently disqualified if, upon its arrival at the destination city, questions arose regarding the procedure in the city of origin.

An agunah whose get was sent from afar was totally dependent on the emissary. Emissaries did not necessarily act in the agunah's best interests, and there were cases of fraud. Rabbi Yehezkel Landau had a case of an agunah whose husband sent her a get by an emissary who held up its delivery for three years.[249] Dov Berish Ashkenazi of Lublin (1801–1852) received a question from the community of Zlatopol (Zlatopil) concerning an emissary for delivery of a get who reneged after inquiries into his age became cause to question the validity of the document. The beit din at the destination city wanted to examine him for signs of physical maturity.[250] The emissary ultimately relented and delivered the get to the wife, but the local rabbi was not certain, given the circumstances, whether the document was valid.[251]

Another problem could arise if the husband, following delivery of the get to his wife, changed his mind and wanted to cancel the divorce. Halakhah deals with this contingency by requiring the husband to confirm in advance that he would not contest the validity of the get. Despite this, a get sent from afar exposed the agunah to claims of procedural error and mistaken identity. On several occasions, the husband exploited this strategy. Correspondence between Rabbi Landau and the rabbis of Bonnhard (Bonyhád) and Paks, Hungary, reveals that a certain divorcing husband appointed an emissary to deliver a get.[252] Once it was delivered, he claimed the emissary had not fulfilled his part in their transaction, which also included delivery of a sum of money and various articles. The validity of the get was questioned. In the synagogue of Konitz, an announcement called on anyone with information about the matter to come forward. No one did.

Landau, learning of the case from fellow decisors, ruled that the husband "was not faithful in his words," since when the get was delivered, the emissary held a valid writ of proxy. Landau did afford the husband thirty days to appear before one of the specific batei din he mentioned to present his case. He also required the wife to have the signatures on the writ of proxy reaffirmed by the beit din of Konitz. Only then would she be allowed to remarry. Landau was unaware that his decision contradicted that of a local rabbi; this rabbi wrote to Landau, arguing with his ruling. Landau replied that if his decision to free the woman from her marriage had preceded the opinion forbidding remarriage, then his own ruling would override the later one. If, on the other hand, the ruling forbidding her remarriage had come first, then that would be the decisive opinion.

We do not know how the events developed, but note that while rabbis disagreed about whether the husband could cancel the get after its delivery, the very act of questioning its validity gained him time and made his wife an agunah, albeit temporarily.

IGGUN: HOW LONG DID IT LAST?

In the premodern era, a person could easily choose to disappear without a trace, and some Jewish men chose to take advantage of this fact. There are no quantitative data regarding the scope of this phenomenon, so I have chosen, in this chapter, to focus on its characteristics. The causes leading up to the act of deserting one's home have been examined, along with the strategies men employed while away from home. We have told the stories of deserting men who refused to divorce their wives and of those who piled up obstacles in the paths of those seeking to locate them. Even when the husband did send a get, a document sent from a distant place did not always help the agunah, for halakhic or other reasons. Many women whose husbands were absent from home for long periods of time did not define themselves as agunot. For a woman who did define herself as an agunah, the length of iggun depended on the specific circumstances surrounding the husband's disappearance and on her ability to find resources for extricating herself from her predicament. Our sources show that some agunot were freed from their marriage a few months after the husband's disappearance; others remained agunot for five, ten, even thirty years.[253] As Kahana has already pointed out, not all long-term agunot made efforts to terminate their status, even when it was possible:[254] some thought the chance of success was negligible, while others did not want to remarry. The underlying presupposition in halakhic discussion is that any woman always prefers marriage over other possibilities,[255] yet this was not true of all women in this period. Even so, in light of the sources analyzed here, it is likely that many agunot held that status involuntarily.

Part Four

The Riddle of the Sources

12 : HETEREI AGUNAH IN BEIT DIN RECORDS AND RESPONSA LITERATURE[1]

Iggun is a halakhic category; sole authority to free an agunah rests with the halakhic decisor. An agunah wishing to extricate herself from that state had to approach a decisor, who was then supposed to review the information about the husband's disappearance and to hear testimony or study testimony heard elsewhere. After weighing the evidence at hand, given the halakhic principles governing the freeing of an agunah, he would rule whether the woman was permitted to remarry or not. Then as now, halakhic ruling took place not in a void but in actual circumstances. What was the approach of decisors to the agunah problem and to the agunot themselves at that time? What factors informed their halakhic activity?

The sources for the study of halakhic activity for freeing agunot are responsa literature and beit din record books, mainly from mid-eighteenth century onwards. Hundreds of heterei agunah (documents permitting an agunah to remarry) appear in responsa literature composed throughout the period, including the years for which beit din records are extant.[2] However, only a very small number of heterei agunah, which document the actual granting of permission to remarry, appear in extant beit din records. This fact can be interpreted in several ways. Before discussing its significance, I will set out my approach to selecting and analyzing the sources.

In order to understand the approaches of decisors, it was necessary to select some case studies from the many hundreds of responsa that discuss agunot. The ensuing methodological problem: How to select those cases that are a faithful representation of typical halakhic activity? What will be the criteria for the choice of cases? There are several options at hand. The first option is to focus on striking cases, those that sparked controversy among the contemporary decisors. The assumption, then, would be that the differing halakhic opinions expressed by participants in the controversy highlight the fundamental differences in halakhic approaches. A second option is to examine those responsa penned by leading decisors who had authority and prestige on the assumption that their halakhic activity represents what was considered appropriate at the time. The third option is to focus on a broad sampling of cases in the hope that the large quantity will reveal emphases, recurring motifs, and patterns of action and discourse that will enable us to outline models of typical halakhic approaches.

The following discussion combines the three options and is based on my in-depth analysis of 435 responsa on the agunah issue.[3] Some of these represent debates involving many decisors. The aim of the analysis was to identify typical structures, stylistic characteristics, recurrent motifs, predominant imagery, theoretical statements, and modes of action. Responsa were selected on the basis of several criteria:

> Geography: Responsa composed by decisors from different parts of the Ashkenazic world.
> Chronology: Responsa penned over the entire span of the period under discussion (1648–1850). Given that the printing of responsa volumes accelerated as time progressed,[4] more responsa from the latter part of the period are represented.
> Status of the decisor: Responsa by decisors recognized as leading halakhic authorities in their own time alongside those by local decisors.
> Ideological affiliation: Responsa by decisors who moved in Hasidic circles as well as those by opponents of Hasidism; responsa by decisors who were close to social circles affected by the Enlightenment (Haskalah) as well as opponents of such tendencies.[5]
> Style: Among the hundreds of responsa dealing with agunot, some report the circumstances of the case in great detail, while others offer only the bare bones of halakhic treatment.

Responsa in the corpus I analyzed are by sixty decisors who were active in the relevant time and region. The sample is not statistically representative in any strict sense of the term. However, we do not know what considerations governed inclusion of any given responsum in a published volume; further, distribution of responsa volumes is not consistent over time and place. Therefore, I doubt that a more representative sample could be built.

RESEARCH APPROACH AND BASIC ASSUMPTIONS

Responsa literature, being halakhic-legal in nature, is a source of information both about the reality of Jewish life and about the processes underlying the development of halakhah to this day. The preceding sections focused mainly on what responsa can teach us of Jewish life; the present section traces halakhic activity. Using responsa literature entails methodological problems, but recent approaches in the study of halakhah, in general, and analysis of responsa, in particular, are likely to be of assistance in dealing with them. For the purpose of the following analysis, I made use of distinctions and concepts developed in the disciplines of halakhah studies and gender studies. A brief overview follows.

INSIDER/OUTSIDER IN RESEARCH
AND IN HALAKHAH

Any research approach to halakhah is grounded — explicitly or implicitly — in a certain view of the nature of halakhah, of the factors involved, and of the processes constituting its structures of thought. These issues become clearer through application of the research term "meta-halakhah," using tools developed in various disciplines.[6] The analysis in the present section is based on the categories of insider/outsider. Let us clarify what these terms mean in the present context.

The consideration of halakhah as an object of critical investigation ostensibly necessitates distancing the researcher from the object of research. Researchers attempt to observe the system of halakhah as a whole and examine it from the outside. But this observation may take place from one of two points of view. One approach is to conduct research while embracing the basic assumptions of halakhah itself, employing the language of halakhic discourse. Researchers examine the object of study with its own tools, not judging them by external criteria (ethical, aesthetic, etc.). As a result, this kind of research is usually descriptive in nature; we may label it "insider research." The other approach examines components of halakhah by applying extra-halakhic concepts and categories. Halakhah is compared to other systems and evaluated through classifications that play no part in the development of halakhic discourse itself. This approach denies that the object of research—namely, halakhah—is a system that cannot be understood or judged by external means. Statements made within the system itself about its own nature and formative processes are treated with skepticism. We may call this the "outsider research" approach.

Both approaches provide explication of intra-halakhic concepts used within the halakhic discourse and clarify its inner logic. Yet, the first approach adopts the system's basic assumptions, whether for methodical purposes or due to a shared worldview, while "outside" research seeks to question the validity of those very assumptions by applying additional criteria. In other words, when a scholar confronts a halakhic text, the research project of the first approach would be "to go with the text," while that of the second approach would be "to go against the text."

WHAT IS HALAKHAH? META-HALAKHIC APPROACHES

In answer to the question, What is halakhah? some would claim it is a system of truths given by God to humanity and, as such, is timeless and unchanging. For proponents of this view, halakhic authorities act on the strength of tradition passed down over generations, which they adopt totally and unquestioningly. Hermeneutically, this approach regards the core of the halakhic text as a locus of absolute truth, where halakhic authorities are called upon to reveal this truth.

In contrast to the aforementioned approach is a way of thinking that was formulated in a different context by the sociologist Karl Mannheim in his discussion of the transfer of ideas from one generation to the next: "Even motifs and aspects simply taken over from a predecessor always become something different owing to this very passage itself, merely because their sponsor is a different one, and relates them to a different situation. Or, to put it more succinctly: change of function of an idea always involves a change of meaning—this being one of the most essential arguments in favour of the proposition that history is a creative medium of meanings and not merely the passive medium in which preexistent, self-contained meanings find their realization."[7]

The hermeneutic approach derived from this viewpoint is that halakhic authorities are charged with investing the halakhic text with meaning in accordance with the concrete social context. It follows that halakhic interpretation is a new creation and not the revelation of an immanent core of the text itself.

As for the processes by which decisors conduct halakhic activity, there are a few approaches. One is the approach known as legal "formalism" (a term borrowed from jurisprudence); it regards halakhah as a closed system that follows its own consistent inner logic. The decisor is consequently seen as bound by formal principles of inference in his rulings, as defined by the system, without imposing on them his external moral judgment.[8] Proponents of this meta-halakhic approach hold that the decisor is governed by halakhic categories, textual tradition formalized into halakhah, and halakhic precedent.

The other approach, known as legal "realism" (again, a term borrowed from jurisprudence),[9] sees in halakhah a system comprising more than just the components recognized by formalism. Rather, it is also influenced by elements that would be termed "external" according to the formalist view.[10] Some would consider these very elements the meta-principles governing the halakhic system and, hence, not actually external to it, even when they are not formulated explicitly within the system.[11] Others consider them intellectual or real entities outside halakhah that nevertheless influence it. Tamar Ross has expressed this succinctly in discussing feminism's contribution to halakhic discourse:

> Beyond formal or moral considerations dictated by the halakhic system itself, there is an extra-systemic *ideological* factor that is likely to influence the nature of halakhic discussion. It draws upon the personal inclinations of the decisor or scholar given their reciprocal relations with the tradition, with the general beliefs and views informing their outlook and with their interpretive environment. It even draws on political constraints defining their field of action.... *The term "meta-halakhah" will be used here to refer to all such extra-systemic factors and their contribution to the process of halakhic ruling and to the reflection upon it.*[12]

A spectrum of factors may impact the way the decisor chooses from among available options in halakhah or creates new options. The insider scholar distinguishes legitimate from illegitimate mechanisms for absorbing external values into halakhah. This type of scholar will explain the inner logic of accepting certain values while rejecting others.

By contrast, the outsider scholar denies the very distinction between legitimate and illegitimate mechanisms, preferring to elucidate the motivations for conferring legitimacy on certain mechanisms as opposed to others. This type of scholar will examine regularities in applying mechanisms to certain content, as well as the ideological bias underlying the choices of the decisor.

The approaches taken by scholars of halakhah and its history reflect a range of "outsider" and "insider" approaches, although the "insider" stance of those with an affinity to halakhah is not always acknowledged explicitly. According to Ross, "Even when theoreticians of halakhah take on the academic role of the external observer, pretense at objectivity cannot conceal the fact that their research work is often accompanied by the hope of influencing the decisor in his rulings."[13]

Ross thus characterizes trends in feminist research of halakhah, but I believe her observations are equally applicable to the study of halakhah before the rise and influence of gender studies. I would venture to add that it is doubtful whether anyone at all in the halakhic conversation is free of the kind of bias noted by Ross. Flawed research claims about freeing agunot, which will be presented in this section, can be attributed to scholars' failing to distinguish between observations of two kinds: those that are an outcome of a distanced, objective stance and those made by people committed to halakhah. It is thus important to place the following analysis of relationships between agunot and decisors within broader scientific discourse. In my analysis I adopted the outsider position, a meta-halakhic viewpoint that denies that halakhah is an unchanging system and the basic assumptions of the legal-realism theory about the processes governing halakhic activity. Throughout the analysis of case histories here, we will see how halakhic development was influenced by social and cultural factors. This, in turn, validates the claim that halakhah is not unchanging, not a mechanism that is sealed off from external influence. Nor do I accept that the halakhic system defies external judgment and evaluation. This was my approach even before studying the sources for the present study, and it is based on studies on the history of halakhah showing halakhic development as influenced by historical circumstances and sociological factors.[14] In addition, I base my approach on feminist research on halakhah that has identified gender bias within the halakhic system and has developed tools to reveal it.[15]

POINT OF VIEW

Feminist criticism has seen the development of two main approaches in recent decades. "Cultural feminism" or the "feminism of difference" holds that men and women are endowed with different qualities by their very nature and demands equal recognition of "feminine" qualities, as defined by feminism or by the patriarchy.[16] The second approach criticizes this essentialist view of men and women, considering the very attribution of different qualities to each sex as the result of mechanisms of control and oppression designed to perpetuate male domination in society.[17]

The young discipline of feminist criticism of halakhah regards halakhah as a system created solely by men, with the ensuing biases.[18] In adopting this position, I will demonstrate where essentialist premises impacted the rhetorical choices of decisors.

In contradistinction to monographs that set out to plumb the thought processes of a specific decisor, I am not interested in investigating the path taken by this or that decisor in his rulings. Nor am I asking what intra-halakhic considerations formed his decisions. I wish, rather, to shed light on recurring patterns on two levels: practical, that is, the actions of the decisors, and rhetorical, that is, their use of imagery and literary patterns. In addition, we will examine the way these relate to the reality in which they are embedded.

RESPONSA LITERATURE

Responsa literature, both generally and when dealing with agunot in particular, contains correspondence between decisors. It is a legal corpus, written in specific technical style; prior knowledge of classical Jewish sources is needed in order to understand its terms. Its content is encoded through the use of phrases taken from sources that are familiar to the readers, comprehended through shared semantic knowledge. In the period under discussion, the necessary knowledge for composing and reading this literature was possessed overwhelmingly by men with Torah knowledge. Quite often, they were the ones responsible — not only in their own opinion but by virtue of their office or status — for the spiritual image of the entire Jewish community and its religious orientation.

On the surface, the purpose of responsa literature is to document the processes of arriving at a halakhic ruling and to transfer halakhic knowledge from respondent to questioner. The questioner could very well be the decisor himself, addressing a halakhic question posed to him by someone else or one he thought up on his own. The responsum was, for him, a means of clarifying halakhah and for documenting his final conclusions. A question could be posed by a fellow decisor, or indeed by any Jew in need of the knowledge possessed by the decisor. The responsum provided necessary knowledge for practical application or for theoretical clarification. This is how halakhic authorities themselves sought to present their activity, and it is how many scholars have engaged with responsa literature. However, as Michel Foucault has taught us, discourse is not limited to documenting or describing reality but also creates reality and hierarchies of concrete structures and meanings in a given social context.[19] Thus, responsa literature does not merely transfer halakhic knowledge. It also has other purposes. One is constructing the decisor's image in the eyes of his peers.[20] According to Jay Berkovitz, from the sixteenth century onwards, decisors' awareness of the role books play in constructing their public image grew constantly. Additionally, publishing responsa was the means for influencing halakhic policymakers and the nature of halakhic activity, whether in general or in a specific context. The decisor, as a participant in the conversation, sought to promulgate his positions, visions, and ideas among the spiritual leadership and, through them, among the wider Jewish public. Indeed, in this way, decisors could create a specific halakhic and social reality.

SOLVING THE RIDDLE

We now return to the discrepancy between the numerous heterei agunah in responsa literature, on the one hand, and the paucity of heterei agunah in beit din records, on the other. How is this discrepancy to be explained?

One possible answer is that there were very few agunot in the given period; in that case, the numerous discussions about agunot in responsa literature would not be a reflection of reality, meaning that many of the accounts are not based on actual events. This is unconvincing for several reasons. First, accounts in responsa literature often provide identifying information about persons known to us from other sources or give detailed descriptions of events that can be corroborated from parallel sources.[21] Second, some of the responsa state explicitly that the question was posed for practical, not theoretical, purposes. A case in point is a responsum by Rabbi Yehezkel Landau in which he emphasizes the importance of a specific question for the lives of many other agunot, many of them very young—adding that he, Landau, would reply promptly because of this.[22] Furthermore, as shown in previous sections, under the living conditions of that time, iggun was in no way an unfamiliar situation. Thus, there is no reason not to give credence to a decisor's description as a whole, even if he altered some detail or another.

Another possibility is that many more agunot received permission to remarry than is indicated by the small number of heterei agunah in extant beit din records, since we have a relatively small percentage of the total number of records from the period in question. This explanation is likely for some cases at least, and we may assume that some heterei agunah were documented in records that have not come down to us. Yet others were probably never documented. This explanation, too, raises difficulties. Extant beit din records come from the largest, most important Ashkenazic communities in the eighteenth century: Frankfurt, Altona-Hamburg-Wandsbek, Kraków, Prague, and Metz, batei din which also served smaller towns in the vicinity. These records document sessions on marital relations. If rabbinic courts did in fact grant more agunot permission to remarry than the extant records show, it is difficult to explain why such permission was not included in court records. Moreover, most extant beit din records contain at least one heter agunah, proof that beit din record books were indeed where rabbinic permission for agunot to remarry was documented.[23] The fact that so few heterei agunah are documented in beit din records makes it unlikely that the very same beit din would have issued many more heterei agunah that remained undocumented.

A third possibility is that despite the numerous heterei agunah referenced in responsa literature, many agunot never obtained formal permission to remarry from the beit din. This assertion challenges the view widely accepted by scholars who have dealt with the freeing of agunot. Before presenting evidence for my assertion, I will look at the opinions of several scholars who have studied this issue.

SCHOLARLY ARGUMENTS ON THE ATTITUDE OF DECISORS TOWARD AGUNOT

As mentioned previously, historians have hardly dealt with the fate of actual agunot. At the same time, both historians and scholars of halakhah and its history have made historical assertions on the nature of the halakhic activity involved in granting an agunah permission to remarry and on the attitude of decisors to agunot. It has often been claimed that decisors generally treated cases of iggun with leniency and did their best, within the limits of halakhah, to enable these women to remarry. Y. Z. Kahana, despite noting the lack of uniformity in halakhic activity concerning agunot, nevertheless made a sweeping generalization regarding the approach of leading Torah scholars to the problem of agunot, characterizing it as "a great endeavor to observe, insofar as possible, the mitzvah of heter agunah [freeing an agunah]."[24] Edward Fram states, "Rabbinic literature throughout the ages displays a marked tendency not only to be lenient in matters of agunot but also to seek ways to grant them permission to remarry."[25] Sarah Breger has claimed that generations of rabbis have been sensitive to the plight of agunot,[26] while Margalit Shilo has observed how famously committed the rabbis were to granting agunot permission to remarry.[27] Yehuda Brandes sees concern for agunot as underlying the final chapters of Tractate Yevamot; he argues for an overriding halakhic principle of preventing iggun.[28] Premised on these arguments is his claim that criticism of halakhic rulings about agunot generally stems from a one-dimensional view of the needs of women.[29] Among the scholars, the exception in his approach is Yedidya Dinari. His overview of the development of halakhic rulings on agunot shows that until late medieval times, some decisors were strict and others more lenient. Starting from the late thirteenth century, Ashkenazic rabbis tended toward stringency. It is therefore surprising to find Dinari claiming that even when permission was not granted, the refusing decisors offered every assistance to such rabbis who were prepared to grant their permission and shared all available information with them.[30]

The opinions cited here are based on two phenomena that arise from the reading of responsa literature. First, in the rhetorical context of this literature, decisors make copious use of images of the agunah as wretched and forlorn and of the decisor as attentive to her distress. The second phenomenon on which scholars have relied is the fact that many responsa, after the characteristic back-and-forth discussion (Aramaic: *shakla ve-tarya*), conclude by granting the agunah permission to remarry. This typical maneuver can be seen in the responsum by Rabbi Yitzhak Katzenellenbogen in the case of the agunah Frieda. After discussing the case details and testimonies, the decisor enumerates fourteen halakhic "doubts" against the testimonies that have occurred to him. There follows a lengthy refutation of the doubts, one by one, based on precedent set by earlier and latter rabbinic authorities (*rishonim* and *aharonim*). He then reaches the conclusion that the agunah may be permitted to remarry.[31] Similarly, some two-thirds of responsa reviewed for the present section reach a similar conclusion, that is, the decisor's ruling that the agunah is permitted to remarry.[32]

The rhetoric of empathy for the agunah, coupled with the many responsa concluding with permission for the agunah to remarry, at first seems to validate arguments for leniency on the part of the decisors. And yet, this conclusion, in my opinion, suffers from four main flaws. First, it attributes a uniform approach to all decisors, whereas in reality they exercised different approaches. Second, it emphasizes certain aspects of the activity of halakhic ruling while completely ignoring others that had a crucial impact on lives of agunot. Third, it is premised on the mistaken assumption that permitting an agunah to remarry is always the lenient option from the agunah's point of view. Fourth, it ascribes to the decisors an ethic that is based on a desire to prevent suffering, while, in fact, it is far from clear that that was actually the ethic guiding the activity of halakhic ruling. Let us examine my contentions one by one.

MODELS OF ATTITUDES TO THE AGUNAH ISSUE

As noted, scholars attribute a uniform approach to decisors with respect to their granting an agunah permission to remarry. In my opinion, such an inclusive generalization about the attitude of all decisors toward agunot over generations, or even in one particular period, is groundless. There are several reasons for this. First, from my study of responsa literature, it emerges that it contained at least four simultaneous models of decisor attitudes toward the agunah. These models are certainly related to the way each decisor conceived of his own halakhic activity. Second, the halakhic field of freeing agunot comprises numerous details and particulars, and a decisor might be stringent in some and lenient in others.

This would render these generalizations meaningless. We must suspect, therefore, that the picture of decisors' tendency to leniency in agunah cases follows a specific aspect of rabbinic rhetoric without adequately reflecting the complexity of halakhic activity in this field.

From the intra-halakhic perspective, treatment of agunot is conducted along an axis of tension between two principles: (1) the prohibition against a married woman's remarrying while her first marriage is still valid and (2) the Talmudic principle of *mishum iguna akilu bah rabanan* (the rabbis were lenient regarding this on account of agunot),[33] interpreted for generations as the need to prevent iggun. However, as Yehuda Brandes has noted, the reasoning for leniency can be understood in two ways. "The first is personal—understandable concern for the woman's welfare—and the second is social—the sages did not look kindly on the presence of unmarried women in society, believing it could undermine the stability of the community and the families within it."[34] Whether a decisor understood the reasoning underlying leniency as personal or social, in ruling on agunah issues, he still had to balance it against the first principle.

A decisor's anxiety over an incorrect ruling was not limited to divine criticism; actual, tragic reality was liable to result from an incorrect decision. If an agunah remarried on the strength of permission from a decisor, and then it emerged that her first husband was still alive, it meant tragedy for the husband hitherto presumed dead, for the woman herself, for her new husband, and obviously for any children born of the second marriage, who would be mamzerim.

Striving for equilibrium between the two principles, decisors fell into different models. At one extreme were those who refused to handle agunah cases at all; at the other were those who sought to grant the agunah permission to remarry wherever possible. The middle ground was occupied by decisors who stressed either the risk entailed in permitting an agunah to remarry or the mitzvah of allowing her to do so, depending on the particulars of the case.

THE STRINGENT MODEL:
REFUSAL TO DEAL WITH FREEING AGUNOT

The decisor Yair Haim Bacharach (Lipnik and Becvou, 1638–Worms, 1702) was asked to join another decisor in granting an agunah permission to remarry. In his book, he tells her story: Two men took passage on a ship from Amsterdam to Portugal. They were lost at sea; nothing was heard of them for ten years. Then a *shetar mekuyam* (validated document; this term refers to a bill attesting to a fact that has been proved to be authentic and valid) came before the beit din in Amsterdam. The question was whether the document sufficed to free the agunah.[35] Other decisors had already granted the woman permission to remarry, based on Maimonides's principle that if a document attesting to a person's death was written by a Jew, the wife could remarry. There was also halakhic precedent. But Bacharach answered that he had never ever freed an agunah, had not even joined as a consenter when other rabbis freed agunot, and did not want any share in such a halakhic ruling. He added that he disputed those who freed her and doubted that anyone had dared to do so.[36] His refusal was based on the disagreement over whether testimony in a writ was sufficient grounds for freeing an agunah. But note that he began his answer with a general statement regarding his attitude towards freeing agunot. His declaration is borne out by his volume of responsa, which contains not a single heter agunah, unlike most responsa volumes of this period. We are looking, then, at a consistent policy. Berkovitz observes that Bacharach compiled his volume of responsa with the greatest care, stressing that his discussion was theoretical halakhah, not to be implemented.[37] Cautious in all areas of halakhic ruling for fear of error, his extreme position — refusal to free agunot as a rule — marked the field of freeing agunot as one of particular stringency.

Bacharach was no minor halakhic figure. His father, Rabbi Moshe Shimshon Bacharach, was the rabbi of Worms, and his uncle was the rabbi in Mannheim.[38] Ordained in Frankfurt, he did not hold any official position. Yet, he composed a volume of responsa and commentary on the *Shulhan arukh*, and he has often been referred to by scholars as one of the greatest Ashkenazic decisors of his time.[39] His ideological position — refusal to allow agunot to remarry for fear of causing someone to violate the extremely serious prohibition against having sexual relations with a married woman — is one pole on the axis of halakhic ruling at that time.

It would seem that other decisors were aware of Bacharach's position. At the end of his responsum, Bacharach reprimands the questioner, saying he would not reply to his letters until the questioner supplied the names of any rabbis who agreed to free the agunah.[40] The message Bacharach sought to convey to the questioner — and, in publishing the responsum, to anyone dealing in agunah issues — was unequivocal: any halakhic ruling on the agunah issue would always come under attack by halakhic authorities and was liable to impact a decisor's relations with his peers. Bacharach's refusal to engage with cases about agunot did not stop him from criticizing others who were active in this area; in the present case he actually overturned their ruling that the agunah could remarry.

We have no way of knowing how many Ashkenazic decisors shared Bacharach's stringent position, but we do know of other decisors who refused to handle cases involving agunot.[41] Obviously, those who refused to handle cases of iggun left no heterei agunah. Hence, responsa on the subject yield a picture skewed in favor of those handling agunah cases. Therefore, we may say that decisors who agreed to deal with agunot, despite the fear of making a mistake, often adopted a lenient approach. However, I believe even this to be an insufficient description. Among decisors who agreed to handle cases involving agunot, different models are discernible. Influenced by Bacharach, a new type of decisor emerged, as will now be described.

THE CO-DECISOR

In reply to an anonymous question, Rabbi Jacob Reischer presented his own approach to freeing agunot: he preferred not to get involved in agunah affairs at all, but would, sometimes, join other decisors in freeing an agunah.[42] Reischer's policy was to not initiate the freeing of an agunah but to occasionally agree to join fellow rabbis who had already given their permission. The responsa *Shevut Yaakov* contains no fewer than sixteen of his agunah cases. Only one of these took place in his own community; all the rest were replies to questions from other decisors. It appears that Reischer indeed rarely took the initiative to free an agunah, which situates him at the stringent pole of halakhic rulings in this area.

The same position is formulated somewhat differently by Rabbi Issachar Dov Ber, head of the beit din of Złoczów. In a responsum he sent to Rabbi Jacob Segal Landau concerning an agunah in Ukraine whose husband had converted, he remarks on the leniency of rabbis of his time in freeing agunot as compared to previous generations. Rabbis of old were more learned, but they knew better than to take such a risk on their own. In fact, he says, it is better to do nothing than to err in this matter.[43]

He describes himself as stricter than the Talmudic rabbis and the decisors in more recent generations. In his view of the development of halakhah, the Talmudic sages sought to free agunot, but the great rishonim (high medieval halakhic authorities) did not want to take such responsibility upon themselves; they agreed to free an agunah only when several decisors joined in agreeing to do so. In his own time, however, such agreement was no longer sufficient, since some rabbis in positions of authority were not suited to the task at hand. For this reason, he advocated refraining from any action. This decisor does go into some detail regarding a case referred to him that ended with his refusal to free the agunah; in other cases, however, he sometimes signed onto the permissions to remarry issued by fellow rabbis.[44]

THE AMBIVALENT MODEL: FREEING AN AGUNAH EX POST FACTO (*bediavad velo lekhat'hilah*)

Unlike Bacharach and Reischer, some decisors of the period penned numerous heterei agunah. Among these were Menahem Mendel Krochmal, Gershon Ashkenazi, and David Oppenheim, Bachrach's former student. Some were published in responsa volumes, and it is quite likely that additional heterei agunah were issued but never published. Some of the aforementioned decisors, as well as those in subsequent generations, continuously emphasized the risk involved in dealing with agunot.

Several kinds of reasoning are given for this risk. Oppenheim was concerned lest he be considered lenient because of freeing several agunot within a short period of time.[45] This reasoning bespeaks a stringent halakhic environment in agunah matters. This was no isolated case. Rabbi Gershon Ashkenazi, with respect to an agunah who became pregnant by a man not her husband, elucidates his reasons: he had already freed an agunah that same year, who had been waiting for the designated brother-in-law to attain maturity, and fears that he will be considered lenient.[46] While Oppenheim was concerned about being thought lenient for freeing several agunot in quick succession, Ashkenazi expressed the same concern over freeing one single agunah in one year. There was also an agunah married to a convert to Christianity, whom he refused to free. In such a grave matter as iggun, observes Ashkenazi, he took the stringent approach.[47]

"Awe in halakhic ruling" (*yirat horaah*) is an expression of humility used in other halakhic contexts. In referring to agunot, many decisors append to it the words "and especially regarding the prohibition of a married woman's remarrying while still bound to the first husband" (*isur eishet ish*).[48] This teaches us that they felt great anxiety at the slightest involvement in agunah issues.[49] We point out that, contrary to Kahana's assumption that decisors viewed freeing agunot as a mitzvah, some decisors actually eschewed agunah cases. They justified their willingness to respond to a question on iggun issues only by appealing to the special circumstances of a specific case. Joshua Heschel Babad (1754–1839), head of the beit din and rabbi of Tarnopol in Galicia,[50] was asked in 1814 by his father-in-law, Rabbi Nahum Hurwitz of Zbaraż, to join him in freeing an agunah. Only because the agunah in question was young, had been waiting for seventeen years, and was of good family did he agree,[51] amid reservations which should perhaps be seen as rhetorical expression of humility, not realistic reflection of willingness to free agunot. In fact, his volume of responsa contains several heterei agunah. A rabbi's reservations were sometimes more than mere expression of humility. Rabbi Yehezkel Landau, in refusing to free an agunah, observes that his reply had been written thirty-six years earlier, in his youth. Being young, he was fearful of making a wrong decision; he preferred stringency to leniency.[52] There is no doubt whatsoever that the aforementioned expressions of humility are meant to mark the field of freeing agunot as dangerous, as one with which not every decisor is worthy of dealing. On the religious level, there was the risk of error and the ensuing transgression of the prohibition of having sexual relations with a married woman; on the social level, decisors had concerns about being considered lenient. I did not come across anything in responsa literature about the implications of erroneous rulings for the agunah herself. We must therefore ask to what extent decisors even took into account the fate of actual agunot. This matter will be elaborated in the subsections "The Practical Meaning of the Decisors' Demands" and "She Weeps, She Grieves, She Sighs." As we shall see, it was the decisor's concern over his own social standing that held great weight in his decisions on the fate of agunot.

THE LENIENT MODEL: SEEKING TO FREE THE AGUNAH

The halakhic system assumes a clear hierarchy of decisors. Those who worked between the eleventh and fifteenth centuries, before the compilation of *Shulhan arukh* (called *rishonim*, lit. "first ones"), were considered superior to those who wrote after *Shulhan arukh* (called *aharonim*, lit. "later ones"). Generally, later decisors based their rulings on those of earlier scholars and are hesitant in disputing the ruling of a rishon.

Decisors sometimes chose to present the freeing of agunot as a mitzvah. These decisors relied on the words of the Rishon Rabbi Asher ben Yehiel (the Rosh; ~1250, Ashkenaz–1327, Toledo), who was in favor of seeking out every possible way to free an agunah.[53] Even ambivalent decisors noted that the Talmudic sages exercised leniency in freeing agunot.[54] This position was given vivid expression by Rabbi Arye Leibush Lipshitz, with reference to an agunah of Briegel (Brzesko), near Kraków. He recounts how fearful he was of erring in releasing a woman from her marriage and permitting her to remarry. Comparing his humble self to the rabbinic colossi of the past, he realizes he cannot take upon himself what they themselves feared to do. He speaks eloquently of the actual agunah sitting before him, forlorn, hopeless. How could he refuse her? If he were to refuse, then even rabbis who had already tentatively agreed to free her were liable to renege.[55] True, erroneous ruling would lead to horrendous results; yet, prolonging the state of iggun was to him no less grave. He cites an image used by Rabbi Menahem Stengi Margaliot (d. 1652) in a question to Rabbi Joel Sirkis (1561–1640), comparing the freeing of an agunah to rebuilding Jerusalem.[56]

In a similar vein, Rabbi Jacob Meir of Alsace was asked to adjudicate the case of an agunah whose husband was on a ship that sank in 1778. He describes the approach of decisors to such cases.[57] Like Lipshitz, Meir attributes his willingness to handle the agunah case, despite the risk involved, to God's demanding it of him. For both decisors, freeing agunot was the will of God. By taking the agunah case, they set themselves opposite decisors who, above all, feared to take the risk when *issur eshet ish* (the prohibition on a married women to engage in sexual intercourse with a man who is not her husband) was involved.[58]

We see that some decisors refused point-blank to take on agunah cases; others would not initiate the freeing of an agunah but would consider requests to join other decisors who had already granted a heter agunah; yet others were ambivalent; and, finally, there were decisors who supported freeing agunot. These models cover the range of legitimate positions in halakhic ruling throughout this period. They highlight how important it was for decisors to make known their position on this issue.

Decisors dealt at great length with their attitude to the agunah problem, primarily because of the sensitivity of the issue and the severity assigned by the halakhic tradition to the prohibition of engaging in sexual relations with a married woman. A decisor declaring his position on freeing agunot was making eminently clear his awareness of the gravity and complexity of this field. Also, he was signaling the legitimacy of being involved, within the limitations of halakhah. At the same time, such declarations reaffirmed the notion that the halakhic field of freeing agunot is an extremely complex one and that utmost caution must be exercised in matters involving agunot, since they pose risk to both individuals and society at large.

THE BUREAUCRACY OF HALAKHIC RULINGS

The pronouncements by Lipshitz and Meir, beyond the personal aspect, reveal the procedural side of halakhic rulings for freeing agunot. Both refer to heterei agunah as the will of God, though it is clear from their words that they would have preferred for someone else to fulfill this mitzvah. Lipshitz, as rabbi of the community where the agunah lived, knows that were he to refuse to handle her plea, greater halakhic authorities than himself would certainly refuse. Meir notes that beyond the fact that God had commanded him to look into the fate of the agunah, he was also under pressure to do so, as no halakhic authority where she lived would free her. Again, it is clear he would have preferred for someone else to do the job. In answer to the question of whether a given decisor would handle the case of an agunah, two main criteria emerge: geographical proximity to the agunah and position in the rabbinical hierarchy. The geographical criterion should have meant that the local rabbi would take the case, easing the agunah's state. However, in the relevant period, tensions were increasing among rabbinic authorities, and certain rabbis deemed their colleagues unfit to take on an agunah case. The resulting rabbinic bureaucracy led to the subordination of the geographical criterion to the hierarchical one. As we have seen, this area of activity was under close social regulation. Most scholars have ignored this fact, despite its far-reaching implications for the agunah's chances of success.

PROCEDURAL ASPECTS OF A DECISOR'S WORK

It will be recalled that many responsa grant the agunah permission to remarry, leading scholars to claim that decisors took a lenient approach on the agunah issue. However, relying on heterei agunah in responsa in support of the leniency claim ignores a fundamental fact with immense impact on the fate of agunot: the decision of an individual decisor as recorded in his responsum was not the end of the process of freeing an agunah. In fact, it was only the beginning, as a number of examples prove.

Rabbi Menahem Mendel Krochmal was approached by Dina, an agunah who requested his assistance in freeing her.[59] Dina's husband, Yehiel, had been killed by villagers, and testimonies were heard by a beit din in Bytom on November 17, 1656. After studying the testimonies, the decisor weighed the halakhic issues at great length. His conclusion was that the agunah should be allowed to remarry. But he qualified this in his final sentence, writing that the entire discussion was not intended for any practical application unless supported and reaffirmed by leading decisors of Vienna. Should the other decisors refuse, he added, his own permission was thereby rescinded.[60]

Nearly all the heterei agunah reviewed for the present study conclude with the same reservation: for the decisor's ruling to be implemented in practice, it would have to be reaffirmed by other decisors.[61] Sometimes the decisor named the fellow decisors who were to be asked to reaffirm his opinion, as in the present case.[62] In other cases, his permission was made conditional on reaffirmation by "two famous leading rabbis [geonim]" or by decisors he described with exalted words of praise.[63]

From the intra-halakhic perspective, the grave ramifications of erroneous halakhic ruling—for agunah, husband, and decisor—justified the need for reaffirmation by an additional expert. Indeed, at times it seems the decisor needed backing because his own conclusion was shaky.[64] However, even when the decisor stated explicitly that testimonies and proofs were completely satisfactory, he still preferred to pass on the question to a colleague for approval.[65] It should be emphasized: the practice of seeking affirmation was a custom—not binding halakhah[66] —that became widespread in the period under discussion. The Talmud already laid the foundations for the idea that halakhic rulings for freeing agunot should come under constant review.[67] Rabbi Joseph Karo expressed this same view in *Shulhan arukh* and previously in a different connection: "Although they were lenient in cases of iggun, there is no advantage in being lenient and releasing an agunah on the basis of suppositions. On the contrary, one must be fearful of ruling, and even if it appears to him that there is evidence to release such a woman, he should not issue this decision to release her from iggun either in writing or orally until all the rabbinic authorities have gathered and all or most of them have agreed."[68]

Despite Karo's stature as a leading halakhic authority in all of Jewish history, my own research shows that, in the relevant period, his instructions were not always followed. Some decisors, in a few cases at least, did not seek the approval of their peers.[69] Hence, the decision to seek affirmation by other decisors was the choice of the individual decisor on a case-by-case basis.[70]

Before proposing a historical explanation for the reversal of this custom and its replacement by one favored by decisors of this period, let us first examine its repercussions for agunot.

THE PRACTICAL MEANING OF THE DECISORS' DEMANDS

On October 25, 1775, in Zbarazh, Rabbi Alexander Sender Margoliot (Satanow and Przeworsk, ~1730–1802) penned a responsum. In it, he provided what he considered sufficient grounds for freeing the agunah Shayna.[71] Testimonies about her husband's death had been heard by a beit din in Zbarazh as early as June 18, 1771 — more than four years earlier. The testimonies had been given to Shayna so that she might approach rabbis with her request to be freed of her marital bond. No explanation is offered in the responsum for the delay of several years. Whether the woman herself put off approaching rabbis, or the delay was caused by some other reason, the decisor agreed to free her. The heter agunah was also signed by three rabbinic judges of Zbarazh. Despite this, Margoliot sent his responsum to another decisor. The latter, in turn, approved, but he, too, qualified his agreement by demanding reaffirmation by a leading decisor. To this, Margoliot replied: "I have seen how hard it is for the agunah to travel hither and thither among batei din to request to be freed from her marriage. For this reason, my permission is hereby granted, provided two learned men of our community agree and sign.

Thereupon, the sorrowful woman will be free of the shackles of iggun and will be able to marry any man she chooses."[72]

The practical implications of the demand for reaffirmation by other decisors is made abundantly clear in the passage by Margoliot. The second opinion, termed "joining others in granting permission" (*tzeruf leheter*), meant the woman had to present the first responsum to other decisors. To do that, the agunah had to travel from place to place seeking out rabbinic courts wherever she went.

Margoliot was not alone in acknowledging the hardship entailed in obtaining reaffirmation. Rabbi Joshua Heschel Babad, on being asked to send his affirmation of permission to free an agunah via emissary, writes as follows: "I could not refuse the request the emissary brought from my relative by marriage, Rabbi Zalman Margaliot of Brody, requesting my affirmation of his permission to free an agunah. All the more so, given how difficult it is for the emissary to travel, in his old age, to other places, to request that someone join this permission."[73]

In order to fully grasp the difficulties entailed in travelling "hither and thither," we must remember that travel was both dangerous and expensive. Even when using an emissary, the agunah had to fund his expenses. As we have seen, the state of iggun brought financial hardship, at least for some agunot. Travelling, or finding an emissary who would travel, was an additional financial burden.

Getting another decisor to join, moreover, was a protracted process, during which the agunah retained her status. The duration of the process depended on how long it took the decisor (or an assistant) to copy out his responsum for delivery to the waiting agunah and on the distance separating the two decisors.[74] We now present some additional factors mentioned in testimonies that appear in the responsa literature.

On February 3, 1758, the rabbi of Lvov, Rabbi Haim Cohen Rapoport, explained the delay of his responsum concerning an agunah: "The testimonies had been delayed by the post" and, therefore, had reached him late.[75] Mail coaches were at the mercy of weather conditions and technical hitches. Thus, delay due to slow postal service is certainly not surprising.

A different kind of delay appears in the following example. Rabbi Yechezkel Landau, replying to his son-in-law's request that Landau join him in freeing two agunot, writes on November 6, 1788: "And I finished reading this letter on the eve of the Holy Sabbath . . . I had planned to review the matter of the second agunah on the Sabbath, but then, I became somewhat weak, as is my constitution, and thus I had no strength to study it. For this reason, I cannot write anything about the second agunah until God in His mercy restores my strength."[76] On another occasion, Landau was prevented from reviewing an agunah's case because, as he put it, he needed his books to review such a grave matter, but they had been sent away following a fire that broke out in the community.[77]

In a responsum Landau addressed to Rabbi Tzvi Hirsch of Brody on April 1, 1778, he gives additional reasons for the tardiness of his reply in the matter of an agunah. Landau asks Hirsch to forgive the delay: Neglecting to read the letter to the end, he missed the question about the agunah. After that he misplaced the letter. It transpires that Tzvi Hirsch, who sent the question to Landau, put the actual question after some other halakhic query. Landau was uncertain how to reply to the first question and never reached the part about the agunah. He put the letter aside. Only after his son pointed out that it was a matter of heter agunah was Landau prepared to review the case, but by then he could no longer find the letter. Before Passover, during the hunt for leavened bread all over the house, the letter resurfaced, at which point he answered it "without delay."[78]

Further examples can be found in the works of other decisors. Responsa literature is replete with such passages. This is no isolated occurrence, nor is it limited to minor decisors. Quite the contrary; decisors of Landau's stature, since they received so many questions, delayed in replying even more than their junior colleagues. Thus, in a question about an agunah from the head of a beit din to the Hatam Sofer in 1832, the writer notes that he has already asked the head of the beit din in Poznań to join in permitting the agunah to remarry. The latter had responded that he was at present too busy to reply.[79]

We see that various circumstances combined to delay replies to requests to join other decisors in granting an agunah permission to remarry. Obviously, in some cases, the decisor would not join because he decided she should not be freed.[80] If that happened, yet another decisor had to be invited to join, making the first rabbi's conditional permission to remarry all the more difficult to realize, as in the following case.

Rabbi David Oppenheim received a question from three rabbinic court judges from a community in Moravia. It concerned three agunot whose husbands had been killed several years earlier. Testimonies as to the deaths had been heard by the beit din of Brod (today Uherský Brod, in the Czech Republic) at various points in the course of 1705, and the rabbis thought the women should be granted permission to remarry. Oppenheim, as district rabbi, was asked to reaffirm their opinion. After reviewing the testimonies, Oppenheim refused, due to supposed contradictions in the witnesses' testimonies. Evidence must be given again, he instructed, and sent to him. He wrote that no agunah could be allowed to remarry unless he was first informed of the precise circumstances of the case.[81] Eventually, Oppenheim did permit one of the three to remarry, based on the new testimonies, after an unknown lapse of time.

Some decisors, at least, were aware of the severe implications of asking a colleague to join in permitting an agunah to remarry. Rabbi Nahum Halevi, head of the beit din of Lubichowo,[82] was asked in 1849 about a certain unnamed agunah. Her husband, Moshe, had been conscripted into military service along with his brother, and reports soon came of his death.[83] The anonymous questioner presented testimonies for and against freeing his wife but refused to take a stand. Rabbi Halevi was asked for his ruling. The questioner attached the opinion of the head of the beit din of Kaminka,[84] granting permission for the agunah to remarry. The respondent, after reviewing the case, gave his permission as well. There were sufficient permissions, he added; no need for further delay or expense in approaching any more rabbis. The letter ended by stating it was a great mitzvah to permit this wretched agunah to remarry.[85]

Some decisors, then, did acknowledge the fact that trying to solicit opinions from additional decisors placed an additional burden on the agunah and made her situation worse. Some responsa state explicitly that decisors did join, reaffirming the first decisor's permission for the agunah to remarry; the woman was freed and subsequently remarried.[86] In the majority of cases, however, the decisor adds nothing of what transpired after his own decision was given. It seems fair to assume that the passage of time, the hardship of travel, and the expense involved in trying to obtain permission from additional decisors prevented at least some of the agunot from realizing the heter agunah they already had from one decisor. This could very well explain my finding of a paucity of heterei agunah in beit din record books.

Why, then, did the practice of seeking affirmation from fellow decisors become so widespread even though it is not mandated by halakhah? Before I give possible answers to this question, it should be recalled that permitting agunot to remarry was not the only halakhic area in which decisors sent responsa to each other. It is, however, the sole area in which halakhah itself demands leniency from the decisor.[87] As Y. Z. Kahana put it, "The halakhah of agunot deviates from the norm, being in a sense the only area in which the decisor is demanded to deliberately attempt to find a way to allow the woman to remarry."[88] If so, decisors might have been expected to do their utmost in order to alleviate the suffering of agunot, but this was not the case, as we have seen. The question remains: Why did the majority of decisors choose to adopt a custom that increased the difficulties of the agunah in realizing the permission already granted for her to remarry?

DEVELOPMENT OF DECISORS' WORK PROCEDURES

One option is that the rabbis' previously described procedure for deciding whether to free an agunah stemmed from halakhic considerations. Akiva Silvetsky has shown that the question of whether a sole decisor may free an agunah, or if only a beit din may do so, is not clarified in the Talmud and has been debated since.[89] Rabbi Moshe Isserles, following the *Shulhan arukh*, addressed the issue only in the context of a woman who marries on the strength of a single witness to the husband's death, in which case a beit din of three decisors is needed. In a dissenting opinion by Rabbi Moshe Lima, author of the commentary *Helkat mehokek* on the *Shulhan arukh*, a sole decisor may grant an agunah permission to remarry, even if there is only a single witness.[90] But what happens when a woman marries without permission from the beit din? There were three opinions among contemporary decisors:

1. The *Shulhan arukh*, and Rabbi Moshe Isserles in his gloss, determined that a priori (*lehatkhila*), a woman who marries on the strength of a single witness must obtain permission from a beit din of three. Yet, ex post facto (*bediavad*), that is, if she marries without such permission, she need not divorce.[91] This opinion did not gain wide acceptance; latter decisors were more stringent.
2. There were decisors who thought that permission had to be obtained from a beit din in any case, and if an agunah married without permission from a beit din, she must divorce.[92]

3. Others thought that a woman who married on the strength of a single witness or of invalid witnesses needed permission from a beit din. However, there are two scenarios in response to the question, What if she marries without obtaining that permission? If, after her marriage, it is proven that her first husband is still alive—she must be divorced from her second husband. Otherwise, her second marriage is valid.[93]

I suggest that decisors who were aware of the debate preferred the most stringent of the previous opinions and, therefore, insisted on obtaining affirmation from colleagues, even though halakhah did not actually require permission from a beit din to enable an agunah to remarry. It is important to know that granting conditional permission is not necessarily siding with any one of the options enumerated here. A decisor could ask others to join for the purpose of distributing responsibility, to protect his interests, even if he did not think that permission from a beit din was necessary. Rabbi Aryeh Leib of Kraków, author of *Shaagat Aryeh*, discusses an agunah whose husband drowned. He agrees with *Helkat mehokek*, namely, that no beit din was necessary for freeing her, adding "all rabbis today follow this practice." This notwithstanding, he made his own permission conditional on another decisor joining him.[94] There were other decisors like him who also made it their practice to get another colleague to join them—and revealed in the process that they, too, did not consider it necessary to obtain permission from a beit din of three in order to free an agunah. Yet it cannot be ruled out that some decisors sought affirmation of their opinion by a colleague because their opinion in the debate was that more than one decisor was needed to free an agunah.

FREEING AGUNOT AND RABBINIC PRESTIGE

The sources and rulings that follow, along with the cases discussed throughout the present book, validate the assertion made by Maoz Kahana that joining another decisor in permitting an agunah to remarry was among "the classic signs of rabbinic prestige."[95]

In his ruling on a woman whose husband had drowned in waters without end, Rabbi Joseph Karo ruled in the *Shulhan arukh*: "A woman for whom a single witness testified that her husband drowned in waters without end, and he did not come up [to the surface], his memory was lost and his name forgotten, she may not remarry on the basis of this testimony, as is explained. And even if a court permitted her to remarry: If she has not yet remarried, she may not remarry. But if she remarried on the basis of this testimony, she does not require divorce."[96]

Rabbi Moshe Isserles glosses this: "Only if she married on the ruling of a wise man or by mistake, thinking that she was permitted to remarry. But if she purposely transgressed and remarried, she must undergo divorce." Whereas Karo ruled that the wife of a man who drowned in "waters without end" and has remarried need not divorce, Isserles is more stringent: only if the woman remarried on the word of a decisor, or mistakenly thought she was permitted to remarry, can she stay married to the second husband. At the same time, according to his gloss, any "learned man" may free an agunah.

Several generations later, Rabbi Samuel ben Uri Shraga Phoebus of Vadislav (author of *Beit Shmuel*, 1640–1698) proposed to qualify Isserles's gloss: the additional decisor must be a renowned halakhic authority.[97]

Krochmal, in *Tzemah tzedek*, quoted in *Beit Shmuel*, was not addressing the context of iggun. Krochmal, returning in 1646 to his congregation after an absence, learned that a certain rabbi was about to marry the wife of his father-in-law.[98] On inquiring who had given permission for this, he was told it was "learned men." Krochmal immediately ordered the local rabbi to separate the couple. After some time, however, he learned that they had married. He was angered, he writes, but said nothing. His silence sparked unease, as people suspected him of keeping quiet because of the high position of the man involved, who had defied his instructions. It was in this context that Krochmal penned the responsum containing the quote cited in *Beit Shmuel*. There he reiterates that only a leading halakhic authority could join a colleague in freeing an agunah; he emphasizes that laws regarding agunot are different from rulings on matters of dairy and meat and suchlike quotidian decisions.[99]

In this, Krochmal was drawing upon Meir ben Yekutiel of Rothenberg (~1260–1298). On an agunah case, the latter writes: If an agunah remarries without obtaining permission from a decisor, she must be divorced, or else the husband shall be excommunicated until he divorces her.[100] It is not enough for some relative of hers to grant permission; it must be a prominent, highly respected decisor.[101]

If we follow Israel Yuval's claims that only in the latter half of the fourteenth century did the rabbinate obtain its monopoly over matrimonial law—previously, halakhic knowledge had sufficed to perform marriage and divorce[102]—then Meir of Rothenberg's student, Meir Hacohen (late thirteenth century), the author of *Teshuvot Maimoniot*, is making a distinction between a rabbi proficient in halakhah and one who lacks that proficiency. If so, Krochmal was innovative with his further distinction between a leading halakhic authority of the generation (*gadol hador*; pl. *gedolei hador*)[103] and "learned men," even ordained rabbis. Formal ordination was not enough, determined Krochmal, reasoning that not all ordained rabbis knew how to issue a halakhic ruling. For this reason, he demanded that the monopoly on matters of personal status (including marriage, divorce, and laws concerning agunot) be transferred to the leading halakhic authorities of their generation. Despite this, he refrained from expressing disapproval a second time to community leadership, in case the woman had become pregnant in the meantime. In such an event, his ruling would besmirch the child's name. Yet, he was unequivocal as to the need for a monopoly of leading halakhic authorities on matrimonial law. He went so far as to prove that the "learned man" who had permitted the marriage lacked the requisite expertise;[104] this "learned man" so harshly criticized by Krochmal remained anonymous. Nor does he name the community where it happened. The background appears to be a widespread campaign by lay leadership to appoint community rabbis, even nominating candidates for rabbinic ordination. The result was an echelon of rabbis who did not necessarily possess broad halakhic knowledge.[105] While Krochmal's discussion does not directly deal with an agunah's case, his requirement of seeking approval by a leading halakhic authority for freeing an agunah was adopted by the *Beit Shmuel*. From that point on, the notion that no one but a leading halakhic authority of his generation may issue a halakhic ruling in an agunah case begins to recur with increasing frequency in responsa literature.

It would seem that the call for restricting the handling of cases involving agunot to leading halakhic authorities appeared in the latter part of the seventeenth century. Yet, deliberations over the type of decisor with the capability and authority for ruling on agunah matters recurs again and again in halakhic writings throughout the relevant period. Some decisors are apologetic for addressing the subject despite lacking a prestigious position in the rabbinic hierarchy. Others reiterate that not just any decisor may handle agunah cases. Rabbi Yechezkel Landau, in a responsum of November 24, 1785, replied to a query about permitting a certain woman to remarry without halitzah. Landau is annoyed by young rabbis, talented though they may be, having the temerity to rule on such sensitive matters of forbidden sexual relations.[106] He advises aspiring young decisors to devote themselves to further study of the Talmud, its commentaries, and the rulings of other decisors before trying to enter the domain restricted to "the great rabbis" (*gedolei harabbanim*).[107] The criteria of advanced years and extensive learning recur in the writings of many decisors as a threshold for handling agunah cases.[108]

True, Landau was writing this in a letter to a fellow decisor. However, criticism of this kind was not restricted to personal conversation; it can be found in Landau's well-known *Sefer hukei haishut* (*Book of Matrimonial Laws*), written at the express command of Holy Roman Emperor Josef II and addressing laws proclaimed by the latter in January 1783. Granting an agunah permission to remarry, writes Landau, is solely for a prominent, leading rabbi possessed of the most extensive Torah learning.[109] This external discourse was aimed at making non-Jewish authorities understand that their institutions could not perform the office of rabbis in these matters. The backdrop for this was the attempt on the part of the absolutist state to transfer monopoly in matrimonial matters from the rabbis to civil officials.[110] The internal Jewish conversation served to establish a rabbinical hierarchy and to confer an image of "expert" on those rabbis who did handle agunah cases, in the eyes of other decisors and of Jewish society as a whole.

There is evidence for saying that a rabbi's desire for prestige as a recognized halakhic authority was the motivation for the practice of requesting affirmation by a fellow decisor for freeing an agunah. Such evidence is found in a responsum by Rabbi Meir Eisenstadt. In 1738, he wrote to Rabbi Moshe of Pressburg concerning an attempt to overturn a ruling on a get, on grounds of over-leniency. In his letter, Eisenstadt criticizes rabbis whose aim is to flaunt their knowledge.[111]

Prestige strengthened one's chances of securing a position as rabbi, a source of livelihood and admiration. Whereas in early medieval times, rabbis were appointed primarily on the basis of familial affiliation and personal contacts,[112] in the relevant period many congregations sought to appoint a rabbi who had earned prestige for extensive halakhic learning.[113] Conflicting interests over the appointment of rabbis are known in this period;[114] yet, more than previously, greater weight was awarded prestige based on supposedly objective considerations. We find this in correspondence from 1759 between Rabbi Levi Fanta of Prague and Rabbi Meir of Frankfurt, concerning the appointment of a rabbi for the latter's community.[115] Rabbi Meir inquired of Rabbi Levi about the character of the candidate, Rabbi Yechezkel Landau. He was assured in superlative terms of Landau's outstanding intelligence and scholarly achievements.[116] The primary quality the Frankfurt congregation was looking for in a rabbi, as Rabbi Levi was aware, was halakhic expertise.

Rabbinic prestige had very real implications for securing a rabbinical position. The practice of soliciting approval from fellow decisors for freeing an agunah expressed the rabbis' wishes to strengthen their professional standing. The following case demonstrates the link between rabbinical prestige and freeing agunot.

In 1691, Rabbi Judah Leib of Pfersee writes of an agunah whose husband was killed; he headed the beit din adjudicating the case.[117] The husband had been doing business in the villages and failed to return home. When he was eventually found, positive identification was made by acquaintances who knew him well, and he was even given a Jewish burial. Rabbi Judah Leib was completely sure that the husband had indeed been killed and duly buried.[118] Therefore, after reviewing the halakhic problems, he concluded that the woman could remarry. He sent his responsum to other decisors,[119] accompanied by an explanation. He had heard that there were some people who held the man to be dead and did not doubt it; therefore, one should see to it that the woman remarry. He believed that the addressed rabbis' authority, unlike his own, would be accepted by the community in question. Once he had given permission for the agunah to remarry, he wanted to make sure other great rabbis agreed with him. If not, they should notify him, because he needed their authority in order to convince the people in the community.[120]

In the context of agunot, there is always possibility of a clash between halakhic authorities and laymen applying "common sense." While an agunah is permitted to remarry if her husband is proclaimed dead, halakhah demands that the death of her husband must be established in accordance with the specific exigencies elaborated throughout this book. Such exigencies may sometimes seem to contradict common sense, visual evidence, and personal experience. Friction is apt to arise when an agunah is certain beyond a doubt of her husband's death, yet the decisor refuses to acknowledge it.[121] This is precisely what Rabbi Judah Leib experienced. The agunah and her circle accepted the death of her husband as a fait accompli; the decisor sought to prevent her remarriage on the strength of this kind of popular conviction. Not that he doubted its veracity; he had himself granted permission for her to remarry, after an investigation. His concern was for rabbinical influence. He feared that in the future, people would rely on popular opinion and dispose with rabbinic rulings altogether. To prevent this, he sought to instill the necessity for rabbis to decree whether a popular belief was indeed true.[122] These higher halakhic authorities have judicial experience and are possessed of superior knowledge and reason.

This was by no means Judah Leib's sole concern. He was worried that colleagues would declare his ruling erroneous by arriving at a different conclusion by halakhic means. It was these two concerns that spurred him to solicit approval from fellow decisors for his own willingness to free the agunah. This was a double-edged maneuver: if they reaffirmed his opinion, they would be backing him in face of any rabbinic opposition; conversely, if they disagreed with him, they wielded the authority over the woman's community and could compel the laymen to obey their ruling — which he lacked the authority to do.

The debate did not arise out of the needs of the agunah, who is described as willing to marry with or without permission. Halakhah for this agunah and her circle was at best a system charged with confirming existing reality, a rubber stamp; at worst, it is a useless system. By contrast, the decisor wished to preserve halakhah as a constitutive system, to determine the woman's legal status and, in so doing, to establish the rabbis as possessors of truths unattainable by mere laymen.

To shed light on the meaning of this source, we must remember that, in this period, the rabbis enjoyed a monopoly on making halakhic decisions. Prestige and status often accompanied this power.[123] During the centuries we are discussing, however, rabbinical functions of judging and ruling were not seldom curtailed by lay leadership or local non-Jewish authorities. Harsh criticism was voiced in certain circles against specific rabbis or against the rabbinate in general.[124] Rabbis had to bolster their position by insisting that special expertise was required for what they did, expertise that they alone possessed. As Israel Yuval put it, as long as social leadership fulfills functions whose value is acknowledged by the rest of society, social stability is assured.[125] One way for a professional group to ensure social recognition of its indispensability is to create professional jargon and keep it obscure.[126]

These matters admirably reflect the processes that took place in the halakhic domain of agunot. A contemporary scholar who unquestioningly accepts the decisors' own explanations as to why this particular legal area requires special expertise will attribute it to the complexities of the laws involved. Critical examination, however, reveals that the very fact that this halakhic domain is so replete with detailed requirements is no coincidence; the decisors themselves were partners in the development of those same requirements. In striving for prestige, rabbis generated extensive responsa on agunot. These questions were sent out all over Europe to display the questioner's erudition before as many renowned decisors as possible. This behavior developed for the purpose of erecting a barrier between rabbis and laypeople.

In conclusion, there is an apt remark by Rabbi Naftali Tzvi Yehuda Berlin, known as NTZYB or "Netziv" of Volozhin (Mir, 1816–Warsaw, 1893). In 1879, he wrote in a responsum concerning freeing an agunah that decisors put too much effort into contrived legalistic solutions of leniency. These merely cause more problems.[127] Though appearing somewhat later than our period, the thought illuminates our topic, all the more so since it was written at a time when more and more men were abandoning their wives, thus rendering them agunot.

AFTERWORD
The Agunah, the Decisor, and the Suffering

The halakhic category of "agunah" comprises women coping with various life situations. Jewish law allows a marriage to end only with the death of a spouse or by the husband's delivering a writ of divorce into his wife's hands of his own free will. Given the realities within the Ashkenazic world of 1646–1850, many women became agunot. Today, most agunot are dealing with their husbands' refusal to grant a divorce. In the period under discussion, wars, persecution, accidents, and natural disasters, as well as travel along dangerous roads, the possibility of assuming a false identity, and conversion to Christianity, all made iggun not uncommon in the least.

In my research, I have attempted to examine the implications of this fact for the lives of the actual agunot themselves and for Jewish society as a whole. The analysis was based on differentiation between types of agunot and aimed to explore the practical significance that iggun had for each type. One of the central conclusions that has arisen from this research is that despite dramatic changes in Jewish society over this two-hundred-year period, no significant changes took place during this entire time in the attitude of decisors toward agunot or toward freeing them.

Part 1 of the book dealt with women in the halitzah trap. These were widows, a group in Jewish society hitherto scarcely studied. A lengthy discussion was devoted to widows and widowhood in Jewish society in this period from an economic and social perspective. The halakhic principle—that the widow of a man who died childless cannot remarry without first undergoing the ceremony of halitzah with a brother-in-law—added an extra burden above and beyond those stemming from the loss of the husband. In those times, it was usual for a married couple to set up house at a great distance from their original families. This made it harder for a widow in need of halitzah to locate the brother-in-law who could perform the ceremony with her. Even if she did find him, it was often difficult to verify his identity.

The study continued in part 2 with stories of women who became agunot after the death of their husbands because the body was never found or was not identified in accordance with the requirements of Jewish law. Contrary to the oft-repeated scholarly contention that many agunot were freed after the persecutions of 1648–1649, it is my contention that we lack data about the number of agunot in those years. Neither do we know the ratio of freed agunot to those who remained in prolonged agunah status. The sources I discussed in this context indicate that decisors were suspicious of agunot who testified to the death of their husbands in wartime. I additionally found that following the persecutions, there developed a kind of mythology that labeled the freeing of agunot and their desire to remarry as dangerous. Other voices opposed the gender inequality in halakhah and protested against the halakhic discrimination—whereas a wife's death does not necessarily preclude a man's remarrying, women face great difficulties in requesting permission to remarry, even when the woman knows for certain that her husband is dead. For women, assertiveness and halakhic knowledge influenced their chances of obtaining permission to remarry. However, marginalization of women in formal education meant they generally lacked knowledge of the laws regarding agunot.

In this period, the risk of iggun was very real, as we have seen, even in peacetime. A married man's disappearance sparked rumor and gossip, as we saw in the cases of the murders in Altona and Hamburg and the fire and drowning events. This had a twofold effect. On the one hand, it heightened the agunah's distress; on the other, it could lead to the information necessary for freeing her. We also saw how Jewish women turned the stereotype of women as irrational to their advantage by performing dangerous acts and breaking through barriers where men could not.

When a dead body could not be identified in accordance with halakhic requirements, and even when the identification process was halakhic, some decisors refused to rely on identification and testimonies, particularly from non-Jewish authorities. In such cases, special importance was attached to eyewitnesses' testifying before the beit din and to their halakhic knowledge and narrative choices. We saw that the procedures for obtaining information about the circumstances of death could be lengthy, which explains why iggun could often last for many years.

Part 3 of the study discussed abandoned women whose husbands summarily went off to distant lands. Then, as today, reasons for friction between husband and wife included the overinvolvement of in-laws in the couple's life, financial difficulties, and complaints by one spouse against the other. When both spouses wished to divorce, rabbinic courts allowed it, sometimes assisting them to reach separation without formal divorce. Nevertheless, like non-Jewish courts at that time, rabbinic courts did not hasten to intervene in a couple's life, even when a marital dispute turned violent.

Yet we found that marital disputes were not the sole cause of a husband's desertion. Part 3 was devoted to deserting men from all walks of life in Jewish society and to the fate of the women left behind. Frequent, prolonged absence of a husband from home was found to be a characteristic of this period. In this reality, many women lived in permanent uncertainty. Being classified an "agunah" depended in large part on a woman's self-perception: a marriage could resume upon a husband's return from an absence of many years, while other abandoned women sought divorce. Given the familial structure enabling a husband's absence, some men stayed away for lengthy periods of time, having no cause for concern over the stability of the marriage. Or a man might abscond with the express intention of ending the marriage without halakhic divorce. Some moved away, sometimes even remarrying, leaving the first wife an agunah. Tracking down a missing husband was an extremely difficult task. Sometimes a missing husband was discovered only after his death in a distant place years after he left home.

The sources reveal that although it was more difficult for women to abandon their spouses, there were those who did so. Jewish society perceived a man who deserted his wife as harming the woman who became an agunah; but a woman's deserting her husband was perceived as a more severe blow against morality and against society as a whole.

The fourth and final part discusses attitudes of decisors to freeing agunot. I have attempted to challenge the metanarrative as presented by some scholars, namely, that decisors for generations tended to be lenient with agunot and made every effort to free them. While responsa literature contains many hundreds of heterei agunah, extant beit din records, mainly from the latter half of the eighteenth century, contain very few. We cannot infer from permission granted to a specific agunah what the decisor's attitude was to agunot in general or even to the individual agunah whose case he handled. Likewise, the fact that a decisor gave his permission for an agunah to remarry did not necessarily lead to her actual freedom. Procedures developed by decisors for agunah cases heaped obstacles in the path of agunot and reduced their chances of obtaining permission to remarry, many of whom never did receive such permission. Decisor policy is elusive; an attempt to characterize decisors' relationships to agunot solely on the basis of the permissions they granted is flawed.

I would like to propose, on the basis of a Talmudic tradition, that decisors dealing with the agunah problem were not necessarily guided by a desire to alleviate their suffering. More than that, they were motivated by concern for the community as a whole.

SHE WEEPS, SHE GRIEVES, SHE SIGHS

On Friday, July 9, 1734, Shlomo husband of Simhah went to bathe in the river in the company of acquaintances. Three witnesses saw him drown. The corpse, found a few days later, was identified by body marks. Testimony of his death was taken down on December 13, 1734, and on August 15, 1735. Rabbi Meir Eisenstadt was asked if the dead man's wife could remarry. He describes a wretched woman who came to him weeping and grieving, an agunah for two years, not even twenty years old. Her husband lived with her only a few months before his death. The woman did not know where to turn for help.[1] This description, and many more like it in responsa literature, depict the agunah as weeping and miserable. This is no literary flight of fancy on Eisenstadt's part. Rhetoric of this kind is typical of discussions of agunot in responsa literature. The agunah Rachel, as described by Rabbi David Oppenheim, is sad, tearful, constantly seeking out halakhic experts to help her.[2] A vivid portrayal of another agunah was penned by the rabbi of Rotterdam: "This woman weeps and wails loudly, all who hear weep with her as she seeks solace and a way out of her predicament."[3] Many other decisors too employed colorful imagery to depict the plight of the agunah, with responsa containing recurring phrases such as "broken-spirited,"[4] "wretched woman,"[5] "forlorn," "lonely,"[6] "grieving for the husband of her youth,"[7] and the like to describe the agunah's suffering.[8] Beside the description of the agunah as wretched is that of the decisor, portrayed as attentive to her suffering, unable to withstand such despair. Rabbi Wolf Epstein of Friedburg sent a question to Rabbi Shmuel Koidonover, describing an agunah as crying out to him to find a way to free her from her marriage and himself as "forced to listen to her cries."[9] Rabbi Jacob Meir of Alsace tells of an agunah who approached him for assistance who was wretched and wailing loudly; he says, "I could not prevent my soul from hearkening to the wail of the lonely and bereaved."[10] Such expressions were, in my opinion, among the causes that led scholars to attribute to decisors sensitivity to the plight of agunot. Y. Z. Kahana, for instance, stated that discussions of agunot issues in responsa literature generally begin and end with an expression of sympathy on the part of the sages of Israel for the misery of the women, as well as describing their efforts to alleviate the women's suffering.[11]

Before asking if decisors were motivated by an ethic of alleviating the suffering of agunot, let us note that scholars who determined that decisors generally tended to be lenient with regard to freeing agunot based this assertion on the assumption that granting an agunah permission to remarry constitutes halakhic leniency and on the assumption that freeing an agunah always constitutes alleviation of her suffering.[12]

Contrary to the picture painted by halakhic rhetoric, and as previously demonstrated by a number of (female) scholars, the terms "stringency" and "leniency" are relative.[13] Not everything regarded as lenient from the halakhic-male point of view is lenient from a woman's perspective. Before we can determine of any decisor whether he was lenient or stringent in halakhic approach, it must be noted that from the point of view of halakhic authorities, permitting an agunah to remarry is always the lenient way. I do not wish to challenge the view that iggun is the more stringent category for the woman; there is no doubt that iggun caused the agunah real suffering in many, perhaps even most, cases. However, my claim rests on the assumption that people's actions do not depend solely on theoretical categories but also on the concrete reality in which they are situated. In that reality, an individual chooses this or that survival strategy from among the available options. The historian must ask: In this period, was a heter agunah always the preferred choice of the agunah? Did it always alleviate her suffering? In light of the sources, we may answer in the negative, for two reasons.

First, in responsa literature, there occur quite a few cases in which iggun is described as prolonged; in many of them, it is difficult to trace the circumstances that caused this. It cannot be ruled out that the women themselves delayed the heter.[14] We propose possible reasons for them doing so. Moreover, it is generally assumed that if the case of an agunah reached a decisor, it was because she wished to extricate herself from that status. Many responsa, however, do not specify who approached the decisor;[15] others explicitly identify the questioner as relatives or heirs of the agunah, who sometimes acted in cooperation with the agunah herself, but not always.[16]

Why would a woman choose to remain an agunah? We have at hand the information presented in the preceding parts. In Jewish society at that time, marriage had great economic significance. Financially, a married woman enjoyed an advantage over a widow, thanks to the livelihood provided by her husband and by virtue of the married state itself. Freeing an agunah was tantamount to declaring her a widow, with all the economic consequences of the distribution of the husband's estate. It was not always the widow who benefited from the termination of marriage.[17] If the couple had children, a wealthy woman might have preferred to remain an agunah; if she remarried, she might be compelled to give up custody of her children. A mother who feared she might not be able to keep her children in a new marriage might very well prefer to remain an agunah. If she kept her children, she might even gain financial support from her late husband's family, who may have preferred that his children remain in her custody.

This is mere conjecture drawing upon indirect information. However, a late-nineteenth-century letter may demonstrate that a woman's preference for remaining an agunah was reasonable. Rabbi Abraham Meir Gitler (1845–1923), the rabbi of Sosnowiec, sent a letter to Rabbi Jacob Joseph, the chief rabbi of New York City's Association of American Orthodox Hebrew Congregations.[18] The letter opens with a portrayal of a woman who came to the rabbi nine years after her husband had left her. She was penniless, with two small daughters and a son. Recently, she had heard that he was in America. She obtained his address. She and her daughters had nothing to eat; her son had already starved to death. The agunah implored the rabbi to write to the rabbi of the congregation where her husband was living to remind him of his wife of many years and of his two daughters and to ask him to send money for their sustenance.[19] Having told her to come back the following week, the rabbi received in the mail a get he was supposed to deliver to an agunah. A special emissary was needed for this task, at great expense, and the rabbi put the get aside. The following week, the agunah returned as instructed. The rabbi, eager to deliver the get he had received, inquired as to her name and the name of her husband. He was astonished to learn that the get was written in her name and her husband's. He was angered at being asked to write to the husband for financial support when she had already asked for a divorce, and, in fact, the get itself had arrived. At hearing this, the woman fainted, and her daughter started to weep. When the agunah revived, she started weeping as well, declaring all was lost and that she had never asked for a divorce. What was she supposed to do now with her two daughters?[20]

Gitler reassured her, saying she need not accept the get. The rabbi in New York was requested to pressure the abandoning husband into providing for his wife and daughters instead of divorcing her.

The letter is apparently from late 1895,[21] some half a century after the period with which this study is concerned. With all due caution in using it to learn about an earlier period, and since no comparable document was found in our period, I nevertheless believe it justifies the assertion that we cannot assume in advance that ending agunah status would always alleviate the suffering of the agunah. Nor can we assume that ending that status was the realization of her own wishes.[22]

ETHIC OF EMPATHY?

The final question I should like to address is whether there is any basis for claiming that decisors applied an ethic of preventing suffering in dealing with agunot. Unlike the empirical nature of the previous discussion, this question does not necessarily relate to the decisors who were active in the period investigated in the present study. It pertains, rather, to the underlying principles that for generations guided halakhic activity concerning agunot.

The metanarrative determines that decisors sought to alleviate the bitter fate of agunot and assist them.[23] Laws regarding agunot and the reasoning of decisors were for centuries supposedly focused on that end.[24] This metanarrative ascribes to the decisors the perception that the agunah's suffering should be taken into consideration within the legal-halakhic activity of freeing them. Such a presumption is based on the personal writings of decisors or on the halakhic sources that guided the decisors.[25] Yehudah Brandes, for instance, claims that "it is important to note that it was the rabbis themselves who put in place the principle of alleviating the suffering of an agunah, and that, therefore, we cannot very well accuse them of indifference to the woman's needs."[26] He acknowledges that there may have been specific times in which decisors were not doing enough to implement this meta-principle. But he suggests examining the possibility that "the tendency to accuse the sages of indifference, reluctance to act, and insensitivity to the distress of the women results from a one-dimensional grasp of those needs." Rabbinic judges, according to Brandes, take into account additional considerations and principles obligating them to exercise the utmost caution with respect to agunot.[27]

What Brandes sees as the exceedingly cautious position of dayanim — their need to balance empathy for the agunah against other fundamental principles — is further elaborated as follows:

> The fact that there exists a principal policy of making every effort to reduce the number of agunah cases and their duration still does not warrant random decision to free an agunah, with no explicit halakhic basis. As relates to agunah laws, there is a general as well as a particular reason for this. The general one is that halakhah, like any legal system, cannot content itself with principles, and must delve into legally valid specifics.... The particular reason pertaining to agunah cases is the contrast between the meta-principle of preventing iggun and another value, requiring no less caution — the value of protecting the woman from being confounded by the horrendous chance that the husband who was pronounced dead should reappear.[28] Such an unlucky event would constitute violation of the prohibition of *eshet ish*, and her children would be mamzerim, with all sorts of further complications. The risk of permitting an agunah to remarry is no less a concern than is iggun itself. The elaborate procedures are aspects of the halakhah designed to prevent a hasty decision regarding the husband's death.[29]

In these words, which reflect rabbinic rhetoric regarding agunot, including during the time period under discussion, Brandes makes selective use of the claim that it was the rabbis who came up with the meta-principle of leniency in agunah issues. Based on that claim, he attributes to the decisors an ethic of empathy for the suffering of agunot. But he presents the other principles, which counterbalance the one for leniency and require the exercise of caution in freeing agunot, as existing a priori; he sees no need to consider the question of how they came to be. At the base of Brandes's argument is the fact that the principle of showing leniency to agunot is rabbinic law, whereas the prohibition against having sexual relations with a married woman—and the prohibitions that derive from that—have the greater force of biblical law. Yet it must be emphasized: not all halakhic meanings of "iggun" or all halakhic outcomes of the return of the husband who was presumed dead derive from biblical law. So, for example, in biblical law, only the children of the second marriage are mamzerim. It was the rabbis who ruled that the children of both husbands were mamzerim. The pecuniary implications for the woman—loss of her ketubah and maintenance monies—are also rabbinic, not biblical, in origin. Just as Brandes regards the leniency of the rabbis in the laws of testimony for agunah cases as a reflection of the principle of sensitivity to the agunah's suffering, we could equally consider the rabbis as callous in this area of halakhah, due to the numerous stringencies they created. It would appear that the picture painted by Brandes is biased.

Brandes fails to inquire how the stringencies designed to prevent outcomes of erroneous marriage came into being; yet he does not ignore the fact that the sages—had they so wished—could have "devised legal solutions of a more or less sophisticated nature to deal with the eventuality of the husband's return, using the means at their disposal." However, the rabbis regarded such solutions with disfavor, as Brandes observes, and as has been proven in the present study. Two major flaws in such solutions, says Brandes, underlie the rabbinic stance: First, the reappearance of the husband presumed dead is a "difficult human situation and grave crisis"; precautions against such an eventuality are more than a mere halakhic position—they are exigencies of reality. Second, such solutions contravene the Torah's tendency "to sanctify and strengthen the marital relationship."[30]

Let us examine these claims. The first is that taking precautions against the reappearance of the first husband whose wife has remarried is an exigency of reality; it is not merely a halakhic position. This is tantamount to saying that the difficulty raised by the first husband's reappearance is not due to halakhic stringencies but to the inherent human tragedy of the situation itself. There would be terrible sorrow and heartbreak even without her being forced to get a divorce from both husbands and without declaring the children mamzerim. There is a degree of truth in this, in my view. Yet we must ask: Is the suffering the woman will experience in such an eventuality necessarily greater than that caused by the halakhic state of iggun? At stake are two kinds of suffering: the suffering of being an agunah and the future suffering if the first husband reappears. The halakhic system has decreed that the suffering that will follow the possible reappearance of the husband is greater than that caused by being an agunah. In other words, potential suffering overrides actual suffering. Contrary to Brandes's presentation, we are not dealing with an assessment of reality but with a gender-biased value judgment, since the suffering of being an agunah is reserved solely for women.

According to Brandes, legal solutions that might have prevented iggun "would weaken the absolute, uncompromising validity of the framework of marriage."[31] This might imply that our sages weighed the institution of marriage against the suffering of agunot, and they found in favor of the sanctity of marriage. Even if we accept the sages' approach, which regards marriage as an institution with benefits for society as a whole,[32] we can nevertheless challenge the assertion that the proposed solutions would have weakened it. It might be claimed, for instance, that such solutions could actually strengthen the institution of marriage by reducing the number of unmarried women and because embedded in such solutions is the notion that an actual marriage is preferable to marriage in name only.

Even if the laws concerning agunot are not founded on an ethic of alleviating the agunah's suffering, this does not rule out the possibility that certain decisors in the relevant period were motivated by such a wish. Many decisors described the agunah's suffering in vivid terms; why not accept what they wrote in good faith? Certainly, we gain the impression that some decisors did, indeed, act out of a wish to alleviate the suffering of agunot. Behind some of the colorful imagery used of an agunah, there was no doubt a decisor who sympathized with her and wanted to assist. However, there is good reason to propose alternative explanations for the vivid imagery used in halakhic literature.

First, depictions of the suffering agunah appear even in cases in which the appeal to the decisor was made by letter, and thus he never actually met the agunah in person and did not know if she was miserable or not.[33] Hence, these are not so much descriptions of an actual encounter between a miserable agunah and an empathetic decisor as they are a literary convention. Second, responsa literature had a readership of decisors and Torah scholars. If decisors were aware of the suffering of agunot, which should be alleviated if possible, why the need for the abundant evocative imagery? Perhaps the recurrent imagery in responsa literature shows that not all decisors were aware of the agunah's plight. The aim of the imagery in that case would be to underscore the suffering for those who lacked sufficient awareness in expectation that they will take the agunah's suffering into account when dealing with her case. But what would "take into account" mean in the context of suffering? What would the decisor be expected to do when faced with a suffering agunah? Let us look at that question with the aid of another example.

On a Thursday in February 1699, Rabbi Yechezkel Katzenellenbogen, then the rabbi of the city of Kaidan (Kedainiai), Lithuania, signed a heter agunah. Like other agunot we have encountered, Frieda's merchant husband was murdered on a business trip. Her husband, Israel, was buried in the community of Taurogi (Tauragė). Witnesses gave evidence in Günzburg as to his death in accordance with halakhic requirements. When Frieda received the written testimonies, she took them to Katzenellenbogen and asked for permission to remarry. The responsum opens with his depiction of the embittered woman before him: "wailing loudly all the while, weeping in a voice of fractured and loud blasts [Hebr., *shevarim u'teruah*, meant to evoke the sounds of the *shofar*], Frieda recounts how her husband Israel was killed, making her an agunah."[34] We have no way of knowing if Frieda did in fact weep and wail loudly in Katzenellenbogen's presence. Be that as it may, his tone cannot be ignored. Assuming decisors were aware of shared associations with their readers, Katzenellenbogen's choice of words was not random. He likens Frieda's weeping to the sound of the shofar — one of the most highly charged images in Jewish tradition. The sound of the shofar is meant to arouse the hearer to inner contemplation and soul-searching, as in Amos 3:6: "Shall the horn be blown in a city, And the people not tremble?" To the responsum's reader, the connotation of the shofar image is of the agunah's cries spurring the decisor into action. The image itself does not spell out any required course of action on the decisor's part, yet it does encode a call for self-contemplation. This was, in fact, one of a decisor's aims in requesting affirmation from a fellow decisor of his opinion to free an agunah. The decisors who joined their voices to the first one who granted his permission are reaffirming his ruling as conforming to halakhic standards.

One result of the practice of asking a fellow decisor to join in granting an agunah permission to remarry was the geographical distancing between agunah and decisor. The first decisor the agunah would approach was likely to be the local rabbi, who thus was acquainted with her. His colleague would usually be a stranger from a different community, often without any prior knowledge of her circumstances — he did not even always meet the agunah in person. I would like to suggest that the practice of requesting affirmation by another decisor in freeing an agunah developed in order to protect the first decisor, the one closest to her and exposed directly to her suffering. Fellow decisors may have been concerned about his susceptibility to pressures that could impair his judgment. The notion that a person's suffering might impair another's judgment appears in the Talmud; one of its most explicit expressions contains some of the most frequently used images of an agunah's suffering. In the context of a Talmudic discussion relating to a verse from the beginning of the book of Lamentations — "Bitterly she weeps in the night, Her cheek wet with tears (1:2)" — appear these homilies:

> Alternatively, the term "at night" indicates that in the case of anyone who cries at night, one who hears his voice is touched by his suffering and cries with him. There was an incident involving one woman, the neighbor of Rabban Gamliel, whose son died, and she would cry over his death at night. Rabban Gamliel heard her voice and cried with her until his eyelashes fell out. The next day his students noticed that he had been crying, and they removed the woman from his neighborhood [so that Rabban Gamliel could sleep]. "Her cheek wet with tears": Said Rabbah in the name of Rabbi Yochanan: "Like the woman who weeps over the husband of her youth."[35]

In this Talmudic story, the deep empathy of Rabban Gamliel for the woman's suffering damages his eyes, the eyes of the spiritual leader — thereby threatening the moderation he needed to correctly assess reality. In order to restore their teacher's faculty of judgment, his students choose to distance the woman from him. The esteemed leader does nothing to stop them. The message is clear: suffering — and perhaps specifically the suffering of a woman — brings failure and is liable to make a decisor work counter to what his role requires of him.

I doubt whether all decisors who dealt with the freeing of an agunah studied this story in any depth.[36] Yet the affinity between some of the descriptions of the agunah's suffering and the story suggests familiarity, at least for some of them. For example, the rabbi of the Sephardic community of Amsterdam, Rabbi Solomon Shlomo (1664–1728), tells of an agunah who came to him for assistance. He sent a question on her behalf to Rabbi David Oppenheim, emphasizing her sorrow and weeping, and stressing the empathy she aroused in himself.[37]

Extant sources on agunot challenge the "metanarrative" presented by some scholars, according to which decisors, in all generations, endeavored to alleviate the suffering of agunot. Critical examination of the claim that an ethics of alleviating the agunah's suffering underlies the halakhic field of freeing agunot reveals that such an ethic does not reflect the rabbinic activity in the period under discussion, nor does it reflect the assumptions underlying the halakhic activity in this field in general. This metanarrative contains several glaring flaws: it overgeneralizes, thereby blurring distinct coexisting models of halakhic activity; it ignores the actions and practices of decisors, some of which made life extremely difficult for agunot; it is gender biased due to the assumption that permission to remarry is always the agunah's first choice; and finally, it attributes to decisors an ethic of preventing suffering where no such ethic exists. This hitherto prevailing metanarrative in scholarship is based, to a great extent, on wishful thinking along the lines that halakhah and rabbinic authority possess the power to satisfactorily resolve cases of individuals with a hard life.

The sources, however, are not always amenable to wishful thinking. Decisors as well as agunot of the time were motivated by ideas and principles but also by desires, drives, impulses, social pressure, and human limitations. Just as some agunot experienced great suffering while others preferred it to available alternatives, so, too, some decisors were affected by the suffering of the agunah and made valiant efforts to help them, while others did not—and even put obstacles in their path. The rabbinate institution tended to make it difficult for agunot who sought permission to remarry, less for substantive halakhic reasons than for pragmatic ones. I see in this fact the primary evidence for the likelihood, supported by the sources, that many agunot whose stories are recounted herein never received permission to remarry.

Introducing his study of the Jewish family in Germany in the modern era, Robert Liberles points to demonstrations of marital fidelity as well as to harsh family frictions and even adultery. He warns historians who would paint a picture of the Jewish family with broad strokes against assigning too much weight to deviations from the norm. In light of Liberles's comment, we must ask: What has the present discussion of agunot contributed to our knowledge of the Jewish family in the early modern era in particular and of Jewish society in this era in general? Should this discussion be located among the increasing number of studies on marginal groups, or can it illuminate aspects of life in Jewish society as a whole?

The answer lies, I believe, not in the number of agunot in this period — data that cannot be derived from surviving sources — but in the understanding of the place of iggun in the perceptions of the institution of marriage in this society. Research shows that Jewish society has always placed the highest value on marriage. Yemima Hovav has even claimed that a Jewish woman's adolescence and maturity were totally focused on the moment of union with her future husband.[38] I believe the unhappy picture emerging from the present study reveals that while men and women alike were brought up to regard marriage as the sole appropriate family unit, implicit, gender-dependent messages instilled a very different understanding of marriage. Whereas men were aware that marriage granted them security, freedom, and control over their wives' fates, women were constantly aware of the lurking threat that marriage would turn into a trap. Men and women alike led their lives among family, community, and non-Jewish society aware of these perceptions, leading their lives knowing that iggun was, respectively, a possibility or a danger. This fact seems to have had far-reaching implications for the status of women in Jewish society in this period and in traditional Jewish society in general. In other words, the very existence of the concept of iggun in the consciousness of members of Jewish society defined their spheres of action, both geographically and metaphorically. This society, with an everyday life characterized by the prolonged absences of husbands from their homes, in which men who abandoned their wives faced few meaningful consequences, sacrificed not only the agunot themselves but, rather, all women on the altar of men's freedom.

GLOSSARY

Agunah
   a woman who is precluded from remarrying because she is still in a marital bond that has not come to an end in accordance with halakhic requirements

beit din/batei din
   rabbinic court(s)

dayan/dayanim
   rabbinic court judge(s)

get
   writ of divorce, the legal document with which a husband divorces his wife

halakhah
   Jewish law

halitzah
   a ceremony voiding the need to perform levirate marriage

heter (pl. heterei)
   a document in which the beit din/decisor declares that the agunah is permitted to remarry

iggun
   the situation of being an agunah

ketubah
   marriage contract

mezonot
   maintenance (lit. "food")

pinkas/pinksim
   record book, register

poskim
   rabbis who gave Jewish legal rulings ("decisors")

responsa
   (Hebr., *she'elot utshuvot*, lit., "questions and answers") answers, typically in the form of letters, written by rabbis in response to questions they had received from their congregants, colleagues, and other followers

shamash
   sexton; a layperson who assisted in the synagogue with religious services and also sometimes kept communal records

shetar
   bill; contract

shetar mekuyam
: validated document; this term refers to a bill attesting to a fact that has been proved to be authentic and valid

shetarot tenaim
: engagement and betrothal contracts

Shulhan arukh
: Code of Jewish law by Rabbi Joseph Caro published in Venice 1566

takanah/takanot
: ordinance/ordinances; Takanot Kehila = communal ordinances

Tzena urena
: a compilation of commentaries and midrashim on the weekly Torah and haftarah portions written by Jacob ben Isaac Ashkenazi of Janów (1550–1624)

yibum
: levirate marriage

NOTES

PREFACE AND ACKNOWLEDGMENTS

1. *Agunot* = plural; *agunah* = singular. Non-English words and phrases in this book are italicized on first use only.
2. Roughly, the situation of being an agunah.

INTRODUCTION

1. The English (1937) translation of Agnon's original *agunah shomemah* as "desolate forsaken wife" does not accurately reflect the Hebrew text.
2. Several of Agnon's works treat the theme of agunot. He actually changed his name from Czaczkes to Agnon following the publication of his first short story, entitled "Agunot," on symbolic iggun. The reason for the change hovers like a riddle over his entire works. On the story "Agunot," see Bernstein (2001).
3. On the poem, see Shamir (2014).
4. See Tal (1948).
5. See Lipking (1988).
6. See Friedman (1974); and Harrington (1995), 268.
7. Kahana (1946).
8. Kahana (1954).
9. Kahana (1954), 7.
10. A detailed list can be found in Shashar (2012), 3–4, n.14.
11. See, for instance, Cohen (2000); and Yael V. Levy (1993).
12. See Golinkin (2000); and more recently, Lubitch (2017); Haneman (2017).
13. See Jackson (2009), 5.
14. The report was published as a book in 2011, under the title *Agunah: The Manchester Analysis*.
15. For the first division, see Grossman (2001), index; Shohet (1960), index; Shilo (2001), index; Hertzberg (1989), 187; Alroi (2008), 124–33; Freeze (2002), index; Salmon-Mack (2012), 215–57. Salmon-Mack dealt extensively with some of the issues that appear in this book as well, but her methodological approach differs from the one used here, and the geographic area she studied is narrower than the one discussed in this book. For the second division, see Keil (2007); Dubin (2007); Sperber (Summer 2010); Baker (1995); Friedman (1982).
16. Katz (1993), 12, 14.
17. Unlike Katz (1993), who considered all of Ashkenaz one unit, others are of the opinion that Jews in different communities did not consider themselves as belonging to a single collective; see Rosman (2009), 15–29.

18. On responsa as correspondence among decisors in Ashkenaz in the early modern era, see Berkovitz (2007), 116.

19. For the implications of the seventeenth-century wars and the riots of 1648–1649 on the lives of individuals and Jewish communities in the Ashkenazic lands, see Teller (2020).

20. On the record books of non-Jewish institutions, see Schilling and Schreiber (1989), introduction.

21. For a definition of "record notebooks," see Litt (2008), 7–11, and references.

22. Although Jewish courts existed in Ashkenaz even before this time period, only in early modern times did the non-Jewish authorities grant them official dispensation to handle civil and family matters involving Jews.

23. Historical record book, Altona and Hamburg; Record book, Altona 17b, fol. 11a.

24. See Shazar (1971), 78; Berkovitz (2014), 3.

25. See the bibliography for a detailed list of record notebooks and their locations symbols in the archives. Two have recently been published: Fram (2012) and Berkovitz (2014). My thanks to these two for allowing me to study the annotated records before having seen the sources themselves.

26. There are very few extant beit din records from premodern times. See Fram (2012), 20, n. 17.

27. Berkovitz, lecture, Jerusalem, May 2011; I thank him for sharing his lecture text.

28. The term "midrash" refers to "a particular genre of rabbinic literature containing anthologies and compilations of homilies, including both biblical exegesis and sermons delivered in public as well as *agadot* [legends] and sometimes even halakhot, usually forming a running commentary on specific books of the Bible." Herr (2007), 182.

29. See Rabinowitz (2007).

30. On the effects of printing on the Ashkenazic elite, see Reiner (1997).

31. In part 4, I explain the structure of the corpus used in the present study, the number of responsa dealing with agunot, and my criteria for selecting representative responsa.

32. For the census of Polish Jewry, see Stampfer (1989); on the census reports from Germany, see Lindemann (1990), 54–55.

33. Mahler (1958).

34. Stern (1962–1975).

35. *Census of the Jews of Alsace, 1784*.

36. An example of an analysis of gravestone inscriptions can be found in Hovav (2009), 466–81.

37. The above was part of a lecture that Berkovitz gave in Jerusalem in May

2011. I thank the author for sharing his lecture text with me. For further reading on this topic, see Berkovitz (2019), 33–35.

38. On the methodological problems of using halakhic literature for historical research, see Soloveitchik (1990).

39. For a survey of feminist methods in this context of this problem, see Alexander (2000).

40. See Dekker (2002).

41. Braudel (2009).

42. Gadamer (1975).

43. Ortner (1974).

44. MacKinnon (1993), 13.

45. See, for instance, Casey (1989).

46. For a concise comparative overview of views on divorce in Jewish law and in other legal systems, see Shereshevsky (1984), 355–57.

47. All biblical translations into English are from the New Jewish Publication Society (NJPS) Tanakh unless otherwise indicated.

48. Usually, halakhah permitted only Jewish men to testify at a beit din, but women were allowed in the case of iggun. For more details, see part 2.

49. Oppenheim (1971–1984), question 43.

50. Gottfarstein (1959), 593.

51. The most comprehensive treatment is Salmon-Mack (2012), 163–214, but it is restricted to Poland-Lithuania.

52. Kasper-Marienberg (2014); Kasper-Marienberg and Fram (2022).

53. Kaplan (2020).

54. Berkovitz (2019).

55. Berkovitz (2019), 356.

56. Berkovitz (2019), 356.

CHAPTER 1: WIDOWS IN THE ASHKENAZIC WORLD, 1648–1850

1. See Rapoport-Albert (2014), 494–95. The term "widow" seemingly refers to all women who remained alive after their husbands died, and it is this group of women that this chapter discusses. However, the meaning of the term is context-dependent; see Buitelaar (1995).

2. See, for instance, Kruse (2007). For an extensive list of bibliography, see Shashar (2012), 32, n. 4.

3. See Salmon-Mack (2012), 163–214; for a brief note about widows within a discussion of other topics, see Hovav (2009), index; Liberles (2005), 59–61.

4. The subject of Glikl and her world has been thoroughly researched; see Turniansky (2019), 1–36, and references there; and, recently, Feiner (2021), 57–69.

5. Glikl as widow, and widowhood in that period more generally, are also discussed by Rapoport-Albert (2014).

6. See McGinn (2008), 78–79; Wiesner (1997), 88.

7. Bogucka (2004), 14.

8. McGinn (2008), 80–84; Ogilvie (2003), 250–51. See also Watt (2001), 125–54, and references there.

9. In the seventeenth and eighteenth centuries, 90 percent of German Jews lived in small communities in rural areas. Urban Jews like Glikl were a minority in Germany and in the wider Ashkenazic world. See Breuer (1996), 173.

10. Turniansky (2019), 66, 91, 97, 180.

11. Turniansky (2019), introduction.

12. Turniansky (2019), 9–31. For methodological problems associated with documents of this kind, see Bar-Levav (2002b).

13. See Ps. 80:6 and Isa. 14:12.

14. Turniansky (2019), 201–2.

15. Midr. Sifre devarim, paragraph 213.

16. I found a single reference relating to an earlier period, in Israel Isserlein's responsa collection, Isserlein (1882), #353.

17. Kruse (2007), 165–81; van Os (2002), 230–46.

18. Bar-Levav (2002a).

19. On apparel worn by Jews in Germany at that time; see Liberles (2005), 161–62.

20. Of special interest is a community regulation passed in Lithuania in 1628 that differentiates between poor women, who wear coarse linen dresses, and the more affluent, whose garments are of finer linen. The regulation further states that female ritual-bath (mikveh) attendants should closely supervise the poorer women. See Dubnow (1924), no. 131.

21. Dress regulations appear in nearly all the community record books that have reached us. For instance, Takanot 3 kehilot 9, 32, no. 185, 5486 (September 8, 1725–September 25, 1726). When a Hebrew year noted in a source can be identified with a Hebrew month, the corresponding Gregorian year can be calculated and will be noted. When only the year is given, however, the Hebrew date could span an approximately two-year span on the Gregorian calendar, as is the case here. The span will be noted as well.

22. On social functions of Jewish customs, see Awiad-Wolfsberg (1957). On the place of customs in Jewish life in Germany in the modern era, see Pollack (1971), xiv.

23. On Jews' awareness of general fashion trends in the surrounding non-Jewish society, see, e.g., Turniansky (2019), 94.

24. Halperin (1952), 183, paragraph 530. Compare Esh (1961), 45.

25. On the union of the Three Communities, see Horowitz (2010), chapter 1. Various record books and registers have survived from these communities,

and I will bring several examples from these throughout this book. Takanot 3 kehilot 9, 33, no. 188.

26. See, for instance, Reischer (1860), 3:115; Segal (1680), 17.
27. Manspach (1987–1992), 103–7.
28. Bnei Gumpel (1767), fol. 16b, 98. Compare Manspach (1987–1992), 252.
29. Sturz, a black kerchief of thick linen, was a typical head-covering worn by women in Germany in the early modern period. See Manspach (1987–1992), 159, nn. 25–26. On the origin of covering one's head during mourning, see Zimmer (2005), 193–210.
30. Kruse (2007), 166, and illustrations 176–81; van Os (2002), 233–34.
31. According to Yemima Hovav (2009), 210–11, widows, more than widowers, were expected to externalize their bereavement.
32. See Levy (2003); Buitelaar (1995).
33. Bremmer and van den Bosch (1995). See also Rapoport-Albert (2014), 497–98.
34. Katz (1945), 22.
35. For an example of Jewish ethical writings, see *Sefer hasidim* (Judah he-Hasid [1957], 412). On commonplace images of widows in non-Jewish society in Europe, and particularly in German culture, see McGinn (2008), 90–99.
36. Turniansky (2019), 177.
37. Turniansky (2019), 267.
38. Community institutions were based on three types of taxation: see Hildesheimer (1992), 64–68.
39. Turniansky (2019), 66, 180.
40. Mishnah Bava Metzia 9:13.
41. See, for instance, Grossman (2001), 470–75; Tallan (1991), 63.
42. The work has been reprinted in over 230 editions to date. On the book and its agenda, circulation, and versions, see Turniansky (2009).
43. Lam. 1:1–2. The association with widows appears in the Babylonian Talmud, Sanhedrin 104b.
44. Ashkenazi (1849), fol. 131a.
45. Shmeruk (1978), 115.
46. Turniansky (2019), 202.
47. See, for instance, Bock (1991), esp. 3–7.
48. On different emphases in research on the financial aspects of widowhood, see Ogilvie (2003), 218, and references there.
49. Rivlin (1999), chapter 3.
50. Shereshevsky (1984), 186–95, 307.
51. An important component of the dowry was a woman's share in her father's estate; see Fram (1997), 81–95. Impoverished young women would

enter domestic service to save up for a dowry; see Shimshi-Licht (2007), chapter 3.

52. Gulak (1926), 22–25.
53. Babylonian Talmud, Ketubot 54b.
54. Babylonian Talmud, Ketubot 81b.
55. On the reasons for this enactment, see Shereshevsky (1984), 314, and the references in nn. 22–23.
56. Freiman (1949); Yuval (1995).
57. Entitlements of widows were restricted in the context of "the market enactment" (*takanat hashuk*); see Shereshevsky (1984), 315. The essence of this enactment is that the woman can claim her share from property and not from chattel.
58. Karo, *Shulhan arukh*, Even haezer, 118:1.
59. Karo, *Shulhan arukh*, Even haezer, 102:1. On the priority of inheritance among widows and creditors and the different practices of Polish Jews and Moravian Jews, see Salmon-Mack (2012), 176–87.
60. Karo, *Shulhan arukh*, Even haezer, 94. See also Shereshevsky (1984), 322–32.
61. See Grossman (2001), 473.
62. Tam (1985), #788; enacted subsequently also in the communities of Speyer, Worms, and Mainz.
63. Yuval (1995), 201.
64. See Moshe Isserles, *Hagahot haRMA al shulkhan arukh*, Even haezer, 52:4. These directives were not always strictly observed, and there were regional differences. See Tzvi Hirsch Ashkenazi (1711), 61; Eisenstadt (1899), 148.
65. Dubnow (1924), 268, n. 981.
66. Avraham Tzvi Hirsch Eisenstadt, *Pithei teshuva al shulhan arukh*, Even haezer, 52, paragraph 14.
67. On these halakhic developments, see Salmon-Mack (2012), 60–64.
68. Turniansky (2019), 202.
69. Turniansky (2019), 66.
70. Glikl and her sister each received a bequest of "half a male heir's share," which they turned over to their respective husbands. See Turniansky (2019), 175, n. 166.
71. Record book, beit din Prague, fol. 87b.
72. The man's surname is illegible in the manuscript.
73. Record book, beit din Prague, fol. 87b.
74. See Ullmann (2000), 93–113.
75. The procedures outlined applied equally to men and women, but their impact was greater for women because a man inherits property from his wife. However, compare Record book, beit din Altona 3, fol. 144a.

76. See Frankfurt dayan record book in Fram (2012), fol. 231b. A 1691 enactment in Warzburg mandated the presence of a government official for sealing off the estate; this was subsequently revoked, and in 1750, Jewish officials were given authority to seal off an estate on their own. See Cohen (1966), vol. 1, 211; in Alsace, see Berkovitz (2010a), esp. 276–77. The same procedure obtained in German non-Jewish society, see Sabean (1997), 167.

77. For instance, Record book, community of Altona 16, 198a, 230; and Record book, beit din Altona 3, fol. 113.

78. Promissory notes (membrana) were in general use for loans in Jewish society beginning in the late sixteenth century; see Fram (1997), 129–43.

79. Roth (1961), 139, n. 193.

80. For the function of shamash, see Horowitz (2010), 26.

81. Record book, shamash of Altona 1. Although the identity of the shamash is not recorded in the notebook, I believe it is Hirsch Lelow; see Shashar (2012), 46, n. 107.

82. Record book, shamash of Altona 1, e.g., fols. 12, 18. Documentation of sealing off an estate can be found also in Record book, Offenbach, fol. 115.

83. Record book, shamash of Altona 1, fol. 22.

84. Abraham Warburg, אברהם אהרן ב' כ' שמואל ווארבורג, https://peace.sites .uu.nl/epigraphy/search/?fbclid=IwAR3uckiObgUoZL_OF6gspAosoqc FGo8KuWs6HnsMmKbzw2PMg-pKY-w8jBk.

85. Record book, shamash of Altona 1, fol. 23a.

86. Jusepe Levi, הנלה רבקה בת // יוזפא יעקב, https://peace.sites.uu.nl /epigraphy/search/?fbclid=IwAR3uckiObgUoZL_OF6gspAosoqcFGo8 KuWs6HnsMmKbzw2PMg-pKY-w8jBk.

87. A regulation passed in Nikolsburg in 5410 (Sept. 7, 1649–Sept. 25, 1650) to the effect that an estate would be sealed off only at the claimant's request; this was subsequently revoked. Most community record books contain a regulation for sealing off the estate independently of the claimants' request.

88. As in the regulation passed in Hamburg in 1710. While I could not find written evidence of this in beit din record books, it could have been implemented nevertheless; see Horowitz (2010), 149; Breuer (1996), 226–27. In Metz, the beit din cooperated with non-Jewish courts; see Berkovitz (2010a), 277–78.

89. The reconstructed text is based on mentions of the Glickstadt family in other sources.

90. Record book, Altona 17b, 11. Appointment of executors is mentioned frequently; see Record book, Altona 17b, 12, 13, and elsewhere. The same holds true for the Record book, Offenbach, fol. 1b, and elsewhere. See also Takanot 3 kehilot 9, takanah 197; Record book, shamash of Altona 1, fol. 17; and Record book, community of Fürth, fols. 12a, 33a, 51a, and elsewhere.

91. Compare Berkovitz (2010a), 283.

92. On appointment of guardians for orphans, see Berner (2018), 189–92.

93. This explains why the position of executor was not always easy to fill; see Record book, shamash of Altona 1, fol. 17; Record book, beit din Altona 4, 70–71a; Berkovitz (2005), esp. 7.

94. See Record book, beit din Altona 1, fol. 39a (62a).

95. Rabbi Horowitz served as rabbi of Altona only for about two years; Record book, community of Altona 16, fol. 8a; see also Duckesz (1903), 53–59.

96. The year was 5527 (Sept. 4, 1766–Sept. 23, 1767).

97. Record book, shamash of Altona 1, fol. 9a.

98. Record book, shamash of Altona 1, fol. 9a.

99. A reichstaler was a coin. Different currencies were used in this period, with exchange rates constantly changing, even in a single territory. This makes it extremely difficult to calculate monetary value. See Nelkenbrecher (1828), 13.

100. Record book, Altona 17b, 31.

101. Examples in Shashar (2012), 48, nn. 127–28.

102. The exceptions are the positions of *mohel* (circumciser) and shohet (ritual slaughterer); contemporary sources show that women occasionally performed both these functions during the period in question.

103. The wife of a community functionary would sometimes be appointed to a "female" position, such as attendant at the ritual bath. For examples, see Shashar (2012), 48, n. 131.

104. See Kaplan (2010), 99.

105. Compare Record book, beit din Poznan, 120 (625), 131 (685), 136 (714). See also Hovav (2009), 400–402.

106. See Grossman (2001), 217–18.

107. In the original: "inventorium."

108. Record book, Altona 17b, 9.

109. Jewish law considers any gift bestowed by the husband on his wife during their married life as her property, to use as she likes.

110. Wills were drawn up in the presence of community officials (shamash, scribe) and witnesses; see Altona wills, Record book, shamash of Altona 1, fol. 23a.

111. Graupe (1972), 13–14 (this is a summary of the will). As opposed to this, two other testators stated explicitly that the wife was to inherit nothing but the ketubah, including its additions. Hirsch Oppenheim (d. 1773) requested that his wife waive part of her rights to the estate in favor of his children. Graupe (1972), 29.

112. On the beit din in the communities of AHW, see Horowitz (2010), 40–41.

113. Record book, beit din Altona 5, fols. 41a–42a.

114. For instance, see the 1624 regulations of the Council of Four Lands

regarding settlement of debts of bankrupt and runaway debtors; on the difficulties this raised for a widow trying to collect her ketubah, see Salmon-Mack (2012), 179; Fram (1997), 143–63.

115. See Kaplan (2010), 110–11.
116. The "gold pieces" were Rheinischer (Rhenish) guilder, a type of gold coin.
117. Halperin (1952), 78, paragraph 235.
118. See Yuval (1995), 193–94; Cf. Ulbrich (2004), 202. A regulation of Bamberg also gave priority to creditors over the widow's claim to her ketubah. Kaufmann (1968), 10.
119. See Fram (2012), introduction, 46.
120. Record book, Offenbach, fol. 121.
121. Record book, Offenbach, fol. 165b.
122. Record book, Offenbach, fol. 169b.
123. Record book, Offenbach, fol. 185b. This custom seems to have been accepted practice in many Ashkenazic communities. See, for example, Nadav (1999), 523, paragraph 788. See also Ullmann (2000), 100.
124. Rosman (2001), 415–34.
125. Rosman (2001), 427–28.
126. Detailed list in Shashar (2012), 51, and notes there.
127. Record book, beit din Altona 3, fol. 23a.
128. See Schacter (1988), 21–22; Feiner (2021), index. See also Record book, beit din Altona 3, fols. 28a, 42b–43a, 81a.
129. A coin.
130. Emden (1896), 162–63.
131. Record book, beit din Altona 3, fol. 43a, 81a. In his memoirs Emden mentions buying several houses; see Emden (1896), 189.
132. Emden fathered twenty children in all: ten with his first wife, of whom only three reached maturity; four with his second wife, of whom only one reached maturity; and six with his third wife, of whom only two reached maturity. See Schacter (1988), 180–82.
133. Emden (1896), 176–77.
134. Emden (1896), 100, 152.
135. It seems that Zalman appealed to the authorities again after the beit din's ruling, but these forced him to comply with the ruling of the beit din. See Record book, beit din Altona 3, fol. 81.
136. Record book, beit din Altona 3, fol. 42b.
137. Record book, beit din Altona 3, fol. 81a. See also Emden (1896), 100.
138. Record book, beit din Altona 3, fol. 81a.
139. Schock was a currency used in some parts of Ashkenaz. See Nelkenbrecher (1828), 190.

140. Record book, Altona community officials, 5a, 16.

141. See Breuer (1996), 156.

142. Thus it was established in enactment no. 25 in Record book, Offenbach. See also Takanot 3 kehilot 10, fol. 28a, no. 128; Baer (1936), 121; Kaplan (2010), 100–101.

143. Baer (1936), 121; Ullmann (2000), 102.

144. Record book, fee collectors of Gochsheim; Record book, Offenbach, fol. 19.

145. Baer (1936), 121.

146. Record book, beit din Poznan, 161, regulation 908; 170, regulation 979. See Record book, Neuzedlisch, no. 12.

147. Halperin (1952), 64, paragraph 192.

148. Kaufmann (1968), 2.

149. Takanot 3 kehilot 9, fol. 21:121.

150. Takanot 3 kehilot 10, fol. 28:128.

151. Takanot 3 kehilot, fol. 50 (this page is missing in the archive copy but is intact in the photocopy edited by Duckesz [1903]).

152. See, for instance, Takanot 3 kehilot 10, regulation 117.

153. Record book, Offenbach, fol. 157b, fol. 142a.

154. Record book, Altona 17a, 36a.

155. Record book, Altona, 38.

156. Record book, Altona, 27 (pages numbered in pencil).

157. See Record book, Altona 17b, 6. There are also many examples in Record book, fee collector of Bingen

158. See Shulvass (1971), 108–9; Friedman (1972), 34–51. On treatment of the poor and the beggars in Hamburg, see Lindemann (1990). The Altona record book for the month of Shevat (January–February) 1728 notes decrees by the authorities of Hamburg intended to restrict begging. Following these decrees, the community allocated regular funding for the poor to prevent begging. See Record book, Altona 17a, fols. 2b, 3b.

159. Kaplan (2010), 98; Ullmann (2000), 97, 109.

160. Liberles (2005), 83; Turniansky, (2019), 176; Emden (1896), 148, 157.

161. See Turniansky (2019), 212; Wischnitzer (1965), 185; Kohler (2010), 129–46.

162. Tevely Lisser died on March 10, 1792, and was buried the next day; see Kaplan (2010), 99, and the photocopy of his gravestone: טעבלי ליסר. https://www.jewishgenorg/databases/cemetery/jowbr.php?rec=J_GERMANY_0151559.

163. Record book, beit din Altona 3, fol. 109a.

164. Record book, beit din Altona 3, fol. 147a.

165. Such as Hayale, widow of Leib Neustadt, appointed midwife in Offen-

bach: Record book, Offenbach, fol. 95b; Record book, Offenbach, fol. 196b. On women and the ritual bath in Ashkenaz, see Shashar (2007), 75–106.

166. Getz (1732), #43. On widows as domestics, see Shimshi-Licht (2007), 59, 118–19.

167. Most were published by Stern (1962–1975).

168. See, for instance, Weinryb (1972), 104; Rosman (2001), 429–33.

169. Hundert (2004), 33.

170. Stern (1962–1975), vol. 3, part 2b, 846.

171. Stern (1962–1975), vol. 3, part 2b, 1012.

172. Ibid., vol. 3, part 2b, 1038.

173. Ibid., vol. 3, part 2b, 1438.

174. Several sources mention women butchers: Record book, beit din Altona 1, fol. 42a (65a).

175. Record book, community of Zülz, fol. 15.

176. Rosman (2001), 426–27.

177. See Ogilvie (2003), multiple pages, esp. 321.

178. Stern (1962–1975), vol. 2, part 2, 102–23.

179. Ibid.

180. Living conditions of Jews in Germany in this period are described in Liberles (2005), 30–34.

181. On community privileges, see Horowitz (2010), 171; Ullmann (2000), 93–94, 100.

182. Turniansky (2019), 497ff.

183. See Soliday (2003), 502; Ullmann (2000), 102–3; Kohler (2010), 136–37.

184. Community records of Worms, no. 85.

185. Compare Ogilvie and Edwards (2000), 965.

186. Turniansky (2019), 180–81; Toch (1995), 83, n. 17.

187. Including children ages twenty, twenty-one, twenty-three, and twenty-five. Soliday (2003), 503.

188. Stern (1962–1975), vol. 3, part 2a, 701.

189. Ibid. vol. 2, part 2, 102–23.

190. Turniansky (2019), 68–69.

191. Liberles (2005), 52.

192. Stern (1962–1975), vol. 3, part 2b, 1434.

193. *Census of the Jews of Alsace, 1784*. See http://www.genami.org/en/lists/alsace/census4-16-50-HAGUENAU.html.

194. Writs of betrothal and of halitzah, AHW, fol. 3a (68c).

195. *Census of the Jews of Alsace, 1784*.

196. Stern (1962–1975), vol. 2, part 2, 102–23.

197. Ibid., vol. 3, part 2b, 1024.

198. *Census of the Jews of Alsace, 1784*.

199. *Census of the Jews of Alsace, 1784.*
200. For instance, Record book, shamash of Altona 1, fol. 14.
201. Turniansky (2019), 69. See also Record book, beit din Altona 3, fol. 55b.
202. Stampfer (1988), 104–5. See also Wasserzug (1911), 2. Compare Harrington (2009), 123–24, 278–83.
203. See Salmon-Mack (2012), 198–204.
204. References in Shashar (2012), 63, n. 268.
205. Hovav (2009), 122–23.
206. Liberles (2005), 59; Wasserzug (1911), 14; Emden (1896), 69, 154; Hovav (2009), 132.
207. This assumption finds expression in Talmudic statements, e.g., Babylonian Talmud, Ketubot 75a: "Better to be with another than to remain a widow."
208. Babylonian Talmud, Yevamot 42a; *Shulhan arukh*, Even haezer, 13, paragraph 1.
209. See Gilat (1994–96); Baumgarten (2004), 186–90, 279; Salmon-Mack (2012), 91–111.
210. Babylonian Talmud, Bava Metzia 84b.
211. Babylonian Talmud, Yevamot 64b.
212. Grossman (2001), 463–70.
213. A widower who has "buried" two wives is not similarly restricted; see Karo, *Shulhan arukh*, Even haezer, 9:2.
214. Isserles, *Hagahot haRMA leShulhan arukh*, Even haezer, 9:1.
215. Horovitz (1901), 295, paragraph 2750, gravestone 4548.
216. See gravestone inscription: https://peace.sites.uu.nl/epigraphy/search/?fbclid=IwAR3uckiObgUoZL_OF6gspAosoqcFGo8KuWs6HnsMmKbzw2PMg-pKY-w8jBk.
217. See Duckesz (1903), 104–6.
218. Emden (1896), 10. That same widow, Shifra, later married Rabbi David Oppenheim.
219. Emden (1896), 154.
220. Compare McGinn (2008), 100.
221. Ogilvie and Edwards (2000), 965; Boulton (1990).
222. Ogilvie (2003), 173, 218.
223. Salmon-Mack (2012), 112–15; Teller (2014), 45.
224. See Wunder (1998), 135; McGinn (2008), 100.
225. Turniansky (2019), 91.
226. Ibid., 180–81.
227. Ibid., 181.
228. Emden (1896), 7, 44, 64, 69.
229. Despite her ambivalence, Glikl did marry a second time. Emden tells

how his younger sister Leah, widowed with one son, remarried and had a child, then was widowed a second time.

230. See Berner (2018), 80–83.
231. See Assaf (1926).
232. Berkovitz (2014), introduction, 13–16. See also Hirsch Oppenheimer in Richarz (1991), 77.
233. Record book, beit din Altona 1, fol. 81.
234. Record book, beit din Kraków, 32.
235. On Kaidanover and his Kav hayashar, see Shahar (1982), 3–6, 80; Shahar observes that the number of Hebrew and Yiddish editions is indicative of the work's popularity in the eighteenth century.
236. Kaidanover (1944), 7:2.
237. Record book, Altona 17b, 4.
238. Record book, shamash of Altona 1, 14.
239. Weil (1982), #42.
240. The Altona record books contain many examples of orphans whose meals were provided by an uncle or other relatives of the father. See, for example, Record book, beit din Altona 3, fol. 72a.
241. Record book, beit din Altona 1, fol. 8a (31a), no. 135.
242. Record book, beit din Altona 3, fol. 50b.
243. Turniansky (2019), 257.
244. For instance, Koidonover (1884), question 2; Landau (1960), 1st edition, Even haezer, #12–#13; Margoliot (1858), part 3, #50; Salmon-Mack (2012), 91–111.
245. Lindemann (1981); Stampfer (1997), 276. Numerous placards warning against employing a married wet-nurse can be found in the communities of Altona-Hamburg-Wandsbek; see Record book of public announcements AHW, fol. 23.
246. Record book, Kraków, v–vi; Sofer (1969–84), part 1, Even haezer, 33; Steinhardt (2004), Even haezer, #4.
247. Ashkenazi (1711), responsa 64–66.
248. Responsa forbidding use of "poisonous" mother's milk appear throughout the eighteenth century; Margoliot (1858), part 3, #27; Eybeschutz, (1819), part 3, fol. 10b. See also Fildes (1988), 79–126.
249. Ashkenazi (1711), responsum 64 (the woman is identified in responsum 66).
250. See Horovitz (1972), 82–83. On Hakham Tzvi and Broda, see Emden (1896), 51.
251. On the use of excommunication in Jewish communities, see Katz (1993), 124–25; Fram (2012), introduction, 62–68.

252. Ashkenazi (1711), responsum 66.

253. On community involvement in the matrimonial issues of the individual and its strict attitude toward marriage that is halakhically forbidden, even in cases where the halakhah conflicts with civil demands, see Horowitz (2010), 71–81. On the weakening of community institutions, see Breuer (1996), 226–27. On developments in the use of excommunication in the communities of Altona-Hamburg-Wandsbek, see Horowitz (2010), 54–56.

254. See references in Shashar (2012), 72, n. 324. On marital age in non-Jewish society, see Pfister (1996).

255. Katz (1944), 26; Reiner (1992), 288–89.

256. Liberles (2005), 50–51; Lowenstein (1994), 167–74.

257. Compare figures in Liberles with those in Freeze (2002), 54–58.

258. Lowenstein (1994), 159–60.

259. Freeze (2002), 53.

260. Studies of widowhood in non-Jewish society show men's preference for marrying a maiden much younger than themselves; see Wunder (1998), 134–35, 139.

261. Gravestone inscription: הרבנית הצנועה
המפורסמת צבי׳ רחל
בת הגאון מו״ה אפרים זצ״ל
ואשת הגאון מו״ה יעב״ץ.
https://peace.sites.uu.nl/epigraphy/search/?fbclid=IwAR3uckiObgUoZL_OF6gspAosoqcFGo8KuWs6HnsMmKbzw2PMg-pKY-w8jBk.

262. Record book, beit din Altona 3, fol. 23a.

263. Gravestones: אסתר אשת כ׳ לעקיש, https://peace.sites.uu.nl/epigraphy/search/?fbclid=IwAR3uckiObgUoZL_OF6gspAosoqcFGo8KuWs6HnsMmKbzw2PMg-pKY-w8jBk; https://peace.sites.uu.nl/epigraphy/search/?fbclid=IwAR3uckiObgUoZL_OF6gspAosoqcFGo8KuWs6HnsMmKbzw2PMg-pKY-w8jBk.

264. שרה מערלא עשקלס, https://peace.sites.uu.nl/epigraphy/search/?fbclid=IwAR3uckiObgUoZL_OF6gspAosoqcFGo8KuWs6HnsMmKbzw2PMg-pKY-w8jBk; אהרן עשקלס https://peace.sites.uu.nl/epigraphy/search/?fbclid=IwAR3uckiObgUoZL_OF6gspAosoqcFGo8KuWs6HnsMmKbzw2PMg-pKY-w8jBk.

265. Rechla Reiss, רייס רעכלה. https://peace.sites.uu.nl/epigraphy/search/?fbclid=IwAR3uckiObgUoZL_OF6gspAosoqcFGo8KuWs6HnsMmKbzw2PMg-pKY-w8jBk.

266. Demographic data on widows can be found in Shashar (2012), 73–77.

CHAPTER 2: YIBUM AND HALITZAH

1. On Rabbi Shlomo Kluger (and a different perspective on freeing this agunah), see Gartner (2013).

2. Kluger (1864), fol. 2.
3. Lev. 18:16.
4. See Brandes (2005).
5. Babylonian Talmud, Yevamot 35b. On this halakhic development, see Shereshevsky (1984), index.
6. Babylonian Talmud, Yevamot 101b.
7. Yaakov ben Asher, Arba turim, Even haezer, #156; see also the commentary of Rabbi Joel Sirkis (Beit hadash ad loc.).
8. Babylonian Talmud, Yevamot 69b and 92b. A minor cannot legally marry; see Shereshevsky (1984), 41.
9. These debates have been extensively discussed by Jacob Katz (1977) and Avraham Grossman (2001), 156–73; see also Salmon-Mack (2012), 49–50.
10. Some Ashkenazic decisors permitted levirate marriage when both parties desired it. See Reischer (1860), part 3, 135, 137.
11. The term "rebellious" refers to a wife who refuses to have conjugal relations with her husband; see Shereshevsky (1984), 244–51.
12. On Rabbenu Gershom's enactment against polygamy in Ashkenaz, see Grossman (2001), 122–34. Grossman has shown that rabbis continued to allow marriage to a married brother-in-law for some time after the enactment (163–64).
13. Katz (1984), 132.
14. Katz (1984), 138; Grossman (2001), 161.
15. See Urbach (1979), vol. 1, 60–113.
16. Katz (1984), 142–55.
17. "Mumar" literally means "apostate." Due to its pejorative connotations, "apostate" is no longer used in scholarly works on this period. As a result, "convert," "convert from Judaism," or "convert to Christianity" will be used in this book unless a source from the period under consideration is being quoted. In that case, I have found it worth preserving the original "apostate" to capture the pejorative meaning that was likely intended by the speaker/writer.
18. See Yuval (1988), index.
19. See Kahana (1954), 67.
20. Mishnah Yevamot, chapter 12; Babylonian Talmud, Yevamot 101aff.
21. See Berkovitz (2007), 117; Davis, (2002).
22. Karo, *Shulkhan arukh*, Even haezer, Halitzah, #169.
23. The widow recites Deut. 25:7: "My husband's brother refuses to establish a name in Israel for his brother; he will not perform the duty of a levir." The levir replies with verse 8: "I do not want to take her."
24. For commentary on the ceremony, see Viberg (1992), 165; Brichto (1973); Leggett (1974), 55; Kruger (1996).
25. Karo, *Shulkhan arukh*, Even haezer, #160, paragraph 1. The husband may

make provisions in his will for his wife to collect maintenance monies from his estate for a longer period.

26. Shereshevsky (1984), 303–4.
27. See Katz (1984), 151, n. 134.
28. Ibid., 152.
29. Isserlein (1882), 220.
30. On halitzah customs in Germany and Austria, see Salmon-Mack (2012), 49–53.
31. Karo, *Shulkhan arukh*, Even haezer, #165, paragraph 4.
32. Jerusalem Talmud, Sanhedrin 1:2; Yevamot 12:6; Babylonian Talmud, Yevamot 39 and 106. See also Gulak (1926), 90–97.
33. On betrothal agreements, see Yuval (1995).
34. For instance, Segal (1680), #22.
35. Halitzah writs, Warburg.
36. Examples of all types of these writs can be found in Gulak (1926).
37. For instance, Halitzah writs, Warburg, 16c.

CHAPTER 3: THE HALITZAH TRAP

1. Record book, beit din Prague (unnumbered page).
2. Record book, beit din Prague (unnumbered page).
3. Karo, *Shulhan arukh*, Even haezer, Laws of Kiddushin, #38.
4. Conditional marriage was performed on the strength of the opinion of Rabbi Moshe Isserles with regard to the apostate brother and in accordance with the enactment of Rabbi Israel Bruna. See Isserles, *Hagahot haRMA le-Shulkhan arukh*, Even haezer, Laws of Yibum, #167, sub-paragraph 4.
5. See, for instance, Reischer (1860), part 1, #127.
6. See Kahana (2015).
7. A letter in this rabbi's name is illegible in the manuscript. The individual in question might be Rabbi Moshe Ginzburg Shapira of Prague, who authored halakhic decisions and endorsements of various works: Maggid (1899), 76.
8. Record book, beit din Prague (unnumbered page).
9. See, for instance, Writs of halitzah, Wallerstein.
10. See Berkovitz (2007), index.
11. Reischer (1860), part 2, 128.
12. Ibid., part 3, 97.
13. Documented in Record book, beit din Metz, vol. 2, 42a; Jay Berkovitz deciphered the manuscript.
14. See Schwartzfuchs (1985); Berkovitz (2007), index.
15. The degree of family relationship of the heirs to the deceased is not specified in the text. According to the order of succession in inheritance, if the deceased had no sons or daughters, the offspring of his father are his heirs; and

if he had no heirs from his father, the heirs are more distant relations on the father's side (Karo, *Shulhan arukh*, Hoshen mishpat, Hilkhot nahalot, #276); in such a case, we cannot ascertain the precise degree of family relationship to the deceased. Since we do know that the widow underwent halitzah, it would seem that the heir according to biblical law was the brother of the deceased; this possibility cannot be ruled out. If so, Nentche was apparently also a descendant of the father of the deceased. Another possibility is that the brother-in-law was not a party to the division of the estate, for some unknown reason. This possibility is supported by the fact that the date of Mayeh's death is unknown. Much time could have elapsed from the payment of the widow's ketubah after halitzah until the division of the estate, since it took time to locate Nentche.

16. Although not mentioned as such in the documents, this seems likely, since halakhah prescribes that the widow stops receiving maintenance payments from the estate ninety-two days after the death of her husband and since we have no record of any further claim on her part.

17. Livres were a type of coin.

18. On the impact on family life, see Liberles (2005), chapter 2.

19. Turniansky (2019), 155, 167, 186, 208; Emden (1886), 104, 153, 186, 188.

20. It was common practice for litigants to deposit a pledge or sum of money with the beit din as security against assets.

21. Ashkenazi (1861), 12.

22. Jacob Goldberg has claimed that Jews were the most mobile group in the population of Poland-Lithuania. See Goldberg (1999), 294. See also Shulvass (1971), 67–74; Breuer (2003), 435–39.

23. For instance, Wasserzug (1911), 9.

24. Turniansky (2019), 160–63; Emden (1896), 187.

25. On the postal service and advances in transportation, see Beyrer (2006), 375–83; Behringer (1990), 148–79. See also Wasserzug (1911), 9, 11.

26. The expression derives from Jerusalem Talmud, Berakhot 4:4.

27. For instance, Halberstam (1874), Even haezer, part 1, #39; Meir (2005), #55.

28. Cited in Kluger (1864), fol. 37b, "Damesek Eliezer," #29.

29. Babylonian Talmud, Sanhedrin 31b.

30. Record book, shamash of Altona 1, fol. 27a.

31. A type of coin.

32. Record book, beit din Altona 5, fol. 66.

33. Record book, beit din Altona 1, fol. 33a. Compare G. Ashkenazi (1861), #12.

34. See his gravestone inscription: Meir Wagner מאיר ואגנר, https://peace.sites.uu.nl/epigraphy/search/?fbclid=IwAR3uckiObgUoZL_OF6gspAosoqcFGo8KuWs6HnsMmKbzw2PMg-pKY-w8jBk.

35. Steinhardt (2004), Even haezer, #13.
36. See Kaplan (2003), index.
37. This was a coin.
38. Non-Jewish public notary.
39. Based on Babylonian Talmud, Yevamot 112b.
40. Ashkenazi (1711), #1.
41. Adelman (1994).
42. Ibid., 111.
43. For a bibliography on religious conversion in Europe in the early modern age, see Shashar (2012), 87, n. 50.
44. Evidence shows that Jews habitually used the services of non-Jewish notaries. See Berkovitz (2014), 12.
45. See Katz (1992), 21–42; Horowitz (2010), last chapter.
46. Record book, beit din Altona 3, fol. 113b.
47. Writs from a later period (end of the eighteenth and early nineteenth centuries) state explicitly that neither the yavam nor his agent may take any remuneration from the widow. For instance, Halitzah writs, Warburg, 16c. I did not find this stated explicitly in earlier writs.
48. Record book, beit din Altona 3, fol. 113b (p. 107).
49. Records of dayan Haim Gunderschein of Frankfurt note no fewer than twelve cases of litigants represented by professional legal counsel. See Fram (2012), 36.
50. Sabean (1997); Ogilvie (2003), 250–51; Ulbrich (2004), 136–37, 206–7.
51. The subject of women appearing before the beit din has not met with adequate study, but see Berkovitz (2017); Fram (2012), 35.
52. Record book, beit din Prague, page marked with letters *yod-het*.
53. Record book, beit din Fürth, fol. 18a.
54. See Shohet (1960), 73; Cohen (1966), vol. 1, 162.
55. See Emden (1896), 89–90.
56. See Cohen (1966), vol. 1, 161–62.
57. Case notes found in the literary estate of Rabbi Shmuel Steg, Community records, Warburg, 10, 10b. This seems to be the individual who died in 1798 and was buried in Arolsen, near Warburg. See his gravestone inscription: מו"ה שמואל ב"ה יוזפא מוורבורג שנו"נ ג' אייר. בט"ג. https://peace.sites.uu.nl/epigraphy/search/?fbclid=IwAR3uckiObgUoZL_OF6gspAosoqcFGo8KuWs6HnsMmKbzw2PMg-pKY-w8jBk.
58. Record book, beit din Fürth, fol. 35a.
59. Record book, beit din Fürth, 22–23.
60. Record book, beit din Fürth, 18.
61. On the income of dayanim in Ashkenaz in this period, see Cohen (1993), 179–92.

62. Compare Fram (2012), 228b–230b, 231a–b.

63. Possibly Wolf son of Meir Troib, tax collector for the community; see his gravestone inscription: Wolf son of Meir Troib זאב וואלף בן הג״צ כה״ר מאיר טרויב. https://peace.sites.uu.nl/epigraphy/search/?fbclid=IwAR3ucki ObgUoZL_OF6gspAosoqcFGo8KuWs6HnsMmKbzw2PMg-pKY-w8jBk. If he is the individual in question, then more than three months elapsed before his brother came to perform halitzah for his widow.

64. Record book, beit din Altona 2, 72a.

65. Record book, community of Altona 16, fol. 81a. His widow, Peschke, died in 1794, apparently without having remarried. See her gravestone inscription: פעסכה מענצר. https://peace.sites.uu.nl/epigraphy/search/?fbclid= IwAR3uckiObgUoZL_OF6gspAosoqcFGo8KuWs6HnsMmKbzw2PMg-pKY -w8jBk. Record book, community of Altona 16, fol. 145a.

66. On Nathan Mez, see Horovitz (1972), 134–43.

67. The letter appears in Responsa of Frankfurt rabbis, fol. 151a; it is referenced in Horovitz (1972), 143.

68. Responsa of Frankfurt rabbis, fol. 151a.

69. Isserles, *Hagahot haRMA leShulhan arukh*, Even haezer, 169:1. The obligation in biblical law is to perform halitzah before a beit din; in this it differs from other legal acts. On the legal development of personal status in Jewish law, see Yuval (1988), 322–435.

70. For instance, Community record book, Oberdorf; Record book, community of Altona 1, fol. 42.

71. More examples in Shashar (2012), 95, n. 86.

72. In some cases, additional judges (dayanim) were added to the beit din's typical three. In Prague, the rabbi heading the tribunal had five dayanim under him; the other two dayanim mentioned in Landau's responsum may fall into that category. On the Prague beit din, see Breuer (1996), 155–56. In Frankfurt, too, more than three dayanim would officiate at the halitzah ceremony. See Fram (2012), no. 154.

73. Landau (1960), 2nd edition, Even haezer, #155.

74. Record book, Altona 17b, fol. 12. See also Landau (1960), 1st edition, Even haezer, #12.

75. Record book, Altona 17, 24.

76. Record book, Altona community officials, 25a.

77. The Altona shamash noted that he was present at nine halitzah ceremonies; see Record book, shamash of Altona 1, 18a, 19, 20, 23, 24a, 27a, 31a, 49. See also Fram (2012), 231b.

78. The Hebrew term used was *muteret lashuk*; it applies to a woman who has had halitzah performed for her; see Babylonian Talmud, Yevamot 119b.

79. Halakhic discussion assumes that the dayan needs to see that the halitzah

is performed in accordance with legal requirements. See, for instance, Reischer (1860), part 1, #126; Landau (1960), 2nd edition, Even haezer, #151.

80. Landau (1960), 2nd edition, Even haezer, #154. The Frankfurt responsa record book contains a question concerning a halitzah ceremony (whether actual or theoretical is unclear) in which one of the dayanim did not actually see the shoe removed; Responsa of Frankfurt rabbis, fol. 57.

81. Reischer (1860), part 1, #129; Bacharach (1678), question 28.

82. Landau (1960), 2nd edition, Even haezer, #136.

83. The first part of the book, printed in Prague in 1776, contains the responsum in question.

84. Zalman Emmerich (1910), pilpul no. 2, fols. 8a–13b. I did not find any mention of this dispute in the Prague beit din records; the arguments apparently grew more heated between the year 1768, that of the final entry for this tribunal, and 1776, the year of publication of the first edition of Landau's *Noda biYehudah*.

85. Landau (1960), 1st edition, Even haezer, #32.

86. The testimony of April 8 was heard after the woman first consulted Landau.

87. On Landau and the rabbis of Brody, see Kahana (2015), 132–52.

88. Landau (1960), 1st edition, Even haezer, #156.

89. Landau (1960), 1st edition, Even haezer, #156.

90. A case from a slightly earlier period concerns the son-in-law of the Maharal of Prague (Rabbi Judah Loew ben Bezalel, sixteenth cent.). After the ceremony, the man claimed that he did it for his father-in-law; he concealed the fact that he was left-handed and purposely removed the shoe with his right hand. According to several decisors, this invalidated the ceremony retroactively. See Friedman (1986).

91. Reischer (1860), part 3,# 97.

92. For instance, Hildesheimer (1992), 239.

93. Cited in Emden (1883), part 1, #29. The name of the agunah appears in Emden (1896), 129.

94. About Yehezkel Katzenellenbogen, see Duckesz (1903), 21–29.

95. Emden (1896), 129.

96. Katzenellenbogen's responsum and Emden's own opinion appear in Emden (1883), part 1, #29. Katzenellenbogen's ruling was printed also in Biala (1803), 35.

97. Emden seems to have penned a separate treatise entitled *Hayta dekitra*; see Avraham Hayim Wagenaar (1868), Toldot Yavetz, 44. Besides the detailed description of the case in *Megillat Sefer*, Emden refers to it also in his *Iggeret Purim* (1991), fol. 32a–b; *Sefer shimush* (1757), 172; *Sefer hitabkut* (1762), fol. 9a;

Akitzat akrav (1752), fol. 14b; *Shevirat luhot haaven* (1758), fols. 42a, 60b; *Beit Yehonatan hasofer* (1762), fol. 12b.

98. Emden (1896), 133.

99. Bnei Gumpel (1767), fol. 16a, 98.

CHAPTER 4: "BITTERLY SHE WAILS":
AGUNOT IN TIMES OF PERSECUTION AND WAR

1. See Yakovenko (2003).

2. Breuer (1996), 82–101.

3. Raba (1994), esp. 182–97.

4. For the impact of the Thirty Years' War on the Ashkenazic realm, see Israel (1983). See also *Jewish History* 17 (2003), an issue devoted to the massacres of 1648–1649 and the historiography of the events.

5. For figures in each category, see Stampfer (2003); and, recently, Teller (2020).

6. Ruderman (2010), 31–32.

7. Salmon-Mack (2012), 216–17.

8. The earliest of these is Meir of Szczebrzeszyn, *Tzok haitim* (1650), followed by Shabbetai ben Meir Hacohen, *Megilat eifah* (1651); Gavriel Schussberg, *Petah teshuva* (1651); Nathan ben Moses Hannover, *Yeven metzulah* (1653); Shmuel Fayvish, *Tit hayaven* (1892, originally published 1655), and the poem printed at a later date; Abraham Shmuel Ashkenazy, *Tzaar bat rabim* (ed. B. Friedberg, Lvov, 1905).

9. See Yakovenko (2003).

10. Meir of Szczebrzeszyn (1650), last page; compare Hannover (1653), 25.

11. For an overview of the scholarship on this subject, see Rosman (2003), 239–42; Stampfer (2003); Yakovenko (2003), esp. 166–67.

12. Halperin referred to this as the Council for freeing Agunot; see Halperin and Bartal (1989), 79.

13. To mention but a few: Krochmal (1674), #88, #101; G. Ashkenazi, Responsa (1861), #106; MiPozna (1985), #130.

14. Salmon-Mack (2012), 217.

15. Salmon-Mack (2012), 217.

16. Kahana (1947), 265.

17. The date given by Krochmal is August 27, 1653, but there is some vagueness as to chronological order of some details in his responsum.

18. See Rosman (2003), 242.

19. It is likely that this is the village in Ukraine known today as Nova Chortoriya; see Mokotoff et al. (1991), 253.

20. Krochmal (1674), #78.

21. For instance, Berkovitz (2010b), 33–66; Kahana (2015), 111–14.
22. For instance, Meir (2005), #70; Margaliot (1975), Even haezer, #7.
23. Estimations vary as to the number of refugees who reached Moravia; see Fram (2007), 408; Stampfer (2003), 217.
24. Raba (1994), 186.
25. Hannover (1653), 22.
26. See Feiner (2021), 82.
27. Oppenheim (1971–1984), Even haezer, question 11.
28. Karo, *Shulhan arukh*, Even haezer, section 17, clause 48.
29. This is not to imply that all men in this period possessed halakhic knowledge; there were different levels of education, and many men lacked Jewish learning. Socioeconomic status was a determining factor of literacy, for women as well as men. Some women possessed halakhic knowledge, but boys could study at an institution (heder and then yeshivah), while girls did not usually have that option. Women would learn from men in the family, not in formal institutions of education. On the education of girls and literature for women in this period, see Hovav (2009), 286–306, 410–15.
30. Blidstein(1976).
31. Isserles, *Hagahot haRMA leShulhan arukh*, Even haezer, 7:11.
32. This case is discussed by Salmon-Mack (2012), 266–67; Fram (2007), 15. The two disagree over the prevalence of such cases; see my own opinion in Shashar (2012), 143, n. 65. Some twenty-five years after Krochmal gave his ruling on Sarah's case, many men were requesting permission to remarry in similar circumstances and succeeding, even though they needed approval from one hundred rabbis.
33. Krochmal (1674), #78.
34. Karo, *Shulhan arukh*, Even haezer, 7:1; and Isserles, *Hagahot haRMA*, 7:11.
35. Raba (1994), 104.
36. Harrington (1995), 89.
37. Harrington (1995), 268.
38. Krochmal (1674), #78.
39. Ibid., end of responsum.
40. See Eliav (1959).
41. Emden (1896), 6.
42. Based on 2 Sam. 15:17.
43. Emden (1896), 7.
44. See Margaliot (1959), vol. 3, 704–7. Joshua Heschel of Kraków probably passed through Moravia on his way back from Vienna, a short while after the pogroms of 1848–1849. He may have given Nehama her permission to remarry during that visit.
45. Emden (1896), 7.

46. The expression is based on Babylonian Talmud, Bava Kama, 74b.

47. Emden (1896), 7.

48. See gloss in Emden (1896), 8–9.

49. The verse is Prov. 12:21. Emden (1896), 8–9.

50. There are no extant responsa authored by Rabbi Joshua Heschel, but they are cited by decisors of both his and subsequent generations. See Krochmal (1674), #103, #108; Eisenstadt (1899), part 1, #1, #105; part 2, #155. In his biography, written by Chanoch Henoch Erzon and printed as an appendix to Heschel's *Hanukat hatorah* (1899), a collection of Heschel's teachings, the description of the events is based on Emden's *Megilat sefer*.

51. Emden (1896), 132.

52. Ibid., 44, 69.

53. Ibid., 98.

54. Rocoles (1683). On the story of Martin Guerre, see Zemon Davis (2002).

55. For instance, Krochmal (1674), #59, #88, #101; MiPozna (1985), #132; Reischer (1860), part 1, #100.

56. See the case in Krochmal (1674), #103; G. Ashkenazi (1861), #106; MiPozna (1985), #130. In none of these did the decisor grant permission to remarry.

CHAPTER 5: TWO TALES OF MURDER

1. Turniansky (2019), 60–61.

2. Ibid., 6.

3. Ibid., 29.

4. On Shmuel Zanvl Heckscher, see Turniansky (2019), 227, n. 111, and references cited there.

5. The representation of the murders in the accounts by Glikl and Heckscher have been extensively discussed in Goldstein (2007), 10–29.

6. See Kaufmann (1896), 394–401.

7. See Grunwald (1903), 14.

8. The date on this man's gravestone inscription in the Hamburg cemetery is the same as in Glikl's account, while Heckscher erroneously dates the man's disappearance to "Isru hag Sukkot 5445." See gravestone inscription of Avraham Metz: אברהם מיץ, https://peace.sites.uu.nl/epigraphy/search/?fbclid=IwAR3uckiObgUoZL_OF6gspAosoqcFGo8KuWs6HnsMmKbzw2PMg-pKY-w8jBk.

9. Turniansky (2019), 226.

10. Three of Avraham Metz's children are buried in the Altona cemetery; the inscriptions do not make it clear if they are the children of his first or second marriage. Given life expectancy at the time, the years of their deaths (1745, 1752, and 1759) suggest that the three were young children at the time of their father's disappearance. See their gravestones (All three should be searched under the

name אברהם מיץ /אברהם מעץ): https://peace.sites.uu.nl/epigraphy/search
/?fbclid=IwAR3uckiObgUoZL_OF6gspAosoqcFGo8KuWs6HnsMmKbzw2
PMg-pKY-w8jBk.

11. The man's name appears only in Heckscher's account.

12. Heckscher begins with his narrow escape from death and offers praise to God for sparing his life. See Kaufmann (1896), 394.

13. See Turniansky (2019), 224–25, and 226, n. 104.

14. Turnianksy (2019), 16–17.

15. There are numerous examples, for instance, the tale of the prince and his so-called friends, Turnianksy (2019), 204–7.

16. Turniansky (2019), 59–260. For the sentence in italics, see 1 Sam. 16:7.

17. Boes (1996), esp. 262–66.

18. Dekker and van de Pol (1989) assert that the phenomenon had all but disappeared by the early nineteenth century.

19. On the spread of this kind of behavior after the Thirty Years' War, see Rublack (1999), 257.

20. Dekker and van de Pol (1989), 99–103.

21. Feiner (2021), 295–310, discusses the tension between science and religion. He refers to 1700–1750, somewhat later than the events discussed here, but may have been present earlier as well.

22. Turniansky (2019), 226–27.

23. Turniansky (2019), 61

24. See Gottfarstein (1959), 593. Intended meaning: A wife who neglects her appearance or her housework risks being abandoned by her husband. When another version of the phrase refers to the husband as the *shlumper* (Yiddish: lout, slob), it implies that his wife does not take good care of him, and he might well leave her and make her an agunah.

25. Turniansky (2019), 227.

26. Goldstein (2007), 19; Turniansky (2019), 226, n. 105.

27. Turniansky (2019), 29.

28. For instance, Gluckman (1963), 307–16.

29. Capp (2003); Sabean (1984), 147–49.

30. Boes (1996), 261–62; Rublack (1999), 16–42.

31. Salmon-Mack (2012), 269–76.

32. Bacharach (1678), #57. On the significance attributed to observance of niddah laws, see Shashar (2007).

33. Record book, Altona 17a, 29a; Record book, judge of Romansweiler, fols. 109b–110a.

34. Record book, community of Fürth, fol. 163.

35. See Rublack (1999), 26, about how a woman without a male relative is more vulnerable to gossip.

36. Turniansky (2019), 228, n. 112.
37. Turniansky (2019), 228.
38. Kaufmann (1896), 397.
39. Turniansky (2019), 227–28.
40. Turniansky (2019), 230. "Oberpräsident" was the title of the official in charge of Jewish affairs in Altona for the Danish crown. See Horowitz (2010), 48.
41. Turniansky (2019), 228.
42. Turniansky (2019), 228; Kaufmann (1896), 399.
43. Kaufmann (1896), 398.
44. Criminals often evaded punishment by escaping to a different jurisdiction; Rublack (1999), 40.
45. On interrogation methods in Germany, see Rublack (1999), chapter 2, esp. 54–60.
46. Turniansky (2019), 230–31.
47. For instance, Ulbrich (2004), 237–78, 279–80; Berkovitz (2010a). The topic of Jewish-gentile relations is currently being revisited; until several decades ago, the prevailing view held that Jewish life did not usually mingle with non-Jewish surroundings. However, recent studies have shown the many points of contact between them; see Teller, Teter, and Polonsky (2010).
48. Dekker (1987), 350.
49. Ulbrich (2004), 245.
50. Turniansky (2019), 231.
51. See Zemon Davis (2001), 124–89.
52. Turniansky (2019), 228.
53. Ibid., 229.
54. Ibid.
55. Zemon Davis (2001); in the context of German literature, see Wiltenburg (1992).
56. Cohen (1708), Sefer gan naul, 15; Feiner (2021), 143–46.
57. Wiltenburg (1992), 253–55.
58. Zemon Davis (2001), 180–83; Dekker (2002), 344. Differential treatment of women criminals also is seen in Glikl's memoirs: the murderer was sentenced to death by breaking on the wheel, while his wife and maidservant got off with exile; see Turniansky (2019), 234.
59. Turniansky (2019), 231.
60. Turniansky (2019), 26–32.
61. Horowitz (2010), esp. 178–80.
62. Rublack (1999), chapter 1.
63. Turniansky (2019), 232–33.
64. Turniansky (2019), 234.

CHAPTER 6: IDENTIFYING THE DEAD IN THE INTEREST OF FREEING THE AGUNAH AND TAKING REVENGE

1. Responsa literature contains many such examples; see, for instance, Meir (2005), #56; Eisenstadt (1899), part 1, #50.

2. Burial society record book, Schwersenz, fol. 13b, paragraph 82.

3. Landau (1960), 1st edition, Even haezer, #44. See similar regulations in Record book, shamash of Altona 1, fol. 27.

4. The question appears in Oppenheim (1971–1984), Even haezer, #9–10; testimonies are appended there.

5. Oppenheim (1971–1984), Even haezer, #9 (28). Of course, the aim was to prevent the woman from becoming an agunah so that she could later remarry.

6. Ibid., 26.

7. Oppenheim (1971–1984), #10.

8. There are many examples; for instance, Koidonover (1884), #9; Meir Margaliot (1791), part 1, 25; Kluger (1910), Even haezer, #92.

9. The date of February 3, 1768, was determined relative to other events recorded in the notebook.

10. Boizenburg was a small town some sixty kilometers from Altona.

11. The lay leader for that month was Hirsch Bressla; see his gravestone: הירש ברעסלא, Zwi Hirsch ben Elasar Halevi, https://peace.sites.uu.nl/epigraphy/search/?fbclid=IwAR3uckiObgUoZL_OF6gspAosoqcFGo8KuWs6Hns MmKbzw2PMg-pKY-w8jBk; see also Duckesz (1903), 84.

12. See Deut. 21:1–8 regarding the procedure if a body is found in an area outside several different towns.

13. Mecklenburg, the county town of Boizenburg.

14. Record book, shamash of Altona 1, fol. 12. Emphasis added.

15. Jellinek (1880), 62. The Altona community recorded expenditures for the year 5570 (Sept. 11, 1809–Sept. 28, 1810) for operations undertaken to find the missing man: search parties, delegations to authorities, burial arrangements. See Record book, ledger for expenses and revenues Altona.

16. Record book, ledger for charity expenses, fol. 2 (marked 2a).

17. See Ullmann (2000), 102.

18. Turniansky (2019), 88.

19. Turniansky (2019), 229.

20. Halperin and Bartal (1989), 547. See also Turniansky (2019), 88, n. 118.

21. Krochmal (1674), 111.

22. Salmon-Mack (2012), 166–168.

CHAPTER 7: "NOTHING OF HIM WAS EVER FOUND SAVE A SHOE AND BELT": FREEING AN AGUNAH WHEN THE CORPSE IS MISSING

1. Lowenstein (2008), 136–37; Sarti (2002), 86–106.
2. A list of fires mentioned in contemporary sources can be found in Shashar (2012), 166, n. 214.
3. See, for instance, Eisenstadt (1899), part 1, #48; Landau (1960), 1st edition, Even haezer, #28; Sofer (1969–1984), part 3, Even haezer, #62.
4. On him and his book, see Breuer (1996), 194.
5. Hahn (1722), fol. 205a (emphasis added).
6. Record book, shamash of Altona 1, 46a.
7. Record book, beit din Heidingsfeld, fol. 8.
8. Record book, Austerlitz; cf. Kahana (1954), 57.
9. Community record book, Forchheim, no. 10.
10. Record book, beit din Prague (pages unnumbered). The rabbi's documents granting the agunah permission to remarry are at the end of the record book. It is not clear why permission to remarry was granted nine years after the letter arrived.
11. Record book, beit din Prague.
12. Margaliot (1791), part 1, #32; Raphael Cohen is quoted in R. Katz (1791), #30; Landau (1960), 2nd edition, Even haezer, #52, #54, #59. See Bieber (1905), 232–33; Tzvi Hirsch Baschko of Zamosc (1816), #106. My reconstructive description is based on several accounts. The variations in details are highly instructive, as will be discussed.
13. Oppenheim (1971–1984), Even haezer, #12 (42–51).
14. See, for instance, Laub and Felman (2008); Wall (1965).
15. Almog (2000), 58.
16. The first was White (1973). See Almog (2000), 11–12, n. 3.
17. See, for instance, Jackson (1991).
18. Bethlehem (2006).
19. Mann (1984); Stow (2011).
20. Berkovitz (2010a), 273; Cf. Hundert (2004), 92–93.
21. Cohen (1966), vol. 1, 33–34, 226; Dubin (2007); Fram (2012), 34, 51–62.
22. Historical record book, Altona and Hamburg; Record book, Altona 17b, fol. 11a.
23. Record book, beit din Altona 3, fol. 148a.
24. See Shazar (1971), 78; Berkovitz (2014), 3.
25. Hebrew was used by dayanim for legal proceedings, at least in writing. Many responsa contain an appendix of verbatim transcripts of testimony. The decisor would translate the testimony, usually given in Yiddish, into Hebrew for his responsum. In extant beit din records, decisions of the judges are generally

written in Hebrew until the early nineteenth century. Gradually Jewish courts in Germany started including a German protocol alongside the Hebrew one. After that, Hebrew is no longer found in the records, nor, presumably, was it used any more in judicial proceedings. Cohen (1966), vol. 1, 213; Fram (2012), 78.

26. See Mishnah Sanhedrin, 4:5.

27. Oppenheim (1971–1984), Even haezer, #12 (43).

28. Ibid., 42.

29. Ibid.

30. The village of Stampfen (Stomfa, Stupava), where the witness resided, is some seventy-five kilometers' distance from Nikolsburg. See Mokotoff et al. (1991).

31. The Morava was the main river of Moravia.

32. Oppenheim (1971–1984), Even haezer, #12. Evidence was given in Yiddish.

33. Mishnah Yevamot, 16:3; see Karo, *Shulkhan arukh*, Even haezer, 17:24.

34. Oppenheim (1971–1984), Even haezer, #12.

35. Based on Babylonian Talmud, Avodah Zarah, 37a.

36. Oppenheim (1971–1984), Even haezer, #12.

37. Landau (1960), 1st edition, Even haezer, #28

38. This village in the Volhynia district in Ukraine had a population of 963 Jews in 1778.

39. Probably the city of Działoszyn, then part of the Kingdom of Poland.

40. This seems to be the same individual mentioned by Bieber (1905), 168–69.

41. On him, see Ibid., 265–66.

42. The expression "leaders and good men" (*rashim vetovim*) was used often in the period under discussion for leaders of the community. This "Eli the leader" may refer to Eli son of Yitzhak, registered as "gabbai" in the burial society record book in the late eighteenth century; see Bieber (1905), 224.

43. Cohen (1966), vol. 1, 226. See also Horowitz (2010), 27.

44. The fire took place in Sukkot (the Jewish fall harvest holiday) of 1776. Bayla gave evidence in 1782. The letter to which she refers arrived sometime in 1781, some four years after the fire.

45. Attitude to knowledge differed among social groups. Throughout this period, there was tension between the elite, who sought to enforce discipline through use of law, and groups who were not always cognizant of legal detail; see Teter (2010), 253; Horowitz (2010).

46. Margaliot (1791), part 1, question 32 (fol. 43b, #11).

47. Karo, *Shulhan arukh*, Even haezer, 17, paragraph 17.

48. On Jewish apostates in Poland, see Teter (2003); Kaźmierczyk (2010). A notable exception is the conversion of the Frankists in the mid-eighteenth century; see Maciejko (2011), 146–201.

49. Hundert (2004), 76.
50. Carlebach (2001), 138–40.
51. Carlebach (2001), 118.
52. See Teter (2003), 258.
53. Although this was true for men and women, it was more pronounced for women who became maidservants or who converted after being deserted by their husbands. See Teter (2003), 262. See also Fram (1996) 320.
54. See Kaźmierczyk (2010), 214.
55. Fram (1996), 321.
56. The attitudes of different segments of Jewish society toward agunot was influenced by both the Haskalah and the increased awareness of privacy issues (which came to Poland decades after they appeared in Germany). See Sinkoff (2003), which deals with Joseph Perl's writings on converts' giving a get.
57. Margaliot (1791), part 1, question 32 (fol. 43b, paragraph 9).
58. For biblical opposition to consulting soothsayers, see, e.g., Lev. 19:31; Deut. 18:10–12.
59. Trachtenberg (1974), 247–48.
60. See Popper (2006).
61. Brosseder (2005).
62. Margaliot (1791), part 1, question 32 (fol. 54b, col. A).
63. Katz (1791), #30.
64. Landau (1960), 2nd edition, Even haezer, #52, #53, #54.
65. Ibid., #59.
66. Ibid., #52.
67. Landau (1960), 2nd edition, Even haezer, #59.
68. Katz (1791), #30.
69. Katz (1791), #30, end of responsum.
70. Bieber (1905), 232.

CHAPTER 8: THE AGUNAH WIFE OF LEMLI WIMPE OF METZ

1. This seems to be the individual mentioned in Turniansky (2019), 274.
2. See Reischer (1860), part 3, #114; Oppenheim (1971–1984), Even haezer, question 4; Katzenellenbogen (1731), question 53.
3. Memory book, Metz, fol. 24.
4. Reischer (1860), part 3, 114.
5. Ibid.
6. Compare, for instance, Turniansky (2019), 120–21; and Emden (1896), 72, 81.
7. Now the city of Châlons-en-Champagne, between Paris and Metz.
8. Reischer (1860), part 3, 114.
9. Items of clothing were habitually marked with initials in case of loss or

theft. On clothing production in Europe in this period, see Sarti (2002), 192–211; on marking items of clothing, Sarti (2002), 216.

10. The lord of the manor was Louis-Bénigne Chasot de Congy, son of the chief justice at the local court in Metz; see Aubert de La Chesnaye-Desbois (1772), 233; Michel (1853), 41, 85.

11. Memory book, Metz, fol. 24.

12. Reischer (1860), part 3, #114.

13. Reischer (1860), part 3, #114.

14. Berkovitz (2007), 43.

15. Oppenheim (1971–1984), Even haezer, question 4.

16. Katzenellenbogen (1731), Kuntres agunot, end of question 54.

17. *Shulhan arukh*, Even haezer, 17:5.

18. Katzenellenbogen (1731), Kuntres agunot, question 54. However, he did not permit the wife or sons to don mourning attire.

19. See Emden (1896), 140–41; see also posters prohibiting the convening of a prayer quorum in private homes in the Record book of public announcements AHW.

20. Emden (1896), 140–41. Emden and Katzenellenbogen had a complicated relationship; while Emden's reminiscences should not be taken at face value, the posters indicate that Katzenellenbogen used his authority to restrict the convening of a prayer quorum in private homes in order to regulate the behavior of the congregation.

CHAPTER 9: DEATH OF A MERCHANT:
GUTTA AND AVRAHAM HECKSCHER OF HAMBURG

1. Hamburg genealogical collection, Staatsarchiv Hamburg, 741–42: *Genealogische Sammlungen, Heckscher*.

2. See, for instance, Horowitz (2010), 113.

3. Record book, beit din Altona, fol. 2, 354 [4 Sivan 5551], and there see fols. 318, 380, 389a.

4. Record book, beit din Altona, fol. 2, 68a.

5. See Record book of appeals to the Hamburg senate. I thank my friend Stefan Litt for deciphering the handwriting for me.

6. Record book, beit din Altona,3 92–93.

7. Identified in the beit din record book as Mordechai Berman Cleve, son of Heckscher's sister.

8. See Horowitz (2010), chapter 4, on arguments used by Jews to convince civil courts to exempt them from the requirement to obey Jewish courts.

9. Record book, beit din Altona 3, page number in pencil, 178, fols. 92b, 102.

10. On the attendance of Jews at the Leipzig fair, see Markgraf (1894).

11. Record book, beit din Altona 3, penciled page number 141.

12. The account of the circumstances of Heckscher's death is based on information written in Reise von Hamburg nach Philadelphia (Journey from Hamburg to Philadelphia), anonymous, published in Hanover in 1800, juxtaposed with information included in a review of the book. On pages 189–90 of this book, there appears a story of a murder committed by a thief, as heard by the author himself on the boat to America. In a book review printed in the literary magazine *Allgemeine Literatur-Zeitung* (October 17, 1801), 118–19, the writer notes that although Heckscher's name does not appear in the aforementioned book, he himself identified the story as a description of his murder.

13. Date of the murder and burial follow Hamburg genealogical collection.

14. According to the genealogy collection, the marriage took place on April 2, 1794.

15. Perhaps Moshe Reuven son of Shlomo Frankl (1726–1834), lay leader of the community. His gravestone inscription appears in Epidat: https://peace.sites.uu.nl/epigraphy/search/?fbclid=IwAR3uckiObgUoZL_OF6gspAosoqcFGo8KuWs6HnsMmKbzw2PMg-pKY-w8jBk. See Joshua Feivush Cohen's gravestone: משה ראובן ב' מהור"ר שלמה אברהם פרענקעל. https://peace.sites.uu.nl/epigraphy/search/?fbclid=IwAR3uckiObgUoZL_OF6gspAosoqcFGo8KuWs6HnsMmKbzw2PMg-pKY-w8jBk.

16. Details of the estate and the settlement as described can be found in Record book, beit din Altona, 3, 141–41a.

17. Record book, beit din Altona, 3, 141–41a.

18. Record book, beit din Altona 3, 141–41a.

19. In Jewish law, a daughter does not inherit from her father. A father gives his daughter a writ called "half a male heir's portion" prior to her marriage. The writ states that the daughter, at the appropriate time, stands to inherit half the inheritance portion of a male heir. See Fram (1997), 81–95.

20. Record book, beit din Altona, 3, 141–41a.

21. Record book, beit din Altona, 3, 153a.

22. As can be understood from the appeal made by Mordechai Heckscher to the beit din on December 7, 1796. See Record book, beit din Altona 4, 128a.

23. Record book, beit din Altona 4, 49a, paragraph 254.

24. Record book, beit din Altona 4, 47, paragraph 248. For details, see 50–51.

25. For instance, Howell (2008), 519–38. Cf. Berkovitz (2014), 13–15.

26. Berkovitz (2005), 10.

27. Horowitz (2010), 161. Lacking research on this subject, we cannot reach a general conclusion, and further study is needed.

28. On the bank, see Mendelssohn (1845), 8.

29. For instance, Record book, beit din Altona, 8, fol. 82a, no. 1039.

30. Record book of the deceased AHW, fol. 1, no. 325.

CHAPTER 10: SCENES FROM MARRIAGES IN CONFLICT

1. Now Lipnik and Bečou.
2. Many towns in Poland and Moravia bear this name (lit. "new town"). From the context, it seems that the reference is to Nove Mesto na Morave (some 60 kilometers northwest of Brno) or Nove Mesto nad Metujf (some 125 kilometers northeast of Prague).
3. Landau (1960), 1st edition, Even haezer, #46.
4. I was unable to identify this town.
5. On the hanging of criminals in general and Jews in particular, see Breuer (1996), 130.
6. For example, Landau (1960), 1st edition, Even haezer, #65; Margoliot (1975), Even haezer, #82.
7. See Bourdieu (1990), 66–79.
8. Lipking (1988), 18–20.
9. Brenner et al. (2000), 92.
10. Liberles (2005), 51; Lowenstein (2008), 148.
11. See Liberles (2005), 92; Teller (1997), 212; Ullmann (2000).
12. On the average size of the Jewish family in Poland-Lithuania, see Stampfer (1997), 274–75; in Germany, see, for instance, Liberles (2005), 51–52. On mortality rates, see, for instance, Berkovitz (2007), 103.
13. Goldberg (1999), 171–216; Liberles (2005), 45–46.
14. See, for instance, Etkes (1991), 63–84.
15. Katz (1993), 123.
16. Breuer (1996), 165; Hundert (2004), 36; Feiner (2010), 91–100.
17. On this long-standing approach in family studies, see Kertzer and Barbagli (2001), ix–xii.
18. Katz (1993), 122.
19. Kraemer (1989).
20. Hundert (2004), 93; Fram (2012), 50.
21. See, for instance, Liberles (2005), 53–59.
22. The Hebrew term is *ezer kenegdo*; see Gen. 2:18.
23. Hovav (2009), 122–53, 237.
24. See, for instance, Turniansky (2006).
25. Liberles (2005), 34.
26. For instance, Segal (1680), 9; on prenuptial agreements, see Salmon-Mack (2012), 66–68.
27. *Nahalat shivah* was written by Samuel son of David Halevi (seventeenth century) and includes most of the bill used by Jewish communities, as well as the halakhot that pertain to their writing.
28. Landau (1960), 1st edition, Even haezer, #67.

29. Polish: Kojdanów, now Dzyarzhynsk, in Belarus, not far from Minsk.
30. Koidonover (1884), question 6.
31. We do have documentation of marital conflict between Jews being heard in non-Jewish courts; see Ullmann (2000), 101.
32. Breuer (1996), 226.
33. This holds true for all of Ashkenazic Jewry in the period under discussion; see Berkovitz (2007), 35, 42.
34. See Shereshevsky (1984).
35. See Shereshevsky (1984), 415.
36. According to halakhah, there are conditions in which a man is obliged to divorce his wife (for example, if she has not given birth after ten years of marriage during her child-bearing years), although men did not always act on this. Halakhah does not stipulate any situation in which a wife is obligated to claim a divorce.
37. *Shulhan arukh*, Even haezer, 154:7.
38. Based on Ex. 21:10, which details what a man owes to his first wife even if he marries a second, the rabbis of the Talmud said that a man has three obligations to his wife: onah (which they interpreted as "conjugal relations"), food, and clothing. See, e.g., Babylonian Talmud, Ketubot, 47b.
39. See sources in Shereshevsky (1984), 402–4.
40. As in all matters of sexual modesty, two halakhically valid witnesses of the adulterous act are needed to prove it happened.
41. The laws of divorce are many, and they are quite detailed. See Shereshevsky (1984), 428–33.
42. The Babylonian Talmud (Kiddushin, 13a) says: "anyone who does not know the nature of bills of divorce and betrothals should have no dealings in them."
43. Harrington (1995), 7.
44. It has been suggested that civil courts were more favorable to women than rabbinic courts; see Dubin (2007). Berkovitz has shown that Metz civil courts gave women custody over their children when rabbinic courts did not. For these reasons, women applied to civil courts. See Berkovitz (2017), 8.
45. Wiltenburg (1992), 97–139.
46. Bogucka (2004), 10.
47. Kertzer and Barbagli (2001), xi; Frick (2007).
48. Watt (2001), 132.
49. Kertzer and Barbagli (2001), 221–56.
50. Goldberg (1978), 28–29.
51. Katz (1993), 122.
52. Ibid.

53. See, for instance, Kaplan (2010); Berkovitz (2017).

54. See Spitzer (1990).

55. Eisenstadt (1899), part 2, #11–#12. The letter is undated.

56. For more on the laws of niddah, see Shashar (2007).

57. In a practice called *libun* (with the same root as "white"), a woman would wear white garments for the seven "clean" days following menstruation.

58. See Shashar (2007) on women's channels of communication concerning ritual purity, the special garments worn during niddah, and the ritual bath.

59. Echoing a Talmudic term meaning that a woman's female neighbors know she is menstruating; see, e.g., Babylonian Talmud, Ketubot, 7.

60. Eisenstadt (1899), part 2, #11–#12. The full text of the letter, translated from Yiddish into English by Adina Liberles, was published originally by Robert Liberles. See Liberles (2005), 34–37, and 393, n. 43.

61. Liberles (2005), 49. The full text of the letter, translated from Yiddish into English by Adina Liberles, was published originally by Robert Liberles, with his detailed analysis. See Liberles (2005), 34–37, and 393, n. 43.

62. Letter-writing in this period was bound by stylistic conventions; special guides for letter-writing called *igronim*, covering various topics, were in widespread use to instruct people as to the style in which to couch their missives. Still, letters were often, as in the present case, relatively free of the stylistic constraints typical of rabbinic and legal writing. For letter-writing by women in this period, see Liberles (2005), 71.

63. Liberles (2005), 35.

64. Similar expectations for marriage to be accompanied by love and amicability were expressed by Yitzhak Tannhauser (b. Bavaria, 1774); see Richarz (1991), 71.

65. Scholars have suggested in the last few decades that it was only in the eighteenth century that love became linked to the institution of marriage in non-Jewish societies. To the best of my knowledge, this issue has not been researched extensively in the context of Jewish societies. For some information on this issue in Jewish society, see Feiner (2021), 57–69.

66. For instance, Shimshi-Licht (2007), 105–7. On the use of the term Zonah, see Carlebach (2010), 298.

67. On the dynamic in the Jewish sources on wife-beating and the relationship of the tradition to this subject, see Graetz (1998).

68. Liberles (2005), 57.

69. Liberles (2005), 36.

70. For instance, Ashkenazi (1711), #41; Ashkenazi (1861), #35, #39.

71. Record book, community of Fürth, 82. In certain places, it was customary for lay leaders (parnasim) to sit in judgment together with rabbinic court judges (dayanim), often with ensuing disagreements between the two groups over lim-

its of jurisdiction of the dayanim and their accountability to community leaders. See Cohen (1966), vol. 1, 31.

72. Record book, community of Fürth, 82.
73. Record book, community of Fürth, 82.
74. Record book, community of Fürth, 82
75. Record book, beit din Kraków, 109.
76. Record book, beit din, Kraków, 109.
77. Record book, beit din, Kraków, 109.
78. Record book, beit din, Kraków, 109.
79. Record book, beit din Altona 1, 18, #329.
80. A certain Ber Frankfurt, married to Sarah daughter of Bonfit, was buried in the Altona cemetery in 1789. This Ber is possibly the father of the husband in the present case, who was perhaps named for his maternal grandfather. A woman by this name, Dusil daughter of Yaakov Glikstadt, wife of Bonfit, died in Altona on December 30, 1769. Perhaps she was the very same woman. See Dussel bat Jaakow ben I(zek) Glückstadt, https://peace.sites.uu.nl/epigraphy/search/?fbclid=IwAR3uckiObgUoZL_OF6gspAosoqcFGo8KuWs6HnsMmKbzw2PMg-pKY-w8jBk.
81. Record book, beit din Altona 1, 22, #381.
82. Record book, beit din Altona 1, 22, #381.
83. Record book, beit din Altona 1, 37, #694.
84. As the two cases occurred twenty-six years apart, obviously the panel of judges in Altona had changed by the time of the second one.
85. Elmshorn is a town some thirty kilometers north of Hamburg.
86. Record book, beit din Altona 4, 28, #161.
87. Record book, beit din Altona 3, 135, 138a.
88. Record book, beit din Altona 2, 452a.
89. Rublack (1999), 33; Boes (1996), 262.
90. Community record book, Kraków, 42 (marked with letters *khaf sofit-aleph*).
91. Community record book, Kraków, 42 (marked with letters *khaf sofit-aleph*).
92. Record book, beit din Fürth, 12.
93. Ibid., fol. 66.
94. Isserles, *Darchei Moshe (Short)*, Even haezer, 154:21. And see Graetz (1998), especially chapters 5 and 7.
95. The Record book, Offenbach, is not exactly a beit din record book, but it does include the proceedings of the beit din in a similar way to how they were recorded in other beit din record books.
96. Record book, Offenbach, 53.
97. Kraków record book, 42 (marked with letters *khaf sofit-aleph*).

98. Kraków record book, 42 (marked with letters *khaf sofit-aleph*).

99. This panel of dayanim in Kraków was keenly aware of the danger of iggun; for extraordinary measures it passed, see the section on runaway husbands.

100. Details of the case are recorded in Record book, beit din Warburg (page numbers illegible). The wife's name appears once, only partially legible; perhaps Heva.

101. Record book, beit din Warburg, page numbers illegible.

102. This was a coin.

103. Record book, beit din Warburg, pages not numbered.

104. Record book, beit din Warburg, pages not numbered.

105. On use of non-Jewish legal terms in beit din registers, see Berkovitz (2014), 6–11; Berkovitz (2010a), 273–75.

106. Sheilagh Ogilvie's study is invaluable for the present discussion, despite its focus on women in Germany's economy. See Ogilvie (2003), 180–94.

107. See Berkovitz (2017), 3.

108. Bonfield (2001), 89.

109. Frick (2007).

110. Bogucka (2004), 18–20.

111. Ogilvie (2003), 180.

112. Wiltenburg (1992), 22.

CHAPTER 11: "CONCERNING THE AGUNAH WHOSE HUSBAND LEFT FOR DISTANT PARTS"

1. Yehoshua (1859), Even haezer, beginning of #57.

2. See Shatzki (1932), 140–47.

3. Shmuel Glick takes this to mean that these men count the days like agunot. Assaf (2001–2009), vol. 1, 234. In my view, it may also mean the women back home are the ones counting the days (despite the plural masculine form; in this period, the masculine form was used when referring to women as well).

4. See Deut. 28:67. This verse comes from a part of the Torah (the tokhehah, or "rebuke") that forecasts the grim fate awaiting the Children of Israel if they do not follow God's commandments.

5. Minden (1696), fol. 17a–b.

6. The low moral standards of melamdim were criticized by others as well, but Minden specifically links the teachers' conduct to their family situations. See Shohet (1960), chapter 6, esp. 131–38.

7. For instance, *Hamagid*, January 5, 1860, 2; and November 18, 1863, 8. On advertisements in the Hebrew press in the 1850s, see Baker (1995); Hayim Sperber (2010).

8. See Salmon-Mack (2012), chapter 5.

Notes to Chapter 11 ::: 307

9. Harrington (2009), 105.
10. The scanty quantitative data raise many methodological problems. See, for instance, Mahler (1958), 80.
11. Harrington (1995), 268; Ogilvie (2003), 254.
12. See, for instance, Landau (1960), 1st edition, Even haezer, #65; additional examples in Shashar (2012), 235, n. 12.
13. See Liberles (2005), 36.
14. See Fram (1997), 129–43; Hundert (2004), 32–33; Breuer (1996), chapter 3 (in Hebrew: 119–25).
15. Emden (1896), 77.
16. Oppenheim (1971–1984), Even haezer, question 22.
17. Emden (1896), 77. See Duckesz (1903), 12.
18. Turniansky (2019), 124.
19. Ibid., 125.
20. Emden (1996), 70.
21. *Seder tehinot uvakashot* of Offenbach (1787), nos. 44–45; compare *Seder tehinot uvakashot* of Vienna (1815), 67.
22. On tehinot books (prayers for women) and their use, see Weissler (1998).
23. Examples in Shashar (2012), passim. Some of these cases were also discussed in part 2 of this book.
24. Yehuda Leib ben Hanokh of Pfersee (1707), question 136 (question undated; in the volume compiled by the son, published in Frankfurt in 1708).
25. The subject of married yeshiva students and their travels has been dealt with previously. See also Breuer (2003), 436–38.
26. Babylonian Talmud, Ketubot, 61b– 63a. A fascinating analysis of the stories can be found in Weiss and Stav (2018).
27. Shohet (1960), 135.
28. Dubnow (1924), 14, paragraph 71; and see enactment of 1632, Dubnow (1924), 53, paragraph 260.
29. Enactments, Fürth (Takanot Fuerda), fol. 105b, paragraph 207. Compare Record book, community of Altona 86, fol. 84.
30. For instance, R. Katz (1791), #31.
31. Belief in demons flourished during this period. Kaidanover (1944), chapter 11, fol. 25b.
32. Maimon (1888), 78.
33. For instance, Katz (1791), #31; Margoliot (1975), Even haezer, #10, #12.
34. Breuer (2003), 437; Assaf (2001–2009), vol. 2, 604.
35. Weil (1982), Yoreh deah, #57.
36. See Slutzky and Kaplan (1967), 17–41, 56–61, 84–122; Bartal (1997).
37. Harrington (2009), 79.

38. Krochmal (1674), #38.

39. Friedman (1972), 46. Friedman (36) notes that this was no literary invention; rather, the writer copied a genuine letter.

40. See Classen (2007).

41. Babylonian Talmud, Ketubot 9b; Shabbat 56a.

42. On the three methods and their halakhic implications, see Zevin (1945), 65–84; Breger (2007).

43. This method aids the agunah by exempting her from levirate marriage and halitzah. In the face of incontrovertible proof of the husband's death, she becomes a widow. In this case, a get dating from before his death is relevant only if he was childless and had no brothers. Without a get prior to death, she would need halitzah. See Zevin (1945), 66.

44. See Urbach (1979), vol. 1, 448–60.

45. Mentioned in Hagahot Mordechai on Babylonian Talmud Gittin, 423, and in Hagahot Rabbenu Peretz on *Sefer mitzvot katan*, mitzvah 184:9.

46. This case of a get signed by a dying man sparked controversy; see Radzyner (2008).

47. Krochmal (1674), #38.

48. See, for instance, Reischer (1860), part 1, #115. Reischer travelled with his tribunal and a scribe to the town where the husband resided to ensure delivery of a valid get. Errors were found in it nevertheless.

49. Record book, beit din Kraków, 21.

50. This halakhic solution is documented also in Duberush Ashkenazi (1858), question 9, with regard to a case in Lublin province.

51. For instance, Landau (1960), 2nd edition, Even haezer, #65; Margoliot (1975), Even haezer, #17, and many other examples.

52. Slutzky and Kaplan (1967), 20–21, 85–86, 103–10; Bartal (1997), 354–55. Note that the Russian army's conscription of adult men (and sometimes older teenage boys) continued at least through the end of World War I. But such conscription should not be confused with the shorter-lived Cantonist movement (1827–1865), in which the Russian government forcibly conscripted Jewish (and other ethnic-minority) twelve-year-olds in the hope (often successful) of converting them to Christianity. For more information, see Olga Litvak (2006).

53. Breuer (1996), 100–133.

54. Slutzky and Kaplan (1967), 56–59.

55. According to Joel Harrington (2009, 106), going off to war was the most common reason for abandoning wife and family in the non-Jewish population of Germany in the seventeenth century.

56. For instance, Margoliot (1975), Even haezer, #8, #17; Deutsch (1874), #35.

57. Harrington (2009), 123–24, notes that German society stressed the financial burden of raising children more than did the societies of neighboring countries.

Yet he rejects the claim that impecunious men were necessarily potential wife-deserters who had no other choices. I believe this is true for Jewish society as well.

58. Bogucka (2004), 20, and index.

59. For instance, Salmon-Mack (2012), 236. Based on the sources I reviewed, I disagree with her conclusion that poor men tended to desert their wives more often than other men did.

60. In Jewish communities in Poland in 1550–1655; see Fram (1997), 144–63.

61. On Jewish beggars in Germany from the seventeenth century onward, see Friedman (1972); for other countries, see Kaplan (2003), 304–6.

62. Krochmal (1674), #108.

63. Eisenstadt (1899), part 2, #114–#115.

64. Community records of Worms, pages numbered as 3–4. This town is some fifty-five kilometers southwest of Frankfurt.

65. See Ulbricht (1994), 173.

66. Volodymyr-Volynskyi is in Volhynia; Jarosław is in west Galicia.

67. Krochmal (1674), #123.

68. For more examples of vagabonds passing on information concerning agunot, see Margoliot (1975), Even haezer, #12; Eisenstadt (1899), part 2, #1.

69. See Dembitzer (1887–1902), vol. 2, 137–39.

70. Rapaport (1861), Even haezer, question 24.

71. Landau (1960), 1st edition, Even haezer, #29 (question and response both undated).

72. See Kahana (2015).

73. Sofer (1969–1984), part 3, Even haezer, #75. For another example of a poor man passing on information, see Ashkenazi (1858), question 22.

74. Ulbricht (1994).

75. Krochmal (1674), #83.

76. Brzesko, like Jarosław, is in west Galicia.

77. Kalbisow is likely Kolbuszowa.

78. Perhaps the town of Kłaj (in Polish).

79. Lifshitz (1873), Even haezer, #13.

80. My thanks to Stefan Litt for his assistance in deciphering these letters, to Chava Turniansky for reviewing the deciphered text, and to Oren Roman for assistance with translation.

81. It emerges later that the writer lived in the town of Gehrden, some ten kilometers southwest of Hannover.

82. The town of Bomst (Babimost), in Poland.

83. Salmon-Mack (2012), 233, based on a case reported in Katz (1875), suggests that in Hungary, an organized system was in place for tracking down missing husbands. In the course of my research, I did not form the impression that the system had been organized for this specific purpose.

84. The small town of Pinne (Pniewy) is some eighty kilometers from the city of Lissa (Leszno), in the district of Poznań.

85. Przemyśl, province of Lvov.

86. Landau (1960), 1st edition, Even haezer, #65.

87. This story was mentioned briefly in part 2.

88. Zemon Davis (1997), 1–22.

89. Kluger (1864a), question 2, fol. 9a.

90. Ibid., fol. 11b.

91. See Goldberg (1978), 198.

92. See Biale (1992), 149–75.

93. On Jewish criminals, see Glanz (1968); the latter study served as the basis for Liberles (2005), 94–96. There is no precise data on criminals for this period. Generally, research suggests that the ratio of Jews involved in criminal acts involving assets was higher than their ratio in society, whereas the ratio of Jews involved in criminal acts such as murder was lower than their ratio in society. There are two main theories in research regarding the approaches to criminals in Jewish society: Glanz claimed that the Jewish leadership handed criminals over to the authorities because they endangered the communities, while Schubert claimed that Jewish community leaders tried to protect the criminals, rather than hand them over, as an expression of Jewish solidarity. See Schubert (1990). Ulbricht has shown that attitudes to criminals depended in large part on their social position; see Ulbricht (1995), 51–52, 61–62.

94. See Egmond (1989), 87–89; Ulbricht (1995), 57.

95. Emden (1896), 108. Emden, who found the man likable despite his criminal cronies, tried to defend him by suggesting that he had never intended to make his wife an agunah. Rather, he claimed, it was she who refused to divorce. This possibility will be discussed.

96. Landau (1960), 1st edition, Even haezer, #46.

97. Liberles (2005) [Hebrew ed.], 95; Egmond (1989), 8; Ulbricht (1995), 56–60.

98. On law enforcement and Jewish criminals, see, for instance, Ulbricht (1995), 65–70.

99. Wolf was the name of the witness preceding the quoted testimony.

100. Landau (1960), 1st edition, Even haezer, #46. Testimony was given in Yiddish.

101. On the hanging of Jewish and non-Jewish criminals in Germany in this period, see Ulbricht (1995), 67; Boes (1996), 430–34.

102. Community records, Mainz, pages unnumbered; according to the testimony, the three men were hanged March 4, 1808.

103. Community records, Mainz.

104. Galhausen (now in Belgium) is 250 kilometers from Weisbaden. At the time of these events, the area belonged to France.
105. Community records, Mainz.
106. Community records, Mainz.
107. Community records, Mainz, last page of testimony.
108. Mishnah Yevamot 16:3: "One may not testify that a person died until his soul actually departs, even if one saw him cut up and severely wounded."
109. The Mishnah addresses the problem of whether the witness actually saw the hanged man at the moment of expiry. The Mishnah posits mistaken identity: a different man could have been hanged instead due to a last-minute switch. See Tosafot, Babylonian Talmud, Kiddushin, 80b. In the present case, the witness claimed he did see the hanging but then left the scene. Hence, there was no proof of the actual expiry.
110. Landau (1960), 1st edition, Even haezer, #47.
111. Carlebach (2001), 138–56.
112. For instance, Yissachar Dov Ber (1797), question 2, deals with an agunah whose husband converted to Christianity in times of persecution in Ukraine.
113. This hope often proved illusory, as non-Jewish society could be equally hostile to converts. See Goldberg (1999), 66–68; Carlebach (2001), 88–125; 170–99.
114. Teter (2003), 258; Carlebach (2001), 124–25.
115. For instance, Katzenellenbogen (1731), question 52.
116. Carlebach (2001), 138; Teter (2003), 262.
117. For an overview of the halakhic history of this issue, see Fram (1996), 300–302; Katz (1984), 255–69.
118. Carlebach (2001), 138–40.
119. Ashkenazi (1861), #39.
120. For instance, Eisenstadt (1899), part 2, #68.
121. Landau (1960), 1st edition, Even haezer, #42.
122. See Oppenheim (1971–1984), Even haezer, question 14.
123. Landau (1960), 2nd edition, Even haezer, #134.
124. Baschko (1816), Kuntres agunot, #15.
125. Landau (1960), 2nd edition, Even haezer, #80.
126. Ibid.
127. Quoted in Carlebach (2001), 139–40.
128. On Perl, see Meir (2013).
129. The essay is entitled "Über die Modifikation der mosaischen Gesetze" ("On the Modification of Jewish law"). See also Sinkoff (2003).
130. See Biale et al. (2018).
131. See Stampfer (2009), 167.

132. Cited in Wilensky (1990), vol. 2, 107. On this treatise and its historiography, see Wilensky (1990), 9–52.

133. It should be recalled that the Vilna Gaon opposed Hasidism on spiritual, not social, grounds. See Etkes (1997), 106. This book has been published in English as *The Gaon of Vilna: The Man and His Image*.

134. See Katz (1993) [Hebrew ed.], 282; Rapoport-Albert (2001), 499–503.

135. The following works of responsa were consulted for the present study, all by well-known opponents of Hasidism: Jacob Meshulam Ornstein, *Yeshuot Yaakov*; Dov Berish Ashkenazi, *Noda bashe'arim*.

136. Rapoport-Albert (1989), 217; Rapoport-Albert (2001), 501, n. 19.

137. See Stampfer (2009), 179; Shashar (2012), 258, n. 179.

138. On the chronology of the spread of the Haskalah, see Feiner and Bartal (2005), 7–12. See also Biale (1992), 149–75; Feiner (2010), 276; Zalkin (1999), 82–83.

139. Feiner (2010), 273; Stampfer (1987).

140. See Goldstein (2007), 29–48.

141. Maimon himself discussed the nature of his autobiography and his narrative decisions, although obviously this, too, should be read critically; see Maimon (2018), 121–25. There is more than one translation of Maimon's memoirs. Most of the English quotations from Maimon in this chapter are taken from Maimon (1888), translated by J. Clark Murray. Yet Murray's translation does not include the introduction to the second part of Maimon's memoirs; when quotations from that are needed, Reitter's 2018 translation is used instead. On the question of the veracity of his autobiography, see, for instance, Teller (1994).

142. Maimon (2018), 124–25.

143. On characteristics of maskilim, see Feiner and Bartal (2005), 9.

144. Maimon (1888), 65.

145. Maimon (1888), 75–78.

146. This incident is recounted in detail in Maimon (1888), 79.

147. Maimon's autobiography (1888), 144, notes that he already had many children when he left home.

148. Maimon, (1888), 80.

149. Maimon, (1888), 144.

150. Ibid.

151. Feiner (2005), 46.

152. Maimon (1888), 72, 89.

153. Maimon (1888), 260.

154. For instance, Maimon makes observations about his father and describes a conversation with his friend about moral choice. Maimon (1888), 72–73, 134–183.

Notes to Chapter 11

155. Goldstein (2007), 33–44, observes that Maimon's wife is seldom mentioned in his autobiography, and only once by name.
156. Maimon (1888), 74.
157. Issues of translation in Maimon's autobiography have often been noted. The present analysis is based on his use in the original German of the verb "can" rather than "want."
158. See Katz (1992), 21–42.
159. Maimon (1888), 262.
160. Maimon (1888), 274–75.
161. Maimon (1888), 276.
162. Trepp (1994).
163. Cited in Freudenthal (2003), 2.
164. In his preface to the second part of the autobiography, Maimon writes: "From the mere fact I left my people, my homeland, and my family to seek the truth, the reader will surely recognize that no petty motivations can have shaped my account of the truth." Maimon (2018), 123.
165. Maimon (1888), 249–50.
166. Trepp (1994), 137–38. Compare Feiner (2021), 57–69.
167. On women's education in maskilic circles in Berlin, see Hertz (1991).
168. Maimon (1888), 251.
169. Maimon (1888), 276–78.
170. Kaplan (2003), 304–6; Wunder (1998), 41.
171. I could not identify this community.
172. Record book, Romansweiler, fol. 86a, for years 1748–1760.
173. A copy of the letter is in the Community records, Metz.
174. See Shimshi-Licht (2007), 45–46, 81–85, 136–51.
175. Takanot 3 kehilot 9, 69.
176. See Halevi-Zwick (1990).
177. Rapoport (1796), letter 11.
178. This is an allusion to the commandment to send the mother bird away from the nest before taking eggs or fledglings (Deut. 22:6–7).
179. Harrington (2009), 96.
180. Oppenheim (1971–1984), Even haezer, question 18.
181. Record book, Altona 17a, fol. 8a.
182. Collection, ADMOR of Stolin-Karlin, document no. 453.
183. See Hovav (2009), 245.
184. Oppenheim (1971–1984), question 14.
185. Regarding the situation in non-Jewish society, see Hull (1996).
186. There are numerous examples of this view; see, for instance, Emden (1896), 82–83; Maimon (1888), 139.

187. See Lipking (1988), xvii.

188. Feiner (2010), 94–100.

189. Shimshi-Licht (2007), 174–76.

190. Record book, shamash of Altona 1, 15.

191. Children born out of wedlock were known as "adultery bastards"; see Record book, shamash of Altona 1, 9, 9a, 17, and elsewhere. On the significance of this phenomenon, see Carlebach (2010).

192. Rublack (1999), 134–62; Hull (1996), 77–89, 100–103, 113–14; Liberles (2005), 152.

193. For instance, Reischer (1860), part 3, #108.

194. On the marking of illegitimate children, see Jacobs-Yinon, Bilsky, and Halperin-Kaddari (2017).

195. Record book, beit din Altona 3, fol. 30.

196. Record book, beit din Altona 3, fol. 223.

197. Meshulam Zalman Hacohen (1806), Even haezer, question 2.

198. This responsum is unique in that it records, verbatim, the questions asked of the agunah by the beit din, as well as her answers.

199. Gelis (1974–1978), vol. 1, 110.

200. Meisels (1745), question 3 (undated).

201. Aryeh Leibush Lifshitz (1873), Even haezer, #22.

202. Sofer (1969–1984), part 3, Even haezer, #10.

203. Freiman (1944), 235–37.

204. That is, sexual relations were prohibited until she could immerse in the ritual bath.

205. Ashkenazi (1711), #2–#3.

206. Benet (1888), #19 (question undated).

207. Contemporary ledgers record amounts paid for deliveries, but I could not find this information for the year and distance in question. Multiple currencies in use at the time compound the difficulty of calculating the cost of delivery.

208. Yehuda Leib ben Kanokh of Pfersee (1707), question 136.

209. Maimon (1888), 260.

210. Salmon-Mack (2012), 232.

211. On the census in Germany, see Lindemann (1990), 52–55.

212. Maimon (1888), 259.

213. Responsa literature documents many cases of agunot who sent messengers, e.g., Deutsch (1874), #106.

214. Bartal and Halperin (1989), 59, paragraph 168.

215. Minden (1696), fol. 16b.

216. Salmon-Mack (2012), 232–35.

217. Margoliot (1975), Even haezer, #82.

218. See Gartner (2013), index.

219. Deutsch (1874), #95; in this case, the distance between the towns was some four hundred kilometers.
220. Ulbricht (1994); Friedman (1972).
221. See Buber (1895), 194.
222. In the responsa volume edited by Joseph Fürst in 1716 based on writings given to him by Moshe Mordechai Ziskind's widow, the question appears as addressed to Moshe (Mordechai's son) but is signed by Mordechai. Based on the dates, it seems this was an error; the question was probably directed to Mordechai Ziskind, not to his son Moshe.
223. The name of the community where she found him is not specified in the responsum.
224. Ziskind Rottenberg (1715), question 26.
225. Boes (1996), 428. On the methodological problems of research into criminality, see Shimshi-Licht (2007), 130–32.
226. Cases of Jewish housemaids who accused their employers of rape are documented; see, e.g., Record book, beit din Altona 4, fol. 178, paragraph 759, and other sources as well.
227. Harrington (2009), 33.
228. Evans (1998), 18.
229. For instance, the case in Hagen (2002), 300.
230. Baines (1998), 72–73, and references there in n. 19.
231. Harrington (2009), 27; Hull (1996), 58.
232. Kahneman (2003).
233. Rublack (1999), 163–96; Hull (1996), 111.
234. Rublack (1999), 163–96.
235. Shimshi-Licht (2007), 173–80.
236. See Sofer (1969–1984), part 4, Even haezer, #1.
237. Salmon-Mack (2012), 230.
238. Literary estate of Rabbi Bing of Würzburg.
239. Record book, shamash of Altona 1, 15a.
240. See Shereshevsky (1984), 429–30.
241. The shamash of the Altona synagogue, who was present at the event, testified to the delivery of the two get documents. See Record book, shamash of Altona 1, 54, and 54a, respectively. Beit din record books of the communities of AHW contain additional examples of get documents that were sent from afar, e.g., Record book, beit din Altona 6, fol. 188a, paragraph 1233.
242. Krochmal (1674), #110.
243. Ashkenazi (1861), #55.
244. Koidonover (1884), question 10.
245. For instance, Landau (1960), 2nd edition, Even haezer, #119.
246. See Brown (2004).

247. Halberstam (1874), Even haezer, 2:133.

248. Halberstam (1874), Even haezer, 2:133.

249. Landau (1960), 2nd edition, Even haezer, #134.

250. In Jewish law, a boy reaches legal majority at age thirteen and one day, provided he can show two pubic hairs. See Maimonides, *Mishneh torah*, Sefer nashim, Hilkhot ishut, 2:11.

251. Ashkenazi (1858), question 11.

252. Landau (1960), 2nd edition, Even haezer, #127–#128.

253. Reischer (1860), part 1, #101; Krochmal (1674), #58; Sofer (1969–1984), part 3, Even haezer, #72; Ashkenazi (1858), question 24. Thirty years is not a conventional length of time in this genre, but many cases of iggun lasted twenty years. See, e.g., Margoliot (1975), Even haezer, #13 (16 years); Hacohen (1684), #104 (twenty years); Deutsch (1874), #106, and many more.

254. Kahana (1954), 16.

255. This is based on the saying "Better to be with another man than be widowed" (Babylonian Talmud, Ketubot 75a).

CHAPTER 12: HETEREI AGUNAH IN BEIT DIN RECORDS AND RESPONSA LITERATURE

1. Heter (pl. heterei) agunah is a document in which the beit din/decisor declares that the agunah is permitted to remarry.

2. It is extremely difficult to pinpoint the precise number of heterei agunah since some are in unpublished manuscripts and others in compilations. As noted by Y. Z. Kahana, the eighteenth-century decisor Rabbi Jacob Emden spoke of "thousands, tens of thousands" of responsa dealing with the agunah problem, though this is probably an exaggeration. Kahana reports finding more than ten thousand responsa in the course of researching his study on Ashkenazic and Sephardic traditions from medieval times to the 1940s—by which time the printing of responsa volumes had become more accessible and less costly, and therefore more widespread, than in the period under discussion. See Kahana (1954), 7–11, 71–76.

3. A list of the decisors and responsa can be found in Shashar (2012), appendix.

4. The seventeenth century saw the printing of a mere handful of responsa volumes in areas of German culture. More were printed in Poland and its territories in this period. See Breuer (1996), 195. On the geographical distribution of responsa literature, see Glick (2006–2009).

5. The ideological positions of decisors are known from their own writings or from secondary sources.

6. For this term, see Rosenak (2011).

7. Karl Mannheim (1952), 187.

Notes to Chapter 12

8. According to some scholars who subscribe to this approach, certain "meta-principles" are external to the system; others consider them internal.

9. Proponents of the stance presented here developed different approaches, each emphasizing different aspects of the judicial process, giving them different names. A clear presentation of the various approaches can be found in Posner (2008), 19–56.

10. "Internal" and "external" causes are explained by Shimshon Ettinger. "Internal" derives from the law itself, while "external" is some aim or goal not inherent to the law itself; it is of a social, moral, or economic nature. It can also be a historical cause that made the law what it is. See Ettinger (1988), 7–9.

11. For instance, Fuss (1988).

12. Ross (2011), 37 (emphasis added). All translations of Ross in this chapter are by this book's translator, Sarah Friedman.

13. Ross (2011), 36.

14. For instance, Soloveitchik (2003).

15. For instance, Irshai (2012).

16. For instance, Gilligan (1982).

17. This approach is applied in the legal context by influential feminist thinker Catherine MacKinnon (2005).

18. Ross (2011), and references there, n. 1.

19. Foucault (1996), 15–29.

20. Berkovitz (2010b); Kahana (2006), 21.

21. Such as the case of Lemli Wimpe, discussed in part 2, chapter 8, based on external sources and three responsa.

22. Landau (1960), 1st edition, Even haezer, #43.

23. The record books of Metz and Frankfurt do not contain any heterei agunah as such, though they do describe several cases of halitzah. I found three heterei agunah in the records of Altona-Hamburg-Wandsbek and several in the Prague beit din records. In the Kraków beit din record, I found not a single heter agunah.

24. Kahana (1954), 18.

25. Fram (2007), 409. The English translation here is by Sarah Friedman.

26. Breger (2007), 10.

27. Shilo (2001), 228.

28. Brandes (2006), 56; see Zevin (1945), 65.

29. Brandes (2006), 61, n. 25.

30. Dinari (1984), 39.

31. Katzenellenbogen (1731), question 52.

32. No precise figure has been given since there is no agreement on whether conditional permission constitutes outright permission or not. Later, I clarify the problematics of cataloguing responsa by this criterion.

33. Babylonian Talmud, Gittin 3a, Yevamot 88a, and parallels.
34. Brandes (2006), 58.
35. Bacharach (1698), #71.
36. Ibid.
37. Berkovitz (2010b), 24–26.
38. Katz (1960), 135.
39. Berkovitz (2010b), 5; Katz (1960), 166.
40. Bacharach (1698), #71.
41. See, for instance, Shimshon Bacharach (father of Yair Haim, the Havot Yair) on the rabbi of Holešov (Holleschau), who did not want to adjudicate agunah cases and would neither permit nor forbid remarriage: Bacharach (1678), question 95. Rabbi Naftali Katz, Rabbi of Frankfurt-an-der-Oder, chose not to write any commentary on *Shulhan arukh*, paragraph 17, Even haezer, since he did not want to rule on practical laws relating to agunot. See Katz (1756), Even haezer, #17.
42. Reischer (1860), part 1, #100. Reischer reiterates his position in part 2, #115.
43. Yissachar Dov Ber (1797), fol. 89b, question 2.
44. Ibid., fol. 101, end of question 4.
45. Oppenheim (1971–1984), Even haezer, question 12.
46. Ashkenazi (1861), #93.
47. Ibid., #39.
48. Halberstam (1874), Even haezer, part 2, #154; Paneth (1999), #80; Hacohen (1684), #118. The context is often the validity of a get.
49. Expressions of anxiety over freeing an agunah can be found, for instance, in Krochmal (1674), #45; Oppenheim (1971–1984), Even haezer, question 9 (the questioner states that he himself saw the dead man, so there was no actual problem), Lifshitz (1873), Even haezer, #14–#15.
50. See Gartner (2013), index.
51. Babad (1828), Even haezer, responsum 88.
52. Landau (1960), 1st edition, Even haezer, #28.
53. Ben Yehiel (1607), 51:2. The Rosh is quoted in Ephraim Hacohen (1684), #101; and in Meir (2005), #45.
54. There are many examples. See, for instance, Oppenheim (1971–1984), Even haezer, questions 4, 9, 11; Eisenstadt (1899), part 2, #114; Paneth (1999), #43.
55. Lifshitz (1873), Even haezer, #14.
56. On the textual and ideational roots of this essay, and for its editions in halakhic literature since the eighteenth century, see Levine (2004).
57. Meir (2005), #66.

58. Rabbi Joshua Heschel of Kraków complained about decisors who caused women to remain agunot for no reason. Heschel (1859), #50.

59. Krochmal (1674), #106.

60. Ibid.

61. As observed by Y. Z. Kahana, without any mention, however, of implications for the agunah. He suggests this custom was practiced especially when a halakhic innovation (*hidush*), one not found in the writings of earlier decisors, was introduced. See Kahana (1954), 44. I disagree with him; many of the requests for a second decisor to join in freeing an agunah relate to extremely simple cases, with no halakhic innovation.

62. See Krochmal (1674), #42, #45, #59, and elsewhere; see also Ashkenazi (1861), #72; Landau (1960), 1st edition, Even haezer, #36; Katzenellenbogen (1731), question 45; Baschko (1816), Kuntres agunot, #8–#9.

63. For instance, Reischer (1860), part 1, #100; and part 2, #115; Eisenstadt (1899), part 2, #32; Rapaport (1861), Even haezer, question 27, and many more.

64. Baschko (1816), Kuntres agunot, #11.

65. Ben Hanokh (1707), question 128.

66. *Otzar haposkim* lists this practice under "Miscellaneous customs in freeing an agunah." The editors note that the section includes items that are not actually law. See *Otzar haposkim* (1981), 102–4.

67. See the Talmudic story about Rabbi Shela in part 2.

68. Karo (1959), Even haezer, Din mayim she'ein lahem sof, 54b. The words were written in the course of a debate with R. Moses Trani (MBYT). Translation edited from that of Hochstein Blass. See Hochstein Blass (2009), 112.

69. For instance, Eisenstadt (1899), part 2, #50; Margaliot (1791), part 1, question 26; Moshe ben Pinhas miKlevan (1818), question 1, 196a, unnumbered question, 199a; Fraenkel-Teomim (1865), questions 7–8.

70. Maoz Kahana, in his book on the Noda Bi-Yehudah (Yehezkel Landau) and Hatam Sofer (Moshe Sofer-Schreiber), has claimed, with respect to their responsa collections, that "the questioners are usually rabbis seeking the solution or support of the rabbi being questioned, which turned, in their [the questioners'] hands, into a kind of higher 'authority.'" See Kahana (2015), 16. This description is imprecise: Although sending a question to a decisor is a private initiative, it does not take place in a void. It results from seen or unseen forces which influence the decisor, where an individual decisor cannot always afford to withstand such appeals to his authority.

71. In Margoliot (1858), part 3, #11.

72. Ibid.

73. Heschel (1828), Even haezer, beginning of question 81.

74. Decisors usually kept a copy of their responsa. Responsa dealing with

agunah issues tended to be lengthy, so copying them out took more time. See Steinhardt (2004), introduction.

75. Rapaport (1861), question 34.
76. Landau (1960), 2nd edition, Even haezer, #64.
77. Ibid., 1st edition, Even haezer, #36.
78. Landau (1960), 2nd edition, Even haezer, #134. Compare Einsenstadt (1899), part 3, #50. For further examples, see, for instance, Meir (2005), #61, #62; Weil (1982), #15; Paneth (1999), #100. Forgetfulness as excuse for a delay in replying to a question can be found in Eisenstadt (1899), part 2, #55.
79. Sofer (1969–1984), part 3, Even haezer, #55. Self-portrayal of a decisor as too busy writing responsa to reply is certainly related to the image he sought to project. Be that as it may, the focus is on the delay itself, not the excuses for it; we may relate to delay as such, not merely to literary convention for delaying.
80. See correspondence of Moshe Shimshon Bacharach and Naphtali Katzin in Bacharach (1678), questions 95–96. See also Eisenstadt (1899), part 2, #55; Landau (1960), 1st edition, Even haezer, #28; we have already mentioned Yair Haim Bacharach's position in Bacharach (1698), #71.
81. Oppenheim (1971–1984), Even haezer, question 15.
82. Apparently the town of Lubaczów, some fifty kilometers northeast of Przemyśl.
83. Gesenbauer (1884), #27–#30.
84. Several towns in the area bear this name; given that the rabbi's name is not mentioned, I was not able to identify the relevant one.
85. Gesenbauer (1884), #30.
86. See Krochmal (1674), #42, #45; Katzenellenbogen (1731), question 51; Hacohen (1684), #101.
87. Not all decisors interpreted the halakhah in this way; however, as we have seen, even among those who did not, some adopted the rhetoric of striving to alleviate the agunah's suffering. From this, we may conclude that they did not regard the human criterion of compassion as external to halakhah.
88. Kahana (1954), 18.
89. Silvetsky (1997), 64–65.
90. As explained in part 2.
91. Karo, *Shulhan arukh*, Even haezer, 17, paragraph 39.
92. This was the position of the Vilna Gaon.
93. This is the position of the Beit Shmuel (Rabbi Samuel ben Uri Shraga Phoebus of Vadislav).
94. Meisels and miKrakow Brisk (1745), question 13 (the second of two questions bearing this number).
95. Kahana (2010), 189.
96. *Shulhan arukh*, Even haezer, Hilkhot ishut (Laws of Conjugal Relations),

17, paragraph 34. The Sefaria website's translation of Karo and Isserles aided mine here.

97. Beit Shmuel (Uri Shraga Phoebus) on *Shulhan arukh*, Even haezer, 17, paragraph 34, #103.

98. Krochmal (1674), #50.

99. Ibid., #40.

100. Meir Hacohen miRothenburg (1879), "Nashim"# 11.

101. Ibid.

102. Yuval (1988), 325.

103. Obviously, Krochmal did not coin this term; it appears in the Talmud. His innovation was its use in the context of freeing an agunah.

104. Lit., "could find neither his hands nor his feet."

105. On the question of whether candidates unworthy of ordination were being ordained anyway—one not limited to Krochmal's generation—see Breuer (2003), 390–96.

106. Landau (1960), 2nd edition, Even haezer, #150.

107. Maoz Kahana devotes a lengthy discussion to what he terms a "return to the Talmud" in Yehezkel Landau's halakhic approach; see Kahana (2015), part 1.

108. For instance, Baschko (1816), Kuntres agunot, #36.

109. Landau (1901), 7, 11.

110. See, for instance, Breuer (1996), 226.

111. Eisenstadt (1899), part 3, #50.

112. Yuval (1988), 336.

113. Breuer (2003), 339. Breuer was referring mainly to criteria for the appointment of yeshiva heads, but the head of the yeshiva (rosh yeshiva) often functioned as the local rabbi as well.

114. See, for instance, Emden (1896), 22–23; Berkovitz (2007), 45–55.

115. On background for the need for a new rabbi, see Horovitz (1972), 119–22.

116. Panta (1989).

117. Details of the case can be found in Judah Leib ben Hanokh (1707), question 128.

118. The author cites Moshe Shimshon Bacharach, with whom he agrees: There was no doubt whatsoever as to the identity of the dead man, yet all the testimonies still had to be thoroughly investigated. Hanokh (1707), question 128.

119. Ben Hanokh's Responsa Hinukh beit Yehudah contains several responsa on this question: from Rabbi Avraham Broda of Prague, Rabbi Shmuel of Fürth, and Rabbi Jacob Reischer.

120. Hanokh (1706), question 128.

121. Tension of this kind can be found in the dialogue of the agunah Sarah and Rabbi Menahem Mendel Krochmal (see part 2).

122. Compare Hacohen (1684), 101.

123. Breuer (1996), 144–55, 228–31.

124. In the mid-eighteenth century, Rabbi Yom Tov Lipman Heller was denounced by his opponents; see Breuer (1996), 228. Glikl quotes her son, who has harsh criticism for the rabbi he was studying with. See Turniansky (2019), 225–26. For criticisms again the rabbinate in general, see, for instance, Feiner (2021), 66–76.

125. Yuval (1988), 422.

126. Yuval (1988), 342.

127. Berlin (1894), part 4, #85.

AFTERWORD: THE AGUNAH, THE DECISOR, AND THE SUFFERING

1. Eisenstadt (1899), part 3, #2.

2. Oppenheim (1971–1984), question 18.

3. Ibid., question 17.

4. Koidonover (1884), question 9; Eisenstadt (1899), part 2, #18, #55; Halberstam (1874), Even haezer, part 2, #173; Kluger (1910), Even haezer, #159.

5. Ashkenazi (1861), #22, #38.

6. Paneth (1999), #93; Ashkenazi (1861), #59, #93; Krochmal (1674), #58; Landau (1960), 1st edition, Even haezer, #20.

7. Krochmal (1674), #101; Gunzberg (1869), Dinei Hadash, #18.

8. See also Deutsch (1874), #35; Krochmal (1674), #38; Landau (1960), 1st edition, Even haezer, #31, #44; Hacohen (1684), #118.

9. Koidonover (1884), question 9.

10. Meir (2005), #60; Gunzberg (1869), Dinei Hadash, #18; Eisenstadt (1899), part 3, #2.

11. Kahana (1954), 18.

12. This is especially marked in the work of Y. Z. Kahana: "The common denominator of iggun of all kinds is the suffering of the agunah." This observation was the basis of his analysis of halakhic activity as intended "to alleviate their bitter fate" (1954, 18). All translations of Y. Z. Kahana in this chapter, as well as in the rest of the book, are by Sarah Friedman, this book's translator.

13. Ilan (1999), chapter 2, shows that the common notion that Beit Hillel were "lenient" and Beit Shammai were "stringent" does not reflect their rulings regarding women. See also Shashar (2007), 6.

14. Y. Z. Kahana realized this possibility, but I believe he applied it too sweepingly. Kahana (1954), 16.

15. For instance, Bacharach (1678), question 72.

16. For instance, Oppenheim (1971–1984), Even haezer, question 21.

17. On distribution of an estate, see part 1 of this volume.

18. On Rabbi Jacob Joseph, see Hertzberg (1989), 143. The entire text of this letter was published for the first time in the Hebrew edition of this book.

19. Sosnowiec at that time was near the meeting point of the borders of Russia, the Austro-Hungarian Empire, and Germany.

20. Literary estate of Rabbi Gitler of Sosnowiec, unnumbered.

21. As is evident from the get appended to the letter, written in New York, October 21, 1895.

22. Yet I believe Y. Z. Kahana exaggerates his claim that in many cases, the agunah herself caused the delay in receiving a heter because she was not interested in remarrying and thus neglected to obtain precise testimony as to her husband's death. Later, when she changed her mind, it was difficult to find witnesses. Kahana (1954), 8. Just as we cannot claim that permission to remarry was always in the agunah's interest, neither can we claim that in a great number of cases, it was the agunah herself who caused the delay in obtaining permission to remarry. As we have shown in this book, there are enough reasons to assume that the conduct of decisors was certainly a contributing factor in iggun's continuing, not infrequently, for many years. Kahana mentions only two possible causes of iggun: the woman's delay and political reasons. He completely ignores the role of decisors in causing the delay.

23. Kahana (1954), 18.

24. Brandes (2006), 62.

25. This is what Y. Z. Kahana did. While he collected the main sources of iggun laws, he did not use them to address the question concerning us here. By contrast, he frequently cites decisors who employed images of the kind presented here: the agunah is suffering, and the decisor is attentive to her suffering. From them, he drew the conclusion that decisors, indeed, endeavored to ease the fate of agunot.

26. Brandes (2006), 61, n. 25.

27. Ibid.

28. Brandes is biased and misleading here, too. Clearly, wishing to prevent the scenario of the first husband's reappearance is not the same as wishing to alleviate the agunah's suffering, as he would have it. He actually declares the risk of iggun no less severe than the risk of producing mamzerim. This anxiety can be understood not only as the desire to protect the woman but—and primarily—as a wish to protect society, for religious reasons, from the creation of mamzerim in its midst. The formulation "her children would be mamzerim" is equally biased; after all, they are also the children of the second husband. And there is no way of determining if we are discussing a desire to protect her above all—or if the weightier factor is to protect him or the children.

29. Brandes (2006), 62.

30. Brandes (2006), 59.

31. Ibid.

32. Predictably, many feminist thinkers have criticized this approach; in their view, the institution of marriage itself is coercive in its unequal power relations between genders. As an institution, it is all too well-known to cause the woman greater suffering than it causes the husband.

33. For instance, Oppenheim (1971–1984), Even haezer, questions 4, 14, and especially the vivid description in question 15.

34. Katzenellenbogen (1731), question 51.

35. Babylonian Talmud, Sanhedrin, 104b and parallels; Lamentations Rabbah, parasha 1; Midrash Eicha zuta, 1.

36. According to Mordechai Breuer, the seventeen tractates included in the regular curriculum (including Sanhedrin, where the story appears) were not studied in their entirety. Many yeshivot skipped the aggadic (not-halakhic) passages of the Talmud. See Breuer (2003), chapter 3, especially 87–89. However, it is difficult to know precisely what was studied in each yeshiva, on every course of learning; it is conceivable that some students did have an interest in the aggadic passages. See also Babylonian Talmud, Rosh Hashanah 33b, for the reference to Sisera's mother, another relevant association. I thank Refael Kroizer for referring me to this source.

37. Oppenheim (1971–1984), Even haezer, question 17.

38. Hovav (2009), 123.

BIBLIOGRAPHY

Adelman, Howard. 1994. "Custom, Law, and Gender: Levirate Union among Ashkenazim and Sephardim in Italy after the Expulsion from Spain." In *The Expulsion of the Jews: 1492 and After*, edited by Raymond B. Waddington and Arther H. Williamson, 107–25. New York: Garland.

Agnon, S. Y. 1937. *The Bridal Canopy* [Hebr. *Hahnasat kalah*]. Translated by I. M. Lask. New York, NY: Doubleday, Doran, & Co. with Schocken.

Alexander, Elizabeth Shanks. 2000. "The Impact of Feminism on Rabbinic Studies: The Impossible Paradox of Reading Women into Rabbinic Literature." *Studies in Contemporary Jewry* (16): 101–18.

Almog, Shulamit. 2000. *Mishpat vesifrut*. Jerusalem: Nevo.

Alroey, Gur. 2008. *Hamahpeha hashketa: Hahagira hayehudit mehaimpiria harusit, 1875–1925*. Jerusalem: Merkaz Zalman Shazar.

Anonymous. 1800. *Reise von Hamburg nach Philadelphia*. Hannover: Ritscher.

Anonymous. 1801. "Reise von Hamburg." *Allgemeine Literatur-Zeitung*, October 17, 118–19.

Asher ben Yehiel. 1607. *Sheelot utshuvot leharav rabenu Asher ZL*. Venice: Alwizi Bragadin.

Ashkenazi, Abraham Shmuel. 1905 *Tzaar bat rabim* edited by B. Feidberg. L'viv: Sallat

Ashkenazi, Duberush. 1858. *SHUT Noda bashearim*. Warsaw.

Ashkenazi, Gershon. 1861. *SHUT Avodat hagereshuni*. Lvov: S. L. Kugel, Lewin, & Co.

Ashkenazi, Tzvi Hirsch. 1711. *SHUT Haham Tzvi*. Amsterdam: Shlomo Proops Mocher-seforim.

Ashkenazi, Yaakov. 1849. *Tzena urena*. Warsaw: Bomberg.

Assaf, Simhah. 1926. "Minuy nashim leapotropsut." *Hamishpat haivri* 2: 75–81.

———. 2001–2009. *Mekorot letoldot hahinukh beyisrael*. 6 vols. New York: Jewish Theological Seminary of America.

Awiad-Wolfsberg, Jeschajahu. 1957. "Minhag und Halacha." *Leo Baeck Institute Bulletin* 1: 27–30.

Babad, Yehoshua Heschel. 1828. *SHUT Sefer Yehoshua*. Zholkva.

Bacharach, Yair Hayyim Moshe Shimshon. 1678. *Hut hashani*. Frankfurt: n.p.

———. 1698. *SHUT Havot Yair*. Frankfurt: Johannes Wust.

Baer, Fritz. 1936. *Das Protokollbuch der Landjudenschaft des Herzogtums Kleve*. Berlin: Schocken.

Baines, Barbara J. 1998. "Effacing Rape in Early Modern Representation." *ELH* 65, no. 1: 9–98.

Baker, Mark. 1995. "The Voice of the Deserted Jewish Woman, 1867–1870." *Jewish Social Studies* 2, no. 1: 98–123.

Bar-Levav, Avriel. 2002a. "Ritualisation of Jewish Life and Death in the Early Modern Period." *Leo Baeck Institute Year Book* 47, no. 1: 69–82.

———. 2002b. "'When I Was Alive': Jewish Ethical Wills as Egodocuments." In *Egodocuments and History: Autobiographical Writing in Its Social Context since the Middle Ages*, edited by Rudolf Dekker, 45–59. Rotterdam: Erasmus University.

Bartal, Israel. 1997. *Giborim o mugei lev: Yehudim betzvaoteha shel polin (1794–1863)*. Vol. 1, *Kiyum vashever: Yehudei Polin ledoroteihem*, edited by Israel Bartal and Yisrael Gutman, 353–67. Jerusalem: Merkaz Zalman Shazar.

Baschko, Tzvi Hirsch. 1816. *SHUT Tiferet Tzvi*. Lvov.

Baumgarten, Elisheva. 2004. *Mothers and Children: Jewish Family Life in Medieval Europe*. Princeton: Princeton University Press.

Behringer, Wolfgang. 1990. *Thurn und Taxis: Die Geschichte Ihrer Post und Ihrer Unternehmen*. Munich: Piper.

Benet, Mordechai. 1888. *SHUT Parshat Mordechai*. Sighetu: Mendel Vider.

Berkovitz, Jay R. 2005. "Civil Law and Justice in the Rabbinic Tribunals of Eighteenth Century Metz." Edited by Baruch J. Schwartz. *Iggud: Selected Essays in Jewish Studies* 14 (1): 87–89.

———. 2007. *Mesoret umahpehah: Tarbut yehudit betzarfat bereshit haet hahadashah*. Jerusalem: Merkaz Zalman Shazar.

———. 2010a. "Acculturation and Integration in Eighteenth-Century Metz." *Jewish History* 24: 271–94.

———. 2010b. "Dyukno shel posek halakhah bemeah ha17: Bein biografia leotobiografia." In *Yosif daat: Mehkarim behistoriah yehudit modernit: mugashim leProf. Yosef Salmon lehag yovelo*, edited by Yossi Goldstein, 33–66. Beer Sheva: Ben-Gurion University.

———. 2014. *Protocols of Justice: The Pinkas of the Metz Rabbinic Court 1771–1789*. 2 vols. Leiden: Brill.

———. 2017. "Women Before the Bet Din in Early Modern France: The Evidence from Metz." In *The Paths of Daniel: Studies in Judaism and Jewish Culture in Honor of Rabbi Professor Daniel Sperber*, edited by Adam S. Ferziger, 47–75. Ramat Gan: Bar Ilan University Press.

———. 2019. *Law's Dominion: Jewish Community, Religion, and Family In Early Modern Metz*. Brill.

Berlin, Naftali Tzvi Yehuda. 1894. *SHUT Meshiv davar*. Warsaw: Meir Yehiel Halter & Meir Eisenstadt Nalewki.

Berner, Tali Miriam. 2018. *Al pi darkam: Yeladim veyeladot beashkenaz*. Jerusalem: Merkaz Zalman Shazar.

Bernstein, Marc S. 2001. "Midrash and Marginality: The 'Agunot' of S. Y. Agnon and Devorah Baron." *Hebrew Studies* 42: 7–58.

Bethlehem, Louise. 2006. *Skin Tight: Apartheid Literary Culture and Its Aftermath*. Leiden: Brill.

Beyrer, Klaus. 2006. "The Mail-Coach Revolution: Landmarks in Travel in Germany between the Seventeenth and Nineteenth Centuries." *German History* 24, no. 3: 375–86.

Biala, Tzvi Hirsch ben Naftali Hertz Ashkenazi. 1803. *SHUT Ateret Tzvi*. Lvov.

Biale, David. 1992. *Eros and the Jews*. New York: Basic Books.

Biale, David, David Assaf, Benjamin Brown, Uriel Gellman, Samuel Heilman, Moshe Rosman, Gady Sagiv, and Marcin Wodziński. 2018. *Hasidism: A New History*. Princeton: Princeton University Press.

Bieber, Menachem Mendel. 1905. *Mazkeret legdolei ostraha*. Berdychiv: Hayim Yaakov Sheftil.

Blidstein, Yaakov. 1976. "Maamadan haishi shel nashim shvuyot umashmadot bahalakhah shel yemei habeinayim." *Shnaton hamishpat haivri* 3–4: 35–116.

Bnei Gumpel, Yisrael Koppel. 1767. *Sefer minhagim dekehilateinu Fuerda*. Furth: Hayim ben Tzvi Hirsch.

Bock, Gisela. 1991. "Challenging Dichtomies: Perspectives on Women's History." In *Writing Women's History: International Perspectives*, edited by Ruth Roach Pierson and Jane Rendall Karen Offen, 1–23. Houndmills: MacMillan.

———. 1996. "Jews in the Criminal Justice System of Early Modern Germany." *Social Science History* 20, no. 2: 259–79.

Boes, Maria R. 1996. "Public Appearance and Criminal Judicial Practices in Early Modern Germany." *Social Science History* 20, no. 2: 259–79.

Bogucka, Maria. 2004. *Women in Early Modern Polish Society, Against the European Background*. Aldershot: Ashgate.

Bonfield, Lloyd. 2001. "Developments in European Family Law." In *Family Life in Early Modern Times, 1500–1789*, edited by David I. Kertzer and Marzio Barbagli, 87–124. New Haven: Yale University Press.

Boulton, Jeremy. 1990. "London Widowhood Revisited: The Decline of Female Remarriage in the Seventeenth and Early Eighteenth Centuries." *Continuity and Change* 5, no. 3: 323–55.

Bourdieu, Pierre. 1990. *The Logic of Practice*. Translated by Richard Nice. Stanford: Stanford University Press.

Brandes, Yehudah. 2005. "Yevamot, arayot, ukrovot: Petihta lemasehet yevamot." *Akdamot* 17: 171–201.

———. 2006. "Agunot: Ekronot-al bahalakhah." *Akdamot* 18: 55–72.

Braudel, Fernand. 2009. "History and the Social Sciences: The Longue Durée." *Review (Fernand Braudel Center)* 32, no. 2: 171–203.
Breger, Sarah Gavriella. 2007. "Sentenced to Marriage: Chained Women in Wartime." Thesis, University of Pennsylvania.
Bremmer, Jan, and Lourens van den Bosch. 1995. *Between Poverty and the Pyre: Moments in the History of Widowhood*. London: Routledge.
Brenner, Michael, Stefi Jersch-Wenzel, and Michael Meir. 2000. *Toldot yehudei germanyah baet hahadashah*. Translated by Raya Nettenbrook-Ginzberg. Vol. 2. Jerusalem: Merkaz Zalman Shazar.
Breuer, Mordechai. 1996. *The Jewish Middle Ages*. Vol. 1, *German-Jewish History in Modern Times*, edited by Michael A. Meyer, 1–255. New York: Columbia University Press.
———. 2003. *Oholei torah: Hayeshiva tavnitah vetoldoteha*. Jerusalem: Merkaz Zalman Shazar.
Brichto, Herbert Chanan. 1973. "Kin, Cult, And Afterlife—A Biblical Complex." *Hebrew Union College Annual* 44: 1–54.
Brosseder, Claudia. 2005. "The Writing in the Wittenberg Sky: Astrology in Sixteenth-Century Germany." *Journal of the History of Ideas* 66, no. 4: 557–76.
Brown, Iris. 2004. "R' Hayim miSanz: Darkhei pzikato al reka olamo harayoni veitgerei zmano." PhD dissertation, Bar Ilan University.
Buber, Salomon. 1895. *Anshei shem: Geonei yisrael, adirei hatorah, rabanim, roshei metivta, morei tzedek, MM, dayanim, parnasim umanhigim asher shimshu bakodesh bair lvov bemeshekh 400 shanah, mishnat 1500–1890*. Krakow: Josef Fischer.
Buitelaar, Marjo. 1995. "Widows' Worlds." In *Between Poverty and the Pyre: Moments in the History of Widowhood*, edited by Laurens Van Den Bosch Jan Bremmer, 1–18. London: Routledge.
Capp, Bernard. 2003. *When Gossips Meet: Women, Family, and Neighbourhood in Early Modern England*. Oxford: Oxford University Press.
Carlebach, Elisheva. 2001. *Divided Souls: Converts from Judaism in Germany, 1500–1750*. New Haven: Yale University Press.
———. 2010. "Fallen Women and Fatherless Children: Jewish Domestic Servants in Eighteenth-Century Altona." *Jewish History* 24, no. 3–4: 295–308.
Casey, James. 1989. *The History of the Family*. New York: Wiley.
Census of the Jews of Alsace, 1784. N.d. http://www.genami.org/en/lists/alsace/census-1784.php.
Classen, Albrecht. 2007. *The Medieval Chastity Belt: A Myth-Making Process*. New York: Palgrave MacMillan.
Cohen, Daniel J. 1966. "Irgunei 'Bnei hamedinah' beashkenaz: Bameot ha17 veha18." 4 vols. PhD dissertation, Hebrew University.

———. 1993. "Kavim ledmutam shel 'Dayanei hamedinah' beashkenaz bemeot ha17-ha18." In *Keminhag ashkenaz uPolin: Sefer yovel leChone Schmeruk*, edited by Chava Turniansky, Ezra Mendelsohn, and Israel Bartal, 179–92. Jerusalem: Merkaz Zalman Shazar.

Cohen, Tovah, ed. 2000. *Nisuin, Herut Ve Shivyon: Hayelchu Yachdav?* Ramat Gan

Cohen (Katz), Tuviah. 1708. *Maase Tuviah*. Venice.

Davis, Joseph. 2002. "The Reception of the 'Shulhan Arukh' and the Formation of the Ashkenazic Jewish Identity." *AJS Review* 26, no. 2: 251–76.

Davis, Natalie Zemon. 1997. *Remaking Impostors: From Martin Guerre to Sommersby*. London: Royal Holloway, University of London.

———. 2001. *Shuvo shel Martin Guerre*. Tel Aviv: Xargol.

de La Chesnaye-Desbois, François-Alexandre Aubert. 1772. *Dictionnaire de la Noblesse*. 2nd ed. Edited by La Veuve Duchesne. Vol. 4. Paris.

Dekker, Rudolf M. 1987. "Women in Revolt: Popular Protest and Its Social Basis in Holland in the Seventeenth and Eighteenth Centuries." *Theory and Society* 16, no. 3: 337–62.

———, ed. 2002. *Egodocuments and History: Autobiographical Writing in Its Social Context since the Middle Ages*. Hilversum: Verloren.

Dekker, Rudolph M., and Lotte C. van de Pol. 1989. *The Tradition of Female Transvestism in Early Modern Europe*. New York: St. Martin's Press.

Dembitzer, Hayim Natan. 1887–1902. *Kelilat yofi: Toldot harabanim . . . asher shimshu bekheter harabanut beir lvov*. 2 vols. Krakow.

Deutsch, Yosef Yoel. 1874. *SHUT Yad Yosef*. Sighetu: Yaakov Greenwald.

Dinari, Yedidyah Alter. 1984. *Hahmei ashkenaz beshelhi yemei-habeinayim: Darkheihem ukhtaveihem bahalakhah*. Jerusalem: Bialik.

Dubin, Lois C. 2007. "Jewish Women, Marriage Law, and Emancipation: A Civil Divorce in Late Eighteenth-Century Trieste." *Jewish Social Studies* 13, no. 2: 65–92.

Dubnow, Shimon, ed. 1924. *Pinkes hamedina, o pinkes vad hakehilot hareishiot bemedinat lita: Kovetz takanot ufsakim mishnat 5383 ad shnat 5521*. Berlin.

Duckesz, Yechezkel. 1903. *Iva lemoshav: Kolel toldot harabanim sheyashvu al kise harabanut shel shalosh kehilot AHV: Altona, Hamburg, veWandsbek*. Krakow: Yosef Fisher.

Egmond, Florike. 1989. "Crime in Context: Jewish Involvement in Organized Crime in the Dutch Republic." *Jewish History* 4, no. 1: 75–100.

Eisenstadt, Meir. 1899. *SHUT Panim meirot*. Lvov: Chaim Rohatyn.

Eliav, Mordechai. 1959. "Kiddush H[ashem] begzeirot 5408–5409." *Mahanayim* 41. http://www.daat.ac.il/daat/kitveyet/mahanaim/eliave.htm.

Emden, Yaakov Yisrael. 1752. *Akitzat akrav*. Amsterdam.

———. 1757. *Sefer shimush*. Amsterdam.

———. 1758. *Shvirat luhot haaven.* Żółkiew.
———. 1762a. *Sefer hitabkut.* Altona.
———. 1762b. *Zeh sefer toledot adam belial: Beit Yehonatan hasofer.* Altona.
———. 1883. *Sefer she'ilat YABTZ.* Lvov: Uri Zev Wolf Salat.
———. 1896. *Megilat sefer.* Warsaw: Szuldberg Bros. and Co.
———. 1991. *Iggeret Purim [Manuscript fascimile].* New York.
Emmerich, Zalman. 1910. *Shisha zironei aruga.* Prague: Waitzen.
Esh, Shaul, ed. 1961. *Pinkes kehilat Berlin: 5314–5483 (1723–1854).* Jerusalem: Rubin Mass.
Etkes, Immanuel. 1991. *Lita biyrushalayim: Hailit halamdanit belita ukehilat haprushim biyrushalayim leor igrot ukhtavim shel R' Shmuel miklem.* Jerusalem: Yad Ben Tzvi.
———. 1997. *Yahid bedoro: Hagaon mevilna—demut vedimuy.* Jerusalem: Merkaz Zalman Shazar.
Ettinger, Shimshon. 1988. "Al mekomah shel hasvarah bamishnah torah laRMBM." *Shnaton hamishpat haivri* 14–15: 1–30.
Evans, Richard J. 1998. *Tales from the German Underworld: Crime and Punishment in the Nineteenth Century.* New Haven: Yale University Press.
Eybeschutz, Yehonatan. 1819. *Sefer benei ahuva.* Prague: Gabriel Eybeschutz.
Feiner, Shmuel. 2005. "Al maslul haprishah min 'hamedinah hayehudit': kriah mehadash betoldot hayav shel Shlomo Maimon." In *Hahaskalah legvaneha: Iyunim hadashim betoldot hahaskalah vesifrutah,* edited by Shmuel Feiner and Israel Bartal, 43–61. Jerusalem: Magnes.
———. 2010. *Shorshei hahilon: Matiranut usafkanut beyahadut hameah ha18.* Jerusalem: Merkaz Zalman Shazar.
———. 2021. *Et hadashah.* Jerusalem: Merkaz Zalman Shazar.
Feiner, Shmuel, and Israel Bartal, eds. 2005. *Hahaskalah legvaneha: Iyunim hadashim betoldot hahaskalah vesifrutah.* Jerusalem: Magnes.
Fildes, Valerie. 1988. *Wet Nursing: A History from Antiquity to the Present.* Oxford: Blackwell.
Foucault, Michel. 1996. *Toldot haminiyut kerekh 1: Haratzon ladaat.* Translated by Gavriel Esh. Tel Aviv: Hakibbutz Hameuchad.
Fraenkel-Teomim, Baruch. 1865. *SHUT Ateret hahamim.* Józefów: Shlomo and Baruch Setzer.
Fram, Edward, ed. 1996. "Perception and Reception of Repentant Apostates in Medieval Ashkenaz and Premodern Poland." *AJS Review* 21, no. 2: 299–339.
———. 1997. *Ideals Face Reality: Jewish Law and Life in Poland, 1550–1655.* Cincinnati: Hebrew Union College Press.
———. 2012. *A Window on Their World: The Court Diary of Rabbi Ḥayyim Gundersheim, Frankfurt am Main 1773–1794.* Cincinnati: Hebrew Union College Press.

Fram, Yechezkel. 2007. "Takdim hilkhati she'einoraui lishmo." In *Al pi habeer: Mehkarim behagot yehudit uvemahshevet hahalakhah, mugashim leYaakov Blidstein*, edited by Hayim Kreisel, Daniel Y. Lasker, and Uri Erlich, 401–12. Beer Sheva: Bialik.

Freeze, ChaeRan Y. 2002. *Jewish Marriage and Divorce in Imperial Russia*. Hanover, NH: Brandeis University Press.

Freiman, Avraham Hayim. 1944. *Seder kidushin venisuin aharei hatimat hatalmud: Mehkar histori-dugmani bedinei yisrael*. Jerusalem: Mosad haRav Kook.

———. 1949. "Shiurei haktubah beashkenaz vetzarfat bimei habeinayim." In *Sefer hayovel lekhvod Alexander Marks*, 371–85. Newark: Jewish Theological Seminary of America.

Freudenthal, Gideon, ed. 2003. *Salomon Maimon: Rational Dogmatist, Empirical Skeptic: Critical Assessments*. Dordrecht: Kluwer Academic Publishers.

Frick, David. 2007. "Separation, Divorce, Bigamy: Stories of the Breakdown of Marriage in Seventeenth-Century Vilnius." In *Lithuania and Ruthenia: Studies of a Transcultural Communication Zone (15th–18th Centuries)*, edited by David Frick, Stefan Wiederkehr, and Stefan Rohdewald, 111–36. Wiesbaden: Harrassowitz.

Friedman, Menachem. 1972. "Mikhtevei hamlatzah lekabtzanim—'Ktavim': Lebaayat hanavadim begermanyah bemeah ha18." *Mikhael: Measef letoldot hayehudim betfutzot* 2: 34–51.

Friedman, Moshe. 1986. "Psakim bedavar halitzah psulah." *Moriah* 15, no. 3–4 (171–172): 24–30.

Friedman, Reena Sigman. 1982. "'Send Me My Husband Who Is in New York City': Husband Desertion in the American Jewish Immigrant Community 1900–1926." *Jewish Social Studies* 44, no. 1: 1–18.

Friedman, Shamma. 1974. "Din haisha ushnei baaleha bahalakhah hatalmudit uvehukei hamizrah hakadum." *Shnaton hamishpat haivrit* 2: 360–82.

Fuss, Abraham M. 1988. "Fact Skepticism in Jewish Law." *The Jewish Law Annual* 7: 125–38.

Gadamer, Hans-Georg. 1975. *Truth and Method*. New York: Seabury Press.

Gartner, Hayim. 2013. *Harav vehair hagdolah: Harabanut begalicia umefgashah im hamodernah*. Jerusalem: Merkaz Zalman Shazar.

Gelis, Yaakov. 1974–1978. *Encyclopedia letoldot hakhmei eretz-yisrael*. 3 vols. Jerusalem: Mosad haRav Kook.

Gesenbauer, Shmuel Nahum. 1884. *SHUT Migdal hashen*. Lvov: Uri Zeev Wolf Salat.

Getz, Eliakim. 1732. *Even hashoham umirat einayim*. Dyhernfurth: Yissachar Ber Katz.

Gilat, Yisrael Tzvi. 1994–96. "Al mi mutelet hovat hahanakah?" *Dinei yisrael* 18: 321–69.
Gilligan, Carol. 1982. *In a Different Voice: Psychological Theory and Women's Development*. Cambridge, MA: Harvard University Press.
Glanz, Rudolf. 1968. *Geschichte des niederen jüdischen Volkes in Deutschland: eine Studie über historisches Gaunertum, Bettelwesen und Vagantentum*. New York.
Glick, Shmuel. 2006–2009. *Kuntres hatshuvot hehadash: Otzar bibliographi lesifrut hashe'elot vehatshuvot mereshit hadfus vead shnat 5760*. 4 vols. Ramat Gan: Bar Ilan University.
Gluckman, Max. 1963. "Gossip and Scandal." *Current Anthropology* 4, no. 3: 307–16.
Goldberg, Yaakov. 1978. "Nisuei hayehudim bePolin hayeshenah bedaat hakahal shel tekufat hahaskalah." *Gilead* 4–5: 2–33.
———. 1999. *Hahevra hayehudit bemamlekhet polin-lita*. Jerusalem: Merkaz Zalman Shazar.
Goldstein, Bluma. 2007. *Enforced Marginality: Jewish Narratives on Abandoned Wives*. Berkeley: University of California Press.
Golinkin, David. 2000. "Gishot shel hatnuah hamesoratit lefitron baayat haagunot bameah haesrim." In *Nisuin herut veshivyon: hilekhu shloshtam yahad?*, edited by Tovah Kohen, 71–80. Ramat Gan: Bar Ilan.
Gottfarstein, Joseph. 1959. *Folklor yehudei lita*. Vol. 7, *Yahadut lita*, 583–627. Tel Aviv: Am-Hasefer.
Graetz, Naomi. 1998. *Silence Is Deadly: Judaism Confronts Wifebeating*. Northvale, NJ: J. Aronson.
Graupe, Moshe. 1972. "Tzvaot shel yehudim bealtona vehamburg mehameah ha18." *Michael: Measef letoldot hayehudim betfutzot* 2: 9–33.
Grossman, Avraham. 2001. *Hasidot umoredot: Nashim yehudiyot beeiropah bimei habeinayim*. Jerusalem: Merkaz Zalman Shazar.
Grunwald, Max. 1903. "Hamburgs deutsche Juden bis zur Auflösung der Dreigemeinden, 1811." *Mitteilungen der Gesellschaft für jüdische Volkskunde* 2, no. 12: 1–88.
Gulak, Asher. 1926. *Otzar hashtarot hanehugim beyisrael*. Jerusalem: Hapoalim.
Gunzberg, Aryeh Leib. 1869. *Sefer shaagat Aryeh*. Warsaw: Yitzhak Goldman.
Hacohen, Ephraim. 1684. *SHUT Shaar Ephraim*. Sulzbach: Moshe Blech.
Hacohen, Meshulam Zalman. 1806. *Bigdei khehunah*. Furth: Itzik ben David Zirndorf.
Hacohen, Shabbetai ben Meir 1651. *Megilat eifah*. Amsterdam [publisher unknown]
Hagen, William W. 2002. *Ordinary Prussians: Brandenburg Junkers and Villagers, 1500–1840*. Cambridge: Cambridge University Press.
Hahn, Joseph Yuspa Nördlinger. 1722. *Yosif Ometz*. Frankfurt: Johann Kelner.

Bibliography

Halberstam, Hayim. 1874. *SHUT Divrei Hayim*. Lvov: Yitzhak Yeshayah Halberstam.

Halevi-Zwick, Yehudit. 1990. *Toldot sifrut haigronim (habriefentstellers) haivriyim (meah 16–meah 20)*. Tel Aviv: Papirus.

Halperin, Israel, ed. 1952. *Takanot medinat Mahren (5401–5508)*. Jerusalem: Mekitze Nirdamim.

Halperin, Yisrael, and Israel Bartal, eds. 1989. *Pinkas vaad arba aratzot: Lekutei takanot, ktavim, urshumot*. Jerusalem.

Haneman, Avigdor. 2017. "Hilkhot agunot: Halakhah behishtanutah." PhD Dissertation, Ben-Gurion University.

Hannover, Natan Nata. 1653. *Yaven metzula*. Venice: Vemdramina.

Harrington, Joel F. 1995. *Reordering Marriage and Society in Reformation Germany*. Cambridge: Cambridge University Press.

———. 2009. *The Unwanted Child: The Fate of Foundlings, Orphans, and Juvenile Criminals in Early Modern Germany*. Chicago: University of Chicago Press.

heHasid, Judah. 1957. *Sefer hasidim*. Edited by Reuben Margulies. Jerusalem: Mosad haRav Kook.

Herr, Moshe David. 2007. *Midrash*. Vol. 14 of *Encyclopdaedia Judaica*, 2nd ed., edited by Fred Skolnik. Detroit: MacMillan Reference USA.

Hertz, Deborah. 1991. "Emancipation through Intermarriage? Wealthy Jewish Salom Women in Old Berlin." In *Jewish Women in Historical Perspective*, edited by Judith R. Baskin, 193–207. Detroit: Wayne State University Press.

Hertzberg, Arthur. 1989. *The Jews in America*. New York: Simon and Schuster.

Heschel, Joshua. 1899. *Hanukat hatorah*. Edited by Hanoch Henoch Erzon. Piotrków: Shlomo Belchatovsky.

Hildesheimer, Meir, ed. 1992. *Pinkas kehilat Shneitakh*. Jerusalem: Mekitzei Nirdamim.

Hochstein Blass, Chagit Beth Amy. 2009. "The Agunah in Jewish Law: Innovations and Limitations." PhD dissertation, University of London.

Horovitz, Mordechai Halevi. 1901. *Avnei zikaron: Haktav vehamikhtav mibeit hakvarot hayashan dekehilah kedoshah Frankfurt al nehar Main*. Frankfurt: J. Kauffmann.

———. 1972. *Rabanei Frankfurt*. Edited by Yosef Una. Translated by Yehoshua Amir. Jerusalem: Mosad haRav Kook.

Horowitz, David H. 2010. "Fractures and Fissures in Jewish Communal Autonomy in Hamburg, 1710–1782." PhD dissertation, Columbia University.

Hovav, Yamimah. 2009. *Alamot aheivukhah: Hayei hadat veharuah shel nashim bahevrah haashkenazit bereishit haet hahadashah*. Jerusalem: Magnes.

Howell, Martha. 2008. "The Gender of Europe's Commercial Economy, 1200–1700." *Gender & History* 20, no. 3: 519–38.

Hull, Isabel V. 1996. *Sexuality, State, and Civil Society in Germany, 1700–1815*. Ithaca, NY: Cornell University Press.

Hundert, Gershon David. 2004. *Jews in Poland-Lithuania in the Eighteenth Century*. Berkley: University of California Press.

Ilan, Tal. 1999. *Integrating Women into Second Temple History*. Tübingen: Mohr Siebeck.

Irshai, Ronit. 2012. *Fertility and Jewish Law: Feminist Perspectives on Orthodox Responsa Literature*. Translated by Joel A. Linsider. Waltham, MA: Brandeis University Press.

Israel, Jonathan I. 1983. "Central European Jewry During the Thirty Years' War." *Central European History* 16, no. 1: 3–30.

Isserlein, Israel. 1882. *Sefer trumat hadeshen*. Warsaw.

Jackson, Bernard S. 1991. *Law, Fact, and Narrative Coherence*. Roby: Deborah Charles.

———. 2009. *Agunah: The Manchester Analysis: Draft Final Report of the Agunah Research Unit*. Manchester: University of Manchester.

Jacobs-Yinon, Nurit, Emily D. Bilsky, and Ruth Halperin-Kaddari. 2017. *Mamzeirim: Siman umhikah*. Edited by Emily D. Bilsky, Ruth Halperin-Kaddari, and Nurit Jacobs-Yinon. Jerusalem: Aluma Films.

Jellinek, Adolf. 1880. *Kuntres hamekonen*. Vienna: David Löwy & Abraham ben David Alkalay.

Kahana, Maoz. 2006. "HaHatam Sofer: Haposek beeinei atzmo." *Tarbiz* 66, nos. 3–4: 519–56.

———. 2010. "MiPrague lePressburg—ketivah hilkhatit beolam mishtaneh: Me'Hanoda biYehuda' al 'Hahatam Sofer' 1730–1839." PhD dissertation, Hebrew University.

———. 2015. *MehaNoda biYehuda leHatam Sofer: Halakhah vehagot lenokhah etgerei hazman*. Jerusalem: Merkaz Zalman Shazar.

Kahana, Yitzhak Zeev. 1946. *Letakanat agunot: Mahut habaayah vehishtalshelotah*. Jerusalem: Mahzikei Hadat.

———. 1947. "Nikolsburg." In *Arim veimahot beyisrael*, vol. 4, edited by Judah Leib Fishman, 265. Jerusalem: Mosad haRav Kook.

———. 1954. *Sefer haagunot: Osef mekorot im peirushim beirurim vehearot*. Jerusalem: Mosad haRav Kook.

Kahneman, Daniel. 2003. "Maps of Bounded Rationality: Psychology for Behavioral Economics." *American Economic Review* 93, no. 5: 1449–75.

Kaidonover, Aharon Shmuel. 1884. *SHUT Emunat Shmuel*. Lvov.

Kaidanover, Tzvi Hirsch. 1944. *Kav hayashar*. Frankfurt: Johannes Wust.

Kaplan, Debra. 2010. "Women and Worth: Female Access to Property in Early

Modern Urban Jewish Communities." *Leo Baeck Institute Year Book* 55, no. 1: 93–113.

———. 2020. *The Patrons and Their Poor: Jewish Community and Public Charity in Early Modern Germany*. University of Pennsylvania Press.

Kaplan, Mordechai, and Yehudah Slutzky, eds. 1967. *Hayalim yehudim betzvaot eiropah*. Tel Aviv: Maarachot.

Kaplan, Yosef. 2003. *Minotzrim hadashim leyehudim hadashim*. Jerusalem: Merkaz Zalman Shazar.

Karo, Yosef. 1959. *SHUT Beit Yosef*. Jerusalem: Tiferet Torah.

Kasper-Marienberg, Verena. 2014. "Jewish Women at the Viennese Imperial Supreme Court: A Case Study from the Eighteenth Century." *Jewish Studies Quarterly* 21, no. 2: 176–92.

Kasper-Marienberg, Verena, and Edward Fram. 2022. "Jewish Law in Non-Jewish Courts. A Case from Eighteenth-Century Frankfurt at the Imperial Aulic Council of the Holy Roman Empire." *Max Planck Institute for Legal History and Legal Theory Research Paper Series* 2021–22.

Katz, Jacob. 1945. "Nissuim vehayei ishut bemotzeei yemei habenayim." *Zion* 10, nos. 1–2: 21–54.

———. 1960. *Bein yehudim legoyim: Yehus hayehudim leshkheineihem bimeihabeinayim uvethilat hazman hahadash*. Jerusalem: Bialik.

———. 1977. "Yibum vehalitzah betkufah habatar-talmudit." *Tarbitz* 51, no. 1: 59–106.

———. 1984. *Halakhah vekabalah: Mehkarim betoldot dat yisrael al medureha veziketa hahevratit*. Jerusalem: Magnes.

———. 1992. *Hahalakhah bemeitzar: Mikhsholim al derekh haortodoksiah behithavutah*. Jerusalem: Magnes.

———. 1993. *Tradition and Crisis*. Translated by Bernard Dov Cooperman. New York: Schocken.

Katz, Naftali. 1756. *SHUT Shaar naftali*. Brno.

Katz, Raphael ben Yekutiel Ziskind. 1791. *SHUT Veshav hakohen*. Altona.

Katz, Yitzhak Avraham. 1875. *Keter kehunah*. 2 vols. Berlin: Yehuda virushalayim.

Katzenellenbogen, Yechezkel. 1731. *SHUT Knesset Yechezkel*. Altona.

Kaufmann, David, ed. 1896. *Zikhronot marat Glikl Hamel: Mishnat 5407 ad 5479*. Frankfurt: J. Kauffmann.

———. 1968. "Pinkas kehilah kedoshah Bamberg." Edited by David Kaufmann. *Kovetz al yad* 7. Jerusalem: n.p.

Kaźmierczyk, Adam. 2010. "The Rubinkowski Family." In *Polin: Studies in Polish Jewry*, vol. 22, *Social and Cultural Boundaries in Pre-modern Poland*, edited by Adam Teller, Magda Teter, and Antony Polonsky, 193–214. Liverpool: Liverpool University Press and Littman Library of Jewish Civilization.

Keil, Martha. 2007. "Aguna ('die Verankerte'): Strategien gegen die Benachteiligung der jüdischen Frau im Eherecht (1400–1700)." *Aschkenas* 17, no. 2: 323–43.

Kertzer, David I., and Marzio Barbagli, eds. 2001. *Family Life in Early Modern Times, 1500–1789*. New Haven: Yale University Press.

Kluger, Shlomo. 1864a. *Shiva Einayim*. Lvov: Avraham Yehoshua Heschel Drucker.

———. 1864b. *SHUT Shiva einayim*. Lvov: Abraham Joshua Heschel Drucker.

———. 1910. *Haelef lekha Shelomo*. Lvov: N. Kronenberg.

Kohen, Tovah, ed. 2000. *Nisuin herut ushivyon: hilekhu shloshtam yahdav?* Ramat Gan: Bar Ilan.

Kohler, Noa Sophie. 2010. "Schutzjuden and Opportunistic Criminality in the Early Modern Period: The Lemmel Family from Neustadt-Eberswalde." *Leo Baeck Institute Year Book* 55, no. 1: 129–46.

Kraemer, David, ed. 1989. *The Jewish Family: Metaphor and Memory*. New York: Oxford University Press.

Krochmal, Menachem Mendel. 1674. *SHUT Tzemah tzedek*. Amsterdam: David de Castro Tartus.

Kruger, Paul K. 1996. "The Removal of the Sandal in Deuteronomy XXV 9: 'A Rite of Passage'?" *Vetus Testamentum* 46, no. 4: 534–39.

Kruse, Britta-Juliane. 2007. *Witwen: Kulturgeschichte eines Standes in Spätmittelalter und Früher Neuzeit*. Berlin: De Gruyter.

Landau, Yechezkel. 1901. *Sefer hukei haishut*. Translated by Zeev Wolf Sheinblum. Mukachevo.

———. 1960. *SHUT Noda biYhudah*. Jerusalem: Halakhah Berurah.

Laub, Dori, and Shoshana Felman. 2008. *Edut: Mishbar haeidim besifrut, bepsychoanalyzah uvehistoriah*. Translated by Dafna Raz. Tel Aviv: Resling.

Leggett, Donald A. 1974. *The Levirate and the Goel: Institutions in the Old Testament: With Special Attention to the Book of Ruth*. Cherry Hill, NJ: Mack.

Levine, Yael. 2004. "Kol hamatir agunah ahat keilu banah ahat mehorvot yerushalayim haelyonah." *Dinei yisrael* 23: 163–97.

Levy, Allison, ed. 2003. *Widowhood and Visual Culture in Early Modern Europe*. Aldershot: Ashgate.

Levy, Yael V. 1993. "The Agunah and the Missing Husband: An American Solution to the Problem." *Journal of Law and Religion* 10, no. 1: 49–71.

Liberles, Robert. 2005. "On the Threshold of Modernity." In *Jewish Daily Life in Germany, 1618–1945*, edited by Marion A. Kaplan, 9–92. Oxford: Oxford University Press.

Lifshitz, Aryeh Leibush. 1873. *SHUT Aryeh devei ilaei*. Przemysl: Hayim Aharon Zupnick.

Lindemann, Mary. 1981. "Love for Hire: The Regulation of the Wet-Nursing

Business in Eighteenth-Century Hamburg." *Journal of Family History* 6, no. 4: 379–95.

———. 1990. *Patriots and Paupers: Hamburg, 1712–1830*. New York: Oxford University Press.

Lipking, Lawrence I. 1988. *Abandoned Women and Poetic Tradition*. Chicago: University of Chicago Press.

Litt, Stefan. 2008. *Pinkas, Kahal, and the Mediene: The Records of Dutch Ashkenazi Communities in the Eighteenth Century as Historical Sources*. Leiden: Brill.

Litvak, Olga. 2006. *Conscription and the Search for Modern Russian Jewry*. Bloomington, IN: Indiana University Press.

Lowenstein, Steven M. 1994. "Ashkenazic Jewry and the European Marriage Pattern: A Preliminary Survey of Jewish Marriage Age." *Jewish History* 8, nos. 1–2: 155–75.

———. 2008. "Reishitah shel hahishtalvut." In *Kiyum beidan shel tmurot: Hayei yom-yom shel hayehudim begermanyah 1618–1945*, edited by Marion Kaplan, 129–241. Jerusalem: Merkaz Zalman Shazar.

Lubitch, Rivkah. 2017. *Misof haolam vead sofo: Masa hayisurim shel nashim bevet hadin harabanit*. Rishon letzion: Yediot Sfarim.

Maciejko, Paweł. 2011. *The Mixed Multitude: Jacob Frank and the Frankist Movement, 1755–1816*. Philadelphia: University of Pennsylvania Press.

MacKinnon, Catharine A. 1993. *Only Words*. Cambridge, MA: Harvard University Press.

———. 2005. *Feminism mishpati betheoreha uvepractikah*. Edited by Daphne Erez-Barak. Translated by Idit Shorer. Tel Aviv: Resling.

Maggid, David. 1899. *Sefer toldot mishpechot Ginzburg*. St. Petersburg: HaMelitz.

Mahler, Raphael. 1958. *Yidn in amoliken poyln in likht fun tzifern*. Warsaw: Yidish bukh.

Maimon, Solomon. 1888. *Solomon Maimon: An Autobiography*. Translated by J. Clark Murray. London: Alexander Gardner.

———. 2018. *The Autobiography of Solomon Maimon*. Edited by Yitzhak Y. Melamed and Abraham P. Socher. Translated by Paul Reitter. Princeton, NJ: Princeton University Press.

Mann, Michael. 1984. "The Autonomous Power of the State: Its Origins, Mechanisms, and Results." *European Journal of Sociology* 25, no. 2: 185–213.

Mannheim, Karl. 1952. *Essays on the Sociology of Knowledge*. London: Routledge & K. Paul.

Manspach, Yosefe. 1987–1992. *Minhagim deKK Worms*. Edited by Juspa Schammes. 2 vols. Jerusalem: Mekhon Yerushalayim.

Margaliot, Alexander Sander. 1858. *Sefer teshuvot haRAM*. Warsaw: Tzvi Yaakov.

Margaliot, Ephraim Zalman. 1975. *SHUT Beit efraim*. Jerusalem: Mosad haRav Kook.
Margaliot, Meir. 1791. *Meir netivim*. Polonne.
Margaliot, Mordechai Meir. 1959. *Encyclopedia letoldot gedolei Yisrael*. Tel Aviv: Tschechik.
Markgraf, Richard. 1894. "Zur Geschichte der Juden auf den Messen in Leipzig 1664–1839." PhD dissertation, University of Rostock.
McGinn, Thomas J. 2008. *Widows and Patriarchy: Ancient and Modern*. London: Bloomsbury.
McKinnon, Catherine A. 1993. *Only Words*. Cambridge, MA: Harvard University Press.
Meir, Yaakov. 2005. *Emet leYaakov*. Jerusalem: Mekhon Beit Aharon veYisrael.
Meir, Yonatan. 2013. *Hasidut medumeh: Iyunim bekhtavav hasatiriyim shel Yosef Perl*. Jerusalem: Bialik.
Meir ben Shmuel of Szczebrzeszyn. 1650. *Tzok haitim*. Krakow.
Meisels, Avraham Natan Neta, and Aryeh Yehudah Leib miKrakow uBrisk. 1745. *SHUT Shaagat Aryeh vekol shahal*. Thessaloniki: Betzalel haLevi Ashkenazi.
Mendelsohn, Joseph. 1845. *Salomon Heine: Blätter der Würdigung und Erinnerung für seine Freunde und Verehrer*. Vol. 2. Hamburg: B. S. Berendsohn.
Michel, Emmanuel. 1853. *Biographie du Parlement de Metz*. Metz: Nouvian.
miKlevan, Moshe ben Pinhas. 1818. *Sefer pnei moshe*. Korets.
Minden, Yehudah Leib. 1696. *Shirei Yehudah*. Amsterdam: Kosman Emmerich.
MiPozna, Yitzhak ben Avraham. 1985. *SHUT Rabenu Yitzhak hagadol miposna*. Jerusalem: Mekhon Yerushalayim.
miRothenburg, Meir Hacohen. 1879. *Teshuvot Maimoniot*. Warsaw.
Mokotoff, Gary, Sallyann Amdur Sack, and Alexander Sharon, eds. 1991. *Where Once We Walked: A Guide to the Jewish Commmunities Destroyed in the Holocaust*. Teaneck, NJ: Avotaynu.
Nadav, Mordechai, ed. 1999. *Pinkes kahal Tiktin, 5381–5566: Haskamot, hahlatot, vetakanot, kefi shehetikan min hapinkes hamekori sheibad beshoah Yisrael Halpern*. Vol. 1. Jerusalem: Israel Academy of Sciences and Humanities.
Nelkenbrecher, Johann Christian. 1828. *J. C. Nelkenbrecher's allgemeines Taschenbuch der Münz-, Maaß- und Gewichtskunde für Banquiers und Kaufleute*. Berlin: Sander.
Ogilvie, Sheilagh. 2003. *A Bitter Living: Women, Markets, and Social Capital in Early Modern Germany*. Oxford: Oxford University Press.
Ogilvie, Sheilagh, and Jeremy Edwards. 2000. "Women and the 'Second Serfdom': Evidence from Early Modern Bohemia." *The Journal of Economic History* 60, no. 4: 961–94.

Oppenheim, David. 1971–1984. *SHUT Nishal David*. Jerusalem: Mekhon Hatam Sofer.
Ortner, Sherry B. 1974. "Is Female to Male as Nature Is to Culture?" In *Woman, Culture, and Society*, edited by Michelle Zimbalist Rosaldo and Louise Lamphere, 67–87. Stanford: Stanford University Press.
Otzar haposkim al shulhan arukh even haezer. 1981. Vol. 8. Jerusalem: Otzar haPoskim.
Paneth, Yechezkel. 1999. *Mareh Yechezkel*. Bene Brak: Tzvi Elimelech Paneth.
Panta, Levi. 1989. "Mikhtav Rabbi Levi Panta ZL miPrague." *Tzfunot* 1989, no. 8: 105–6.
Pfister, Christian. 1996. "The Population of Late Medieval and Early Modern Germany." In *Germany: A New Social and Economic History*, vol. 1, *1450–1630*, edited by Bob Scribner, 46–50. London: Hodder Education.
Pollack, Herman. 1971. *Jewish Folkways in Germanic Lands (1648–1806): Studies in Aspects of Daily Life*. Cambridge, MA: MIT Press.
Popper, Nicholas. 2006. "'Abraham, Planter of Mathematics': Histories of Mathematics and Astrology in Early Modern Europe." *Journal for the History of Ideas* 67, no. 1: 87–106.
Posner, Richard A. 2008. *How Judges Think*. Cambridge, MA: Harvard University Press.
Raba, Yoel. 1994. *Bein zikaron lehakhhashah: Gzeirot 5408 ve5409 bereshimat benei hazman uwire'i haktivah hahistorit*. Tel Aviv: Tel Aviv University.
Rabinowitz, Louis Isaac. 2007. "Shulhan Arukh." In *Encyclopaedia Judaica*, vol. 18, edited by Fred Skolnik, 529–30. Detroit: Macmillan Reference USA.
Radzyner, Amichai. 2008. "Milvov letel aviv: Psikut get muteh beshel hafarat heskeim hageirushin bevatei hadin harabaniyim: Beikvot tik." *Mishpatim* 39: 155–231.
Rapaport, Chaim Kohn. 1861. *SHUT rabenu Hayim Hacohen*. Lvov: S. Back & A. J. Menkes.
Rapoport, Shlomo Ashkenazi. 1796. *Itur sofrim*. Grodno: Barukh ben Yosef.
Rapoport-Albert, Ada. 1989. "Hatnuah hahasidit aharei shnat 1772: Retzef mivni utmurah." *Zion* 55, no. 2: 183–245.
———. 2001. "Al hanashim behasidut: S. A. Horodezki umsorat habetulah melodymyr." In *Tzadik veedah: Heibetim historiyim vehevratiyim beheker hahasidut*, edited by David Assaf, 496–527. Jerusalem: Merkaz Zalman Shazar.
———. 2014. "Glikl hamel kealmana." In *Hasidim veshabtaim, anashim venashim*, edited by Immnuel Etkes and David Assaf, 492–507. Jerusalem: Merkaz Zalman Shazar.
Reiner, Elchanan. 1992. "Hon, maamad hevrati vetalmud torah: Hakloyz

behevra hayehudit bemizrah eiropa bemeot ha17-ha18." *Zion* 58, no. 3: 287–328.

———. 1997. "The Ashkenazi Élite at the Beginning of the Modern Era: Manuscript versus Printed Book." In *Polin: Studies in Polish Jewry*, vol. 10, *Jews in Early Modern Poland*, edited by Gershon David Hundert, 85–98. Liverpool: Liverpool University Press.

Reischer, Yaakov. 1860. *SHUT Shevut Yaakov*. Lvov.

Richarz, Monika, ed. 1991. *Jewish Life in Germany: Memoirs from Three Centuries*. Translated by Stella P. Rosenfeld and Sidney Rosenfeld. Bloomington, IN.

Rivlin, Yosef. 1999. *Hayerusha vehatzavaah bemishpat haivri*. Ramat Gan: Bar Ilan University Press.

Rocoles, Jean Baptiste de. 1683. *Les imposteurs insignes, ou histoires de plusieurs hommes de néant, de toutes nations, qui ont usurpé la qualité d'empereurs, roys et princes*. Amsterdam: Chez Abraham Wolfgang prés la Bourse.

Rosenak, Avinoam. 2011. "Meta-halakhah, philosophiah shel hahalakhah veYosef Schwab." In *Halakhah, meta-halakhah uphilosophiah: Iyun ravtehumi*, edited by Avinoam Rosenak, 17–34. Jerusalem: Magnes.

Rosman, Moshe. 2001. "Lihiyot isha yehudiya bePolin-Lita bereishit haet hahadashah." In *Kiyum vashever: yehudei Polin ledoroteihem*, vol. 2, edited by Israel Bartal and Yisrael Gutman, 415–34. Jerusalem: Merkaz Zalman Shazar.

———. 2003. "Dubno in the Wake of Khmel'nyts'kyi." *Jewish History* 17, no. 2: 239–55.

———. 2009. "Jewish History Across Borders." In *Rethinking European Jewish History*, edited by Jeremy Cohen and Moshe Rosman, 15–29. Littman Library of Jewish Civilization, Liverpool University Press

Ross, Tamar. 2011. "Trumat hafeminism lediyun hahilkhati: 'Kol beishah ervah' kemikreh mivhan." In *Halakhah, meta-halakhah, uphilosophiah*, edited by Avinoam Rosenak, 35–64. Jerusalem: Magnes.

Roth, Avraham Naftali Tzvi, ed. 1961. *Sefer takanot Nikolsburg*. New York: Yeshiva University.

Rottenberg, Mordechai Ziskind. 1715. *SHUT MHRM Ziskind*. Hamburg.

Rublack, Ulinka. 1999. *The Crimes of Women in Early Modern Germany*. Oxford: Oxford University Press.

Ruderman, David B. 2010. *Early Modern Jewry: A New Cultural History*. Princeton, NJ: Princeton University Press.

Sabean, David Warren. 1984. *Popular Culture and Village Discourse in Early Modern Germany*. Cambridge: Cambridge University Press.

———. 1997. "Allianzen und Listen: Die Geschlechtsvormundschaft im 18. und 19. Jahrundert." In *Frauen in der Geschichte des Rechts: Von der*

Frühen Neuzeit bis zur Gegenwart, edited by Ute Gerhard, 460–79. Munich: Beck.

Salmon-Mack, Tamar. 2012. *Tan du: Al hanisuin umishbereihem beyahadut polinlita, 1650–1800*. Tel Aviv: Hakibbutz Hameuchad.

Sarti, Raffaella. 2002. *Europe at Home: Family and Material Culture 1500–1800*. Translated by Allan Cameron. New Haven: Yale University Press.

Schacter, Jacob J. 1988. "Rabbi Jacob Emden: Life and Major Works." PhD dissertation, Harvard University.

Schilling, Heinz, and Klaus-Dieter Schreiber, eds. 1989. *Die Kirchenratsprotokolle der Reformierten Gemeinde Emden, 1557–1620*. Köln: Böhlau.

Schubert, Ernst. 1990. *Arme Leute, Bettler und Gauner im Franken des 18. Jahrhunderts*. Vol. 2. Neustadt an der Aisch: Degner.

Schussberg, Gavriel ben Yehoshua. 1651. *Petah teshuvah*. Amsterdam: Immanuel Benvenisti.

Schwartzfuchs, Shimon. 1985. "Tanay harabanut shel haShaagat Aryeh beKK Metz." *Moriah* 15, no. 1–2: 81–90.

Seder tehinot uvakashot. 1787. Offenbach: Tzvi Hirsch Spitz of Pressburg.

Seder tehinot uvakashot. 1815. Vienna: Anton Schmid.

Segal, Shmuel ben David Halevi. 1680. *Nahalat shiva*. Frankfurt.

Shahar, Yeshayahu. 1982. *Bikoret hahevrah vehanhagat hatzibur besifrut hamusar vehadrush bePolin bemeah ha18*. Jerusalem: Merkaz Dinur.

Shamir, Zivah. 2014. *Hakol biglal kotzo shel yod: Al shir ehad shel YLG berei hayetzirah haivrit*. Israel: Safra.

Shashar, Noa. 2007. "Mekoman shel hilkhot nidah behayei hayom-yom shel yehudei hamerhav haashkenazi bemeot ha17-19." Master's thesis, Hebrew University.

———. 2012. "Agunot ugvarim neelamim bemerhav haashkenazi 1648–1850." PhD dissertation, Hebrew University.

Shatzki, Yaakov. 1932. "Yehuda Leib Zelechower un zayne 'Shirei Yehudah.'" *YIVO-bleter* 3: 140–47.

Shazar, Shneur Zalman. 1971. *Urei dorot: Mehkarim vehearot letoldot yisrael bedorot haahronim*. Jerusalem: Bialik.

Shereshevsky, Bentzion. 1984. *Dinei Mishpaha*. 3rd ed. Jerusalem: 1984.

Shilo, Margalit. 2001. *Nesikha o shevuyah? Hahavayah hanashit shel hayishuv hayashan birushalayim, 1840–1914*. Haifa: University of Haifa.

Shimshi-Licht, Tamar. 2007. "Mesharetim umesharetot yehudiyim begermanyah bereishit haet hahadashah." PhD dissertation, Ben-Gurion University of the Negev.

Shmeruk, Chone. 1978. *Sifrut yiddish — prakim letoldoteha*. Tel Aviv: University Publishing Projects.

Shmuel Fayvish. 1892. *Tit hayaven*. Krakow: n.p.

Shohat, Azriel. 1960. *Im hilufei tekufot: Reshit hahaskalah beyahadut germanyah*. Jerusalem: Bialik.

Shulvass, Moses A. 1971. *From East to West: The Westward Migration of Jews from Eastern Europe during the Seventeenth and Eighteenth Centuries*. Detroit: Wayne State University Press.

Silvetsky, Akiva. 1997. "Hanimukim lekolat HZL beheiter agunah." Master's thesis, Bar Ilan University.

Sinkoff, Nancy. 2003. "The Maskil, the Convert, and the Agunah: Joseph Perl as a Historian of Jewish Divorce Law." *AJS Review* 27, no. 2: 281–300.

Sofer, Moshe. 1969–1984. *SHUT Hatam Sofer*. Jerusalem: Mekhon Hatam Sofer.

Soliday, Gerald L. 2003. "The Jews of Early Modern Marburg, 1640s–1800: A Case Study in Family and Household Organization." *History of the Family* 8, no. 4: 495–516.

Soloveitchik, Haym. 1990. *SHUT kemekor histori*. Jerusalem: Merkaz Zalman Shazar.

———. 2003. *"Yeynam": Sahar beyaynam shel goyim—al gilgulah shel halakhah beolam hamaaseh*. Tel Aviv: Koren.

Sperber, Hayim. 2010. "Tofaat hanashim haagunot bahevrah hayehudit bemizrah eiropa uvituyah baitunot hayehudit, 1857–1896." *Kesher* 40: 102–8.

Spitzer, Shlomo Y. 1990. "Al peilut ha'Panim meirot' b'sheva hakehilot." *Tzfunot: Rivon torati* 10: 83–87.

Stampfer, Shaul. 1987. "Hamashmaut hahevratit shel nisuei-boser bemizrah eiropah bemeah ha19." In *Kovetz mehkarim al yehudei Polin: Sefer lezikhro shel Paul Glikson*, edited by Ezra Mendelsohn and Chone Schmeruk, 65–77. Jerusalem: Merkaz Zalman Shazar.

———. 1988. "Remarriage among Jews and Christians in Nineteenth-Century Eastern Europe." *Jewish History* 3, no. 2: 85–114.

———. 1989. "The 1764 Census of Polish Jewry." *Bar-Ilan: Annual of Bar-Ilan University* 24, no. 5: 41–147.

———. 1997. "Gidul haukhlusia vehagira beyahadut polin-lita baet hahadashah." *Kiyum vashever: yehudeiPolin ledoroteihem*, vol. 2, edited by Israel Bartal and Yisrael Gutman, 263–85. Jerusalem: Merkaz Zalman Shazar.

———. 2003. "What Actually Happened to the Jews of Ukraine in 1648?" *Jewish History* 17, no. 2: 207–27.

———. 2009. "Hashpaat hahasidut al hamishpahah hayehudit bemizrah eiropah: Haarhah mehadash." In *Yashan mipenei hadash: Mehkarim betoldot yehudei mizrah eiropah uvtarbutam, shay leImmanuel Etkes*, vol. 1, edited by David Assaf and Ada Rapoport-Albert, 165–84. Jerusalem: Merkaz Zalman Shazar.

Steinhardt, Yosef. 2004. *SHUT Zikhron Yosef.* Jerusalem.
Stern, Selma. 1962–1975. *Der preussische Staat und die Juden.* 4 vols. Tübingen: Mohr Siebeck.
Stow, Kenneth. 2011. "Jewish Pre-emancipation: Ius Commune, the Roman Comunità, and Marriage in the Early Modern Papal State." In *Tov Elem: Memory, Community and Gender in Medieval and Early Modern Jewish Societies: Essays in Honor of Robert Bonfil,* edited by Amnon Raz-Krakotzkin, Roni Weinstein, and Elisheva Baumgarten, 79–102. Jerusalem: Bialik.
Tal, Shlomo. 1948. "Haget miklibah." *Sinai* 24: 152–67, 214–30.
Tallan, Cheryl. 1991. "Medieval Jewish Widows: Their Control of Resources." *Jewish History* 5, no. 1: 63–74.
Tam, Rabenu Yaakov ben Meir. 1897. *Sefer hayashar: Helek hashe'elot vehatshuvot.* Berlin: Tzvi Hirsch Itzkowski.
———. 1985. *Sefer hayashar: Helek hahidushim.* Vol. 4. Jerusalem.
Teller, Adam. 1994. "Sefer zikhronot shel Shlomo Maimon: Behinat meheimanut." *Galed* 14: 13–22.
———. 1997. "Hapeilut hakalkalit shel hayehudim bePolin bemahatzit hashniyah shel hameah ha17 uvameah ha18." In *Kiyum vashever: Yehudei Polin ledoroteihem,* vol. 1, edited by Israel Bartal and Yisrael Gutman, 209–24. Jerusalem: Merkaz Zalman Shazar.
———. 2014. "Jewish Women in the Wake of the Chmielnicki Uprising: Gzeires Taḥ-Tat as a Gendered Experience." In *Jewish Culture in Early Modern Europe: Essays in Honor of David B. Ruderman,* edited by Richard I. Cohen, Natalie B. Dohrmann, and Adam Shear, 39–49. Pittsburgh: Hebrew Union College Press.
———. 2020. *Rescue the Surviving Souls: The Great Jewish Refugee Crisis of the Seventeenth Century.* Princeton, NJ: Princeton University Press.
Teller, Adam, and Magda Teter. 2010. "Introduction: Borders and Boundaries in the Historiography of the Jews in the Polish-Lithuanian Commonwealth." In *Polin: Studies in Polish Jewry,* vol. 22, *Social and Cultural Boundaries in Pre-modern Poland,* edited by Adam Teller, Magda Teter, and Antony Polonsky, 3–46. Liverpool: Liverpool University Press and Littman Library of Jewish Civilization
Teller, Adam, Magda Teter, and Antony Polonsky, eds. 2010. *Polin: Studies in Polish Jewry,* vol. 22, *Social and Cultural Boundaries in Pre-modern Poland.* Liverpool: Liverpool University Press and Littman Library of Jewish Civilization .
Teter, Magda. 2003. "Jewish Conversions to Catholicism in the Polish-Lithuanian Commonwealth of the Seventeenth and Eighteenth Centuries." *Jewish History* 17, no. 3: 257–83.

———. 2010. "There Should Be No Love Between Us and Them: Social Life and the Bounds of Jewish and Canon Law in Early Modern Poland." In *Polin: Studies in Polish Jewry*, vol. 22, *Social and Cultural Boundaries in Premodern Poland*, edited by Adam Teller, Magda Teter, and Antony Polonsky, 249–70. Liverpool: Liverpool University Press and Littman Library of Jewish Civilization.

Toch, Michael. 1995. "Aspects of Stratification of Early Modern German Jewry: Population History and Village Jews." In *In and Out of the Ghetto: Jewish Gentile Relations in Late Medieval and Early Modern Germany*, edited by R. Po-chia Hsia and Hartmut Lehmann, 77–89. Washington, DC: German Historical Institute.

Trachtenberg, Joshua. 1974. *Jewish Magic and Superstition: A Study in Folk Religion*. New York: Atheneum.

Trepp, Anne-Charlott. 1994. "The Emotional Side of Men in Late Eighteenth-Century Germany (Theory and Example)." *Central European History* 27, no. 2: 127–52.

Turniansky, Chava, ed. 2006. *Glikl: Zikhronot 1691–1719*. Jerusalem: Merkaz Zalman Shazar.

———. 2009. *Yayin hadash bekankan yashan: Girsaot maskiliot shel 'Tzena urena.'* Vol. 2, in *Yashan mipnei hadash: mehkarim betoldot yehudei mizrah Eiropa uvtarbutam: shay leImmanuel Etkes*, edited by David Assaf and Ada Rappaport-Albert, 313–44. Jerusalem: Merkaz Zalman Shazar.

———, ed. 2019. *Glikl: Memoirs 1691–1719*. Translated by Sarah Friedman. Waltham, MA: Brandeis University Press.

Ulbrich, Claudia. 2004. *Shulamit and Margarete: Power, Gender, and Religion in a Rural Society in Eighteenth-Century Europe*. Translated by Thomas Dunlap. Boston: Brill.

Ulbricht, Otto. 1994. "The World of a Beggar Around 1775: Johann Gottfried Kastner." *Central European History* 27, no. 2: 153–84.

———. 1995. "Criminality and Punishment of the Jews in the Early Modern Period." In *In and Out of the Ghetto: Jewish-Gentile Relations in Late Medieval and Early Modern Germany*, edited by R. Po-Chia Hsia and Hartmut Lehmann, 49–70. Washington, DC: Cambridge University Press.

Ullmann, Sabine. 2000. "Poor Jewish Families in Early Modern Rural Swabia." *International Review of Social History* 45: 93–113.

Urbach, Ephraim E. 1979. *Baalei hatosfot*. 4th ed. Vol. 1. Jerusalem: Bialik.

van Os, Geertje. 2002. "Widows Hidden from View: The Disappearance of Mourning Dress Among Dutch Widows in the Twentieth Century." In *Between Poverty and the Pyre: Moments in the History of Widowhood*, edited by Jan Bremmer and Lourens van den Bosch, 230–46. London: Routledge.

Viberg, Åke. 1992. *Symbols of Law: A Contextual Analysis of Legal Symbolic Acts in the Old Testament*. Stockholm: Almqvist & Wiksell.
Wagenaar, Abraham Hayim. 1868. *Toldot YABTZ*. Amsterdam: Yisrael Levinson.
Wall, Patrick M. 1965. *Eye-Witness Identification in Criminal Cases*. Springfield, IL: Charles C. Thomas.
Wasserzug, Moshe. 1911. *Korot Moshe Wasserzug*. Berlin.
Watt, Jeffrey R. 2001. "The Impact of the Reformation and Counter-Reformation." In *The History of the European Family*, vol. 1, *Family Life in Early Modern Times, 1500–1789*, edited by David I. Kertzer and Marzio Barbagli, 125–54. New Haven: Yale University Press.
Weil, Yedidyah Tiah. 1982. *SHUT Yedidyah Tiah Weil*. Jerusalem: Genuzot.
Weinryb, Bernard D. 1972. *The Jews of Poland: A Social and Economic History of the Jewish Community in Poland from 1100–1800*. Philadelphia: Jewish Publican Society of America.
Weiss, Haim, and Shira Stav. 2018. *Shuvo shel haav haneedar: Kriyah mehudeshet besidrat sipurim min hatalmud habavli*. Jerusalem: Bialik.
Weissler, Chava. 1998. *Voices of the Matriarchs: Listening to the Prayers of Early Modern Jewish Women*. Boston: Beacon Press.
White, James Boyd. 1973. *The Legal Imagination: Studies in the Nature of Legal Thought and Expression*. Boston: Little, Brown, & Co.
Wiesner, Merry E. 1997. *Gender, Church and State in Early Modern Germany: Essays by Merry E. Wiesner*. London: Routledge.
Wilensky, Mordechai. 1990. *Hasidim umitnagdim: Letoldot hapulmus shebeineihem beshanim 5532–5575*. 2nd ed. 2 vols. Jerusalem: Bialik.
Wiltenburg, Joy. 1992. *Disorderly Women and Female Power in the Street Literature of Early Modern England and Germany*. Charlottesville: University of Virginia Press.
Wischnitzer, Mark. 1965. *A History of Jewish Crafts and Guilds*. New York: Jonathan David.
Wunder, Heide. 1998. *He Is the Sun, She Is the Moon: Women in Early Modern Germany*. Translated by Thomas Dunlap. Cambridge: Harvard University Press.
Yakovenko, Natalia. 2003. "The Events of 1648–1649." *Jewish History* 17, no. 2: 165–78.
Yehoshua, Heschel ben Yosef miKraków. 1859. *SHUT Pnei Yehoshua*. Lvov: Zalman Leib Flecker & Co.
Yehudah Leib ben Hanokh of Pfersee. 1707. *SHUT Hinukh beit yehuda*. Frankfurt.
Yissachar Dov Ber ben Aryeh Yehudah Leibush. 1797. *SHUT Bat eini*. Dubno: n.p.

Yuval, Yisrael Yaakov. 1988. *Hahamim bedoram: Hamanhigut haruhanit shel yehudei germanyah beshelhi yemei habeinayim*. Jerusalem: Magnes.

———. 1995. "Hahesderim haksafiyim shel hanisuin beashkenaz bimei habeinayim." In *Dat vekhalkala — yahasei gomlin: kovetz maamarim, shay leYaakov Katz bemloat lo tishim shanah*, edited by Menahem Ben-Sasson, 191–207. Jerusalem: Merkaz Zalman Shazar.

Yitzhak ben Yoseph miCorbeil, 1401. *Sefer Mitzvot Katan*. N.p.

Zalkin, Mordechai. 1999. *Baalot hashahar: Hahaskalah hayehudit beimpiriah harusit bemeah hatshah esreh*. Jerusalem: Magnes.

Zevin, Shlomo Yosef. 1945. *Leor hahalakhah: Beayot uveirurim*. Jerusalem: Mosad haRav Kook.

Zimmer, Yitzchak. 2005. *Olam keminhago noheg: Prakim betoldot haminhagim, hilkhoteihem, vegilguleihem*. Jerusalem: Merkaz Zalman Shazar.

Manuscripts and Archival Sources

ALTONA, HAMBURG, AND WANDSBEK

Hamburg genealogical collection, Staatsarchiv Hamburg, 741–42: *Genealogische Sammlungen, Heckscher*.

Historical record book of Altona and Hamburg, CAHJP (The Central Archives for the History of the Jewish People), AHW/16b.

Record book, Altona 17, CAHJP, AHW/17.

Record book, Altona 17a (1727–1732), CAHJP, AHW/17a.

Record book, Altona 17b (1760–1776), CAHJP, AHW/17b.

Record book, Altona 86 (1664–1810), CAHJP, AHW/86.

Record book, Altona community officials, CAHJP, AHW/18.

Record book, beit din Altona 1 (1768–1771), CAHJP, AHW/121/1.

Record book, beit din Altona 2 (1777–1796), CAHJP, AHW/121/2.

Record book, beit din Altona 3 (1781–1796), CAHJP, AHW/121/3.

Record book, beit din Altona 4 (1769–1800), CAHJP, AHW/121/4.

Record book, beit din Altona 5 (1799–1800), CAHJP, AHW/121/5.

Record book, beit din Altona 6 (1799–1802), CAHJP, AHW/121/6.

Record book, beit din Altona 8 (1804–1808), CAHJP, AHW/121/8.

Record book, community of Altona 1 (1641–1731, 1750), CAHJP, AHW/1.

Record book, community of Altona 16 (1764–1810), CAHJP, AHW/16.

Record book, ledger for charity expenses, Altona, CAHJP, AHW/52.

Record book, ledger for expenses and revenues Altona (1706–1812), CAHJP, AHW/89.

Record book, shamash of Altona 1 (1767–1792), CAHJP, AHW/20.

Record book of appeals to the Hamburg senate, CAHJP, microfilm HM2/1170.

Record book of public announcements, AHW 5484-5504 (1724–1744), CAHJP, AHW/85a.

Record book of the deceased, AHW (1811–1835), CAHJP, AHW/4.
Takanot 3 kehilot 9 (1693–1724), CAHJP, AHW/9; (1698–1872).
Takanot 3 kehilot 10 (1698–1872), AHW/10.
Writs of betrothal and of halitzah, AHW (1773–1778), CAHJP, AHW/68 and AHW/69.

AUSTERLITZ

Record book, Austerlitz, the record book is included in the Prague collection, CAHJP, HM2/8201.1.

BINGEN

Record book, fee collector of Bingen, Record book, collector of expenses and revenues of Bingen (1776–1795), CAHJP, D/Bi2/11.

FORCHHEIM

Community record book, Forchheim, CAHJP, D/Fo1/26, item #8.

FRANKFURT

Responsa of Frankfurt rabbis, Responsa and novellae of the rabbis and gaons of Frankfurt from 1565 to 1810, YIVO Archive, Gershon Epstein collection, MK414, facsimile in CAHJP, HM2/4447.

FÜRTH

Record book, beit din Fürth, CAHJP, HM2/672, HM/674; the source is in the Jewish Archives in Cincinnati, OH (precise reference not available).
Record book, community of Fürth, HM2/677; the source is in the Jewish Archives in Cincinnati, OH (precise reference not available).
Takanot Fürth, Takanot Fürth, CAHJP, Inv. 3428

GOCHSHEIM

Record book, fee collectors of Gochsheim, CAHJP, D/Gio1/1.

HALBERSTADT

Community record book, Halberstadt, CAHJP, Microfilm HMF/332 (1).

HARBURG

Community record book, Harburg, Community records and writs of Harburg, CAHJP, GA/a161.18.

HEIDINGSFELD

Record book, beit din Heidingsfeld, pages from the record book of the beit din of Heidingsfeld, CAHJP, He 3 (7).

KARLIN

Collection, ADMOR of Stolin-Karlin, Institute of Microfilmed Hebrew Manuscripts, National Library of Israel, film F49264, document #453.

KRAKÓW

Record book, beit din KK Kraków 1764–1805, CAHJP, HM2/5743; the original is in the Kraków district archive, III/11/2.

MAINZ

Community records, Mainz, CAHJP, D/Ma7/12

METZ
Community records, Metz, CAHJP, Fme/264.
Memory book, Metz, Jewish Theological Seminary of New York, JTS MS 3670.
Record book, beit din Metz, YIVO Archive, Gershon Epstein collection, #8. This record book was later published; see Berkovitz (2014).

NEUZEDLISCH
Record book, Neuzedlisch (1752–1764), CAHJP, HM2/8201.4; Jewish Museum of Prague #123795.

OBERDORF
Community record book, Oberdorf, CAHJP, D/Ob1/7.

OFFENBACH
Record book, Offenbach, CAHJP, GA/Offenbach/KGE14/5.

POSEN/POZNAN
Record book, beit din Poznan, CAHJP, P1/Po5.

PRAGUE
Record book, beit din Prague (1755–1768, and added are records from the 1780s and 1790s), CAHJP, HM2/3868; Jewish Museum of Prague #123804.

ROMANSWEILER
Record book, judge of Romansweiler, JTS MS 8545.

SCHWERSENZ
Burial society record book, Schwersenz, CAHJP, P/SW/36.

SOSNOWIEC
Literary estate of Rabbi Gitler of Sosnowiec, CAHJP, P233/14.

WALLERSTEIN
Writs of halitzah, Wallerstein, CAHJP, Ga/Wallerstein 27 (2).

WARBURG
Community records, Warburg, from the archives of Rabbi Shmuel Steg of Warburg, CAHJP, D/Wa/8.
Record book, beit din Warburg, CAHJP, D/Wa/8/5.
Halitzah writs, Warburg, CAHJP, D/Wa8/7; writ of obligation re the halitzah of Warburg, CAHJP, D/Wa8/16c.

WORMS
Community records of Worms, CAHJP, R/W/XII 3, 52.

WÜRZBURG
Literary estate of Rabbi Bing of Würzburg, CAHJP, D/Wu1/1.

ZÜLZ
Record book, community of Zülz, 5552–5574, CAHJP, Zülz/7.

INDEX

abandoned wives, xxx, 3, 141–43, 160, 176, 179–82, 183, 188, 203–4, 205, 214–15
accessibility in decision-making, 212–13
act of ugliness (*maaseh kiur*), 151
additional monies (*tosefet ketubah*), 14
Adel daughter of Avraham Halle, 204
Adelman, Howard, 59
adultery, xxix, 143–44, 151, 180, 205–7, 210–11, 213, 303n40
age: elderly widowhood, 29–30, 57; love and marriage debates among young people, 201–2; marriage age, 38–40, 143, 190; young men, 55; young widowhood, 6, 11, 31–33, 37, 72, 116
agent to deliver a get, 183–84, 215–18
Agnon, S. Y., xv–xvi, 271nn1–2
agunot, xv–xvii; additional strategies, 122–25; Avraham and Gutta Heckscher, 133–37; battered women, 160; beggars, 183–84, 209; bureaucracy of halakhic rulings, 240–53; choosing to abandon a wife, 141–43; converts to Christianity, 45, 119–21, 193–95; criminal activity, 190–93; decisors as colleagues, 125–26; documentation, importance of, 108–10; domestic service, 203–4; emissaries appointed to find missing husbands, 208–9; empathy for the agunah, 233, 261–67; financial difficulties, 47–50, 134, 136–37, 170–71, 203–4; geographical area of Ashkenaz, xix–xx; Glikl and Heckscher anecdotes, 91–97; halakhah relevant to, xxviii–xxx; halakhic authorities, 251–52; halakhic basis for halitzah, 41–50; halitzah and community dispute, 72–73; halitzah ceremony, 51–73; Hasidim, 195–96; identification of a body, 102–7; identifying the brother-in-law, 54–56; imposters and scoundrels, 89, 184–93; Jewish men in the military, 179–82; legal status, 46–47, 252; length of iggun, 218–19; looking for missing husbands, 175, 209–12; maskilim, 196–202, 215; merchant husbands, 176–77; mitzvah, freeing seen as a, 238, 239; models of decisor attitudes, 233–40; mourning customs, 73, 131–32, 275n29; *mumar* brothers-in-law, 45; murdered infants, 213–14; murders, 90–107; new studies, xxxii–xxxiii; out-of-wedlock pregnancy, 205–7; pogroms of 1648–1649, 86–89; preference for remaining an agunah, 48, 260–61; prolonged travel, 176; rabbinical power struggles, 129–31; remarrying before being free of previous marriage, 207; as a research topic, xvii–xviii; responsa literature, xxiv; revenge, 105–7; Sarah and Leah cases, 79–86; scholarly arguments on decisor attitudes, 232–33; sending a get by proxy, 215–18; sources, xxi–xxv; suffering of, 79, 233, 246, 258–67, 320n87, 322n12, 323n25, 323n27; as threat to the social order and community morals, 205–7; in times of persecution and war, 77–89; Torah study away from home, 177–79; and widows, 3–4; witnesses and testimony, xxix–xxx, 110–25; *yibum* (levirate marriage), 44, 52, 308n43. *See also* heterei agunah; ketubah (marriage contract)
AHW (Altona, Hamburg, and Wandsbek), 9, 26, 63, 68, 104, 133–37, 231, 317n23

349

Akiva, Rabbi, 202
alimony. *See* maintenance
Almog, Shulamit, 110–11
Alsace, xix, xxv, 29–30, 99, 203, 239
Altona, 22–23, 25, 26, 34, 37, 72, 90, 91–97, 100–101, 131–32, 133–34, 204, 296n15
Altona, Hamburg, and Wandsbek (AHW), 9, 26, 68, 104, 133–37, 231, 317n23
Altona record books, 283n240
ambivalent decisors, 239
ambivalent model, 237–38
Amsterdam, 35, 54, 56, 77, 89, 174, 183, 198, 210, 235, 267
annulment, 123
anthropology, xxvii–xxviii, 10
appeal to halakhic authorities, 122–26
aristocracy, 5, 8
army, 93, 179–82, 184, 308n52
Asher ben Yehiel, 239
Ashkenaz, geographical area of, xix–xx
Ashkenazi, Dov Berish, 217
Ashkenazi, Jacob, 87
Ashkenazi, Rabbi Gershon, 54–55, 85, 194, 216, 237
Ashkenazi, Rabbi Meshulam Zalman, 204
Ashkenazi, Rabbi Tzvi, 37
Ashkenazi, Rabbi Yaakov, 86–87
Ashkenazi, Rabbi Zvi, 32, 37–38, 57–59, 88
Ashkenazic communities' records, xxi, 231
Ashkenazic practice of binding, 44
asset value tax, 24–25, 28
assistance from community leaders, 214–15
astrology, 121–22
Aszód, Hungary, 194
attitudes of decisors, 232–40
Austria, xix
Avraham son of David Shohet of Altona, 163
Avraham son of Shimon, 82

Avram son of Moshe Tiplitz, 191–93
"awe in halakhic ruling" (*yirat horaah*), 237–38
Ayllón, Rabbi Shlomo, 58, 267

Baal Shem Tov. *See* Eliezer, Rabbi Israel ben
Babad, Rabbi Joshua Heschel, 238, 243
babies. *See* infanticide; mamzerim; nursing the child of another man
Babylonian Talmud, 49
Bacharach, Moshe Shimshon, 95, 235–36, 321n118
Bacharach, Rabbi Avraham ben Yosef, 18
bachelors, 4
Bachrach, Yair Haim, 234–35
Bamberg, 25
Bar-Levav, Avriel, 8
basic assumptions, xxvii–xxviii, 225–26, 228
basic ketubah, 14
batei din (rabbinic courts): assistance from community leaders, 214–15; Avraham and Gutta Heckscher, 134–37; betrothal contracts (*shetarot tenaim*), 146–48; children from previous marriages, 33–36; collecting testimony, 80, 111–12, 273n48; community records, xxi–xxii; converts to Christianity, 195; crime, 191–92; dividing up estates, 20; divorce imposed by, 170–72; documentation for agunot, 109–10; fate of an abandoned wife, 203; get received from a distant place, 217–18; gossip, 95; halakhah relevant to agunot, xxviii–xxx; halakhic divorce, 148–52; halitzah, 45, 51–53, 66–68, 72, 289n69; hearing evidence, 113–17; heterei agunah in beit din records, 223–53; imposters and scoundrels, 188; involvement of third parties in marital conflict, 165–67; Jewish men in the military, 179–82; lien on husband's property, 16–17; maskilim,

199–202; marital violence, 167–69; martial disputes, 146–48, 160–72; as mediator and arbitrator, 163–65; Metz beit din, xxxii–xxxiii, 129, 277n88; Offenbach, 169, 305n95; out-of-wedlock pregnancy, 206–7; poverty, 183–84; practical meaning of decisors' demands, 242–45; rabbinical power struggles, 130; representation of women by men, 63–64; Sarah and Leah cases, 82, 85; security against assets, 287n20; sole decisor debate, 246–47; transgressing the Law of Moses, 151, 155–58; translation of testimony, 297–98n25; widows in beit din records, 22–23, 26, 30, 38; writ of halitzah, 49, 52, 61–66, 69. *See also* dayanim (rabbinic court judges); responsa literature
battered women, 158–60, 167–69
Bayla, 57, 117–20, 298n44
Bazalia, Ukraine 70
beggars, 26, 183–84, 209
begging, 280n158
behavior, 94, 142–43, 150–51
Behrend, Hyman Samuel, 133–34
beit din. *See* batei din (rabbinic courts)
Beit Shmuel (Uri Shraga Phoebus), 248–49
Bela, widow of Meir Oppenheim of Offenbach, 25
beliefs, xx, 4, 8, 93, 100, 121, 193, 212, 252, 307n31
Benet, Rabbi Mordechai, 207
Ber, Zalman, 66
Bereu, Lippman, 66
Berkovitz, Jay, xxii, xxv, xxxii–xxxiii, 130, 230, 235, 286n13, 303n44
Berlin, Germany, 39
Berlin, Rabbi Naftali Tzvi Yehuda, 253
Berlin, Zanvil and Miriam, 166
Berl, 113–15
Bethlehem, Louise, 111
betrothal contracts (*shetarot tenaim*), 29–30, 49–50, 146–48

Beyle, 184
Beyle, the widow of Shimon, 64–65
biblical image of widows, 10–13
biblical law, 263
biblical law(s), xxviii, 3, 13, 31, 42–43, 47, 67, 149, 195, 287n15, 289n69
Bieber, Menachem Mendel, 126
bigamy, 184, 207
Bing, Rabbi Avraham, 214
Binyamin Ze'ev of Arta, 168
birth. *See* giving birth
black kerchief, 9, 275n29.
   See also garments of mourning
Blimele daughter of Moshe, 141, 190–93
Boes, Maria, 92
Bogucka, Maria, 172, 183
Bohemia, 77, 209
Bomsil, Rabbi Mendel, 51–52
Bonfit son of Ber Frankfurt, 163–67
books, 22, 25, 129, 130, 230. *See also* beit din record books; community records
books of customs, xxii, xxiv, 9
books of homiletics, xxii, xxiv
Bourdieu, Pierre, 142
Bourse, 96–97
Brandes, Yehuda, 232, 234, 261–64, 323n26
Braudel, Fernand, xxvi
Breger, Sarah, 232
Brendl, widow of Leib Berl, 64
Breslau/Wrocław, Poland 200
Breuer, Mordechai, 321n113, 324n36
Brisk (Brześć Litewski), Belarus 41
Brod, 103, 245
Broda, Rabbi Abraham, 37
Brody, Ukraine, 19, 23, 41, 54–55, 70, 123–25, 243–44
brothers-in-law: coercion into halitzah, 44; cost of halitzah, 47–50, 58–67; exploiting halakhic expertise, 70–71; identifying, 54–56; legal ties, 47; withholding communal religious services, 72
Bruna, Rabbi Israel, 45, 286n4

Brzesko (Briegel), Poland, 239, 309n76
Buchsbaum, Shainele and Yosefe, 21
Budapest, 81, 106
bureaucracy of halakhic rulings, 240–53
burial arrangements, 102–5

canon law, 85–86, 149, 154
cantors and teachers (*melamdim*), 174–75, 306n6
captivity, 8, 77–78, 85
Carlebach, Elisheva, 120–21, 194–95
census data, xxiv–xxv, 27, 29
central Europe, xix, xx, 77
ceremonies. *See* halitzah
childbearing, xvi–xvii
children: born from adultery, 205–7; born out of wedlock, 314n191; business partnerships, 28; fate of an abandoned wife, 203–4; halakhic divorce, 149; halitzah, 43; Hasidim, 195–96; living conditions of widows, 29–30; marriage of, 26; matchmaking, 54; nursing the child of another man, 36–37; poverty, 183–84; preference for remaining an agunah, 260–61; from a previous marriage, 4, 33–36; rights of, 15–16, 19, 22–24; roles of beit din in divorce settlements, 161–63; *yibum* (levirate marriage), 43; young widowhood, 31–33. *See also* child support; family life/networks
children born from adultery. *See* mamzerim
child support, xxix, 36, 149, 162–63, 205–6
Christianity, 45, 119–21, 193–95
circumstances of death, 108–9
civil courts, xxxiii, 34, 136, 172–73, 300n8, 303n44
"the Cleves *get* [writ of divorce] affair," xvi
clothing, 8–10, 15, 20–22, 299–300n9
co-decisors, 236–37, 265–66
cohen (of priestly lineage), 85

Cohen, Eli, 26
collecting testimony, 111–12
commerce, 176–77
communal fees, 24–25
community aid, 19, 25–26
community and the agunah awaiting halitzah, 72–73
community archives, xxiii
community documents, xxii, 133
community institutions, 38
community leaders, 18–19, 26, 27, 106, 117, 214–15
community records, xxi–xxiii, xxxii, 15, 20, 22, 25, 35, 109, 127–29
community treasurer (*gabai*), xxii–xxiii
condemned men, 191–92
conditional marriage, 45, 51–52, 286n4
conditional permission to remarry, 244, 247, 317n32
conduct. *See* behavior
conjugal intimacy, 156–57
converts to Christianity, 45, 119–21, 193–95
coping strategies, 11, 144
correspondence. *See* letters
correspondence between decisors. *See* responsa literature
correspondences and controversies, xix–xx
cost of halitzah, 47–50
Council of Four Lands, 78, 105, 209, 278–79n114
Council of the Land of Lithuania, 15, 177
counting the days, 175, 306n3
court fees, 67–68
crime, 92, 95, 97, 190–93, 211, 295n44, 295n58, 310n93
Crown of Poland-Lithuania, xix
cultures of testimony, 110–11
currencies, 278n99, 279n139, 314n207
custody, 149, 163, 303n44
customs. *See* lifting the man's foot as she removes his shoe; mourning customs; reaffirmation of other

Index

decisors; social networks; widow's oath

David of Makov, R., 195–96
David son of Eliyahu, 82
David son of Samuel Halevi Segal, 85
dayanim (rabbinic court judges), xxii, 45–46, 67–68, 112, 262, 289n72, 297–98n25, 304–5n71
death, xvi; ambivalence about the remarriage of widows, 31–33; beggars, 183–84; circumstances of, 108–10; documentation for agunot, 108–9; gravestones, xxv; halakhah relevant to agunot, xxix; halitzah, 46–47, 57; by hanging, 191–93, 311n109; Heckscher's murder, 133–37, 301n12; identification of a body, 102–7, 114–15, 128–30; martyrdom, 86–89; mourning customs, 8–10, 20, 73, 131–32, 275n29; nursing the child of another man, 37; orphans, 36; practical meaning of decisors' demands, 244–45; rabbinical power struggles, 130–31; rabbinic prestige, 251–52; revenge, 105–6; suffering of agunot, 258–67; in wartime, 78–86; while travelling, 108–10; widow's claim to late husband's estate, 13–25; *yibum* (levirate marriage), 43
decision-making, 212–13
decisors, xvii, xix–xxi, 223–25, 319n70; co-decisors, 236–37, 265–66; as colleagues, 125–26; conditional marriage, 51–52; delay, 242–45, 320n79; ethic of empathy, 261–67, 320n87, 323n25; hierarchy of, 238–39, 240; legal documents, xxvi; leniency, 116, 232–34, 236, 237, 239, 241, 246, 259, 262–64; massacres of 1648–1649, 78–79, 88–89; meta-halakhic approaches, 227–28; models of attitudes toward the agunah, 233–40; point of view, 229; practical meaning of decisors' demands, 242–46;

procedural aspects, 241–42, 246–47, 258; public image, 80–81; rabbinical power struggles, 129–31; rabbinic prestige, 247–53; reaffirmation, 241, 242–43, 245–46, 248; remarriage after childbirth, 37; responsa literature, 229–30; scholarly arguments on decisor attitudes, 232–33; sending a get by proxy, 216–18; social order and community morals, 205; sole decisor debate, 86, 131, 246. *See also* responsa literature

Dehan, Aaron, 36
Dehan, Izak, 36
Dekker, Rudolf M., 92–93, 98, 100, 294n18
delaying halitzah, 64–66, 69–71
delay of burial, 105
delivering a get, 308n48; beggars, 183–84; converts to Christianity, 194; delay, 155; from a distant place, 215–18; halakhic divorce, 152; imposters and scoundrels, 185; transgressing the Law of Moses, 155–56
Denmark, 77
deserted women, xvi–xvii
deserting husbands, 190, 194, 215, 218–19
destitute women, 11, 16, 28, 57, 204
Deutsch, Rabbi Yosef Yoel, 209
deviant behavior, 142–43
Dina, widow of Shimon, 58–59
Dina, widow of Yehiel, 241
Dinari, Yedidya, 232
disappearance of Avraham Metz, 91–97
Disorderly Women (Wiltenburg), 153–54
disputes, 19, 22–24, 35–36, 47–49, 58–62, 63–64, 65–66, 69, 72–73, 133–37. *See also* marital disputes
distance and the halitzah ceremony, 46
distance and Torah study away from home, 178
distance between decisors, 243
diverse legal models, 5

divorce, xvi; *batei din* (rabbinic courts), 161–63, 195; canon law, 85–86, 149, 154; economic implications, 154–55; halakhah relevant to agunot, xxviii–xxix; halakhic authority, 248–49; halakhic divorce, 148–52; imposed by the beit din, 170–72; Jewish men in the military, 179–82; marital violence, 167–69; non-Jewish courts, 172–73; roles of beit din in, 161–63; sending a get by proxy, 215–18; State of Israel, xviii; traditional Jewish society, 143–45; transgressing the Law of Moses, 151, 155–58
domestic service, 27, 203–4, 214
domestic violence, 167–69
dowry, xxix, 5, 13, 15, 26, 155, 159
dress regulations, 274nn20–21
drowning, 108–9
duality of widowhood, 4–8, 11–12
duration of widowhood, 38–40
Dusil daughter of Yaakov son of Itzik, 163–67

eastern Europe, xix, xx, 25, 55
Eastern European Jewry, 195
economic implications for widows, 13
economic implications of divorce, 154–55
Edele, 65–66
Edele of Nikolsburg, 110–16
edited printed volumes, xxii
Egmond, F., 190
"ego-document" type, xxvi
Eisenstadt, Rabbi Avraham Zvi Hirsch, 15
Eisenstadt, Rabbi Meir, 155–58, 183, 250, 258
Elia Balin of Worms, 29
Eliezer, Rabbi Israel ben (Baal Shem Tov), 195
Eliezer Innsbruck of Neuwied, 67
Ella, wife of Shmuel, 63–64
emancipation, xx
Emden, Rabbi Jacob, 22–24, 32–33, 39, 54, 72–73, 86–89, 132, 176–77, 190, 279n131, 300n20, 310n95, 316n2
emissaries, 113, 129, 174–75, 183–84, 208–9, 216–18, 243
emotions in family disputes, 35
empathy for the agunah, 233, 261–67
Emrich, Rabbi Zalman, 69
entitlements, 53
Epstein, Rabbi Wolf, 258–59
estates, distribution of, 13–24, 35–36, 52–54, 65, 134–37, 278n111
Essen, 27
Esther, the widow of Lekish, 22, 39
Esther daughter of Meir Austerlitz, 110
Esther daughter of Moshe, 162–63
Ettigen, Meir, 215
Even haezer, xxiii
excommunication, 37–38, 95, 181–82, 215
expulsion of the Jews from Hamburg, 90
extortion, 44, 47, 50, 61–62, 66, 188–89

false identity, 92–94
family life/networks: attitudes to married life and marital conflict, 153–54; battered women, 158–60; children from previous marriages, 33–36; criminality, 190–93; fate of an abandoned wife, 204; financial security, 13, 16; Hasidim, 196; heirs, 286–87n15; ideal Jewish family, 143–45; identifying the brother-in-law, 54–56; institution of marriage, 264, 268; involvement of third parties in marital conflict, 165–67; living condition of widows, 30; looking for missing husbands, 209; maskilim, 198–202; mourning customs, 131–32; public interest, 148; social status, 10–11; timeframe, xx–xxi. *See also* marital disputes
Fanta, Rabbi Levi, 251
Faygele, Rachel, 216
Faygele daughter of Zanvil, 161–62
fee collectors, xxii–xxiii

Index

Fegerscheim, Shlomo, 64–65
Feivel son of Aaron, 182
female sexuality, 180
female solidarity, 99
feminist research, xviii, 227–29, 324n32
financial aid, 19, 24–26, 68–69, 180
financial difficulties of agunot, 47–50, 134, 136–37, 170–71, 203–4
fires, 108
Fleckeles, Rabbi Elazar, 109
Fokselheim, Mordechai, 64–66
formalism, 227
Foucault, Michel, 230
Fram, Edward (Yehezkel), xxxii, 121, 232, 292n32
Frankfurt, 63, 231, 317n23
French judicial system, xxxiii, 34
Frick, David, 172
Frieda daughter of Michl, 185–87, 233, 265
Friedche (midwife), 205
Friedl daughter of Yitzhak, 170
friendship with converts, 119–20
Frumet daughter of Meir, 204
Fürst, Joseph, 315n222
Fürth, 9, 63–64, 95, 178

Gadamer, Hans-Georg, xxvii
Galhausen, 192, 311n104
Gamliel, Rabban, 265
garments of mourning, 8–10, 73, 275n29
gender, xx, xxvii, 83, 93–95, 99, 157, 160, 212, 228–29
gentiles, 89, 98–99, 119–22, 127–28, 156–57, 295n47
geographical area of Ashkenaz, xix–xx
geographical proximity to the agunah, 240
German Jews, 182
Germany, xix, xxxii, 4–5, 18, 28, 32, 38–40, 77, 85, 90, 95, 97, 120–21, 153–54, 166–67, 172–73, 175, 178, 182, 183, 193, 203–4, 274n9
Gershom, Rabenu, 44, 185, 285n12
get, 308n43; choosing to abandon a wife, 141–43; halakhah relevant to agunot, xxviii–xxix; halakhic divorce, 149–52; marital violence, 167; over-leniency, 250; permission to give a get against her will, 207; received from a distant place, 215–18; requiring the wife of a convert to obtain before she could remarry, 195; sent by proxy, 215–18; unconditional, 181–82
Getz, Rabbi Eliakim, 27
Ginzburg, Carlo, xxvi
Ginzburg, Rabbi Aryeh Leib, 53
Gitler, Rabbi Abraham Meir, 260–61
Gittel, wife of Haim son of Rabbi Tzvi, 70
giving birth, 27, 31, 37, 43, 151, 164, 166, 192, 205–6, 210–11, 303n36
Glick, Shmuel, 306n3
Glikl Hamel. *See* Hamel, Glikl
glosses (*Mapah*), xxiii
Goldberg, Jacob, 287n22
Goldstein, Bluma, 198–99
Gomperz, Aaron Umrich, 20
good-luck charm (*segulah*), 108
goods, 18, 26–27, 64, 133–35
Gordon, Judah Leib, xv–xvi
gossip, 93–96
granting an agunah permission to remarry. *See* heterei agunah
gravestones, xxv, 18, 32, 39–40, 293–94n10, 293n8
grief, xv, 7. *See also* mourning customs; suffering of agunot
Grona, widow of Zalman, 56, 61–63
Grossman, Avraham, 44, 47, 285n9, 285n12
grounds for divorce, 150, 152, 154, 166, 168–70, 180
grounds for freeing an agunah, 80–83, 235
guardianship, xxxii, 33–34, 72, 134–36
Guerre, Martin, 89, 189
Guggenheim of Offenbach, Rabbi, 21
Gutrad, widow of Tevely Lisser, 26

Hacohen, Rabbi Joshua Falk, 181
Hacohen, Rabbi Meshulam Zalman, 206
Hacohen, Rabbi Raphael, 122–24, 125, 199–200, 206
Hacohen, Rabbi Shmuel Shmelke, 116–23
Hacohen, Rabbi Yaakov, 32
Hacohen, Rabbi Yitzhak, 141
Hagenau, Alsace, 29–30
Hahnasat kalah (Agnon), xv–xvi
Hakham Tzvi. *See* Ashkenazy, Rabbi Zvi
halakhah, xv–xvii; adultery, 210–11; agunot as research topic, xvii–xviii; basis for halitzah, 41–50; brother-in-law exploiting halakhic expertise, 70–71; bureaucracy of halakhic rulings, 240–53; captivity, 85; child support, 162–63; converts to Christianity, 45; death in wartime, 80–82; delivering a get, 215–18; dividing up estates, 17–24, 52–54, 134–37; divorce his wife, 303n36; economic implications of divorce, 155; entitlements, 53; ethic of empathy, 261–67; geographical area of Ashkenaz, xix–xx; halakhic divorce, 148–52; halakhic knowledge, xx, 70–71, 83, 118–19, 123, 249–50, 292n29; identification of a body, 102–7, 114–15, 128–30; identifying the brother-in-law, 55–56; imagery of the widow, 10–13; insider/outsider in, 225–28, 317n10; ketubah payment, 16–17; mamzerim, 152, 205–6, 262–64; meta-halakhic approaches, 226–28; models of decisor attitudes, 232–36; nursing the child of another man, 31, 36–37; practical limitations, 36–38; precedents, 131, 213, 235; reaffirmation of other decisors, 245–46, 248; relevant to agunot, overview, xxviii–xxx; remarriage, 31–32, 223; responsa literature, xxiv, 230; treatment of widows, 5; validity of a get, 217–18; widow's claim to late husband's estate, 13–25; widow's finances, 13; witnesses and testimony, 110–25; writing and delivering a get, 216
halakhic authorities, xv, xx, xxviii, 122–25, 129–31, 194, 211, 226–27, 230, 236, 240, 248–52, 259
Halberstadt, Judah Leib, 66
Halberstam, Rabbi Chaim, 217
Halevi, Rabbi Nahum, 245
Halevi, Rabbi Yitzhak, 182
halitzah, xvi, 51–73, 289n69; brother-in-law exploiting halakhic expertise, 70–71; ceremony ritual, 45–46; community dispute, 72–73; cost of, 47–50, 57–67; delay, 64–66, 69–71; dividing up estates, 52–54, 286–87n15; expenses of ceremony, 67–69; identifying the brother-in-law, 54–56; takes place after three-month waiting period, 57; and widows, 3–4; without remuneration, 47–49, 57, 61–62, 65–66; *yibum* (levirate marriage), 44, 59, 308n43
halitzah shoe, 46, 69, 290n80, 290n90
Hamagid (weekly), 175
Hamburg, Germany, 25, 90, 93–94, 99–101, 133–37, 208, 277n88
Hamburger, Mordechai, 176
Hamel, Chaim, 6–8
Hamel, Glikl, 295n58; disappearance of Avraham Metz, 91–97; financial security, 16; imagery of the widow, 10–11; informal women's networks, 97–99; living conditions of widows, 29–30; matchmaking, 54; merchants, 176–77; remarriage, 32–33, 36; revenge tale, 105–6; Rivkah, Lipman's wife, 97–101; widowhood, 4–8, 25
Hamel, Hertz, 169, 192
Hannah, widow of Yaakov bar Manis, 56

Hannah the wife of Rabbi Lazar, 116
happiness, 144, 186
Harrington, Joel, 153, 183, 204, 308n55
Hasidim, 195–96
Hasidism, xx, 143
Haskalah (Jewish Enlightenment), xix, 143, 196, 215
Hatam Sofer. *See* Sofer-Schreiber, Rabbi Moshe
Havah, 194
Haya, 72–73
Haya Rachel of Brody, 41, 54–56
Hayim, Rabbi Shmuel, 70–71
Hebrew and Yiddish books, xxiv, 283n235
Hebrew language, xxii, 112, 134, 297–98n25
Hebrew year, 274n21
Heckscher, Avraham Marcus and Gutta, 133–37, 301n12
Heckscher, Mordechai, 134–37
Heckscher, Reuven, 57
Heckscher, Shmuel, 90, 91–98
Heine, Salomon, 137
heirs, 15, 19, 21, 22, 26, 49, 52–53, 65, 260, 286–87n15
Helkat mehokek (Lima), 246–47
help and the suffering of agunot, 258–67
helpmeet role, 145
Hendele daughter of Yosef Stathagen of Altona, 37–38
Henele daughter of Joseph Segal of Leutershausen, 146
herem derabeinu Gershom, xxviii, 149
Heschel, Rabbi Joshua, 87–88, 319n58
heterei agunah, xix, 223–53, 316nn1–2, 317n23; agunot in 1648–1649, 79–86, 88–89; in beit din records, 223, 230–31, 245; bureaucracy of halakhic rulings, 241–53; confirming death, 191–93; delay, 260, 320n79, 323n22; faced with a suffering agunah, 265, 320n87; gossip, 96; halakhah relevant to agunot, xxix; halakhic limitations, 37; meta-halakhic approaches, 226–29; models of decisor attitudes, 233–40; procedural aspects, 246–47, 258; rabbinic prestige, 247–53; research approach and basic assumptions, 225–31; in responsa literature, 230–31; scholarly arguments on decisor attitudes, 232–33; seeking affirmation, 106; testimonies, 323n22; witnesses and testimony, 108–10
hierarchy of decisors, 238–39, 240
Hildesheim, Saxony, 27
Hinde daughter of Raphael, 167
Hinde of Ostrog, 116–26
historical contexts, xviii
Hollender, Wolf and Hannah, 166
Holocaust, xvii
Holy Roman Empire, 77
home, Torah study away from, 177–79
home prayer services, 131–32, 300nn19–20
homes of the wealthy and poor, 108
homiletics, books of, xxii, xxiv, 272n28
Horowitz, Rabbi, 19–20, 68, 278n95
horses, 81, 128
Hoshen mishpat (legal issues, both civil and criminal), xxiii
householder tax, 24–25
Hovav, Yemima, 145, 268
humility, 237–38
Hundert, Gershon, 27
Hungary, 55, 77
Hurwitz, Rabbi Nahum, 238

identification, belated, 189–90
identification and imposters, 184–85
identification and testimonies, 192–93
identification of a body, 102–7, 128–30
identifying the brother-in-law, 54–56
identity, confirmation of, 45–46, 54–56, 69–70, 93
identity of a murderer, 92–94, 97–98
iggun. *See* agunot
imagery of the widow, 10–13, 275n35

images of agunot, 232, 266, 323n25
images of rebellious women, 153
images of women in rabbinic literature, 145
impersonation, 189–90
imposters and scoundrels, 89, 184–93
independence, 11–13, 17, 29, 136, 144
indifference, 35, 83, 97, 262
individual decisors, 241–42, 319n70
infanticide, 210–11, 213–14
informal women's networks, 97–99, 118
inheritance, xxxiii, 5, 13, 25, 35–36, 60, 62, 276n75, 278n111, 286–87n15, 301n19
insanity, 99–101
insider/outsider in research, 225–28, 317n10
institution of marriage, 11, 195, 304n65, 324n32
inventory, 17–20, 135, 171
Israel son of Peretz, 109
Issachar Dov Ber, Rabbi, 236
Isserlein, Rabbi Israel, 47–48, 274n16
Isserlein, Rabbi Moshe, 168
Isserles, Rabbi Moshe, xxiii, 15, 31, 48–49, 67–68, 85, 131, 181, 246, 248, 287n22

Jackson, Bernard, xviii
Jacob ben Isaac Ashkenazi, Rabbi, 11–12
jealousy, 126
Jerusalem Talmud, 49
jewelry, 20, 146, 165, 170
Jewish burial society (*hevra kadisha*), 102
Jewish population, xxiv–xxv
Jewish society, xv–xvii, xx–xxi; attitudes to married life and marital conflict, 153–54; attitudes toward the agunah, 91–93, 299n56; beggars, 26, 183–84, 209; converts to Christianity, 194; ideal Jewish family, 143–45; infanticide, 214; institution of marriage, 268; Maimon's memoir, 196–202; marriage age, 38–40, 143, 190; mourning customs, 8–10, 20, 73, 131–32, 275n29; out-of-wedlock pregnancy, 205–7; poverty, 183–84; social structures, xxvii; traditional lifestyle, 143–45, 157; treatment of widows, 5
Josef II, 250
Joseph, Rabbi Jacob, 260–61
judicial process, 110–12
justice, 105–6
Jutta daughter of Reuven, 49–50

Kahana, Maoz, 247, 319n70, 321n107
Kahana, Yitzhak Ze'ev (Y. Z.), xvii–xviii, 79, 232, 238, 246, 259, 316n2, 319n61, 322n12, 323n22, 323n25
Kahneman, Daniel, 212–13
Kaidanover, Rabbi Shmuel, 259
Kaidanover, Rabbi Tzvi Hirsch, 35, 178
Kalman, Yosef, 29
Kaplan, Debra, xxxii
karet (being cut off from the community), 42
Karo, Rabbi Joseph, xxiii, 241–42, 247–48
Kasper-Marienberg, Verena, xxxii
Katz, Hertz and Tipkhe, 21
Katz, Jacob, xix, 10, 44, 47, 143–45, 153, 154–55
Katz, Rabbi Yonatan, 203
Katzenellenbogen, Rabbi Aryeh Leib, 56, 300n20
Katzenellenbogen, Rabbi Yechezkel, 72–73, 131–32, 265
Katzenellenbogen, Rabbi Yitzhak, 233
Kaufmann, David, 90
Kav hayashar (Kaidanover), 35, 178
ketubah (marriage contract): Avraham and Gutta Heckscher, 135–36; dividing up estates, 19–23, 53, 137; economic implications of divorce, 155; exact amount to be paid for halitzah, 67; extortion, 66; halakhah relevant to agunot, xxix; halakhic divorce, 149–51; halitzah fees, 68;

involvement of third parties in marital conflict, 166; legal status of agunot, 47; lien on husband's property, 16–17; marital violence, 168–69; parental interference, 163; securing children's welfare, 34; value of estate, 14, 26, 48–49, 62, 65; when halitzah takes place, 57; widow's claim to late husband's estate, 14–15
Khmelnytsky Cossack uprisings. *See* massacres of 1648–1649
Kiddush Hashem, 86
"killer wife" (*katlanit*), 31–32, 60
Kleve, 24
Kluger, Rabbi Shlomo, 41, 55–56, 189–90
knowledge, 142–43, 229–30, 298n45
Kostrzewski, Franciszek, 120
"Kotzo shel yod" (Gordon), xv–xvi
Kraków, xxii, 22, 34, 87, 162, 167, 170, 182, 194, 231, 239, 247, 292n44, 91, 306n99, 317n23, 319n58
Krochmal, Rabbi Menahem Mendel, 79–86, 105–6, 179–81, 183–84, 216, 237, 241, 248–49, 292n32, 321n103. See also *Tzemah Tzedek* (Krochmal)
Kruse, Britta-Juliane, 8
Kulm law (or, Chełmno law), 5
Kushner, Aaron and Rachel, 22

labor market, 26–28
Laminitz, Itzek, 134–36
Lancom, Zanvil and Tzerli, 21
Landau, Rabbi Jacob Segal, 236–37, 289n72
Landau, Rabbi Shmuel, 109–10, 190–93
Landau, Rabbi Shmuel Segal, 204
Landau, Rabbi Shmuel Yosef Halevi, 214–15
Landau, Rabbi Yechezkel, 52, 68, 69, 70–71, 102, 116, 124–25, 141, 146, 184, 188–89, 194, 217–18, 231, 238, 243–44, 249–51, 319n70. See also *Noda biYehudah* (Landau)
Lansburg, Itzik, 186
law code, xxiii

laypeople, 251–53
"leaders and good men" (*rashim vetovim*), 298n42
Leah daughter of Yitzhak of Budapest, 79–86, 89
legal documents, xxv–xxvi. *See also* get
legal status, xxxiii, 14, 46–47, 61, 63, 93, 252
Leib, Rabbi Aryeh, 247
Leib, Rabbi Judah, 251–52
Leidesdorf, Egla, 32
Leipzig, 134–35
leisure, 181–82
Lember Levi of Metz, 127–31
Lemberg/Lvov/Lviv, Ukraine, 182, 183–84, 188, 195, 243
Lemli Wimpe of Metz, 127–31
length of time a Torah scholar could be away from home, 177–79
length of time legitimate for travel, 176
lenient decisors, 116, 232–34, 236, 237, 239, 241, 246, 259, 262–64
lenient model, 238–39
letters, xxiii, xxvi; assistance from community leaders, 214–15; battered women, 158–60; betrothal contracts (*shetarot tenaim*), 148; delivering a get, 218; documentation for agunot, 109; false identity, 92–93; fate of an abandoned wife, 203–4; Lemli's widow, 127–29; model letter requesting financial aid, 180; poverty, 183; practical meaning of decisors' demands, 243–45; preference for remaining an agunah, 260–61; rabbinic prestige, 250–51; stylistic conventions, 304n62; transgressing the Law of Moses, 155–58; two letters, 185–87. *See also* emissaries; responsa literature
Levi, Nahshon, 69
Levi, Yeshayah, 67
Levi, Yosefe, 18
levirate marriage. See *yibum* (levirate marriage)

Libba, widow of Haim Otitz, 51–52
Liberles, Robert, 39, 145, 158–59, 268
liboun, 304n57
Lifshitz, Rabbi Aryeh Leibush, 185, 206
lifting the man's foot as she removes his shoe, 69
Lima, Rabbi Moshe, 131, 246
Lipnik, Rabbi Yitzhak Hacohen, 193
Lipshitz, Rabbi Arye Leibush, 239–40
Lisser, Tevely, 26, 280n162
literary estates, xxiii
Lithuania, 55, 274n20
living conditions of widows, 28–30
living with married children, 29–30
love and its role in marriage, 200–202, 304nn64–65
Lübeck, 133–34

Maas, Rabbi Nathan, 67
Mabit (Moshe ben Yosef di Trani), 130–31
MacKinnon, Catherine, xxvii
madness, 99–101
Magdeburg law, 5
Magnus, Marcus, 133
Mahler, Raphael, xxv
mail coaches, 55, 127, 243
Maimon, Salomon, 178, 196–202, 208–9
Maimonides, 121, 235
maintenance, 15, 47, 53, 149–51, 162–63, 165, 169, 170–71, 287n16
Mainz, 47, 192
male authority, 153–54
mamzerim, xxix, 84, 152, 205–6, 262–64, 323n28
Mann, Michael, 111
Mannheim, Karl, 226
Manspach, Yosefe, 9
Mapah, xxiii
Margaliot, Rabbi Ephraim Zalman, 209
Margaliot, Rabbi Meir, 110, 116, 119–20, 121, 122–25
Margaliot, Rabbi Menahem Stengi, 239
Margaliot, Rabbi Zalman, 243

Margaliot, Rabbi Alexander Sender, 242–43
marital disputes, xxviii, 160–73; battered women, 158–60; beit din as mediator and arbitrator, 163–65; betrothal contracts (*shetarot tenaim*), 146–48; divorce imposed by the beit din, 170–72; Jewish attitudes, 153–54; marital violence, 164–65, 167–69, 172–73; nature of, 142–43; in non-Jewish courts, 172–73; parental interference, 163–65; roles of beit din in divorce settlements, 161–63; third-party involvement, 165–67; traditional Jewish society, 143–46; transgressing the Law of Moses, 151, 155–58
marital violence, 173
marriage age, 38–40, 143, 190
martyrdom, 86–89
maskilim, 196–202, 215
massacres of 1648–1649, xx–xxi, 77–89
matchmaking, 54
material culture: assets, xxv, 13, 21, 24–25, 28, 135, 287n20, 310n93; clothing, 8–10, 15, 20–22, 299–300n9; household articles, 15, 18, 20, 53; houses, 16–17, 28–30, 108, 279n131; property, 5, 13–25, 134–36, 165, 170–73
Matityahu Aptiker of Altona, 56
Matityahu son of Israel, 82
matrimonial law, monopoly over, 249
Mayeh, Seligman, 52–54, 287n15
Megillat sefer (Emden), 89
Meir, Rabbi Jacob, 239–40, 259
Meir ben Gedalyah (Maharam) of Lublin, 131, 181
Meir ben Samuel of Szczebrzeszyn, 78
Meir ben Yekutiel, 248–49
Meir Hacohen, 249
Meir of Frankfurt, Rabbi, 251
Meir Oppenheim of Offenbach, 25
Meir son of Mendel Ullmann, R., 65–66

Meisels, Rabbi Avraham Natan Neta, 206
memoirs, xxiv, xxv, xxvi, 22; Glikl Hamel, 4–8, 25, 90–99, 118, 295n58; Jacob Emden, 22–23, 32, 279n131; Salomon Maimon, 178, 196–202, 312n141
memory, 56, 189, 193
memory books, xxii, 127–29
Menahem Mendel, son of dayan in Działoszyn, 116–21
Mentzir, Yosefe, 67
merchants, 176–77
Merchingen, Yozel, 52–54
messengers. *See* emissaries
meta-halakhic approaches, 226–28
meta-principles, 227, 262, 317n8
methodological problems, xxiv, xxv–xxviii, 31, 126, 223, 225
Metz, xxxii–xxxiii, 39, 63, 127–29, 231, 317n23
Metz, Avraham Zimla, 91–97, 293–94n10
microhistory, xxvi
midrash, xxii, 8, 272n28
military, 179–82
Minden, Yehudah Leib, 174–75, 209
Mindl, wife of Itzik Hacohen, 116
Mishnah, 11, 43, 193, 311n109
missing husbands, xxix, 84, 94–96, 108–26, 175, 184, 189–90, 194, 208–12, 214–15
mistaken identity, 217, 311n109
mitzvah, freeing agunot seen as a, 238, 239
models of decisor attitudes toward the agunah, 233–40
money. *See* child support; cost of halitzah; dowry; extortion; financial difficulties of agunot; ketubah (marriage contract); maintenance; poverty
Moravia, 9, 20, 24–25, 77, 302n2
Mordechai son of Meir, 161–62
Moshe son of Avraham, 203
Moshe son of Nissan, 192
Mourner's Kaddish, 131
mourning customs, 8–10, 20, 73, 131–32, 275n29
mumar, 45
murders, 90–107, 310n93
mutual consent, 149

Nahalat shivah (Samuel son of David Halevi), 146, 302n27
Naphtali Hertz of Offenbach, 104–5
Nathan of Göddern, 109
Nehama daughter of Rabbi Ephraim Hacohen, 86–89
Nehemiah son of Ephraim, 95
neighbors, 95, 156–57, 165–67
Nentche, 53, 287n15
Neumark, Meshulam Zalman, 68
Neurlingen, Yosef Hahn, 108
niddah, 95, 155–57, 304n58
night, 12, 45, 266
Nikolsburg, 17–18, 79, 110–16, 277n87
Noda biyehudah (Landau), 69, 126
non-Jewish authorities, xxv, xxix, 4, 16–17, 28–29, 97, 102–4, 106, 128–29, 194, 205–6, 215, 250, 252, 272n22
non-Jewish courts, xxxii, 23, 60–61, 111–12, 137, 153, 172–73, 191
non-Jewish refugees, 85–86
non-Jewish society, 3, 4, 8–9, 24, 91–94, 118–21, 143, 153, 189, 304n65
non-Jewish sources, 78
non-Jewish surroundings, xx, 63, 119–21, 295n47
non-Jewish widows, 28, 32
Nouvelle Gallia Judaica project, xxv
nursing the child of another man, 31, 36–37

objective circumstances, 150–51
object of research, 225–26
Ogilvie, Sheilagh, 28, 32, 63, 172–73, 306n106

online databases, xxv
Oppenheim, David, 81–82
Oppenheim, Hirsch, 278n111
Oppenheim, Rabbi David, 103–4, 106, 110, 113–16, 131, 176, 203, 204, 205, 237, 244–45, 258, 267
Orah hayim, xxiii
orphans, 18, 20, 22, 24–25, 26, 204, 283n240
Ortner, Sherry, xxvii
Ostrog 110, 116, 119–23, 125–26, 209
out-of-wedlock pregnancy, 205–7, 212–14
outward appearances, 92–93
over-leniency, 115, 250

pain. *See* battered women; suffering of agunot
Pais son of Meir of Elmshorn, 166
Paks, Hungary, 68, 218
parental interference, 163–65
peers, decisors relations with his, 230, 236, 242
Perl, Joseph, 195
Perl, Yosefe, 64, 66
Perle Issa of Trebbin, 28
permission to remarry. *See* heterei agunah
personal notices, 175
personal status, xxviii, 148, 149, 151, 194, 249, 289n69
Petshele daughter of Nathan, 218
Peusner, Hirsch, 61–63, 66
Phoebus, Rabbi Samuel ben Uri Shraga, 248
physical revulsion (*ma'is alai*), 150, 170
Pinne (Pniewy), 188–89, 310n84
placards, xxiii, 283n245
pledges, 141
Poland, xix, xx, 5, 22, 27–28, 32, 39, 78, 108–10, 119–20, 121, 154, 172, 181–82, 183, 193, 214, 302n2
Poland-Lithuania, xix, 106
Polonnoye/Polonne 79–81
polygamy, 44, 184, 185

population census, xxiv–xxv
positive commandments, 42, 47
poskim. *See* decisors
poverty, xxix, 37, 183–84, 204, 280n158
practical meaning of decisors' demands, 242–46
Prague, 16–17, 51–52, 63, 231, 289n72, 317n23
prayer of "supplication" for women in Yiddish, 177
prayer quorum (*minyan*), 131–32, 300nn19–20
Preger, Shimshon, 22
pregnancy by rape, 210–13
pregnancy out of wedlock, 205–7, 212–14
pregnant by a man not her husband, 237
prenuptial agreements, 13, 34–35. *See also* betrothal contracts (*shetarot tenaim*)
"presumption of danger" (*hezkat sakanah*), 55
printed Jewish sources, xxiv
privacy, 156–57, 299n56, 319n70
probate process, 17–20, 135
professionalism. *See* rabbinic prestige
prolonged travel, 176
promissory notes (*membrana*), 53, 176, 277n78
property. *See* estates, distribution of
Prussia, xix, xxv, 27, 28
Przemysl, 188–89
public and private spaces, 12, 93, 98

quarrelling. *See* marital disputes
quarrelsome wives, 93–94, 96

rabbinical hierarchy, 250
rabbinical power struggles, 129–31
rabbinic bureaucracy, 240–53
rabbinic enactments, 13–15, 20–21, 45, 46, 47–49, 66, 78–79, 148–49, 152
rabbinic prestige, 247–53
Rabenu Tam, 15, 44

Rachel daughter of Israel, 166
Rachel Miriam of Hamburg, 216
Raizele daughter of Zvi Hirsch, 182
rape, 210–13, 315n226
Raphael Cohen, Rabbi, 61
Raphael son of Kalman, 95
Rappaport, Rabbi Haim Hacohen, 184, 243
Rappaport, Rabbi Itzik Kahana, 68
Rashi, 44
reaffirmation of other decisors, 241, 242–43, 245–46, 248
realism, 227–28
reappearance of the husband, 186–87, 262–64, 323n28
rebellious women, 100, 153–54
Rechele, widow of Leib Reiss of Frankfurt, 40
record books (*pinkasim*). *See* beit din record books; community records
refugees, 81, 84–86
refusal of halitzah, 47
refusal of levirate marriage, 43, 44
refusal to divorce in accordance with halakhah, 194
refusal to grant a get, 199
refusal to permit an agunah to remarry, 72–73, 79–86, 110, 234–37
Reischer, Rabbi Jacob, 52, 72, 127–31, 236
religious conversion, 193–95
remarriage, xvi; based on the erroneous assumption, 84–86; before being free of previous marriage, 207; children from previous marriages, 4, 34–36; child support, 162; conditional marriage, 51–52; converts to Christianity, 195; dividing up estates, 20; duration of widowhood, 39; halakhah relevant to agunot, xxix; halakhic limitations, 36–38; halakhic rulings, 223; mourning customs, 9; refusals to permit an agunah to remarry, 79; of widows and widowers, 24, 30–33. *See also* heterei agunah

residency rights, 28–29
Responsa Binyamin Zeev, 168
responsa literature: agunot classification due to procedural error, 3; choosing to abandon a wife, 142; financial difficulties, 204; geographical distribution, 316n4; get received from a distant place, 217; Hasidim, 196; heterei agunah, 223–25, 230–31; as historical sources, xxiv, 59; imagery, 264–65; imposters and scoundrels, 185; infanticide, 214; Jewish men in the military, 182; Lemli's widow, 127–29; marital disputes, 160–61; merchant husbands, 177; methodological problems, xxv–xxvi, 126, 225; models of decisor attitudes, 233–40; overview, 229–30; practical meaning of decisors' demands, 243–45; public image of the decisor, 80; refusal of levirate marriage, 44; religious converts, 193; remarry before a child was two years old, 36; research approach and basic assumptions, 225; scholarly arguments on decisor attitudes, 232–33; suffering of agunot, 259–61; Torah study away from home, 178–79
revenge, 105–7
ritual bath (*mikveh*), 155–57
Rivash (Isaac ben Sheshet), 131
Rivkah, Lipman's wife, 97–101, 105–6
Rivkah, wife of Hertz Hamel, 169
Rocoles, Jean-Baptiste de, 89
Romania, 77
Rosh Hashanah, 9
Rosman, Moshe, 22, 27–28
Ross, Tamar, 227–28
Rothschild, Shmuel, 35
Rottenberg, Rabbi Mordechai Ziskind, 209–13, 315n222
Rublack, U., 214
rumors, 94–96, 117–19
Russia, xix

Sabean, David W., 63
Salmon-Mack, Tamar, 32, 78–79, 106, 187, 208, 214, 271n15, 292n32
Sapperstein, Hillel, 204
Sarah daughter of Rabbi Mordechai of Nova Chortoriya, 79–86, 89, 292n32
Sarah Merla, widow of Aharon Eshklas of Bonn, 40
Sartil daughter of Akiva, 203
scholarly arguments on decisor attitudes, 232–33
seal off an estate, 277n76
seat in the synagogue, 21, 65
Seder halitzah (order of halitzah), 45
Sefer haagunot (Kahana), xvii–xviii
Sefer hukei haishut (*Book of Matrimonial Laws*) (Landau), 250
Segal, Aharon, 183
Segal, Rabbi Israel, 103
Sender son of Yosef, 167
Sephardic traditions, 59, 316n2
sexuality, 180, 205, 211–13
sexual relations and halakhic divorce, 150–51
sexual relations and levirate marriage, 42
sexual relations and niddah, 155–57
sexual relations with a married woman, 235, 238, 240, 263
sexual relations with anyone other than a husband, 205–6, 210–11
Shaar Ephraim (Emden), 86–87
Shabtai Tzvi, xx, 89
Shahor, Hirschel, 112–16
shame, 158–59, 210, 213
Shapira, Rabbi Aharon Shimon, 86
Shayna, 242
shetar mekuyam (validated document), 235
Shevut Yaakov (Reischer), 236
Shilo, Margalit, 232
Shimshi-Licht, T., 214
Shirei Yehudah (Minden), 174
Shlomo Elbe of Altona, 20
Shlomo husband of Simhah, 258

Shlomo Zalman son of Eliyahu Segal, 162–63
Shmeruk, Chone, 12
Shmuel son of Yaakov, 171–72
Shmuel Zanvil son of Isaac of Harburg, 146
shofar image, 265
Shofet, Anthony, 119
Shulhan arukh, xxiii, 14, 31, 45, 48, 67–68, 181, 239, 242, 247–48
Silberman, Eliezer Lipman, 175
Silvetsky, Akiva, 246
Sirkis, Rabbi Joel, 239
social networks, 97–99
social order, 8, 10–11, 93–94, 97, 100, 205–7
social structures, xxvi–xxvii
Sofer-Schreiber, Rabbi Moshe, 184, 206, 244, 250, 319n70
sole decisor debate, 86, 131, 246
sorrow. *See* suffering of agunot
sources, xxi–xxv
spaces. *See* public and private spaces
"speaking innocently" (*mesiah lefi tumo*), 103–4, 118, 120, 122, 130
Speyer, 47
Stampfer, Shaul, 30–31
standardization, 111
State of Israel, xviii
Steg, Rabbi Shmuel, 64–65, 185–87
Steinhardt, Rabbi Yosef, 57
Stern, Selma, xxv
Stow, Kenneth, 111
stringent model, 234–38
suffering of agunot, 79, 233, 246, 258–67, 320n87, 322n12, 323n25, 323n28
Sweden, 77

Takles, Shimshon Wolf, 214–15
Talmud, xxiii, 14–15, 31, 43, 44, 181, 246, 250, 265
Talmudic academies (*yeshivot*), xx, 55
Talmudic rabbis, 236–37, 239
Taufenburg, Friedrich Wilhelm, 195

taxes, 12, 24–25
teaching and studying Torah in a distant yeshiva, 177–79
testimonies, 110–25; choosing to abandon a wife, 141; circumstances of death, 108–9; community dispute, 72; community records, xxii; criminals, 191–93; cultures of testimony, 110–11; delay, 323n22; doubts about identity, 70; gender, 157; halakhah relevant to agunot, xxix–xxx; halakhic activity, 223; by a non-Jew, 103; practical meaning of decisors' demands, 242–45; procedural aspects, 241; rabbinical power struggles, 130; Sarah and Leah, 80–86; scholarly arguments on decisor attitudes, 233; verbatim transcripts, 80, 297n25; widows and heirs, 22. *See also* witnesses
Tevely of Koblenz, 109
third-party involvement in marital conflict, 165–67
Thirty Years' War, xx, 77
Tilh, Arnaud du, 189
Tobias Cohen of Metz, 100
Torah, xv
Torah study away from home, 177–79
Trachtenberg, Yehoshua, 121
Tractate Yevamot, 31, 232
transgressing against Judaic law, 151
transgressing the Law of Moses, 151, 155–58
transgression of halitzah, 47
travel/journey: death while travelling, xxix, 108–10; false identity, 93; geographical area of Ashkenaz, xix; halitzah expenses, 61–62, 68–69; Jewish men in the military, 179–82; Lemli Wimpe Halevi, 127–29; length of time legitimate for, 176; looking for missing husbands, 208–12; practical meaning of decisors' demands, 245; practical meaning of the decisors' demands, 242–43;

prolonged travel, 176; Torah study away from home, 177–79
treatment of agunot. *See* attitudes of decisors
Trepp, Anne-Charlott, 200–201
trustee, 203
Turniansky, Chava, 92
Tzemah David (Heckscher), 90
Tzemah tzedek (Krochmal), 79, 248
Tzena urena (Rabbi Jacob ben Isaac Ashkenazi of Janów), 11–12
Tzerlin (battered woman), 158–60
Tzirl daughter of Gimpel, 203
Tzok Haitim (Difficulty of the Times) (Meir ben Shmuel of Szczebrzeszyn), 78
Tzvi Hirsch (Baschko) of Zamosc, 194, 297n12
Tzvi Hirsch of Brody, Rabbi, 244
Tzviya Rachel, 22–24, 39

Ukraine, 77, 84–87
Ulbrich, Claudia, 99
Ulbricht, Otto, 183–84, 310n93
Ullmann, Mendel, 65
unconditional get, 181–82
Unwanted Child (Harrington), 183

vagrancy, 26, 209
validity of a get, 216–18
van de Pol, Lotte C., 92–93
Vilna, 39
violence, 158–60, 164–65, 167–69, 172–73
virginity, 122–24

Wagner, Leib, 57
waiting period, 46–47, 49, 57, 86, 131
Wandsbek, 25
war and persecution, xx, 77–89
Warburg, Germany, 49, 64, 171, 185
Warburg, Avraham, 18
Warburg, Gedalya, 20
warning witnesses, xxix–xxx, 112
Warzburg, 277n76

weather conditions, 55, 243
Weil, Rabbi Yedidyah Tiah, 35, 178–79
Wenig, Lippman, 64
Wertheim, Yeruham Fischel, 214–15
Wertheimer, Rabbi Akiva, 32
western Europe, xix, xx, 39
wet nurses, 36–37, 283n245
widows, xvi, 3–40; children from previous marriage, 4, 33–36; communal fees, 24–25; community aid, 19, 25–26; duration of widowhood, 38–40; entitlements of, 15, 53, 276n57; halakhic limitations, 36–38; in historical documents, 3; imagery of, 10–13; labor market, 26–28; living conditions, 28–30; of merchants, 19, 26, 32; ordinary *vs.* businesswomen, 25; of rabbis, 19; remarriage, 30–33. *See also* halitzah
widow's oath, 15, 18–19, 23, 49
Wiltenburg, Joy, 153–54
witnesses, 110–25; adultery, 303n40; beggars, 183–84; choosing to abandon a wife, 141; circumstances of death, 108–9; community records, xxii; converts to Christianity, 194; criminals, 191–93; fate of an abandoned wife, 203; gender, 157–58; get document, 152; get received from a distant place, 215–17; halakhah relevant to agunot, xxix–xxx; massacres of 1648–1649, 88; procedural aspects, 246–47; rabbinical power struggles, 130; Sarah and Leah, 80–82; warning, xxix–xxx, 112. *See also* testimonies

Wolf son of Meir of Hamburg, 67
women's education in maskilic circles, 202
Worms, 9, 47
writ of halitzah, 49–50, 52, 61–66, 288n47

Yaakov son of Itzik, 163–65
Yaakov son of Mordechai Segal, 185–87
Yechiel Michl of Warburg, 49–50
Yehiel, Rabbi, 181–82
Yehiel son of Shlomo Zalman, 72–73
Yehudah Leib ben Hanokh of Pfersee, 177, 208, 307n24, 321n119
Yeshayah son of Leible Leshni of Leipnik, 141, 191–93
Yetcha, widow of Leib Weiler of Bingen, 40
yibum (levirate marriage), 42–50, 52, 59, 308n43
Yom Kippur, 9
Yoreh deah, xxiii
Yosef, Rabbi, 203
Yosef son of Lazer Shohet, 167–68
Yosef son of Zvi Hirsch, 170
young marriages, 190
Yuval, Israel, 248–49, 252

Zamosc, Rabbi Zvi Hirsch,
Zelechow. *See* Minden, Yehudah Leib
Zemon Davis, Natalie, 99–100, 189
Zot torat hakenaot (R. David of Makov), 195–96
Zülz, community records, 27–28